# Keepers of Our Past

Recent Titles in
**Contributions in American History**
*Series Editor: Jon L. Wakelyn*

# Keepers of Our Past

## Local Historical Writing in the United States, 1820s–1930s

## David J. Russo

Contributions in American History, Number 129

**GREENWOOD PRESS**
New York • Westport, Connecticut • London

**Library of Congress Cataloging-in-Publication Data**

Russo, David J.
    Keepers of our past : local historical writing in the United
States, 1820s-1930s / David J. Russo.
        p.   cm. — (Contributions in American history, ISSN 0084-9219
; no. 129)
    Bibliography: p.
    Includes index.
    ISBN 0-313-26236-5 (lib. bdg. : alk. paper)
    1. United States—History, Local—Historiography.   I. Title.
II. Series.
E175.R875   1988
973'.072—dc19                                        87-36095

British Library Cataloguing in Publication Data is available.

Library of Congress Catalog Card Number: 87-36095
ISBN: 0-313-26236-5
ISSN: 0084-9219

First published in 1988

Greenwood Press, Inc.
88 Post Road West, Westport, Connecticut 06881

Printed in the United States of America

The paper used in this book complies with the
Permanent Paper Standard issued by the National
Information Standards Organization (Z39.48-1984).

10 9 8 7 6 5 4 3 2 1

**Copyright Acknowledgments**

The author and publisher are grateful to the following for granting the use of their material:

Essex Institute, Salem, Massachusetts. "Felt, Lewis, and Coffin Papers."

The Historical Society of Pennsylvania, Philadelphia, Pennsylvania. "John Hill Martin Papers."

Maine Historical Society, Portland, Maine. "William Willis Papers."

Maryland Historical Society Library, Baltimore, Maryland. "J Thomas Scharf Collection, MS. 1999."

Massachusetts Historical Society, Boston, Massachusetts. "Shattuck Papers."

The State Historical Society of Wisconsin, Madison, Wisconsin. "Gregory Papers" (1930); "Thwaites Papers."

University of Maine, Orono, Maine. "Babb's thesis on Abby Maria Hemenway."

University of Virginia Library, Charlottesville, Virginia. "Papers of John Wayland" (#2386); "Papers of Oren Morton" (#6888), Manuscripts Department.

University of Washington Libraries, Seattle, Washington. "Clarence Booth Bagley Papers."

For my mother and my father

# Contents

# Preface

When I grew up in Deerfield, Massachusetts, in the 1950s, the physical remains of the remoter past seemed to be everywhere. There were many eighteenth-century homes along the main street (restored by a historical foundation and opened to the public as museum houses); a museum filled with colonial and nineteenth-century artifacts donated over the years by villagers and others from the area; a cemetery or "burial ground" with grave markers dating from the earliest settlement in the late seventeenth century; an old town well of indeterminate origins; a stone memorial dedicated to those who had died in several wars, including an early Indian massacre and the Civil War; and an academy founded in the 1790s and, though turned into a private secondary school in the 1920s, open to the town's young people, such as myself, who attended as day students.

By contrast, when I left Deerfield to enroll in the nearby state university at Amherst, the history I studied was largely national and political in orientation. Even though I had already assimilated a local past through history's physical presence, real history became something with much larger dimensions. Like many history majors of my generation, I took courses in modern history that were usually focused on nations and politics. I even became the research assistant of a professor working on American politics during the 1830s. The subject of my doctoral dissertation at Yale was of a very similar nature. I then secured a position at the University of Massachusetts in Amherst and organized my own course on "U.S. History." As time passed, I sensed the inadequacy of such an approach to historical study. Was political life necessarily the most important aspect of life? Did economic, social, cultural, and intellectual life change in unison with political life? Which was cause and which was effect? Did the nation offer the most meaningful perspective from which to study the past in any case?

In 1971 I learned that the historical foundation in Deerfield had opened a library to house the documents collected over the years by the local historical society. George Sheldon, Deerfield's nineteenth-century antiquarian (whose life had almost spanned the century: 1818-1916!), had originally opened the local museum in 1880 and had ransacked the area for available documentary material. (It was said that when the coffin was carried out the front door, Sheldon could be seen climbing the back stairs headed for the attic.)   Sheldon was president of the local society from 1870 to 1916 and wrote a massive two-volume history of the town, serialized in the local newspaper during the 1880s and published in book form in 1895-96. He had been a local historical impresario of the first order.

I began to appreciate the accomplishment of antiquarians like Sheldon, and this book is the result of a long and full investigation of the entire antiquarian enterprise.   I believe that amateur local historians are worthy of our attention for several reasons.   First, most historical writing in the United States before the 1930s was written by amateurs and was local or at least subnational in its dimensions.   Moreover, what these amateurs wrote mirrored what ordinary people thought was most important about both their past and their present:   namely, the personal and close-to-home.   Historical consciousness in North America since the initial European migration has had a popular dimension, and these amateur local historians have been its scribes. That is, they recorded what they and others around them believed the past was primarily about.

This antiquarian enterprise has not, however, been popular in the sense that just anybody wrote local history.   Such individuals have been rare and have usually constituted a kind of local elite of leisured or prominent persons, just as academic historians now make up a nationally — and internationally — oriented intellectual elite.   What has made amateur local historical writing popular is that these antiquarians, situated in localities strewn across the continent, have been academically untrained, have been nearly always unknown outside of their own communities, and have been involved with others from the area who have served as contributors and subscribers and who usually have also achieved local prominence. Even those hired by the commercial presses that turned out formula local history in the late nineteenth and early twentieth centuries were typically anonymous individuals.

The academic historians who have increasingly dominated historical writing in the twentieth century are of quite recent origin as a species, given the whole span of such writing since North America was first settled by European immigrants.   Though now in a dominant position, academic scholars would benefit from an increased awareness that historical consciousness on this continent has had a deep-rooted, popular, amateur, and local dimension.   The great antiquarian enterprise that is delineated here has abated, but the legacy of the amateurs is very great, and the debt academic scholars owe them commensurately high.   The antiquarians were the first great collectors and preservers of the artifactual and documentary evidence of the past in modern North America, and, without their strenuous efforts, much of the source material on which North American historical scholars base their research simply would not exist.   It was this strong antiquarian impulse to preserve the remains of the past that led to the founding of many of the historical societies, museums, and archives now managed by professionally trained staffs.

Furthermore, the amateur local histories themselves, for all their imperfections from the standpoint of modern academic scholarship, were the first histories to define the past as comprehensively as evidence and the capability of the particular author would allow. Theirs was history that was social, cultural, intellectual, and economic as well as political. The academic scholars of the American past who now collectively study various levels of community from the local to the national and beyond should recognize that their antiquarian predecessors were broad-ranging in what they tried to encompass in their histories, and almost never tried to chop the past of their towns and cities and counties into political epochs, as academic national historians are wont to do, to their seemingly everlasting confusion.

What is more, the antiquarians, for all their failings as historians from our current vantage point, in the act of focusing on what was near and familiar, perceived the reality of the past in a way scholars are in danger of losing. The amateurs devoted much time and energy to *their* past: there was only one Deerfield, Massachusetts, and only one Sheldon family, the ancestors of George Sheldon. When Sheldon wrote about family and community, he was emphasizing what was distinctive, unique, unrepeatable, and real. When scholars write about types of towns and cities, and types of families, they are in danger of presenting mental constructs as social reality. "Cattle towns" are not real: Abilene, Kansas is. Amateur historical thinking, without any capacity for abstraction, has been mired in historical reality in ways scholars are losing sight of as they become increasingly involved with concepts, models, processes, and patterns.

It is precisely because academic historians currently enjoy such an easy domination that there is a need for them to become aware of the brevity of their own past and their still briefer ascendancy, a need for them to recognize that historical consciousness in modern North America has long assumed shapes and forms that have been popular, and amateur, and local in nature. The real danger is that such scholars will forget — or will not sufficiently remember — from what they emerged, and who it is they have come to dominate. They, as historians above all others, should be aware of the shallowness that characterizes any group (even an intellectual elite) forgetful of major dimensions of its own past.

I would like to thank the librarians and staffs of the twenty-one manuscript repositories ranging from coast to coast where I examined the surviving papers of particular antiquarians, as well as the librarians of the local history and genealogy room of the Library of Congress, where I looked at the histories themselves. I am grateful to two colleagues, Ezio Cappadocia and Charles Johnston, for reading and commenting on earlier versions of the manuscript for this book, as well as to other colleagues who discussed with me certain aspects of this subject while I was working on the project. I am appreciative of the generosity of the Social Science and Humanities Research Council of Canada, which provided me with two research grants. I would like to thank Manon Ames and the Humanities Word Processing Center for their excellent production of the manuscript from its initial stages to the camera-ready copy. And finally, I would also like to thank Sheila Turcon who prepared the index.

# Introduction

People have always had an interest in studying the past, seeking, in the words of J. H. Plumb, "the meaning of time when related to themselves, with its harsh facts of birth, growth, and death."(1) An awareness of history is innate, inescapable, something essential to human identity. Certainly there is a close connection between the urge to know "who am I?" and genealogical investigation.

Plumb, in a more restrictive vein, stresses "the personal ownership of the past [as] . . . a vital strand in the ideology of all ruling classes. The authoritarian purposes of genealogy for society," Plumb argues, can be seen in the "acquisition of the past by the ruling and possessing classes and the exclusion of the mass of the peasantry and labouring classes," something he claims "is a widespread phenomenon through recorded time," adding: "Nor is it merely Kings and Pharaohs or high priests who have acquired the authority of an ancestral table. All aristocracies have, very sensibly, made a cult of genealogy in order to underpin their special status."(2)

But this perennial search for the historical sources of legitimacy, authority, and status has also been taken up by people whose inclusion under the rubrics "ruling class" and "aristocracy" would stretch the meaning of such terms beyond recognition. I am referring here to people whose prominence, if at all evident, was modest, local. The typical amateur genealogist and local historian has not been a scribe-in-hire to some Sanhedrin of yore, but a lone individual who believed, as one of them so aptly put it, that "[there] is something so natural in enquiring into the history of those who have lived before us, and particularly of those with whom we have any connexion, either by ties of relation or place, that it is surprising anyone should be found by whom this subject is regarded with indifference."(3)

In that portion of the British Empire that became, in 1776, the United States of America, genealogical and historical writing from the seventeenth to the twentieth centuries was produced by amateurs, who, before the rise of the historical profession in this century, were "Keepers of Our Past," antiquarians whose untechnical, descriptive writings were accessible to any literate person. History was then the common property of a large and significant segment of the population.    The past portrayed was local in character, rooted in particular families and communities, mirroring the relative strength and influence of the groups and settlements that provided the context for individual lives.    As I argued in *Families and Communities,*(4) the mass societies of our time are of recent origin. Through most of recorded time, most people have lived and died in largely isolated villages and rural settings.    The great enlargment in the scale of human organization spurred on by technology, has been a long-term, complicated, even contradictory and inconsistent historic process, but one that was plainly visible by the nineteenth century.    What was local and regional in range and reach has typically become national and international. This enlargement of scale has not been neatly progressive, however, and each facet of human life in all parts of the world has not developed in lockstep with all the others, but at its own rate, with its own mixture of persisting local and global influences.    Empires that embraced continents, like ancient Rome, and religious faiths or economic systems, like medieval Christianity or modern capitalism, are obvious examples of organizations of great magnitude that have flourished through the centuries.    Large-scale political empires, religious faiths, and economic organizations produced elites (priests, officers, politicians, merchants, businessmen) who had a perspective, horizons, interests, awareness, and contacts as wide as the political, economic, and religious worlds themselves. But these large entities did not bind and unify in a way that ended the isolation of the vast majority of the world's population.(5) Only recent technological innovations and the rampant urbanization of the last century and a half have succeeded in breaking down this isolation and truly conquering space.    I am referring here to such developments in transportation and communication as air-travel, the telephone, radio and television, the vast and growing systems of telecommunications, as well as the hording of an increasing portion of humanity into urban areas.

In a rough sort of way, historical inquiry, in the American context, at least, has reflected these changes.    The antiquarians who have written about a personal, familial, or local past were thus commenting on those levels of groups and communities that most influenced their ancestors' lives. To write a history of one's family, town, city, state, or even region was both natural and important.    In Daniel J. Boorstin's apt words: "The history of states and regions seemed primary; the history of the United States contrived and derivative. Many years would pass before Americans would see their history the other way around . . . . Not until after the Civil War would a national perspective on American history seem normal."(6)

The exponential growth of academic historical writing through the decades of this century has paralleled the vast enlargement of national influences and organizations and the corresponding decline in the importance of the local dimensions of life.    Professional historians assumed the task of explaining why and how the American nation attained its special, preeminent place in the world.    Their technical, analytical monographic studies have typically dealt with thin slices of national life.

In textbooks from the 1920s onward, generations of students have been exposed to general accounts of how and why the United States became powerful and influential. Thousands of high school teachers have further distilled this analysis for millions of school children.(7)

But these recent developments must not be allowed to obscure two features of American historical writing that stand out with clarity in the long view: history as written in the United States, until recently, was written mostly by amateurs and typically was local (or at least subnational) in its range and coverage.

What follows is an assessment of the writings of these rare individuals — antiquarians — whose interest in the local past was of such magnitude that they felt compelled to expend considerable time and energy to produce accounts of their community's history. Antiquarians were academically untrained collectors and preservers of reminiscences and documents and artifacts, founders and officers of historical societies, and compilers, editors, and writers of local history.

Historical consciousness and awareness were not in any sense confined to the authors of such histories, or even to those who contributed material and who subscribed to the published result. Various writers of fiction — from James Fenimore Cooper (*Pioneers*) to Harriet Beecher Stowe (*Old Town Folks*) to Gore Vidal (*Burr, Lincoln*) — have written about the past as well. But, practically all the antiquarians who have penned local histories during the nineteenth and twentieth centuries have done so in pursuit of factual truth and have tried hard to separate verifiable information from myth, anecdote, and story. Indeed, these amateur local historians have usually eschewed dramatic narration altogether, preferring to compile compendia of fact, sometimes arranged chronologically, sometimes topically, not infrequently both. In this, their writing has contrasted strikingly from that of literary historians like Bancroft and Prescott or, more recently, from that of academic scholars with their increasingly analytical and conceptual language. Those most affected by the antiquarian impulse have almost never had a theoretical or analytical cast of mind, and it is difficult to find evidence that these amateurs have had any interest in or capacity to articulate a theory or concept concerning the communities whose past they have so lovingly uncovered.

In comparison to accomplished writers of all kinds, these antiquarian authors were subliterary in the sense that their principal occupation was with few exceptions something other than writing for publication, which means that their literary labors were both strenuous to achieve and rare. Very few have had the stamina and speed and interest in other localities to be "repeaters," to write histories of different communities at various times in their lives.

But, the antiquarians, from another perspective, have been "prominent" as well. They have often been widely known in a local context and have usually tried to recover a past that sustained and gave historical dimension to the lives of their own family and of other families, which together comprised a kind of local elite. Their search for both genealogical and historical information directly attests to their deep personal concern for those in their community who have persisted or have become successful, and not for the much larger drifting, transient, unsuccessful element in the local population.

Even though their readership was local and their histories usually unknown outside of the area they wrote about, collectively the antiquarians presented the only historical accounts of the communities that mattered most in the lives of individuals both in North America and everywhere else in the world before this century: rural areas, villages, towns, cities, and not nations or empires. It is ironic and important that these crude chroniclers, in nearly total obscurity, wrote hundreds of histories from the 1820s until the 1930s with exactly the proper focus, at the same time that Bancroft and a long line of national historians, followed in this century by a vast corps of academically trained "American historians," wrote about the past of a nation whose preeminence was obvious only as recently as the 1930s and 1940s.

In one fundamental aspect, the amateurs, with a passionate concern to recover *their* past in the context of their community, have been the better historians. Academic scholarship has been largely misdirected, yet another indication of the distorting power of nationalism in this century, as scholars until quite recently have cast backward onto the nineteenth, eighteenth, and seventeenth centuries a unit of historical study (the United States of America) that was non-existent before 1783 and of relative unimportance to most of those who inhabited that portion of the North American continent until the twentieth century itself. Adopting a national perspective that was becoming important during the very time academic scholarship developed, scholars projected onto earlier centuries the increasingly obvious centrality of the nation-state of their own time.

Why the earliest local histories appeared in the 1820s; why the forms, content, manner of writing, publication, and sale evolved as they did; and why the entire antiquarian enterprise lost momentum by the 1930s are difficult questions for which to provide clear answers. The chapters that follow explore such questions, but I have from the outset been mindful of a basic kind of anarchy that has usually prevailed in amateur local historical writing that, in turn, makes safe generalizing a hazardous undertaking. Antiquarians often worked in isolation from others who were embarked on similar enterprises elsewhere, resulting in a lack of collegiality, an absence of prescribed form. But there are notable exceptions to even these observations. The earliest antiquarians in New England, at least to some extent, did work together and did create a recognizable kind of local history. And, later, during the last decades of the nineteenth and earliest decades of the twentieth centuries, local historical writing, at least in the midwest, did become reducible to a commericalized formula.

This study is based primarily upon the surviving papers of various amateur local historians that are available in research libraries from coast to coast and on the local histories themselves, lining, as they do, many shelves in the Library of Congress. Most of the authors singled out for extended treatment are those whose papers happen to have survived. Fortunately, these individuals lived in and wrote about towns, cities, and counties in all parts of the United States and in both the early (pre-Civil War) and later (to the Great Depression) periods. As a group, their efforts are representative of a vast, sprawling folk movement to recapture and retain the past, a movement that needs to be understood in order for us to gain a fuller awareness of the nature of historical consciousness in modern America.

Earlier studies of the history of historical writing in the United States ignore the local antiquarians. Michael Kraus' *The Writing of American History*(8) and Harvey Wish's *The American Historian: A Social-Intellectual History of the Writing of the American Past*(9) focus on major national historians. David Van Tassel's *Recording America's Past: An Interpretation of the Development of Historical Studies in America, 1607-1884*(10) equates local history with colony- and state-wide historical activities and writing and includes only a few references to genuine local historians, to those who actually wrote of villages, towns, cities, and counties. Similarly, George H. Callcott's *History in the United States, 1800-1860: Its Practice and Purpose*(11) deals with historians of colonial empires, European nations, and the United States, and not with their local counterparts, whom he fleetingly refers to in a brief chapter entitled "Antiquarianism in the Age of Literary History."

However, in the study that follows, I share with Callcott a concern for such subjects as the rise of a historical consciousness in the United States during the early nineteenth century (and its later evolutions), the reasons people studied the past, and what the past meant to them. My focus throughout is on the general histories of towns and cities and on their authors, and not on such other manifestations of historical interest as fictional accounts, speeches, pamphlets, guides, and commemorations. I believe that such a focus provides the best opportunity for the study of local historical writing in that the antiquarians who wrote full local histories were at the very center of what was a many-faceted enterprise.

# PART I
# The Early Antiquarians

# CHAPTER 1
# The Early Setting

There is an abundant promotional literature on particular British North American colonies written by various explorers, organizers, and apologists, containing richly varied knowledge of a new and strange land.(1) These writings were later used by the antiquarians who attempted to recreate their locality's past. Such promoters unwittingly produced source material for the wide-ranging "social" history that characterized local historical writing in North America from its inception in the early nineteenth century.(2)

The specifically historical writings that British colonists presented were histories of particular colonies, usually partisan accounts focused on controversies with Britain. By contrast, the Puritan historians of colonial New England typically cast their accounts in a religious mold. Theirs was a Christian view of history. Believing that they were among God's elect and the builders of model religious communities, the Puritans wrote history whose theme was that "God carried on His work through ... His chosen people" who planted his churches in the new world and whose faith and endurance were constantly tested by God's enemies and theirs.(3)

The New Englanders' histories were written from a colony-wide perspective, even though the Puritans organized themselves in planned towns given wide autonomy.(4) And yet the Puritans made no effort during the colonial period to provide overall histories of particular towns. The only form of writing by the colonists that can be regarded as even related to truly local history was the "captivity story," accounts of the Indian massacres of frontier villages, and the subsequent captivity of the survivors who were held for ransom but who sometimes remained with their captors, adopting their culture. However, such accounts were about a specific event, and in no sense dealt with the development of a community over time. The massacres were traumas, seared into the memory of the survivors, whose written recollections were limited to descriptions of an unforgettable calamity.(5)

Neither the Puritans nor the other British colonists copied the "chorographers" or "antiquarians" in England who had been producing historical, genealogical, and topographical accounts of particular counties and towns since the late sixteenth century.(6) During the seventeenth and eighteenth centuries, such publications became commonplace and could have served as a model for the colonists if they had been interested in perceiving their own settlements in the same manner, as a past worth recalling.   The simplest explanation for their failure to draw on this model is that the colonial villages and seaport towns seemed of too recent origin to be written about in a historical manner.   As John Farmer, a pioneering North American genealogist, explained to Joshua Coffin, an early town historian from Massachusetts: "What labour and what expence are bestowed upon the county and *town* histories of Great Britain . . . .     These generally go back beyond the conquest and have full scope in antiquarian research."(7)

The people who fought and won their political independence from Britain from 1775 to 1783 entered nationhood without any developed form of local historical writing.     Promotional tracts to woo settlers, partisan accounts of controversies between Britain and particular colonies, recollections of Indian massacres, religious accounts of the testing and endurance of a group who believed they were God's chosen people — such was the legacy for those who would attempt, after independence, to fashion historical accounts of the communities they lived in and identified with. Local historical writing was thus a phenomenon of the nineteenth century, of a time that provided those who undertook the task with a sense of a past.     For by then, villages, towns, cities, and states (erstwhile colonies) had existed for a century and more.

When the rebelling British colonists succeeded in gaining their political independence from Britain in the peace treaty of 1783, they created a new nation-state, distinctive in its republican character.   But, in forming a new central government to replace the old provincial ones, they left intact the federal nature of colonial life.   The inhabitants of what became the United States of America thus identified with their local community, state, region, and nation in a hierarchy of loyalty and involvement, in a fashion strikingly similar to their colonial forebears.   The nation replaced the empire; Washington (after a brief interval) replaced London.   What was trans-Atlantic in scale would before long become continental in scope.   This federalism infused all aspects of life, even historical writing, for one of the basic features of historical inquiry as it evolved after the Revolution was the on-going tension between local and national perspectives and allegiances.   Whether the study of the past should focus on the nation and its inhabitants' common experiences or on localities in all their distinctiveness and peculiarity was a question never resolved because, by its nature, it could not be.

The interplay of national and local influences on those who wrote history is clearly revealed in the founding and development of historical societies in the decades between the Revolution and the Civil War. These organizations provided a continuous, institutionalized means for the collection of documents and artifacts and for the publication of writings. Such societies were forums for group effort, a reassuring backdrop, and sometimes a useful resource for the lone author or compiler. Historical inquiry was thus, from its inception, both a group and individual enterprise, with one spurring on the other.

The early state historical societies – those of Massachusetts, New York, and Pennsylvania were all organized by individuals who emerged from the Revolution as nationalists in outlook, wanting to foster study of the nation's past. Jeremy Belknap, founder of the first of these, the Massachusetts Historical Society, in 1792, was a Congregational minister from Dover, New Hampshire, who had written a history of his state, moved to Boston after the Revolution and devoted time and effort promoting cultural nationalism in such forms as an "American language" and a national education system.

In devising a plan for a historical society, he drew heavily upon the examples set by the London Society of Antiquaries (1572) and the Society of Antiquaries of Scotland (1790) for the organizational structure and constitution of what he and his colleagues changed from a "Society of Antiquaries" to a "Historical Society." The object of the new society was "to rescue the true history of this country from the ravages of time and the effects of ignorance and neglect."(8) Belknap tried, but failed, to make an arrangement with Congress for copies of all documents printed by the federal government; collected materials concerning the national past; sponsored a periodical, *The American Apollo*, to diffuse and preserve the Society's collections; and "dreamed of a nationwide network of branch societies founded by corresponding members of the Massachusetts parent, which would become a clearing house for communications from all over the country." (9)

Similarly, John Pintard, a wealthy dry goods merchant from New York City, in 1804 won the support of members of the New York state legislature for his plan to found a historical society whose constitution was patterned after the Massachusetts society's. Like the older group, whose priority in the field was acknowledged, the New York society sought to gather material "towards the study of our national history."(10) And, in Worcester, Massachusetts, in 1812, Isaiah Thomas, a printer and bookseller, founded the American Antiquarian Society, whose name and purpose were both avowedly nationalistic and whose membership came to include persons from all parts of the nation.(11)

But, by the 1820s, the objectives of such organizations were becoming state oriented. When, in 1824, a group of wealthy Philadelphians organized the Historical Society of Pennsylvania to replace the Historical Committee of the American Philosophical Society, they pledged themselves to "repairing the injuries which the early history of Pennsylvania sustained by reason of [the] inattention" of the early inhabitants.(12) During the decades through the Civil War increasing numbers of state, county, and local historical societies were organized as the American nation spread across the continent. Most were entirely private in character, but some of the state societies, particularly those in the Midwest, were supported with public funds from their inception.(13)

But the nationalist impulse of such early organizers as Belknap, Pintard, and Thomas gave way, by the 1820s, to narrower concerns. All forms of nationalism generated by the Revolution were short lived, basically because of the bottom-heavy federated character of life during the century and more after the achievement of political independence. Local, state, and regional attachments were too powerful for any summons to support national enterprises of the sort made by Belknap and his contemporaries to be successful.

As historical societies relinquished geographic scope, they collected a vast array of documents and artifacts and investigated a wide range of subjects within their narrow purview. Repositories of government documents, institutional records, private manuscripts, Indian artifacts, geological specimens, and geographic maps, the historical societies served a very useful and practical purpose: to collect and disseminate information that could be used to promote a given town, city, county, or state "to attract settlers and new capital."(14) To the extent that those active in historical societies promoted their community in order to induce further immigration and growth, they carried on the work of the earlier colonial promoters and gave additional evidence of the profoundly practical character of the gathering and spreading of information in North America.

Another consequence of the historical societies' eclectic approach to collecting and publishing (which they also shared with those same colonial promoters) was that the early local histories were naturally broad-ranging in their coverage, based as they were on material providing much information on the details of everyday life relating to many individuals, families, institutions, and activities.(15)


Biographical and genealogical writings on individuals and families were also affected by the crosscurrents of national and local influences during these years. Taking a filiopietistic view of figures of national significance, biographers after the Revolution used eulogy and fictionalized anecdote to illustrate character and to create heroes encased in legend who would serve as models of moral character for youths and adults as well and who would inspire patriotism in everyone for a new and special nation. In the absence of other forms of historical writing, biography became "very nearly the exclusive medium for records of America's past. . . . [Many] parents, ministers, and pedagogues felt that biography had greater instructional value than other forms of literature."(16)

Parson Mason Locke Weems, an Episcopalian minister who was also a traveling book agent for Matthew Cary's Philadelphia publishing house, established the model with his biography of George Washington, which appeared in 1800, soon after the former president's death. Washington was presented in idealized form as a national hero, a model of virtue, who personified the rebel cause during the revolution and became the moral and political father of his country.(17) Weems influenced biographers of other national figures, most notably William Wirt in his treatment of Patrick

Henry (1818).(18) The most influential example of group biography of the same type was George Lippard's *Washington and His Generals or Legends of the American Revolution* (1847), which first appeared in serialized form in the Philadelphia *Saturday Courier*.(19)

Such writings were challenged by those who developed a fact-oriented form of biographical writing.   Jeremy Belknap's purpose was to present a factual "recital of events," and he included "Adventurers, Statesmen, Philosophers, Divines, and other remarkable characters" as his subjects. During the 1790s, he lived long enough to publish two volumes, presented in chronological order, of his *American Biography*.   John Eliot, a congregational minister in Boston and a friend of Belknap's, published in 1801 a two-volume *Biographical Dictionary*.   William Allen, who was later a president of Dartmouth College, in 1809 presented *An American Biographical and Historical Dictionary*.   The greatest enterprise of collective biography was Jared Sparks' *The Library of American Biography* (1833-1849, 25 volumes).   Sparks—a Unitarian minister, editor-owner of the *North American Review*, and editor of the papers of George Washington—designed a series of biographical sketches of the most prominent Americans so as to "serve in some degree as a connected history of the country as well as to illustrate the character and acts of some of the most illustrious men of the nation."(20)

By the 1820s and 1830s a growing number of the prominent inhabitants of the old communities along the Atlantic coast devoted considerable time to genealogical investigation.   Persons of local  eminence turned to family history as a source of status and for evidence of ancestral heroism in the same manner that biographers sought to define a nation through the lives of its heroes.   John Farmer, a New Hampshire printer and first secretary of the New Hampshire Historical Society, published *A Genealogical Register of the First Settlers of New England* in 1829, reflecting this trend and referred in his preface to the "curiosity among many of the present generation to trace their progenitors in an uninterrupted series to those who first landed in New England."(21)

By the 1840s, the influx of Irish and German immigrants encouraged various forms of native-born American exclusiveness, and genealogists sought such documents as "church records, ships's passenger lists, lists of town fathers, muster rolls, and other proofs of lineage and a place among the early settlers."(22) In 1845, the very year the Native American Party was formed, there were sufficient adherents of genealogical research for the founding of a journal whose purpose was to further their interests: *The New England Historical and Genealogical Register*.

Joshua Coffin, an early local historian who was as interested in genealogical investigation as he was in the history of local communities, advertised in the new journal, prompting inquiries with reference to "a notice (published sometime since, in the *Genealogical Register*) of your willingness to supply genealogical information concerning the families of Essex county, [which] encourages me to solicit your good office in the matter."(23) Another wrote to Coffin that "there seems to be a growing taste to recover from utter forgetfulness the names of our ancestry.  You will pardon me an utter stranger in person to you from troubling you with so many queries, when I state I have in this respect done by you as others sometimes do by me. If you can only answer a few of these many queries for that much I will be thankful, and be as liberal in giving the information to others as I have been in questioning you."(24)

At the same time that biographical writing with a national perspective was making room for historical accounts of a broader scope, the biographical impulse was finding outlets at the local level in the form of genealogical investigation. Alongside the heroic individual in the nation's past stood the prominent family in the local community's past. Heroism and prominence became central features of both national and local history.

From the time of the Revolution and through the Civil War, historical writing itself bore the marks of the interplay of national and local influences. David Ramsay — a medical doctor from Charleston, South Carolina, a leader of the rebels in that colony during the Revolution, and a delegate to the Continental Congress — wrote a *History of the American Revolution*, which appeared in 1789 in two volumes and quickly became the first successful treatment of the Revolution and the Constitution. Ramsay's account, presented from a partisan rebel point of view "attempted to make the revolution a symbol of national unity and to demonstrate that the constitution was the most natural and perfect embodiment of the purposes of the war."(25) Ramsay's achievement was to bring a national perspective to a historical literature that hitherto consisted largely of partisan accounts of particular British North American provinces. This perspective was maintained by Abiel Holmes, a Congregational minister from Boston, whose popular *American Annals*, which surveyed the history of all the colonies from their beginnings through the eighteenth century, was published in two volumes in 1805.(26)

The first widely read and influential, large-scale national history was George Bancroft's, which appeared in ten volumes over the forty year period from 1834 to 1874. Bancroft, initially a headmaster of a private academy in Northampton, Massachusetts, was distintive among early American historians in that he received formal academic training in historical study in Germany. He brought to his writing a developed concept of history as the depiction of the dramatic actions of individuals whose collective activities exemplified an overall theme. Bancroft organized the massive manuscript sources he gathered in support of the thesis that the American past revealed God's plan for human progress. Starting in the 1830's with a colony-by-colony survey of colonial life, Bancroft went on to present a detailed account of the American Revolution, which he believed placed the victorious rebels in the vanguard of the enduring human struggle for freedom. American history was, therefore, "the study of that succession of events by which the American colonies, in their march from repression toward liberty, in their advance from scattered settlement toward unified republic, illustrated the progress and unity of humanity under God's direction."(27) Bancroft's account, by turns descriptive, dramatic, and philosophical, was immensely popular, and his volumes went through many editions.

During the same years that Holmes and Bancroft provided accounts of the new nation's past for adult readers, the authors of textbooks introduced school children to the same subject. The awakening of patriotism and nationalism among the young was a goal fostered first by educational theorists, such as Johann Pestalozzi, whose method "was to teach from the particular to the general, from the familiar to the unfamiliar, and from the tangible to the abstract,"(28) or, in this case, the history of one's own country before that of the rest of the world; second by organizations like the American Academy of Language and Belles Lettres, which, in 1822, offered a prize for the best history of the United States designed for schools; and third by state governments in Massachusetts, Vermont, New Hampshire, Rhode Island, and Virginia, which enacted legislation requiring the teaching of American history.(29) Salma Hale (1822), Charles A. Goodrich (1823), and Noah Webster (1832) wrote the most popular of these texts.

But nationalist feelings were not easily aroused and sustained. Holmes' *American Annals* and the school texts that drew heavily upon it had a distinctly New England bias in the sense that they created the impression that "in New England lay the foundation of the nation."(30) Bancroft was confident he had gone beyond a New England centered portrayal and had truly embraced the colonies that became a nation. But, as his volumes came out in the years after 1834, criticism mounted from commentators in the South and the mid-Atlantic area who argued that Bancroft had slighted or distorted in some way the history of their colonies or regions.

A common resentment toward New England broadened and deepened into sectional antagonism between Northerners and Southerners as Richard Hildreth (1849-1852, six volumes) and George Tucker (1856-1857, four volumes) wrote national histories to compete with Bancroft's. Hildreth, a New Englander, wrote from a Federalist perspective, and Tucker, a Southerner, from a Jeffersonian one. Each brought his coverage into the post-Revolutionary decades.(31) Neither rendering of the nation's past received praise — or even attention — from all parts of the union. Reviewers in Southern journals, such as *De Bow's Review* and the *Southern Quarterly Review*, or in Northern journals, like the *North American Review*, favored local, state, and regional histories, and abused or simply neglected the writings of Hildreth and Tucker, who sought, like Bancroft, to rise above a regional bias and perspective.(32)

Bias of another kind marked the early state histories written after the Revolution. Some former Loyalists wrote histories of their own colonies, favoring the Loyalist position. These included Thomas Hutchinson (Massachusetts), William Smith (New York), Samuel Peters (Connecticut), Robert Proud (Pennsylvania), and Alexander Hewatt (South Carolina and Georgia).(33) By contrast the state histories written from a rebel standpoint were nationalistic in that their authors believed "that the history of any state in the nation could be used effectively to illustrate the principles of the United States."(34) These rebel-oriented nationalist-minded historians — Jeremy Belknap (New Hampshire), Samuel Williams (Vermont), James Sullivan (Maine District), John Daly Burk (Virginia) — anticipated

Bancroft by arguing "that human society tended toward freedom and that Americans, the chosen people of God and Nature, were to lead the world into freedom's path."(35)

But these nationalist-oriented state histories gave way after 1815 to those of a state-wide perspective. Just as the national historians—with the large exception of Bancroft—failed to develop an audience for the history of the United States after independence and under the Constitution, so too did those state historians who sought to present their state's history as a microcosm of American history fail to establish a pattern that could be sustained by their successors who dealt with the various states of the nation after 1783.

The nationalist perspective created by the Revolution was not a natural one when writers dealt with the more recent past. The Revolution as a historical event could be portrayed as a cataclysmic event of historical importance to all "Americans"; by extension, the colonial past of each state in the new nation could also be interpreted as a prelude to political independence and the establishment of nationhood. But the nationalist perspective was increasingly less evident to those who wrote national and state histories in the decades after the 1780s. The nation in reality was a loose federation, its government small and weak, nationalism and patriotism ill defined. The local, state, and regional perspectives were dominant in the minds of those who wrote history, as well as to subscribers, readers, and critics. Only Bancroft, who imposed a thesis on a sprawling literary canvas and thus provided a kind of unity and who had the good sense to end his account with the Revolution, produced a national history that largely withstood the powerful attraction of the local—or at least sub-national—perspective.

All of these developments involving historical societies and historical biographical-genealogical writing need to be viewed together in order to understand why local history assumed the shape it did in the decades after the Revolution. The earliest histories of towns and cities are intricately bound up with the activities of the founders of historical societies, national and state historians, biographers, and genealogists.

Local historical writing from the beginning was nurtured by historical societies. Even the earliest ones, founded to foster study of the nation's past, did not neglect the state and its localities. Jeremy Belknap, first Corresponding Secretary of the Massachusetts Historical Society "travelled through the New England states collecting manuscripts . . . [and] sent out a questionnaire to ministers of towns throughout New England and to all corresponding members in the country, asking for information on each town, instances of unusual longevity, beneficial effects of the climate, and accounts of the deeds of unusual people. The result was that most of the town histories written in New England between 1792 and 1815 were published in the collections of the Massachusetts Historical Society."(36)

These "histories" were, in reality, sketches or short accounts often of only five, ten, or twenty pages in length, with such titles as "Topographical and Historical Sketch of . . . ," "Geographical Sketch of . . . ," "Historical

Sketch of . . . ," "Statistical Account of . . . ," "Topographical Description of . . . ," "History and Description of . . ." – or more simply: "Description of . . .," "Account of . . . ," "History of . . ." Longer-than-ordinary pieces appeared on Boston (sixty-five pages in 1794) and on Cambridge (sixty-six pages in 1800). In the introduction to the Boston sketch, the editor of the society's collections referred to the "Geographical Gazetteer of the towns in the Commonwealth of Massachusetts" begun earlier in the *Boston Magazine*,(37) which only included a few towns before it ended. It was this task the Historical Society assumed shortly after its founding, with the aim of presenting a complete gazetteer of all the towns in Massachusetts.

To that end, members were asked to send "Communications" to the society, which would become a repository for them and the publisher of "accurate descriptive accounts."(38) By the early 1820s many sketches had appeared, with a smattering on towns in other states. Typically, the editor acknowledged the contributor(s), as in the case of the first sketch, "A Topographical Description of Worcester": "the following particulars relating to Worcester, in the State of Massachusetts, were communicated by Timothy Paine, William Young, Edward Bangs, and Dr. Samuel Stearns to whom the Historical Society acknowledges themselves much obliged."(39)

The topics dealt with were: Situation, Extent and Boundaries, Soil and Produce, Woods, Hills, Air, Minerals, Ponds, Brooks and Rivers, Mills, Manufacturers, Means of Subsistence, Number of Inhabitants, Houses, Roads, Religion, Settlement. As other pieces appeared, the prominence of geographical and topographical subjects continued, but even in the first sketches, such headings as Settlement and Religion were naturally treated with a historical dimension. Contributors did not separate geography from history, or the past from the present, as their objective was to present a factual account that included everything they knew about their community.

In the broader, transatlantic perspective, these earliest efforts in local historical writing in North America were a direct continuation of the British tradition of "chorography" with its strong basis in topographical or geographical description. There is no direct evidence, however, that either the editors at the Massachusetts Historical Society or their contributors had either seen or were influenced by the antiquarian researches and sketches that had been produced in Britain since the late sixteenth century.

Early genealogists, like John Farmer, whose *A Genealogical Register of the First Settlers of New England* was a pioneering effort, encouraged and assisted such early local historians in Massachusetts as Alonzo Lewis, Joseph Felt, and Joshua Coffin, who, in turn, aided genealogical projects like Farmer's. Indeed, Farmer insisted that families and communities must be studied together. On September 20, 1827, he wrote to Joseph Felt: "In the progress of your work, I hope you will give the names of the first settlers of Salem, whence they came, and when arrived, as in the present curiosity for local histories, the curious inquirer is not satisfied merely with the history of a corporate community, but is anxious to have some account of the individuals composing it."(40)

That the genealogist and the historian should share their common sources was obvious to Farmer, and it was with enthusiasm that he worte to Felt a year or so later: "Your letter, containing notices of the wills of various persons of distinction among our first settlers was duly received, and from them I glean some useful facts.    There are perhaps no documents which at once let us into a knowledge of the circumstances and relations of an individual or family so fully and so intimately as these testamentary ones."(41)  Farmer repeatedly requested the assistance of Felt and others in his own genealogical compilations: "Annexed to this sheet is a prospectus of a Register of the first settlers of New England, in which I have been happy to cite you as an authority in several instances, and should be under obligations for more extensive reference to your labours.    I wish to obtain the names of all of your early settlers . . . that I may enter them on my ms. together with any facts, such as the time of their fixing their residence in Salem, when they married, their children, and the times they died, etc."(42)

Joseph Felt was quite responsive and was continuously encouraged by a gratified Farmer to pursue his researches further.(43)  Joshua Coffin of Newbury was also eager to assist: "Had I known four months ago that you [were] collecting materials for such a work as you announced, I should have been more particular in my communications and could have furnished you with many particulars proper for your work I have passed by without writing down, as they appeared in the papers on file in the clerk's office. . . . When will your book be printed? I wish I could see you before it goes to press or could see the manuscript.    I think I could assist you in some particulars, but now I cannot tell in what. . . . Mr. Lewis can give you the name of the first settlers of Lynn and Rev. Joseph B. Felt of Salem."(44)

Such assistance flowed in both directions, with Farmer, in turn, providing various kinds of information and steady encouragement to Felt(45) and to Lewis.(46)   But Farmer, as eager as he was for these antiquarians to write and publish local histories, never lost sight of his own primary interest: genealogy.    At the same time that he encouraged Felt and Lewis in their work, he reminded them of the intricate connection between biography and history.    To Felt: "I was glad to hear from you after so long an interval and am happy to learn that your labors of late have been bestowed on so important a town as Ipswich.    I hope you will find room for the genealogies of some of the more distinguished of the early settlers."(47) To Lewis: "In your researches you must have collected many very interesting facts, which will give your history a particular interest.    Let us have as many biographical sketches and genealogical details as are consistent with your plan."(48)

This close relationship between Farmer – the pioneering genealogist – and Felt, Coffin, and Lewis – the early local historians – mirrored the intricate connection between historical and genealogical inquiry at the time local historical writing assumed its initial form.

The same kind of relationship existed between librarians and the early antiquarians who wrote histories.    In a "My Dear Josh" letter, Christopher C. Baldwin, librarian at the American Antiquarian Society, wrote to Joshua Coffin in 1832, requesting that he act as a referee so that Baldwin could "beg books and the like" for his library from such local historians as Joseph Felt.(49)  And, of Coffin himself, Baldwin asked for "all the pamphlets, books, maps, and manuscripts that may fall in your way.    Your situation is such as to enable you to render us very important business. [Everything] that has a name and a date is worth something. . . . And I cannot but think it an object with editors and publishers who have any ambition to be thought well of by future antiquaries or to be thought of at all, to deposit with us a copy of their labors that they and their works maybe transmitted in safety to succeeding generations."(50)

A few weeks later, after receiving a copy of Alonzo Lewis' just-published history of Lynn, Baldwin was prompted to write: "What have you done with the ancient manuscripts employed in your account of Lynn? Should there be any among them that may be worthy of preservation, which you can conveniently part with, the members of the antiquarian society would be very thankful if you would deposit them among its collections. And should you have it in your power to secure for us any books, maps, or pamphlets they would always be acceptable. A series of newspapers published in your place from the beginning would be regarded as valuable."(51)

Similarly, in 1851, Samuel C. Jackson, Assistant Librarian of the Massachusetts State Library wrote to Coffin that "when you were in the State Library this winter, I observed that you had in your possession as Town Clerk some ancient copies of the *Journals* and *Laws of Mass.* May I trouble you. . . to look on these journals, etc. and ascertain their *dates* and give me the information. They may be of value to a library like this when they would be of little value elsewhere and, if *preserved here*, they may be of benefit to many towns. They will be accessible to all. You may thus confer a favor on the commonwealth which will be duly acknowledged."(52)


There is some evidence that the earliest local historians were aware of the literature on the history of English towns and cities and, indeed, on occasion, casually referred to it as a model to emulate or depart from. When, in 1824, John Farmer "supposed" Joshua Coffin was devoting what leisure time he had "to the collection and arrangement of materials for your History of the Town of Newbury," he imagined it would be "one of the best town histories which have appeared in our country, and bearing a close affinity with similar histories in the old world."(53)

Farmer even kept up with the reviews of English local histories. While praising Alonzo Lewis' *History of Lynn* in 1829, he referred to the reviewer of Surtee's *History and Antiquities of the County Palatine of Durham* as saying, appropriately in his view, that "[the] local historian is sure of obtaining the gratitude of posterity, if he performs his task with fruitful diligence: his name becomes far more intimately and lastingly connected with the place, the memorials of which he has collected, than that of any personage however illustrious, who derives his title from it, and he erects for himself a more durable monument in perishable paper than could be constructed of marble or brass."(54)

But others stressed an important distinction that could be drawn between local histories of the old world and those of the new. When P. C. Brooks learned from Lemuel Shattuck that he was "engaged in our early history — Nothing can be more commendable — While the accounts of other countries run back into fable—ours can be traced with as much certainty almost as any fact within our knowledge."(55)

There is not much direct evidence that the early antiquarians in North America were conversant with local historical writing in England, but there is abundant evidence that those in Massachusetts knew one another, or at least corresponded with one another in a tone of familiarity.   Joshua Coffin, Lemuel Shattuck, Alonzo Lewis, and Joseph Felt—all knew of each other's researches and writings in intimate detail, and, indeed, actively assisted one another.

This awareness of and participation in the work of others engaged in the same kind of task was not entirely restricted to Massachusetts. Genealogist John Farmer keenly felt his isolation as a pioneering antiquarian as first secretary of the state historical society in New Hampshire.   He wrote to Lewis: "I often think of the pleasures and advantages which would be derived from having the aid, counsel, and encouragement of some literary friend, fond of and engaged in similar pursuits.   Though I occasionally receive calls from congenial minds, I am located [in Concord] near no one who feels an especial interest in historical inquiries."(56) But he rejoiced, after receiving letters from Lewis and Coffin, that "we are all members of the parent Historical Society of all similar ones in the U.S., and we are all somewhat linked together by the similarity of our past and present pursuits."(57)

In Pennsylvania, John F. Watson, the self-advertised premier antiquarian of the midatlantic states, also felt isolated and expressed his need to interact with his brethren from Massachusetts.   He wrote to Lewis in July, 1831, that he had read "some extracts" from his *History of Lynn*. "[It] will not surprise you if I should claim you as an intellectual kinsman — I having myself been sometimes engaged in unearthing old records." Conscious of his isolation, Watson suggested that "[p]erhaps an interchange of books may impart to us severally, new ideas on our favorite topics, and mutually assist each other in case of further researches."   To this end, Watson sent Lewis copies of his *Annals* of both New York and Philadelphia, asked for a copy of Lewis' *History of Lynn*, and added:   "Help me then what you can to still better understand and feel an interest in [the New Englanders'] *early* history. . . ; and if you have any means to furnish me with anything, . . . from other *olden time* writers, I will ask you to do so."(58)

In Maine, another pioneer, William Willis, corresponded with Alonzo Lewis (during the 1830s) and with Joshua Coffin and Lemuel Shattuck (during the 1850s) about genealogical matters relating to Portland.(59) A bond of a stronger kind was revealed in John F. Watson's letter to Willis, written on February 22, 1850: Watson's son and Willis' daughter had gotten married.   "It pleases me," Watson said, "that my son should have been impelled to a choice of one of the daughters of that intellectual and steady habit land.   I inherit this bias from my mother, of the Fanning and Miner race in Stonington [Connecticut].   I remember graphic tales of Yankee-land with cherished affection."   He went on to thank Willis "for your gift of a copy of your interesting Portland History.   It presents internal evidence that our minds have been moulded in the same class of affections and bias.

It is gratifying to see among us a growing regard for the preservation of such relics and reminiscences of olden times."(60) Watson then sent Willis a copy of his *Annals of New York*(61) and later added: "I feel myself personally flattered by your good feelings toward my history of New York in the olden time. It is something to us severally to feel congenial interests and emotions in consideration of the things that are past."(62)

In Connecticut, Frances Caulkins, still another pioneer, wrote to Watson in 1850 "in the spirit of kindred influences" (as Watson had put it in an earlier letter) and said: "We must become mutual friends — I am won by your pictorial delineations — many of them are as familiar to me as household words, and equally belonging to the personages and things occupying my drama."(63)

These communications among Lemuel Shattuck, Alonzo Lewis, Joshua Coffin, William Willis, John Farmer, Frances Caulkins, and John Watson constitute quite graphic evidence that the earliest local historians knew of each other's work and, at times, actively assisted in its furtherance. This correspondence reveals a kind of comradeship, an awareness that all were engaged in a novel and common enterprise: the preservation and recording of the past of a new people.


Without an established native tradition of historical writing to draw on, the early local historians were forced to forge their own forms and, in doing so, they drew upon a variety of literary genres, producing an amalgam: a composite, which was never stable for long, and was far from ever becoming a mechanical formula, a ready-made prescription to which all who wished to record their community's past would easily refer.

The histories produced after the Revolution, and especially after 1815, were formed in part out of a rejection of myth, folklore, hearsay, anything that was not factual or incontestable. Whether oral or written or printed, such forms of folklore as jokes, anecdotes, and tall tales encased the past of individuals, families, and communities alike. Then, as now, this story-telling impulse had in it a propensity toward exaggeration, distortion, and overdramatization. The early antiquarians sought to cleanse their histories of all such imperfections in an endless quest for truth, which they equated with the gathering of factual information.

As C. C. Baldwin, the Secretary of the American Antiquarian Society, put it to Lemuel Shattuck: "I am of our friend [Joshua] Coffin's opinion in this matter, which is that an antiquary should never back out from the truth, even though the consequences should be as disasterous as an earthquake."(64) Or, as Coffin himself said, "Every fact, however trivial, ought to be recorded as in its connection with other facts it may be of consequence. Things which we now consider of no moment may be of great importance some years hence, and very few antiquarians at the present day are sufficiently particular in the [recording] of *names* and *dates*."(65) Someone Coffin knew wrote to him that "[indeed] I have imbibed a little of that spirit of antiquarians which delights even in little scraps of information which to other people is of no interest."(66)

   This passion for factual accuracy often erupted into written comment
in the prefaces of the histories themselves.    J. W. Hanson said that in
preparing a *History of Gardiner, Pittston & West Gardiner*, Maine, that
"[his] constant effort has been to crowd and compress his facts into the
least possible space; so that the reader looks for any felicities of diction,
he will be disappointed.    He will only behold a plain, unvarnished account
of literal facts."(67)  Or, as Frances Caulkins put it in the preface of her
pioneering *History of Norwich*, Connecticut, in 1845: "The great point kept
in view through the whole composition of the work, was *accuracy*.    It was
the aim of the author to be minutely accurate.    Not a fact, name, or date
has been given without careful inquiry and examination."(68)  This was
clearly the goal, even though such statements were usually followed by
others indicating an awareness of the impossibility of attaining it.

   This factual orientation sharply delineated local historical writing from
popular fiction in the years between the 1820s and the 1860s.    The
melodramatic, sentimental "domestic" novels of these years were usually
produced by women authors and were immensely popular, especially during
the 1840s and 1850s.    These fictional portrayals of family and domestic life
contained plots that were "chains of episodes, which, taken together, served
to show the reader that bliss could come from suffering; that conventional
morals were best; that church, home, and family were anchors against
unhappiness and evil. Soft and lachrymous as most of these stories were,
they had nonetheless a real social function, in that they defined the moral
boundaries of life, delineated some of its problems, and gave advice on how
to cope with them."(69) Thus, family and domestic life was widely regarded
as a fit subject for fictional treatment during the same years that fact-
oriented genealogical investigations proliferated, even though novels rarely
focused on the context of family life, in villages, towns, or cities, as was
the case in the historical writings of the early antiquarians.

   Similarly, at the same time that both national and local historians
were insisting upon the validity of factual, truthful accounts of the past,
biographers like Weems and Lippard were producing myth-laden accounts of
national figures that served as historical depictions.    However much their
means differed, myth-making biographers and historians shared one goal: to
praise their ancestors for the great task of successfully building a
community or a nation.    The early antiquarians did not expect the truth
that their factual information disclosed to reveal anything other than
praiseworthy forebears, just as Weems and Lippard created heroes to
illuminate the glorious origins of the new nation.    Whether through fact or
myth, historians and biographers wrote out of sense of pride.

   But which facts? One form of writing that influenced the kind of
information the first local historians included in their histories was the
"gazetteer" or "statistical view" or "account," which were collections of
"descriptive facts about the civil relations of men. . . [i.e.] about
population, wealth, trade, industry, occupations, and civil and religious
institutions. . . . [They were] descriptive books the purpose of which was
to inform the public and especially men in public life—statists—about the
nature of American society."(70)    A variant of writings on geography,
travel, and natural or civil history—more specifically of the "topographical"

sketches that appeared during the same years in the Massachusetts Historical Society's *Collections*, the gazetteer flourished from the 1790s to the 1820s, when it made way for statistical manuals or collections stripped down to numerical tables.(71)  The gazetteer was one result of a passion for "authentic fact" arranged in an orderly manner. Various compilers surveyed the nation, regions, states, counties, cities, and towns.(72)

Typical was John Farmer's and Jacob Moore's *Gazetteer of the State of New Hampshire*, which appeared in 1823 with the prefatory remark that "[it] is unnecessary to offer an apology to the public for the appearance of a work, the utility of which, if well executed, no one will question." Farmer and Moore organized the work at the level of the state, its counties, and its towns.(73)

Early state historians, such as Jeremy Belknap of New Hampshire (1792), James Sullivan of Maine (1795), and David Ramsay of South Carolina (1809) were sufficiently influenced by this statistical approach to include gazetteer-like segments in their histories.  Belknap "devoted the final book of his three volume *History of New Hampshire* to a compendium of facts which he gathered by an intensive one-man investigation.  He scoured the countryside, talked to prominent local people, searched public record offices, sometimes surveyed land himself, and circulated a letter of inquiry to local clergymen and 'other gentlemen of public character', so 'that no sources of information might be left unexplored.' "(74)

The early antiquarians shared with the gazetteers a concern for verifiable facts, which the authors of gazetteers "carefully distinguished from opinions and estimates, and several authors printed wildly eclectic data as if to prove that no preconceived theory dictated their selection.  Some compilers went so far as to boast that they had eliminated commentary altogether: facts should be permitted to speak for themselves, without interpretation or amplification."(75)

The close relationship that sometimes existed between compilers of gazetteers and the earliest local historians is revealed in a letter from John Hayward, one of the most prominent of these compilers, to William Willis, the most important of the early antiquarians in Maine: "I herewith enclose copies from my old gazetteer of my description of some of the most important towns in your county to aid you in the performance of your kind offer of assistance in my new gazetteer of Maine. . . .  I beg you to exercise your own judgment and give me such information as you may deem most suited to the work. . . . P.S. I have just returned from Augusta [the state capitol] where I found gentlemen from almost every county of Maine who kindly offered to correct and amend my old gazetteer of N.E."(76)

The gazetteer served as a model for the range of subjects that the first local historians found it natural and congenial to treat, but the historical literature of the colonial period—the histories of particular colonies—was so thoroughly partisan, so much the product of selectivity and interpretation, that the successors of pioneer state historians like Belknap did not attempt to reduce historical writing after independence to a random compilation of facts, with "commentary eliminated altogether."

Another limitation on the gazetteer as a model was that it was a contemporary survey, usually without a significant temporal dimension and thus lacking in information involving change and continuity over significant periods of time. It is clear that the early antiquarians were influenced by a particular format or arrangement for historical writing in fashion during the colonial period: history in the form of annals, or a strictly chronological frame. Thomas Prince's *A Chronological History of New England in the Form of Annals* (Boston, 1736) was the most notable example. Prince, a Congregational minister, saw himself as a chronologist in the tradition of J. J. Scaliger in France and Archbishop Usher in England,(77) and turned out forty-three "numbers" or sections before ceasing publication of his excerpts from other writings.

Another manifestation of the annals form was the practice of early printers in the colonies of presenting news as a "history of the times," even if it meant falling behind in their presentation and displacing more recent occurrences. John Campbell of the *Boston News-Letter* and other, later, colonial editors, perhaps influenced by historical chroniclers like Prince, included items "only in strict chronological sequence – a logical procedure if one viewed a newspaper as a species of historical tract."(78)

When Joseph Felt chose to cast his history of Salem in "annals" form, genealogist John Farmer wrote Felt that "[the] labours of no one in New England have approximated so near those of the laborious and careful Prince as do your Annals of Salem, the last number of which I have examined with much interest. The work will be not only interesting to the people of Salem, but to all lovers of historical research and inquiry in this section of the country."(79)

Whether strictly in the annals form or not the whole corpus of early local historical writing in North America reveals the lasting influence of annalists like Prince. History was as much a chronology as it was a wide-ranging catalogue of subjects relating to community life. These two elements jockeyed for position, vied with each other for dominance during the entire century after local historical writing assumed its earliest recognizable shape.

State histories were written regularly after the Revolution, with the earliest authors continuing in various forms what their predecessors had started as histories of the British North American provinces. In sharp contrast was the rather sudden appearance of book-length local histories during the 1820s. To explain why such histories originated during that particular decade is difficult, for direct evidence is scanty.

In praising Lemuel Shattuck for his research on Concord, John Farmer told him that "[it] is desirable that histories of all our ancient towns should be written before the lapse of two centuries from their settlement."(80) But why *two* centuries? Farmer did not explain. When Dr. Caleb Snow presented the first overall history of Boston in 1825, a recipient of a free copy wrote that "[a] publication of the kind [that] appears to me would be very interesting as likewise advantageous to a large portion of the citizens of Boston, when events of the present day are contrasted with those 50 or 60 years past."(81) In other words, those who came of age during the Revolution, with political independence, were, by the 1820s, old men who had the perspective to view the contrast in their community's life between colonial times and the years after the revolution.

Another, far more typical explanation was that offered by Rufus C. Torrey in the preface to his history of Fitchburg (1836): "The writer has been induced to undertake the present work by a desire to save from the oblivion to which they were hastening, some of the events connected with the history of this town—Many of these are treasured up in the memories of a few aged people, and must, in the course of nature, soon be inevitably lost, if not preserved in a connected and tangible form. Though the number of these relics of other days is now small, much information has been derived from them, and much more might have been obtained had enquiries been commenced a few years earlier."(82)

Such inducements did not lead antiquarians to rush forth to have their researches and writings appear in print, however. In 1831, when William Willis presented his pioneering history of Portland, Maine, his publisher, George Folsom, noted that "[there] is a woeful ignorance prevailing everywhere, even among antiquarians, on the subject of the settlement and history of the eastern parts of New England, owing doubtless to the insignificance entertained by the early writers and perpetuated by later ones. Your volume must inevitably disperse in great measure this mist, dense as it is."(83)

But, by 1843, Edwin Stone saw fit to write in the preface of his history of Beverly, Massachusetts: "It is gratifying to perceive that the interest of late awakened in town histories is increasing."(84) And by 1847, in the introduction to his history of Framingham, Massachusetts, William Barry referred to "[the] public taste [that] has created a demand for such publications."(85) A year later, Caleb Butler prefaced his history of Groton, Massachusetts, with the comment that such chronicles "have become almost universal"(86) —at least in Massachusetts.

But not elsewhere. In 1830, John F. Watson advertized his *Annals of Philadelphia* as a work "without example for its imitation, [which] may be deemed *sui generis* in its execution."(87) And in Connecticut, in 1845, Frances Caulkins maintained that her history of Norwich "is not founded on previous histories—it has no predecessor. . . . It is an independent, original work."(88)

In 1846, Hermann Ludewig, in the earliest bibliography of local history in North America, indicated in his introduction that "there is no lack of local histories, especially in New England, whose sons may justly be called a 'documentary people.' . . . There is hardly a town of some extent in New England, the historical events of which have not been recorded in some work, particularly written for that purpose, or in centennial sermons, lectures, or notices garnered up in the collections of their historical societies."(89)

But, in New England—or just Massachusetts? Here Ludewig kept alive a tradition of linguistic exaggeration perpetuated by writers who equated developments in Massachusetts with *all* of New England. Spawned in a period when Massachusetts dominated the surrounding colonies politically, economically, and spiritually—most clearly in the seventeenth century—authors like William Hubbard, in *General History of New England* (finished in 1682), Daniel Neal, in *The History of New England* (1720), and Thomas Prince, in *A Chronological History of New England* (1736), focused on events in Massachusetts while purporting to give the history of the entire region.(90) If Ludewig had replaced "New England" with "Massachusetts," his statement would have been far more accurate.

# CHAPTER 2
# The New England Pioneers

The domination of early local historical writing in North America by authors from Massachusetts can be somewhat explained by reference to several interrelated factors. The founding of Puritan towns as special, planned, model religious communities was a phenomenon—temporally—mostly of the seventeenth century and—spatially—largely of the coastal region of New England centering on Boston. Here were the towns that in the 1820's had (1) the age and family continuity, (2) the records, (3) a tradition of historical writing stretching back to the religiously oriented Puritan accounts, and (4) a still-important Congregational clergy who, along with others of long-term connections, continued to view their communities as sufficiently special and religious to be worth writing about. What moved these men to act by the 1820s and thereafter was their sense that such towns (and cities) were old enough and worthy enough to have their past recalled, especially before their origins and early development were permanently distorted in folklore or irretrievably lost with the destruction of badly secured records.

Many of the fifty-seven men and two women who wrote book-length histories of towns and cities in Massachusetts before the Civil War were of such little prominence that no biographical information has survived. It was rare for these early local historians to be marked out for posterity unless their achievements went beyond the confines of antiquarian research and historical writing. Even membership in the Massachusetts Historical Society, the New England Historical and Genealogical Society, of the American Antiquarian Society did not guarantee an extended obituary or "memorial," unless more than exceptional service had been rendered.

The fifty-nine names read like a roll call of early settlers: Allen, Snow, Worthington, Lincoln, Lewis, Abbot, Biglow, Deane, Hudson, Thacher, Graves, Shattuck, Bliss, Read, Willard, Mitchell, Gage, Field, Draper, Stone. All shared a strong sense of identity with the places they wrote about;

none could in any obvious sense be regarded as newcomers or outsiders. Though not all were born in the communities they wrote about, they all had at least a long-standing association.  It is obvious that antiquarianism was a male-dominated task, with only two women — Euphemia (Blake) Smith (on Newburyport, in 1854) and Electa Jones (on Stockbridge, in 1854) — to be counted among the early antiquarians from Massachusetts.  However, women were not in any way ever formally barred and, indeed, were never completely discouraged.    For example, in nearby Connecticut, Frances Caulkins clearly regarded herself as the pioneering antiquarian for her state.

Many of those about whom biographical information exists were trained for the ministry, and, in most cases the Congregational or still-dominant ministry, and were thus apt to have a community-wide perspective not shared by anyone else, with the possible exception of the selectmen. Others became school teachers, at least for a time, or, more rarely, college professors, usually at Harvard.  A few studied law or medicine — occasionally both — or embarked on "mercantile" or business careers, or became booksellers.    Still others combined such pursuits with political office, sometimes at more than one of the national, state, and local levels.  Some were of prominent or wealthy families. Justin Winsor's father was a prosperous merchant; Josiah Quincy's was a "mercantile family" of considerable wealth, as was Daniel Ricketson's, to the point that he never had an occupation from which he derived needed income.  But others were from families of modest means: Peter Whitney's father was a minister, Joseph Felt's a shipmaster, Convers Francis' a baker, and James Thacher's parent was labeled as a farmer.(1)

Typical of the better known local historians was a life of many dimensions, with antiquarian pursuits one of a list of undertakings.  There is not a single known instance of any of the fifty-nine who actually derived his principal income from personal literary endeavors.  Joseph Felt was unusual in that he achieved prominence largely for his historical work, but it is important to note that he came to focus on such undertakings because ill-health forced him to retire from the ministry while still in his forties. After writing two full-length town histories — of Salem in 1827, and of Ipswich in 1834 — Felt was hired by the Massachusetts state government to arrange the papers in the state archives and went on to serve as the Librarian of the Massachusetts Historical Society from 1842 to 1854 and as an early president of the New England Historical and Genealogical Society from 1850 to 1853.    Characterized at his death in 1869 as a "diligent annalist" with an extraordinary zeal for discovering and reading old manuscripts, Felt was presented by the 1930s in the *Dictionary of American Biography* as, simply, an "antiquarian," the only one so characterized among the group of fifty-nine.(2)

Of the forty-six whose birth and death dates are known, the age at which their first local history was published is as follows: one — Justin Winsor — was in his teens, five were in their twenties, eleven in their thirties, eight in their forties, five in their fifties, seven in their sixties, seven in their seventies, and one — Josiah Quincy — in his eighties.   Or, seventeen were young, thirteen middle-aged, and fifteen old—which demonstrates that age was as much a variable as chief occupation.

Justin Winsor (1831-1897), the child prodigy of the group who later became the enormously influential Librarian of the Boston Public Library (1868-1877) and of Harvard (1877-1897), developed an early interest in history. As one memorialist put it: "Even as a boy he attended meetings of the New England Historic Genealogical Society and began to collect materials for his first book, A History of the Town of Duxbury, which was published in 1849 during his freshman year at Harvard."(3) He made his way—as he himself admitted "to many of the aged inhabitants of the town, to whose tales I have listened with interest and whose words I have taken from their lips."(4) In his college journal, Winsor recorded a remarkable scene of himself, as an incoming freshman, hard at work on the proofs of his history, noting on October 27, 1849: "Got some of my books [bound] for the first time. . . . I received my first proof Saturday, July 14, 1849, just fifteen weeks ago."(5) Neither Felt nor Winsor—neither making antiquarian pursuits one's major occupation nor showing signs of doing so as a teenager—was typical of the early local historians in Massachusetts, however.

How certain individuals took up "antiquarian pursuits," as they often put it, is sometimes referred to, usually in a tantalizingly brief way, in the prefaces of the first local histories on Massachusetts towns and cities. John Daggett revealed that his history of Attleboro, which appeared in 1834, was in its earliest version, a lecture delivered at the Lyceum in Attleboro in 1830. His subject, "being entirely *new* to the hearers, excited much interest." At the earnest request of many of the most respectable citizens of the town, Daggett decided to prepare his lecture for publication. But as his research continued, "new materials were found, and the work multiplied upon my hands."(6) Similarly, Lemuel Shattuck collected many materials relating to the history of Concord. "[I]n the process of his investigation, the quantity of interesting matter increased so much" that, instead of preparing them for serialization in a newspaper, as he originally intended, Shattuck decided to publish a book-length history.(7)

Leonard Bliss revealed in his history of Rehoboth (1836) that his original purpose was to furnish the Massachusetts Historical Society with another in its series of brief "town sketches," which had been appearing since the turn of the century. But the materials were far more extensive than he had imagined, and, "encouraged by the example of several town histories which had recently made their appearance, determined, if I found sufficient patronage to warrant the expense of publication, to extend my sketch to a more complete history, and publish it in a separate volume."(8) A book-length treatment of Worcester's history was justified in 1837 by William Lincoln as "desirable, while it was yet possible, to gather the fast fading traditions and scattered records of the past, and preserve a more full view of our local history, than was permitted by the limits of religious discourse and festival address, or accorded with the plans of former writers."(9) David Willard, the first to attempt a history of an inland town, pointed to "the establishment of a new press" as creating "the opportunity of offering [his history] to my fellow townsmen, the publishers volunteering its publication on fair terms, requiring no *security*, (which means entangling one's friends), beyond the subscription list."(10)

The writing of local history was unquestionably a demanding and laborious task, so much so that a few of the early antiquarians from Massachusetts referred directly to the fact in their prefatory statements. John Daggett wrote in 1834 that "the attempt was indeed at first discouraging. The field was new and unexplored. There was no light to lead my blind way through the dark labyrinths of the past. Little or nothing was contained in other works to which I could refer for aid. The spot had almost escaped the prying curiosity of the antiquarian. I found, however, after diligent and laborious research, facts enough to make up the present volume."(11)

Lemuel Shattuck was blunter: "Those only who have been engaged in similar works can be aware of the great labor required to collect the materials for a volume like this, and arrange them both for the press."(12) Blunter still was James Draper when he let his readers know that "[however] satisfactory or acceptable this may prove, and however much it may be esteemed, it has cost a great deal of time and labor, indeed so much, that had it been known and realized at the commencement, it would have been abandoned before it was undertaken."(13)

Deteriorating health sometimes resulted, as in the case of George Faber Clark, who revealed that "[when] we issued our subscription paper, May 1, 1855, we supposed the book would go to press in about fifteen months. But, in the attempt to carry out that plan, our eyes (which had been weak for years) became so affected in the autumn of 1856, that all labor upon the book was suspended for several months; and since it was resumed, we have been able to work but a small portion of the time upon it."(14)

The correspondence of Joshua Coffin contains the best surviving evidence of how time consuming and frustratingly slow work was, especially if researching and writing a book-length history was the objective. On June 3, 1824, Coffin wrote to John Farmer: "I have made but little progress in my history of Newbury, or old Dunstable, solely for want of time. All my leisure moments after I have finished transcribing the Newbury Records for which the town have agreed to pay me."(15) In 1826, Coffin must have learned that J. Dudley was also interested in doing a history of Newbury, for Dudley wrote on August 20, thanking Coffin for his suggestion that Dudley deal with the nearby towns of Ipswich, Rawley, and Salisbury, reaffirming that "I shall call [my work] a history of *Newbury* and nothing more." It is likely that Coffin felt Dudley had been poaching on his territory. In any case, a history of Newbury by Dudley never appeared.

On February 13, 1827, Coffin wrote to Farmer that "I am in no hurry to print. . . . If I publish in haste I shall repent at leisure. . . . My business has been this winter in talking with old people, rummaging [through] old trunks, and trying to save what would otherwise be lost very soon." In response, on February 24, Farmer tried to goad Coffin on: "[You] can revel at your ease—and surely, you who have such advantages ought to give the public a volume of collections which might be easily made up from the records I have mentioned." On August 10, Coffin responded by saying that "[Y]ou err in supposing that I am so situated as to give much leisure to attend to subjects of an antiquarian nature, when the facts are that I have to steal all the time that I devote to researches of the nature." Coffin went on to catalogue his activities: "This summer I am keeping school, taking care of a few acres of land, house, a tan-yard, walk 2½ miles to school and return at night, have two children and myself to provide for, and have *no wife* to help *yet*."

A few months later, on February 22, 1828, A. Gerrish wrote to ask: "How do you progress? When do you expect the work will [be] ready for the press?" A year or so after that, on June 21, 1829, Farmer was after him again: "I am solicitous to know how advances the preparing of the History of Newbury. [Then, the not-so-subtle hint:] that of Lynn [by Alonzo Lewis] I suppose is in the press." By April 8, 1835, Farmer could no longer hide his exasperation: "How are your Antiquarian pursuits? Have you abandoned them altogether? Not so with me. I suspect I was born an antiquarian, and that it will be impossible for me to change my nature. Do inform me something about your Newbury mss. You are duty bound to place them in some important hands, who will give the long expected and desired history. [Then:] Would not Mr. Felt be a good man?" With or without further goading Coffin persevered, undoubtedly at his own pace: he published a history of Newbury in 1845!

Daniel Ricketson tried to explain the difficulties confronting the early local historians: "The labor of an original work of this kind," he wrote, "is much more arduous and difficult than many more important works of history where the labors of others can be brought into requisition."(16) It is true that the pioneer antiquarians in Massachusetts labored alone in the sense that they were the sole authors of their histories, but Ricketson — responding to the difficulty of the undertaking — claimed too much. Even he expressed his "warmest thanks . . . [to] the friends who have afforded me assistance in the preparation of my task."(17)

Far more typical was the practice of naming those who helped. For example, Alonzo Lewis prefaced his early history of Lynn (1829) with "the sincere expression of my gratitude" to such individuals as James Savage, Secretary of the Massachusetts Historical Society; John Farmer, Secretary of the New Hampshire Historical Society; and Joshua Coffin, "author of a manuscript History of Newbury, an animated and interesting sketch, which I hope he will soon present to the public[!]"(18)

Others referred directly to the earlier histories of particular historians as models for their own. In 1837, William Lincoln, in presenting his history of Worcester, revealed that "[the] general plan of arrangement, affording convenience in tracing the course and connection of events, and facility of reference, has been imitated from Mr. Shattuck's History of Concord. It would have been greatly desirable that the excellence of this model could have been more fully copied."(19) In 1848, J. W. Hanson, in presenting his history of Danvers, indicated to his readers that "[it] will be seen that he has followed the general plan of Stone's History of Beverly, a well-arranged work."(20) In 1854, Samuel Drake, in prefatory remarks to his history of Boston, went further: "How many persons have had it in contemplation to write a History of Boston is unknown to the author; but the only one, probably, who, in the last thirty years, has seriously thought of it, was Mr. Alonzo Lewis. That gentleman was very competent for the task, and had he been at liberty to persecute it, agreeably to his announcement about twenty-five years ago, it would have rendered this undertaking unnecessary."(21)

At least several of the early local historians in Massachusetts corresponded, had detailed knowledge of each other's work, and even provided needed material on occasion. For instance, evidence that Joshua Coffin kept himself informed of what others were doing is contained in his letter to John Farmer on January 9, 1828: "Mr. Felt will soon have his second number [of his serialized *Annals of Salem*] out which will be valuable. I have lately received a letter from Alonzo Lewis giving me the names of the first settlers of Lynn."(22) On March 23 of that year Coffin sent Lewis verbatim copies of various documents, with the salutation of "mi frater" and the signature of "Yours antiquarially and truly."(23) On May 4, Lemuel Shattuck wrote to Lewis: "I have been informed by several eminent antiquarians . . . that you are engaged in compiling the History of Lynn. Being engaged in a similar employment on the history of Concord, you will pardon me I hope if I trouble you with a few inquiries about which I wish information."(24)

Being informed sometimes extended to active assistance, as when, in December, 1831, Shattuck wrote to Coffin: "I propose to go to Boston next week and shall leave the bundle you speak of and shall I hope to have pleasure of seeing you and answering personally the other queries in your letter."(25) Similarly, William Lincoln wrote to Shattuck in October of the same year "of my great desire to read the history of Concord in its printed form. . . . Allow me to aid in any mode in which I can be useful."(26)

Just how extensively involved in each other's work these antiquarians became at times is revealed in Alonzo Lewis' letter to Joseph Felt on May 1, 1830: "The following anecdote exhibits a striking instance of magnanimity and is a noble illustration of human disinterestedness. It is so good that I was about to include it in my history, but thinking you would be best pleased to have it in yours where it more properly belongs, I send it to you."(27)

Queries were even passed around, as Samuel Drake indicated to Felt on April 7, 1832: "Gave your letter to Mr. Coffin this morning (was not able to see him before) and he said he would attend to your request *immediately*. If, however, you do not hear in a reasonable time, I will attend to it with pleasure, on your dropping me another line stating with what you desire, as may not be able to get the other without loss of time."(28)

Beyond the assistance other antiquarians were in a position to provide, the early local historians regularly solicited information from fellow inhabitants of their towns and cities. Some of these contributors were willing and eager to help and did so with alacrity. But others provided information only after some delay, purportedly caused by the press of other business or the inaccessibility of pertinent sources of information.(29)

The scattered antiquarians who worked on local history elsewhere in the United States in the years before the Civil War did so in a context markedly different from that of the Massachusetts group. Nowhere else in the young union was the enterprise of research and writing local histories of such a large scale that an antiquarian could expect the encouragement and assistance of others. Nowhere else could a local historian receive reassurance from the sheer weight and number of previously published works. In Massachusetts what was a group activity elsewhere involved the labor of solitary individuals.

However, in all parts of New England, early antiquarians relied on material contributed by volunteers. In 1819 and for several years thereafter, William Williamson sent out a circular letter to prominent citizens in each of Maine's towns, asking them to contribute information to his proposed history of the new state.(30) The responses to Williamson's repeated requests for information were varied, but numerous, and, examined in their entirety, reveal a lot about the attitudes and perceptions of those with an interest in local history who lacked the talent and perseverence to be an antiquarian or a genealogist. Practically everyone who responded praised Williamson for undertaking such a task.(31) Williamson must have experienced frustration waiting months, even years, for responses, having to send out two or more copies of his circular to certain individuals. The explanations Williamson received on how the requested information came to be gathered reveal something of the circumstances within which those with a layman's interest in their community's past operated during these years. Respondents referred to the mislaying of Williamson's letter, to poor health, to the need for compensation, to ignorance, to the want of leisure time, to the amount of time needed for such a compilation, to the transfer of the letter to others who were more knowledgeable.(32)

Most of the respondents were keenly aware of their limitations as compilers and sketchers. They looked to Williamson to transform their jottings into real historical writing. Some were so self-effacing or lacking in confidence that they requested that their names not be made public.(33) Others asked Williamson to edit, improve, correct, or write out in stylistically proper language what they had submitted.(34) This is, in fact, what Williamson did. In a memorandum accompanying the "alphabetical list of towns and names of the gentlemen to whom circulars concerning history of Maine were sent", Williamson indicated the stages of research and writing that led to the creation of his history of Maine, published in 1832.(35)

Williamson refers in his preface to the "letters from 150 correspondents, residing in different parts of the state [and] . . . to [the] topographical notes upon towns [scattered through the two-volume history that] contain facts which could not with propriety be incorporated with the text, and yet were thought too valuable to be lost; for descriptions of these municipalities are not only interesting to their respective inhabitants they are collectively the local chronicles of the State."(36) In a special appendix, Williamson provided an indexed "List of *Counties* and *towns* within the State, at the time of Separation [from Massachusetts, in 1820] with references to the settlement, incorporation, or description." He added a note of thanks for "the numerous epistolary communications from the pens of his obliging correspondents," adding that "fuller descriptions of many towns would have been given, had the *Circulars*, repeatedly sent to them, drawn from the gentlemen addressed, the information requested."(37)

George Folsom—a peripatetic lawyer later active in the American Antiquarian Society, the New York Historical Society, and the Vermont Historical Society—lamented in his pioneering history of Saco and Biddeford (1830) that "the settlements of Maine have been almost wholly neglected by New England historians," even ten years after Maine's separation from Massachusetts (as a district) and entrance into the Union as a state.(38) And when, in 1831 and 1832, William Willis presented a two-part history of Portland, the young state's first city, he revealed that "[in] 1820, when Maine became an independent State, no historical work, nor any other of literary value, had been published in the State."(39) He added that "[the] entire loss of the records in the destruction of the town by the Indians in 1690, has deprived me of many valuable materials for the present work, and rendered my task at the same time more difficult and more unsatisfactory."(40)

Willis was unquestionably the most influential local historian in Maine from the 1830s through the 1860s and the many dimensions of his life as antiquarian are revealed in his well preserved correspondence and diary. Of a leading merchant, ship-owning family, a graduate of both Philips Exeter Academy and Harvard, he became a distinguished lawyer in Portland, where for fifty years (1820-1870) "he filled the role of 'substantial citizen.'" Willis was a state Senator; mayor of Portland; a bank commissioner; chairman of the State Board of Railroad Commissioners; a director and vice president of a Portland bank; President of the Maine Central Railroad; active in the Unitarian church; a busy humanitarian; a member of a literary club called the "Portland Wits"; a contributor to newspapers of pieces on old houses, detailed obituaries, and "episodic accounts of Maine history"; Secretary, Treasurer, and President of the Maine Historical Society; and editor of the first six volumes of its collections (1831-1850).(41) It is hard to imagine a single figure so prominent in so many dimensions of a community's economic, political, social, cultural, and intellectual life.

By the 1840s, Willis' reputation as an antiquarian was high and far-reaching. Another pioneer within the state, Charles Folsom, wrote that he hoped "you will be induced to keep 'your hand in' and go on to other historical labors, for which you have proved yourself to have a vocation [and] by now repeated conspicuous achievements."(42) From Massachusetts, the chief citadel of antiquarian endeavor, the very active Nahum Mitchell, historian of Plymouth, revealed: "We of the historical society esteem your Portland the best local history we have."(43)

George Preble, formerly of Portland, passed on a scrapbook and list of deaths compiled by his father with the note that "I feel I could place it . . . in no better hands than yours," and urged Willis to use the material "when you make up a new edition of your history of Portland, which I much hope to see. It is now more than a quarter of a century since . . . your valuable and interesting book was published, and quite enough events I should say in that period of time have happened to make up a very interesting third volume if the labor of altering the whole work to conform to the present time is [not] too much for you."(44)

Preble need not have worried.  Willis in all these years had indulged in what a successor in the historical society called "relentless study and incessant note-taking.    His notes for these years, contained in forty huge volumes at the Maine Historical Society, are paragons of organization and enabled [him] to know precisely what he wanted to correct, amend, and elaborate."(45) On March 1, 1865, Willis revealed in his journal that during the past year "I prepared a new edition of the history of Portland, in one large octavo volume of over 900 pages, bringing the history down to the present time, and adding a copious index.   This work is now in the hands of the binder and will be issued in a few days." On March 16: "My history of Portland is out today and goes off rapidly — the whole edition will be exhausted in a few days here." On March 24: "My history of Portland meets with general acceptance and is much praised by discriminating persons."(46)

Willis' eminence as an antiquarian was revealed in a variety of ways. John Johnston wrote as an aspiring local historian: "I am glad that so much interest is taken in my native place, Pemaquid, and that the compilation of its ancient history is recommended by so competent [an] authority as yourself. . . .   [My] principal object in writing is to inquire whether you cannot from your experience give your suggestions with regard to the best course to be pursued in collecting materials and perhaps inform me where important documents may be found."(47)

Willis' central position in the world of Maine's antiquarian activity was acknowledged in other ways as well.   Charles Folsom occasionally forwarded material for Willis to distribute "among such gentlemen of your acquaintance, as you think will take an interest in the subject."(48) Harvard's librarian, John L. Sibley, whose sketches of Harvard graduates made him famous, wrote about his history of his hometown, Union, Maine: "I go immediately to Union with numerous copies of my book, conscious that at least I must sacrifice on it $100 or $200.   If you are disposed to give it a notice in the Portland Advertiser at a very early date, it may help the sale somewhat.   The Daily Advertiser is not taken in Union, but the weekly or semi-weekly into which I shall be glad to have it go.   However, I wish you to act your pleasure about it and feel free to write a notice or not."(49) And, a few weeks later: "The commendation of my history [in the *Advertiser*] was vastly greater than I could have anticipated and is peculiarly gratifying, and I owe you many thanks for your favorable notice of it.   The book has occupied my leisure for six years, and though I am aware of its many imperfections, I have been particularly careful to make it as exact as circumstances would warrant.(50)

Willis' many-faceted activities with the Maine Historical Society also attest to his prominence.   R. H. Gardiner wrote on several occasions, seeking Willis' advice on the best place for the state's historical society to hold its meetings.(51) Charles Norton, an "Agent for Libraries and Colleges" supported Willis in his plan to prepare a bibliography on historical writings about Maine.(52) In his diary, Willis described the historical society's meetings, listed the speakers and their subjects, and referred to the dinners and overnight stays he shared with other members, on one occasion revealing that they "were fully occupied in discussing historical and ecclesiastical subjects until near tea-time: the day and evening were most agreeably spent."(53)

With a prominence unequalled in any of the other New England states, Willis kept busy right up until his death. November 27, 1869: "Wrote this afternoon my introduction to the bibliography of Maine, in which I gave a history of the earliest literary attempts among us." December 3, 1869: "I am making daily progress in my bibliography and hope and expect to see the end of it before the end of January." January 8, 1870: "I am getting along well with the bibliography, am nearly through P." January 22, 1870: "Wrote Mr. Dawson yesterday that my bibliography was finished except a revision which I am now engaged in." February 9, 1870: "Had a very sick day — Dr. Gilman going to Augusta called in Dr. Wood in consultation; they have not changed their remedies — Finished my bibliography and packed it up ready for printer." He died eight days later, on February 17.(54)

The antiquarian impulse in New Hampshire found its earliest significant expression in the writings of Jacob Moore. Moore acknowledged the preeminence of the Massachusetts group by printing his own *A Topographical and Historical Sketch of the Town of Andover* in 1822,(55) clearly modelling it after the sketches that had been appearing in the *Collections* of the Massachusetts Historical Society.

Moore joined with the pioneering genealogist, John Farmer, to produce *A Gazetteer of the State of New Hampshire*, which Moore himself published in 1823. A founder of the New Hampshire Historical Society with Farmer, Moore became its librarian in 1823, a position he occupied until 1830,(56) and became co-editor with Farmer of the first three volumes of the Society's *Collections*. In 1824, Moore published his own *Annals of the Town of Concord*, pioneering in the annalistic form that the earliest Massachusetts antiquarians also favored in the late 1820s and early 1830s.(57)

Nathaniel Adams' *Annals of Portsmouth*, was written in 1824, but not published until the following year.(58) Whether Adams and Moore worked independently, or, if not, who influenced whom, is not known. Moore, who combined journalism, publishing, mill operations, and landowning, left New Hampshire in 1839, a bankrupt man. His departure, coupled with Farmer's early death, left the state without active antiquarians, and indeed no book-length local history appeared between Adams' history of Portsmouth, in 1825, and 1840, when Charles James Fox was appointed chairman of the Committee upon Histories of the Towns at the annual meeting of the New Hampshire State Historical Society.(59)

Fox, a lawyer from Nashua, had already prepared the revised statutes of New Hampshire while a member of the state legislature,(60) and shortly after his appointment as chairman of the Committee upon Histories of the Towns, he prepared (with Rev. Samuel Osgood) the "New Hampshire Book," "a collection of pieces in prose and verse from the writings of natives and adopted citizens of this state."(61) Fox chose "Old Dunstable," a township that was in both Massachusetts and what became New Hampshire. Having to draw on sources in Massachusetts, he expressed his indebtedness "for many accommodations in examining and copying the records [to] Rev. Joseph B. Felt, who has been employed for many years by the State in arranging and binding them."(62)

Fox's committee does not appear to have inspired others to produce local history. Indeed, the influence of the pioneers, Farmer and Moore, lived on only in the work of Rev. Nathaniel Bouton, who was for forty-two years (1825-1867) the minister of the First Congregational Church in Concord. It was natural for Bouton, first trained as a printer, to meet Moore and Farmer when he came to Concord out of Andover Seminary in the mid-1820s.(63) Nor was it surprising that they asked him to join the New Hampshire State Historical Society when his historical interests became evident.(64) Bouton served on the publications committee for a number of years and was president of the society for two years.

His son later recalled that "[it] was not long before John Farmer, Jacob B. Moore . . . and other kindred spirits found him out." Farmer and Moore and others "often called at his house and were glad to enlarge their own stock of lore [from information] which he was always picking up in his rides and walks about the parish and his examination of the oldest inhabitants. In return they would tell him of anything interesting they had seen or heard." His son thought that he "had the knack of putting this or that [document or artifact] together."(65)

Or, as Professor Henry E. Parker of Dartmouth College recalled in a "Memorial Discourse": When Bouton made pastoral visits as a young minister "through every hill and valley nook and corner of the wide township," he became acquainted with all the inhabitants of the area and developed an interest in family and town history. "A score of years were spent in diligent gatherings of materials, and then three more of untiring labor with the pen in preparing those materials for the press."(66)

Still, Bouton's *History of Concord* is a good example of how antiquarians everywhere in New England continued to rely on the assistance of others. In his preface, he provides an unusually detailed description of all those who had assisted him: Richard Bradley and Nathan Stickney, "for valuable information relative to the civil affairs of the town, with which they have long been intimately acquainted"; Benjamin Parker and Stephan C. Badger, "for the exact description they have given of localities and distances"; Moody Kent, "for an account of the ancient trees which are the ornament of our main village, and for many facts respecting professional men who are deceased"; William Prescott, M.D., "for his contributions to the chapter upon Physical History"; Jacob Hoyt, George Abbot, Simeon Abbot, and Benjamin Rolf, "for the entertaining incidents and anecdotes they have furnished relative to ancient times"; Chandler E. Potter, "for friendly aid in furnishing me copies of original documents"; "a young lady of our own city, for results of her careful researches into our Indian history."(67)

When Bouton retired, in 1867, the office of state historian was created for him, and, before his death in 1878, he edited and had published ten volumes of state documents pertaining to the colonial and revolutionary periods.

In both Rhode Island and Connecticut, even though the oldest towns were founded and settled in the seventeenth century, the earliest local histories date from the 1840s, twenty years after the pioneering efforts in Massachusetts, Maine, and New Hampshire.

William Staples, a judge in Rhode Island from 1835 to 1856 and one of the founders of the state's Historical Society in 1822 (as well as being its first librarian and cabinet-keeper),(68) remarked on the absence of local historical writing in Rhode Island in the preface of his long, pioneering *Annals of the Town of Providence* (1843). Staples went on to provide at least a partial explanation for the neglect Rhode Islanders had exhibited toward the past of their own communities. He admitted that in his *Annals* he had drawn on an admixture of material from both state and town sources because "in the early times, the dividing line between the state, or rather the colony, and town history was, by no means, so distinctly defined as now."(69)

But Providence, as the colonial and then state capital, was an exception. What Staples ignored in his remarks was any reference to the wide autonomy and authority Rhode Island's towns had exercised throughout the colonial period,(70) something that could well have served to induce antiquarians to delineate the past of well defined communities. But, for whatever reasons, Staples' *Annals* did not serve as a model for others. Only one other local history was published in Rhode Island before the Civil War: Guy Fessenden's 125-page history of Warren, in 1845.(71)

In Connecticut, Frances Caulkins was keenly aware of her role as a pioneer when she presented her history of Norwich in the same year. She indicated in her preface that her history "is not a compilation from published documents, is not founded on previous histories,—it has no predecessor, and therefore cannot appeal to works which are generally accessible. As a History of Norwich it is an independent, original work; but it makes no claim beyond that of a faithful purpose to give a more enduring form to a mass of local information, that would be lost if left much longer in the charge of mouldering paper, fading ink, and fast dropping age."(72)

In Connecticut, the work of other early antiquarians was published by the Hartford firm of Case, Tiffany, and Co., which appears to have taken a special interest in local historical writing. Frances Caulkins' second volume, a history of New London (1852), was published by Case, Tiffany & Co., as were Charles Sedgewick's Sharon (1842), Noah Phelps' Sunsbury (1845), and Payne Kilbourne's Litchfield (1859).

There is no obvious explanation for why the antiquarian impulse found expression later in Rhode Island and Connecticut than it did in Maine and New Hampshire, given that both sets of states contained towns of comparable age and were equally close to Massachusetts. However, the work of Willis in Maine and of Moore and Adams in New Hampshire was the work of individuals, not the product of sustained group effort. The pioneer antiquarians in New England—outside of Massachusetts—were lone individuals prompted to labor away in an effort to recover the past out of a personal concern to do so, and not because it was fashionable or common. Nowhere in New England—outside of eastern Massachusetts—was there continuous effort to produce local histories, involving many individual antiquarians, sometimes aware of and indeed assisting in the work of others. Before the Civil War, the antiquarian impulse in the United States clearly centered on Boston and its environs.

Younger than communities along the New England coast, in fact settled only from the mid-eighteenth century onward, the earliest Vermont towns did not contain active antiquarians until almost the time of the Civil War. However, in Vermont, the earliest local historical writing developed out of efforts to produce gazetteers, and the planning and production of gazetteers was done by individuals who were not especially concerned about the age or longevity of the places they dealt with.

As early as 1814, Josiah Dunham sent out a circular from Windsor to "gentlemen of science and information.," to gather accurate material on incorporation and territorial size, topography, man-made structures, churches, schools, statistics, and biographical sketches on the inhabitants. Dunham added, "[The] members of the legislature are respectfully and particularly requested to assist in this business as soon as may be; to consult, if necessary, their respective Clergymen, other Professional men, or town clerks; to procure what number of subscribers they can. . . . Representatives from the several towns, also, Post Masters, Printers, Booksellers, and others are respectfully to receive subscriptions and to encourage the work."(73) Though Dunham received some responses, he did not go on to issue a gazetteer.(74)

By October, 1823, Zadock Thompson revived the proposal,(75) and went on to send out subscription sheets and lists of queries to hoped-for contributors in the various towns, making a plea for subscribers and for answers to questions about town charters, proprietors, first settlers, town governments, churches, schools, professions, various buildings, and topography. The responses varied, but one preoccupation distinctive to those who aided Thompson in his project was their concern that there be an adequate number of subscribers.(76)

In any case, Thompson persisted, and in 1824 E. P. Waton published his gazetteer in Montpelier, the state capitol. The section consisting of sketches on the towns was by far the longest one. In his preface, Thompson acknowledged that "[when] this work was commenced, we were aware that the accomplishment of our design would be attended with much labor and difficulty. . . . In the execution of it, we have, however, had to encounter unexpected obstacles, which would probably have deterred us from the undertaking had they been fully anticipated." He went on to indicate that "[the] materials for the following pages have been derived principally from personal observations, and from written and oral communications. We have visited most of the townships in person, and have likewise received a great number of written communications from gentlemen in different sections of the state."

Asking his fellow citizens to "recollect that this is the first attempt to collect facts relating to the settlement and history of our townships," Thompson cleverly added: "[Should the gazette] be patronized with the liberality which will warrant the publication of a *second edition*, we flatter ourselves that our fellow citizens will cheerfully lend their assistance in correcting the errors and supplying the deficiencies in this."(77)

Thompson's "second edition," when it came in 1842, took on the form of a state history, rather than another gazetteer. His decision to alter the description of what he presented to the public is a good indication of the shift in emphasis away from gazetteers toward histories that occurred between the 1820s and the 1840s. But, in fact, the content of Thompson's 1842 history remained basically the same in form as that presented in his 1824 gazetteer. The sketches of the towns continued to dominate. In both gazetteer and history, the state-wide sections were brief accounts of the geography and natural history and of the civil or political and social and religious history of Vermont, obviously meant to be introductory to what followed.

Thompson asked hoped-for contributors from the various towns to examine the sketch of their town that had appeared in the gazetteer and to note any errors it contained and to bring it up to date.(78) In making additions to the original sketches, some contributors relied on others.(79) Thompson's reliance on the survivors of the first generation of inhabitants created problems, especially by the 1840s, when such survivors were very old.(80) Thompson's 1840s respondents appear to have been more sanguine about the prospects of finding subscribers than their 1820s forbears; certainly they were more persistent.(81)

In the preface to his history, Thompson confessed that "[ever] since the publication of his Gazetteer of Vermont in 1824, the author has contemplated a longer work, which should embrace, not only the Gazetteer, but a general History of the state, both Natural and Civil." For four years Thompson had been collecting material preparing the new work for publication. Thompson expressed the hope that the history "may be found to answer the reasonable expectations of all."(82) It did, to the extent that Thompson published a second edition in 1853.

But not everyone interested in local history was satisfied with Thompson's brief sketches. During the 1840s, the historical society in Middlebury in Addison County became the first in the state to support book-length histories of towns within the larger context of their county's history. Samuel Swift explained this development in his pioneering history of Middlebury (1859). Because the members of the young Historical Society of Middlebury believed it was important to have histories of the towns in the county, they appointed, at their annual meeting in 1846, a special committee to consider the subject. The committee appointed agents who were sent out to the towns with copies of a circular describing the society's plan. But the committee found to its dismay that some of the agents failed to perform their duties and others delayed for so long that the committee gave up hope of their ever acting. Some new agents were appointed. The committee was also unable to find a publisher who would undertake to publish all of the proposed town histories "on account of the limited sale which must attend the work." Then, in 1858, the state government passed an act requiring towns to give financial support if anyone could be found to prepare a history. The Middlebury Historical

Society was given overall direction, but "none of the credit or responsibility of the composition. These belong exclusively to the several authors."(83)

Swift provided a brief "Statistical and Historical Account of the County of Addison" as an introductory unit for whatever volumes on particular towns within the county might appear. In a "Notice," he was anxious to convey that "it has not been my intention to interfere with the histories of the several towns . . . nor state any facts or statistics, except such as have some reference to the county generally. . . . I am unwilling to take these out of the hands of the historians of the several towns, which may be better qualified to describe, and which are more properly within their province."(84)

Following Swift's history of Middlebury, histories of other, contiguous towns in Addison County followed in quick succession: John Weeks' Salisbury (1860), Rev. Josiah Goodhue's Shoreham (1861), and Rev. Lyman Matthews' Cornwall (1862). Weeks, who finished his manuscript in 1850 and died long before it was published, in 1860, dedicated his history of Salisbury to the Historical Society of Middlebury, "it having been prepared at its request." In an appended, unsigned memoir of Weeks, who died in 1858, we learn that "[having] been a resident of Salisbury from his infancy, and thus made personally acquainted with most of the settlers, and having an unusual inclination to historical research, both general and local, he was peculiarly fitted to gather together the long-forgotten facts of early years."(85)

Rev. Josiah Goodhue faced an even more perilous task than Weeks had in putting together a history of Shoreham. Goodhue had been asked to take on the responsibility by the Middlebury Historical Society only after the death of Governor Silas Jemson, the original proposed author. But, Goodhue left Vermont in 1857 and parcelled out his material "to persons able in his opinion to prepare the work." These individuals, "finding greater difficulties than had been anticipated, declined the task." The town then made an appropriation to pay someone to write the history. "At their request, I ventured to undertake it. Had I then understoood its intrinsic difficulties as I now do, I should have shrunk from the attempt."(86)

Rev. Lyman Matthews' experience in preparing a history of Cornwall, which appeared in 1862, was less tumultuous. Matthews noted that "the publication of this volume has been secured by a generous appropriation from the town treasury." Though "[the] work [has been] delayed beyond his intentions by the ill health of the writer," the Middlebury Historical Society's series of Addison County town histories (to which Matthews' history was another contribution) had advanced to the point that Matthews discerned a widespread" desire increasingly manifest in many communities, especially in New England, to rescue from the ravages of time the incidents of our early history, and so to embody them as to secure their preservation."(87)

Thus, the antiquarian impulse first found expression in Vermont in the efforts of a single individual, Zadock Thompson, someone with a state-wide perspective who sought to persuade individuals in the various towns with a serious interest in their community's past and present to provide sketches that would serve gazetteers and histories alike. In Vermont, what followed the pioneering project was not a profusion of book-length local histories, but the organized attempt of an early county historical society to find individuals who would prepare such histories for towns in that particular county.    Early antiquarianism in Vermont was a state- and county-wide enterprise, not a local one.    Lone antiquarians did not, on their own initiative, undertake the arduous task of producing a history of their community.

# CHAPTER 3
# Their Histories

Though assisted by each other and by others, the antiquarians who actually wrote the early local histories were extremely rare individuals who had to have some abiding objective or purpose to sustain them through a characteristically long and arduous task. At first, histories were presented with a certain hesitancy, with some doubt in the author's mind as to their worth or appeal.

Erastus Worthington was quite candid when he offered for public sale his history of Dedham in 1827. Worthington admitted that "[s]ome facts related to the following sketch will appear trivial." Nor was he "certain that a sufficient reason can be given for extending the history of a town of no considerable extent to so many pages." But, "a town like Dedham, having its first settlement at an early date, having copious materials for a history, and nearly resembling a much longer extent of country around it, in its character and past transactions," could have its history "[s]o arranged, that it may afford some views of society not exhibited in more general histories." In particular: "It may bring us nearer the homes, and enable us to see more distinctly the doings of the inhabitants."(1)

Nevertheless, John Daggett introduced his history of Attleboro in 1834 with the statement that "[this] little work is designed principally for the citizens of this town. The subject is not presumed to be of sufficient interest to attract the particular attention of strangers. I have, therefore, entered into details and local descriptions which will not be interesting to readers in general, but only to those who are connected with the same by association or locality."(2) As local historical writing became a well established form of writing, this apologetic tone all but disappeared from prefatory commentary. Some of the early antiquarians felt confident enough about the value of what they were doing to reflect on the question of why it was natural for people to have an interest in local history.

Alonzo Lewis was the first to probe the significance of the antiquarian impulse. He wrote in the preface of his history of Lynn (1829):

There is something so natural in enquiring into the history of those who have lived before us, and particularly of those with whom we have any connexion, either by ties of relation or place, that it is surprising anyone should be found by whom this subject is regarded with indifference.
. . . To trace the settlement and progress of our native town – to read the history of the play place of our early hours, and which has been the scene of our maturer joys – to follow the steps of our fathers through the course of centuries, and mark the gradation of improvement – to learn who and what they were, from whom we are descended – and still further, to be informed of the people who were here before them, and who are now vanished like a dream of childhood; and all these in their connexions with the history of the world and of men – must certainly be objects of peculiar interest to every inquisitive mind.(3)

Such musings were singled out for comment among those who wrote to him after the book appeared. One wrote that "the Introduction with some slight exceptions, surpasses anything I ever saw from your pen. . . ."(4) John Farmer was even more emphatic, disclosing his reaction to Joshua Coffin: "I must say that the Introduction is one of the most felicitous and best written productions which I have ever seen annexed to any work of the kind. My love and esteem for the author of such sentiments have been much increased since I read it, which has been more than once, besides hearing parts of it read twice. Rev. Mr. Thomas was quite gratified with it and felt an accession of fervour and sentiment on perusing it."(5) A few days later Farmer told Lewis directly: "The introduction I have read several times, and admire it more and more."(6)

By the 1840s, comments like Lewis' were less exceptional or noteworthy. Charles Ellis introduced his history of Roxbury in 1847 with the statement that "[we] love to know the origin of those we spring from, what they did, how they dressed, labored, and worshipped. Most men have local attachment so strong that it invests some spot, endeared by association, with controlling interest. The old church, the old homestead, the old school, or something of the sort, bring back dear recollections to every man, and he will find pleasure in all that relates thereto."(7)

In the same year, Andrew Ward made the point with greater force: "Who has not a desire to know something of the *people* of a town, as well as of its location, its ponds, hills, and natural advantages."(8) Here Ward is, in effect, saying that the early linkage of local historical writing with geographical inquiry – all those topographical sketches and gazetteers from the 1780s through the 1820s – must no longer constrain purely historical investigation and curiosity.

By the 1850s, the value of local historical inquiry was so established that Daniel Ricketson felt free to state flatly that "[it] behooves every American to be acquainted with the history of the place which gave him birth." Ricketson believed that the time had come for such action. The "youthfulness" of settlement, which thirty years earlier had been offered as an explanation for the absence of local historical writing, Ricketson argued was a reason for an exponential growth of such writing: "The history of this country is neither wrapped in obscurity, nor hidden in uncertainty; there are no fictitious names, no fabled accounts of heroes; everything is authentic, and much within the memory of people yet living. . . . While other nations are boasting of their antiquity and exulting in the mysterious deeds of their ancestors, we pride ourselves in the recency of our origin, and the well known achievements during the struggle for liberty, as well as for the rapidity of our increase."(9)

But Ricketson was exceptional in his consideration of a nation-wide perspective. Most of the early antiquarians whose gaze extended at all beyond the vicinity they wrote about, brought a regional, not a national, frame of reference to their work. If the history of an early Massachusetts town were to be seen as a Puritan town, if a particular locality's past were presented as an instance of a region-wide pattern of community-building, then any place was a subject worthy of study.

What sustained the early antiquarians in New England more than anything else and gave their labor its purpose and worth was the collective gratitude they felt toward their Puritan ancestors whom they greatly admired — an admiration that bordered on a kind of reverence. The antiquarians were the beneficiaries, the inheritors of the flourishing communities the early settlers had worked very hard to build. By writing local history, they paid homage to their forbears and became recorders of a past that filled them with pride.(10)

As Charles J. Fox put it in the introduction of his history of Dunstable (1846): "Of such descent we may well be proud. We wish to know who they were, and when, and where, and how they lived. Their toils and privations, and sufferings, their opinions and peculiarities to us should be important. From them is derived all that is peculiar to the New England character; its energy, its ingenuity, its perseverance, and its hatred of tyranny in all its forms and manifestations."(11)

William Barry, the next year, referred to "[the] examples [our Puritan ancestors] display of heroic faith, of invincible courage, of generous self-sacrifice, of bold and untiring enterprise, the illustration they afford to the genius of the age, . . . [the] extraordinary spectacle everywhere presented of rising schools, amidst popular ignorance, or a stern morality amidst general degeneracy, of a devout and inflexible faith amidst widespread unbelief, of a jealous and enlightened love of liberty, amidst universal despotism, all reflect honor on the past."(12)

Overdrawn statements like Barry's reveal how keenly the early antiquarians felt about their strongly atavistic enterprise: to recover and recreate what to them were the heroic efforts of the Puritan settlers. This ancestral worship created in the minds of at least some of these writers a model to be emulated. As Edwin Stone surveyed the obvious and notable material progress that separated the inhabitants of Beverly, Massachusetts in the 1840s from the wilderness setting of the original settlers, he also emphasized the lasting legacy of the town's founders — namely, their virtuous character. This legacy lived on in the form of the "integrity," "industry," "prudence," "stability," "love of order" or "reverence for law," "public spirit," "piety," and "patriotism" of his contemporaries. "To the young," he concluded, "the pages of the past are replete with practical suggestions. In the [character] of their ancestors, they may perceive the index that points their own course to usefulness, respectability, and happiness."(13) Material progress and moral stability: the past brought to mid-nineteenth century New Englanders the best possible combination—Puritan rectitude and Yankee ingenuity.

Most of the antiquarians did not comment on or moralize about specific aspects of Puritan community life. Exceptions were Joseph Felt and Alonzo Lewis, both of whom were known and esteemed by the cluster of local historians situated around Boston and its hinterland. Felt's and Lewis' reflections—while idiosyncratic and certainly their own—are probably also an index to the views held by their contemporaries, who, lacking a penchant or capacity for such musings, would doubtless have appreciated or respected efforts like these, especially if made by fellow antiquarians. To some extent, the views of Felt and Lewis are an unusually refined expression of what the early antiquarians felt about particular dimensions of their ancestors' lives from the vantage point of the early to mid-nineteenth century. Felt's and Lewis' reflections are a mixture of positive and negative reactions to the historical experiences they chronicled.

As to Indian-white relations, Lewis included an extended commentary in his preface. He tried hard to be balanced and fair,(14) and keenly felt the ambivalence produced by reverence for heroic ancestors who also obliterated the preexisting civilization of those whose land they settled. Unable to question the value of the Puritan legacy, Lewis at least appreciated its devastating human cost. His fellow antiquarians did not—at least in print. For example, Felt's prefatory comment was simply: "Before we fully attend to the various concerns of the English, it may not be out of place to give a parting notice to the Indians, who owned and occupied the land, on which their more intelligent and powerful successors entered. . . . When we look back on the Aborigines, as the sole proprietors of our soil, on the places which once knew them, but are now to know them no more forever, feelings of sympathy and sadness come over our souls."(15)

As for the religious focus of their ancestors, Felt asserted: "No concerns, when considered as to the highest good of a community, are so vitally important as these. . . . To enjoy these institutions with purity of conscience and liberty of person, our ancestors sundered the ties of relationship, submitted to losses of property, forsook the home of their nativity, braved perils by sea, and endured sufferings by land."(16) But Lewis was concerned about the continuing record of religious disputes and divisions that besmirched the past of the early Puritan towns: "Though many years have passed, the diversities of opinion respecting the faith and order of the Gospel, seem in no degree to have lessened; but surely if peace and happiness are objects of regard, then it is desirable that men should be united in their view of the subject, which of all others is the most important. The benefits of Christianity might have been as industrious in promoting union, as they have been in devising ways by which they might differ."(17)

Both Felt and Lewis condemned their ancestors' involvement with witchcraft, which was no longer regarded by these writers to have been a genuine religious phenomenon, involving demonic or satanic possession. Felt lumped witchcraft under "Remarkable Events," and at the end of his section on the witchcraft craze of Essex County (1692-93) intoned: "Thus closed one of the darkest, deadliest infatuations, which ever fell upon New England. Its criminations were so indiscriminate; its excesses carried so far, as to break the spell, which had long given it credibility and victims, to wrest it, as a dreaded instrument, from the hand of fiendish revenge, and trample it down with the forbidden follies of human[ity]."(18) Lewis exclaimed: "It was an awful time for New England. Superstition was abroad in her darkest habilments, scourging the land with the judgment of God."(19)

As for the role of education among the Puritans, Felt had no doubt that "[t]hey were deeply impressed with the importance of having the young well educated, as a main support of the political and religious liberty, for which they had exchanged the joys of their native home, for the perils, uncertainties and toils of the wilderness." Felt, himself a school teacher at times, provides a rare summary comment on the history and "progress of common education."(20) In this way, he created a time-frame for educational history that linked education with progress and that enabled him to go beyond a mere chronological listing of activities without an overall direction.

As for the wars the Puritan settlers had been involved in, Felt drew a moralistic conclusion: "It is perceived that, with no small treasure, suffering, and blood, Ipswich [the town whose history he had written] has assisted in the defence of our country's rights, from its beginnings to our own age. From the scenes of trial and woe, through which she, as well as other communities, must have passed, while compelled to protect her territory, homes, and families, against the invasion of desolating foes, we may justly wish, 'then perish war! detested war!' "(21)

Felt's moralizing was of a positive kind when he commented on the evolution of economic activity from the time of the Puritan migrations to his own time (the 1830s). Of "manufacturers" he writes: "In proportion as they flourish in any place, so does its prosperity abound. They are arts essential to the comfort of society and should never be frowned on so long as they are useful." He spoke out against those, who in the 1830s, at the beginnings of industrial development, create "the too prevalent inclination to hold them in low repute [as] erroneous, and calculated to keep them from the advancement which they should make and from being so profitable as they might be." But, in dealing with the older "trades," Felt cautioned: "In this, as in every calling, honesty is the best policy. They who make haste to be rich by unjust dealing, generally lose their reputation and die poor. It is far better for peace of conscience and durable estimation to have one penny of honest gain, than one pound of fraudulent profit."(22)

Alone among the early antiquarians Felt cast a backward glance at the behavior of his fellow townsmen through the years and saw unmitigated decline. In his view the original settlers had a moral rectitude that his contemporaries lacked.(23) When he examined "immoralities and crimes", he proclaimed: "Vigilance and retribution—for transgressions of wholesome laws, denote a healthful state of morals, and prevent the abounding of iniquity."(24) And his commentary on disease was that "these, like all our afflictions, are mercifully and divisely intended for our spiritual benefit."(25)

Felt's and Lewis' moralistic commentaries on particular aspects of Puritan life certainly do not coalesce into a comprehensive assessment of the historial experience of New Englanders in their early towns. These observations are incomplete, disparate, quite strongly felt reactions—some positive or praiseworthy, others negative or critical—to particular dimensions of their community's past. What makes these musings noteworthy is their rarity. They constitute hints of or clues to what the antiquarians thought about their ancestors. But most of the early local historians lacked the inclination or the ability to summarize, reflect, interpret, or moralize.

In general, the local histories that the early antiquarians in New England produced served, in their minds, the purpose of recapturing a past offered to their contemporaries as an inspirational model. What seriously hampered this goal was that their mode of writing worked against the creation of a dramatic, didactic presentation in which the Puritan settlers were made to appear heroic and virtuous. For, a second passion the antiquarians shared—equal in strength to the first—was for accuracy, for precise fact or information.

In preface after preface we learn of their abiding devotion to and never-ending search for the truth.(26) This unequivocal quest for the truth ordinarily did not lead to troubling questions concerning the propriety of what would be revealed about the early New Englanders. The common assumption was that only examples of virtue and heroism would be uncovered. Erastus Worthington was distinctive in displaying his concerns in print. Offering a "retrospect" of Dedham in 1827, 190 years after its founding, he admitted that "I have endeavored on the one hand, to avoid the error of bestowing extravagant or unmitigated praise, and on the other, to give no just cause of offence, by an improper narration of private affairs, having no relation to general character." Worthington tried "to make known the substantial virtues and the real merit of the present and past generations of this town," but refused to produce a history "suppressing all notice of the errors and follies of past times, as some have suggested ought to be done."(27)

So immersed were the early antiquarians in the task of presenting factually accurate information that at first there was an identity problem: were they being historians, or something else? In 1829, Abiel Abbot felt no hesitation in presenting himself in his history of Andover as "The Compiler, for he does not assume the name of author."(28) In 1835, Lemuel Shattuck introduced his influential history of Concord with the assertion that "[the] details, which it is the appropriate province of the local historian to spread before the public, are not so much history itself as the materials for history."(29) But, most of the early antiquarians referred to themselves as "authors" or "writers," even when presenting what they thought of as "compilations." A statement that the author (or compiler) had carefully examined all available sources quickly became a prerequisite for presumed reliability.

Boston, because of its size, presented special problems for its historians, and Caleb Snow, the earliest of them, told his readers (in 1825) that "I have endeavored to select from the mass of records, which numerous hands have left to us, those facts which appear to have excited any great or general interest among the inhabitants of this metropolis."(30) Nearly thirty years later, the antiquarian, collector, bookseller, and publisher Samuel Drake referred in his, the second history of the city, to the town records as "full and perfect" from their beginning in 1634, material to which he was granted full access by the city clerk. Drake also drew on his own massive collection of materials, amassed over more than a quarter of a century, and pointed especially to his pamphlets, numbering "above five thousand" and consisting of public documents, reports of societies, speeches, handbills, and the like.(31) The abundance of Drake's materials was exceptional and no doubt won him the admiration and envy of the other antiquarians whose work focused on much smaller communities.

Typically, the early local historians utilized the town and church records that remained in the town clerk's office and in the Congregational Church at the time they wrote. Such records, however incomplete or imperfectly preserved, formed the basis for an on-going chronology of events relating the "civil and ecclesiastical" history of the town. Erastus Worthington used these records for his early history of Dedham (1827), admitting that "I have carefully perused [them]."(32) Samuel Deane "diligently consulted [them]" for his history of Scituate, in 1831.(33)

Many of the Massachusetts antiquarians used other material in an effort to take account of anything that would add information about the past and extend their inquiry beyond the realms of politics and religion. Charles Hudson, for his brief history of Westminster, also in 1831, "examined the records in the Archives of the State, County, and Town and also the papers of deceased individuals. He has also availed himself of all the information which the elderly inhabitants could impart."(34)

Not all were clear or specific about their sources. John Daggett said: "I have gathered 'here a little and there a little' from a mass of voluminous records and other manuscripts. I have left nothing unsearched which might throw light on the early history of the town [Attleboro]."(35) Others were quite specific and orderly in listing the full range or amount of examined material. William Lincoln referred to " the files and records of the colonial and provincial governments; of the original proprietors; of the town, and its parishes, Churches, and societies; of the county courts and registries; and the series of newspapers from their commencement[,] . . . private journals and papers, the recollections of aged inhabitants, the treasures of garrets."(36)

Edwin Stone indicated that "[in] the preparation of this volume I have made a thorough examination . . . amounting in all to nearly twenty thousand manuscript pages."(37) J. W. Hansen revealed that "[the] compiler . . . has spent about a year and a half in researches, during which time he has travelled about 600 miles on foot, to different parts of Danvers and Salem, besides several other journeys—examined twenty-thousand pages of manuscript—perused several historical works, and made many pilgrimages to antiquated sires and matrons, and to moss grown grave-yards."(38)

But others mourned the paucity of records. Joshua Coffin thought "[it] is . . . much to be lamented, that so small a number of the first settlers were in the habit of recording the transactions of the day, and that journals or diaries of those who made a record, should have been in so many instances lost or destroyed."(39) Unquestionably, the availability of records varied considerably from town to town in Massachusetts. However, all the early antiquarians experienced the scarcity of written sources relating to the Indians, the native population. Joseph Felt registered his frustration: "Had letters flourished among Agawames [Indians], many of their transactions, fitted to excite pity and admiration, to draw forth censure and approval, would have been recorded on the pages of history. But such a privilege, with which a kind Providence has favored us, was not theirs."(40) Restricted to scattered town or colony records and to a few surviving personal accounts, Felt utilized—as did others—the remaining Indian artifacts.(41)

Elsewhere in New England the situation was similarly mixed. Nathaniel Bouton, in the preface of his *History of Concord* referred with evident satisfaction to the reminiscences of aged inhabitants, newspapers, original records and documents in the town clerk's and Secretary of State's office and in the archives of the New Hampshire Historical Society, and "choice family papers which have been generously placed in my hands."(42)

By contrast, John Weeks, at the outset of his *History of Salisbury*, Vermont, indicated that "[v]ery few of the early records . . . are now to be found."(43) Similarly, Josiah Goodhue, in his *History of the town of Shoreham* [Vermont] lamented the "absence of records dating back to beyond the year 1783. His only resource, therefore, was to consult the only living man who had been here before the Revolution and few of the older inhabitants who came soon after."(44)

Indeed, there is much evidence that Vermont's towns did not rigorously strive to preserve their records, even thought the earliest of the towns were founded and settled in the late eighteenth and early nineteenth centuries, during the same years the Massachusetts Historical Society fostered awareness of the importance of preservation through the presentation of its topographical-historical sketches of Massachusetts towns. Unable to draw regularly on documents, the early local historians in Vermont relied considerably on the personal reminiscences of aged pioneers, thereby linking local historical writing and personal recollection to a greater extent than antiquarians farther to the east—in the older towns of Massachusetts, Maine, and New Hampshire—had, but anticipating the mixture of records and reminiscences that characteristically served as sources for local history west of the Appalachians after the Civil War.

The form and contents of the early local histories in New England were never set, fixed, or a well designed model shared by all. Certain types emerged, but are noticeable only after an examination of dozens of histories exhibiting various mixtures and a considerable degree of individuality.

In 1819, William Williamson's circular mixed topographical, archaeological, physical, historical, and personal kinds of inquiry, revealing that his format for the study of local communities had changed very little from the 1790s, when Jeremy Belknap, as Secretary of the Massachusetts Historical Society, had sent out a similar kind of circular to individuals in various Massachusetts towns to solicit topographical-historical sketches for the collection of the society.

Not everyone understood what kind of book Williamson wanted to prepare, his circular having consisted of queries rather than a prospectus for the actual publication. B. Johnson of Jackson conveyed the confusion over just what shape local history should assume in the 1820s: "I perceive by your circular that you intend something like a Gazetteer. I have thought for some years past that a complete Gazetteer of Maine which would be but a small volume would meet with a ready sale, but a history and some statistical view of the state added would increase its value."(45)

But, beginning in the 1820s, in Massachusetts, historical forms began to emerge in the writings of the antiquarians grouped in and around Boston. Some adopted a straight-forward "annals format," namely, a strictly chronological account based on town and sometimes church records already arranged in that manner. Joseph Felt's Salem (1827) and Alonzo Lewis' Lynn (1829) were the earliest of these efforts, but the durability of the form is evident in John Daggett's Attleboro (1834), Joshua Coffin's Newbury (1845), and Herman Mann's Dedham (1847). Others developed variants of the form.(46)

Several built their accounts directly on the town and church records and presented what Edwin Stone called in the subtitle of his history of Beverly a "Civil and Ecclesiastical History." Others chose a strictly topical arrangement, a format derived from the gazetteer. Abiel Abbot's Andover (1829) was the first, but Joseph Felt, in his history of Ipswich (1834), developed the form. Felt—almost totally abandoning the annalistic structure of his earlier history of Salem—turned his treatment of Ipswich into brief passages on a great array of subjects, all titled in his table of contents. By the 1840s and 1850s the topical approach led to the production of some rather highly organized local histories.(47)

Others were unable to separate the history of individuals and families from their community's past. Starting with Jacob Moore's *Concord*, ( N. H.) (1824), biographical sketches of early or prominent inhabitants appeared, usually as the last section. Moore had just jointly presented a gazetteer of New Hampshire with John Farmer, the pioneering genealogist of the earliest white settlers of New England. Moore explained that in noticing "some of the most distinguished citizens of this town, who have decessed [,] . . . the writer is activated by no motive than a wish to perpetuate their good fame, and with it, the salutory influence of their examples . . . [for] the generations that are to come."(48)

Samuel Deane's Scituate (1831) included "Family Sketches," in whose preface he wrote: "There needs to be no apology for attempting to preserve the genealogies of those families who occupied these hills in those early times: it is all the nobility we have; and it is nobility enough, when we can trace our descent from the fathers of New England."(49) Lemuel Shattuck's

Concord (1835), Leonard Bliss' Rehoboth (1836), and William Lincoln's Worcester (1837) all contained biographical sketches and, by 1847, no fewer than five local histories were published with similar arrangements.

In 1840, the genealogical or biographical section—called a "Family Register"—was the largest part of Nahum Mitchell's history of Bridgewater. "There is," he wrote in his preface, "an increasing attention to the biography of our fathers and the first planters of New England. Each one finds a pleasure in knowing something of his own particular ancestor, who first left the old world and set his foot on the new; and in being able to trace accurately his own descent from him." Indeed, Mitchell asserted that the "principle purpose of the present publication is to afford the inhabitants of Bridgewater, and those who were born or early resided there, whenever they may now live, some knowledge of those from whom they are descended, and if possible to enable them to see every link in the chain connecting them with their first American ancestor." The "short history" preceding the "Family Register" was explained by reference to the "great similarity in the general history and internal management of public affairs in all our New England towns the recital of which, therefore, to most readers, would be dull, repetitious, and uninteresting details. Very little of this nature is inserted here."(50)

Mitchell's was the most extreme case of genealogical interest taking precedence over inquiry into a community's past, but others followed his lead in providing far more impressive genealogical sections than local histories. Andrew Ward, in presenting his history of Shrewsbury in 1847, stated that "to furnish a Family Register of the inhabitants of the town . . . was the chief, if not the sole cause of this undertaking."(51)

Henry Brooks, in the preface to his history of Medford (1855), indicated that he had sent out circulars inviting all of the living descendants of our ancestors and all the present inhabitants of the town to provide him with genealogical registers of their families, "promising to insert all they might send." Brooks regretted that many did not comply with his request and thereby withheld the requisite information that they alone possessed: "It is a serious loss to our history and may hereafter be regretted by themselves."

Just how much they would regret their negligence in a time of a hostile nativist reaction to the heavy immigration from Ireland and Germany during the 1850s, Brooks went on to explain: "These registers of early families in New England will contain the only authentic records of the true Anglo-Saxon blood existing among us; for, if foreign immigration should pour in upon us for the next fifty years as it has for the last thirty, it will become difficult for any man to prove that he has descended from the Plymouth Pilgrims."(52)

Rarely did the antiquarians explain why they chose the particular form their histories assumed. The mixture of annalist chronology, topical treatments, and biographical-genealogical sketches evolved during the 1820s, 1830s, 1840s, and 1850s out of earlier forms of writing, such as gazetteers and topographical sketches, and out of standard sources, like town and church records, which themselves suggested a certain shape to the writings that ensued.

Thus, local historical writing in its earliest phase in North America was so loosely defined that it contained elements of what the late twentieth century scholar defines as geographical, anthropological, and archaeological inquiry.    Indeed, the only fixed point of past time of which all such histories took account was the founding and initial settlement of a community.    Thereafter, continuous reference to historical time was the organizing principle of an account only if the author chose an annalistic or chronological format.    Therefore, this was historical writing that was not necessarily entirely linked to either a time sequence or documentary evidence, and it sometimes contrasted sharply with contemporaneous national histories, which were chronological narratives of political life based upon the written record.

As in the case of their form, the contents of the early local histories also revealed an overall pattern.    But, once again, that pattern was never fixed or static, and there was much variation from history to history.    The availability of sources, the particular interests of the author, the extent to which he was concerned about constructing a broad survey of his community's past, his capacity to select description and detail from his sources – all these factors influenced what went into a given local history.

Usually, the first section was on the town's topography with the author providing a brief account of the geographical setting – features of the land and water, and less frequently, the local roster of plants and animals. These accounts of the physical setting also sometimes included references to the human-built artifacts of the town's landscape:   houses, public buildings, transportation facilities.    But, unless these artifacts survived or their shape and uses were recalled by the antiquarians or their contributors, such references did not include descriptions, but consisted of listings of the political decisions made by the town respecting houses, buildings, and public works.

Nonetheless, there was a widely shared awareness that what we call the "material culture" of the early settlers as well as the geographical or topographic setting of the town – together comprising the community's total physical setting – was something appropriate to include in a local history.    In this, the amateurs were following the lead of the writers of the essays on the towns published by the Massachusetts Historical Society around the turn of the previous century, who, in turn, had sustained a tradition with deep roots in local historical writing in England, dating from the seventeenth century.    In all of these accounts, the local community was given a "physical" dimension.

The naming of the town sometimes received a separate treatment. Usually the name chosen was one with an obvious English reference – such as Duxbury or Newbury – even if it meant the older Indian name for the area was overridden.(53) That the colonial assemblies chose names "more familiar and dearer to Englishmen"(54) is readily attested to when the names of all the early towns of New England are examined.    But, that the names of areas given by the local Indian tribes were sometimes retained also shows: for example, Agawam, in Massachusetts.

The early local historians also dealt with the Indians themselves. These accounts are usually brief, since Indian-white relations were primarily the responsibility of colonial governments, and focused on descriptions of Indian life or on those occasions when a particular town was engaged in some way with a nearby tribe or its members.(55) Frontier towns attacked by hostile tribes were not among those about which the early antiquarians wrote general histories before the time of the Civil War.

The founding and settlement of Puritan towns was also under provincial jurisdiction.  But the early local historians described at length the beginnings of their communities — even if similar in character to those of many other places — because the founders were their ancestors, and it was the achievement of those pioneers that the antiquarians were interested in commemorating above all else.  So, it was typical for there to be a section on the land grant from the colonial assembly to the original settlers or proprietors, whose records were used as the basis for a description of the early land divisions, house lots, and commons, sometimes followed by a full list of the original settlers.(56)

All the early local historians assigned a prominent place to religion and the churches in their histories.  A connected, chronological treatment of the churches and their ministries — one by one, minister by minister, church by church — was fairly standard, given the conviction that what defined a Puritan town's past was as much its religion as its government. Typically, the accounts were a blend of information of a biographical and institutional nature; that is, both ministers and churches were traced chronologically.  Certain phenomena were patterned and repeatable, such as the founding of particular churches, the "calling" of particular ministers, or the creation of new parishes as townships, sprouted in newly settled areas. But other happenings were quite unusual and were referred to at greater length:  doctrinal  disputes,  outbreaks  of  witchcraft,  the  effects  of evangelical preaching.  However, typical accounts also provided information on such subjects as the construction and organization of meetinghouses; the ordination, salaries, and settlement of ministers; and various forms of community fasting.(57) The main concern of all these writers was to uncover the ordinary rhythms in the religious life of the community.

So too, with civil or municipal history.  Whether chronological or topical — or a mixture of the two — treatments of political affairs usually consisted of descriptions of actions taken at the town meetings or by town officials.  Typical accounts convey the broad range of regulatory activities of the town's government by quoting various "REGULATIONS" enacted at town meetings, dealing with such subjects as products, labor, family life, worship, and the consumption of alcoholic beverages.(58)

Far less standard was any treatment of crime as dealt with by the judicial agencies of government, which in any case were organized on the county level.  A few of the early antiquarians did include a section on, say, "immoralities and crimes"(59) and many at least made occasional reference to criminal behavior.  As much of military life was under the control of provincial governments, accounts of such activity varied considerably in length and detail, though some antiquarians focused on the local militia or a town's role in particular wars.(60)

References in the local histories to economic activity were irregular, sporadic, typically based on accounts of political actions. Some of the antiquarians singled out agriculture and manufacturing for topical treatment; others interspersed chronological or annalistic sequences with information of this kind. Aware of the limitations of examining economic life by means of references to political action, one of the antiquarians added: "It is very probable that some of the following trades were practiced here before the time of their being seen on record, and that part of them were more extensively carried on than appears from the list."(61)

Such "lists" include references to municipal decisions relative to craft, milling, and even early factory production,(62) an amassing of evidence that, though largely political in character, when seen as a whole, conveys a sense of the many dimensions of economic life as early New England towns slowly shifted from providing fertile ground for the crafts to becoming a seed-bed of American industry. The picture that emerges is of a local government actively regulating the economic life of the town from its inception as a community.

Of all the social or cultural institutions of the town, none was more important than the schools, and it was fairly standard for the antiquarians to include a section on education in their histories, or at least, in annalistic accounts, to refer to actions taken by the town or the school districts the towns were divided into. Singling out education as a subject worthy of separate treatment was appropriate in the sense that the colonial government in Massachusetts was the first to require its towns to provide for schooling, reflecting the Puritans' emphasis on literacy and the comprehension of scripture on the part of the faithful. How the school was organized, what property the town provided the school and its master, what fees the students were charged, what the schools looked like, what their "rules" and "reports" consisted of were all duly recorded.(63)

Beyond education and the schools, information on and descriptions of other institutions and groups and activities in the town was spotty, and certainly not part of a standard format. A section most typically called "Remarkable Events" was incorporated in some fashion into early local histories, almost without exception. Rare, bizarre, sometimes inexplicable happenings were too dramatic, too obviously a means of sustaining the interest and curiosity of readers for any of the antiquarians to ignore. What did the unusual mean, portend, reveal? This was an important question for author and reader alike at a time when human life was not reduced to rational explanation. That such events were not typical and did not illustrate the ordinary, on-going, slowly changing life of the community was never regarded as a sufficient reason for omission or deletion. In this context, the antiquarians referred specifically to such objects and occurrences as handicapped persons, pests, droughts, storms, severe winters, lightning, fires, eclipses, earthquakes, accidental deaths, and visits from famous people.(64)

A few antiquarians also included specific information on births, baptisms, marriages, obituaries, funerals, and burying places.(65) A section on "Diseases" is an example of a subject almost all took notice of by cataloguing incidents of such epidemic illnesses as smallpox, "throat distemper," typhus, fevers, and scarlet fever.(66)

Though many of the early local historians in New England knew of each other's work, either because they read it when published in book form or because they knew others and corresponded with or actively assisted them, the actual contents of their published histories are notably varied. Information and description and listings are mixed with bits of moralizing and reflection. The sources used varied considerably. What was culled from them differed from one antiquarian to another. Historical writing in the hands of these keen amateurs lacked a firm pattern, a settled form. Their motivation and purpose was so clearly linked to their particular interests in their own community that information was gathered and presented as an extension of their own curiosity about the past of their family and its setting, and not to satisfy the prescriptions of talented pioneers like Lewis and Felt.

What we learn from these histories is vast in its range and in the variety of its detail. What we read is a byproduct of curiosity, the result of a long, loving, atavistic search by scions of the early Puritan towns. These histories were not offered as critical, dispassionate assessments of these communities. The early antiquarians were, however, aware of the overall form of their ancestors' Puritan culture, aware of the wider context, within which towns like Ipswich and Lynn fitted.

But their portrayal of their community's past looks almost random in its lack of form. Some awareness of change through time — especially in a civil or religious realm — coexisted in their minds with an interest in delving into the past of something that still had tangible form — like buildings, streets, bridges, roads, wharves. What had led others to produce natural histories or gazetteers, led them to put together a potpourri of information, some of which had a historical dimension, some of which was presented without reference to time or change, but all of which was designed to appeal to others who shared with them a curiosity about everything that would extend their knowledge of their family and their community.

Though they lacked the capacity to use language in a theoretical and conceptual way, what the early amateur local historians in New England presented in these accounts of the past was profoundly conservative. All that they recovered was in homage to their ancestors, whose lives they memorialized, and whose heroic and successful creation of Puritan towns and cities they showed to be a priceless legacy. For the antiquarians, the founders and their descendants provided a model for life in the future. Above all, what these earliest local histories displayed was individual and family life embedded in community, special communities formed on the basis of covenants, created to sustain a godly life for all their inhabitants, meant to be coterminous with life itself. And though a few, such as Joseph Felt, emphasized the moral decline that they believed had set in by the early nineteenth century, most wrote in hopeful, positive tones, their faith largely unshaken in the midst of undoubted material progress.

The early antiquarians were very sensitive to the question of appeal, of who would be interested in reading about what, because it was almost always the case that they sought subscribers, those who would commit themselves to the purchase of one or more copies of the published volume. Local historical writing was from its inception a facet of subscription publishing.(67)

Few among the pioneering Massachusetts writers followed Joseph Felt's lead in actually including a list of the subscribers, replete with the number of copies to which each had subscribed.(68) But, from the outset, publishers made contracts with local historians on the assumption that there would be subscribers. Caleb Snow's agreement with the Boston publisher Abel Bowen, in 1824, refers to "publishing by subscription" for Snow's history of the city.(69) The laborious process of proofreading is clearly revealed in letters between Alonzo Lewis and his publisher, John H. Eastburn, and others.(70) Lewis asked Joshua Coffin to participate in the process, something Coffin did with enthusiasm, even jocularity: "What a glamorous thing it is to be a critic, and to have the supreme felicity of 'tearing to rags to very tatters' the works of those who are so much our superiors."(71)

That the aid of such a friend could come at a price is indicated when Coffin disclosed that his negligence had led to a delay in publication.(72) Delays were not unusual, however, and involved both authors and publishers. For example, the agreement between Caleb Snow and Abel Bowen was twice extended.(73) George Folsom, the publisher paid by Felt for his history of Ipswich (1834) admitted that "I should have sent you the printed sheets earlier but for a little accidental delay, arising principally from the sad state of the time in regard to money matters, and this leads me to say that if it were convenient for you to advance me a portion of the pay by the first of July, I should esteem it a great kindness."(74)

The earliest local histories were sometimes produced in parts issued over several years and ultimately collated by subscribers as the "finished" book. For instance, Caleb Snow's agreement with Abel Bowen indicated that Snow "agrees to compile . . . a History of Boston, which when completed will make from twelve to sixteen numbers of twenty-four pages each."(75) Similarly, Joseph Felt's annals of Salem were published in 1827 in several parts, as was Alonzo Lewis' history of Lynn in 1829.

Such a format could create problems, however, and Snow admitted in his preface that "[to] enable [the publisher, Abel Bowen] to fulfill the terms of those proposals, I was obliged to let the first number appear, on the first of July, before I could possibly know what the succeeding number should contain. The case has been similar with all other numbers. I have found it necessary to put notes, almost in the same form in which I had taken them, at the hazard of being compelled afterwards to exclude other matter, perhaps more important."(76) Whether for this or for other reasons, few — beyond the 1820's — chose to continue the practice of issuing a local history in parts.

The vexing question of how many copies should be published was dealt with anew with each publication. Subscriptions provided an assured sale. But how many copies beyond that number would sell? Boston was uniquely large. In the Snow-Bowen agreement, Snow was to be paid a certain sum

($300) for the first thousand sold, and another sum (10 cents) for every copy over that amount.

But what about smaller communities? Joshua Coffin advised Alonzo Lewis that it was Eastburn's (Lewis' publisher) opinion that Lewis ought to print 500 to 600 copies, instead of 300 (which Lewis himself must have originally suggested). "Books of this kind will always sell at some price or other for above the cost—and the sale, though slow, after subscribers are supplied, will always be sure."(77)

Some of the original press runs of the early local histories sold out rather quickly, prompting authors to bring out second editions a few years later. James Thacher, whose history of Plymouth first appeared in 1832, boasted in the preface to his second edition (1835): "The author of these pages feels great pleasure in acknowledging his obligations to the public that the whole of the first edition, consisting of 1,250 copies, was disposed of within a few months after publication."(78) James Thacher put out a second edition of his history of Spencer in 1860, informing his readers that the original 1841 edition "has long been out of print, but three hundred copies having been published. This little publication having been received with more favor than was expected, many calls have been made for copies, and as none could be supplied, at the urgent solicitation of many of his friends, the author has been induced to rewrite the book with additions and improvements."(79)

The issuance of a second or even additional editions after the original had sold out was a fairly common practice among the early antiquarians: Caleb Snow's Boston (1825 and 1828); Alonzo Lewis' Lynn (1829 and 1844 and 1865); James Thacher's Plymouth (1832 and 1835); William Lincoln's Worcester (1837 and 1862); James Draper's Spencer (1841 and 1860); and others, in later years, long after the deaths of the authors.

Sales could only be estimated, of course, and there is evidence that additional subscribers bought copies through the authors directly, shortly after publication. When Alonzo Lewis published his history of Lynn in parts in 1829, John White wrote: "I see by the papers that the first number of your history of Lynn is published and am sincerely glad to find you intend to prosecute the undertaking with vigor—You have my best wishes—I wish to be considered a subscriber for two copies."(80)

John Farmer revealed how personal and varied the arrangements for a sale could be: "The *3rd* No. of your Annals of Lynn I have not seen. A copy will come to me safe if enclosed to Francis Jackson, Esq., of Boston (my name being written on the book) and left at No. 31 South Market Street to the care of John L. Emmons. I am indebted to you for the first two numbers. When I receive the whole I will pay you for them."(81) Another wrote to Lewis that "I should like six copies each of the History and map, to distribute—one to our Atheneum, to Mr. Burroughs, my minister, to my brothers in N. Carolina and Tennessee, . . . but I cannot afford to buy them. If you will send them to me I will put the value on the note."(82)

Some purchasers were quite eager—and persistent. In 1835, Waldo Higginson, five years after the appearance of Joseph Felt's history of Salem, wrote to the author: "I was fortunate a short time since as to meet with your highly valuable work, Annals of Salem.   Being very desirous of owning the book, I have applied to the booksellers of Boston and Salem for a copy and find to my regret that there none is to be had in either place — I am induced therefore, sir, to make a similar application to you.   If you have a spare copy in your possession, or if you can put me in a way to get one elsewhere, I shall hardly consider any price too high for it and you will greatly oblige."(83)

A desire to own his own copy even after reading Felt's history, animated George Folsom to write from Maine: "I had the pleasure of reading the first numbers of your 'Annals of Salem' from the Atheneum in Portland, but have not found them for sale.  I understood from Col. Baker, whom I saw at Saco a year since that you will favor the public with a new enlarged edition in that it may become accessible to the numerous class of individuals who take an interest in historical inquiries, whose penchant your work is so admirably adopted to gratify."(84)

The swapping of copies with fellow antiquarians must have brought the greatest satisfaction.   Lewis wrote to Felt that "I have received, by the kindness of Mr. Ives, the four numbers of your history of Salem already published, which for their particular reference, I regard as a treasure.   I have requested Mr. Ives to furnish you with the numbers and map of the history of Lynn."(85)

Distribution to libraries was an important means beyond direct sales by which the local histories found an audience (as Folsom indicated in his letter to Felt).   That historical societies and their librarians thought a collection of local histories accessible to their users and members was of importance is indicated in a letter C. F. Birney, of the New England Historic Genealogical Society, wrote to Joshua Coffin.(86)

Sales were only one measure of the influence, popularity, and impact of the early local histories.  The question of how they were received, what readers thought of them, how much they made of them, and what the opinions of reviewers in magazines and newspapers were is also of importance to an assessment of the place of such histories in the development of an informed historical consciousness among New Englanders.

Sometimes readers were simply grateful, as when Charles W. Morse wrote to Joshua Coffin: "I think much of your History of Newbury and it must have cost an amount of labor that but few can conceive of.   I hope you may be amply rewarded for giving the descendants from Newbury such a clear view of their ancestry."(87)   Another, with a far less direct interest, nonetheless wrote: "When I had the pleasure to see you for a moment at my counting-house last summer,   . . .   I scarcely at first recognized you,   . . .   [but] I have since looked through your history of Newbury with a good deal of interest."(88)

Occasionally, readers found fault, though expressed their criticisms cautiously.   After joining with others in praise of Alonzo Lewis' introduction to his history of Lynn, one went on to note: "If it will not seem hyper-critical, I would suggest as a fault a want of minuteness in describing locality — for instance it would be difficult for most readers to understand what is the situation of 'Strawberry Brook,' 'Willis Hill.'"(89)

It was standard — though not automatic — for local and regional journals to present a brief notice of a local history when it was published. Such notices were usually terse summaries of what was in the book and were not at all meant to be assessments or critiques. But, on occasion, critical remarks were offered by those who wrote the notices. When Alonzo Lewis' history of Lynn was criticized in the *National Aegis* in Worcester, Massachusetts, for maintaining that the founders of New England were Separatists from the Church of England (as indeed the Pilgrims, at least, were), John Farmer sprang to Lewis' defense: "The [notice] on you in the Aegis, altho' I have not seen it, strongly excited my feelings. I had received some intimation of it from a friend in Worcester County, who is also a friend of the editor of the Aegis, before you sent me the Lynn Mirror, containing your vindication, and on receiving *that*, I immediately sent it to my friend."(90)

However, criticism of this kind was unusual, its place in such reviews unsettled, and the response of authors and their partisans prickly. Indeed, notices were sometimes paid for by the writer or his publisher and thus took on a form murkily located between outright advertising and an honest appraisal.

The most flattering notice was one appearing in the press of London, the cultural capital of the English-speaking world. John H. Eastburn, Alonzo Lewis' publisher, wrote exuberantly about a piece on Lewis' history of Lynn in the *London Courier*, "the most influential and widely circulating journal in the world." Eastburn, still sensitive to the cultural inferiority of Americans and the attendant difficulties of their publishers, exclaimed: "It has been often asked who reads an American Book. We can now ask who publishes a notice of an American Book and a Yankee history too." But how and why was Lewis' history so honored?: "[The *Courier*] contained verbatim the notice of the History of Lynn, Part I as published in the [Boston] *Columbian Centinel* viz.: 'The History of Lynn by ALONZO LEWIS has just been published ·from the press of Mr. Eastburn, City Printer, etc., etc.' Hudson of the Centinel says we must pay him fifteen guineas, as that is the price for being Gazetted in London. It was somewhat pleasing to see one's name in the extra large type in a far distant quarter of the globe."(91)

From "being gazetted" to having a brief, unpaid, but uncritical notice took in a great deal of the spectrum of the way early local histories were reviewed. Ordinarily, only in the papers, collections, and journals of historical societies and in the pages of respected literary reviews did this process verge toward genuine assessment and criticism. And, of all these publications, the most prestigious was Boston's *North American Review*, with its regional, indeed, national audience of well read subscribers. The *Review* selected only a few of the local histories published before the Civil War for the accolade that came from one of its detailed, reflective critiques. Of the early Massachusetts histories, only Lemuel Shattuck's *Concord* (1835), Edwin Stone's *Beverly* (1843), Charles Brooks' *Medford* (1855), Henry Bond's *Watertown* (1855), Samuel Drake's *Boston* (1856), and John J. Babson's *Gloucester* (1860)(92) were so singled out.

The long review of Lemuel Shattuck's history of Concord, which appeared in the April 1836 issue, emphasized Shattuck's great devotion to

accuracy:    "Accuracy    .  .  .    is  the  *sine-qua-non.*    A  history  not  accurate,
is,  in  other  words,  no  history."(93)  Praising  Shattuck's  history  as  "the  fruit
of  laborious  research,  the  most  so,  in  its  class,  which  American  literature
has  produced",(94)  the  reviewer  went  on  to  refer  again  to  "the  value  of
town  histories,  and  especially  of  the  value  of  accuracy  in  them  ....  It  is
among  the  chief  of  [Shattuck's]  merits  that  he  has  not  only  done  a  good
thing,  but  that  he  has  set  a  good  example,  and  given  almost  a  model."(95)

In  reviews  like  this,  the  premier  journal  of  New  England  helped  to
establish  what  made  for  good  local  history  and  who  its  best  practitioners
were,  making  models  of  Shattuck,  Stone,  Brooks,  and  Bond,  and  emphasizing
the  importance  of  accuracy  in  whatever  antiquarians  were  able  to  recall  of
their  community's  past.

The  conservatism  of  the  pioneer  antiquarians  is  also  manifest  in  their
practice  of  choosing  subscription  publishing.    With  very  few  exceptions,
they  did  not  even  try  to  contact  the  commercial  publishers  that  were
beginning,  during  this  period,  to  find  a  lucrative  market  for  popular  forms
of  fiction.    The  early  local  histories  were  clearly  intended  for  an  elite  of
families  whose  hallmarks  were  longevity  of  residence  and  a  high  local
status.    Contributors,  subscribers,  and  readers  were  all  meant  to  be  involved
in  the  recovery  of  a  past  that  gave  meaning  to  their  lives,  but  not  to  the
lives  of  the  far  more  numerous  portion  of  the  community  that  drifted  in
and  out  of  particular  localities  within  relatively  short  periods.(96)

This  was  history  for  "persisters,"  not  for  "movers,"  and  the  inclusion
of  biographies  and  genealogical  sketches  was  a  deliberate  effort  to  link
family  history  with  community  prominence.    Private  publishing  arrangements
were,  thus,  the  appropriate  means  of  preserving  in  print  the  shared  lives  of
particular  families  in  particular  communities.    An  assumed  lack  of  interest
by  most  people  living  elsewhere,  coupled  with  an  indifference  toward  that
element  in  the  community  without  deep  roots,  produced  an  attitude  among
the  early  antiquarians  that  the  best  way  to  publish  their  findings  was  by
means  of  an  assured  subscription  list,  and  not  the  larger  commercial  presses
that  writers  of  fiction  often  found.    Local  history  thus  failed  to  attract  the
wide  national  audience  that  melodramatic  fictional  stories  reached.

# CHAPTER 4
# Elsewhere: John F. Watson

Outside of New England, early antiquarian activity was dominated by a single individual: John F. Watson of Philadelphia, who, at his death in 1860, was called "the pioneer in antiquarian research — the father of local historians — the 'Homer of his Class, as Washington Irving styled him"; "the distinguished annalist, so well and universally known"; "the author [who] enjoyed popularity both far and near."(1)

Watson was a bookseller and a bank cashier who grew up in Stonington, Connecticut, where, he told William Willis, the historian of Portland, "I remember [my mother's] graphic tales of Yankee-land with cherished affection."(2) Watson's mother "[transmitted] to him her faculty for lucid remembrance of names, persons, and places encountered in her youth."(3) Watson, who got into the habit of noting what he observed by keeping diaries during his travels, turned his attention to the collection of historical materials on Philadelphia after the American Philosophical Society created a Committee of History, Moral Science, and General Literature, in 1815. On March 6, 1821, he published a letter in Poulson's *American Daily Advertiser* in which "he suggested that elderly inhabitants relate facts respecting manners and customs of early times as they recalled them."(4)

Two years later, on April 8, 1823, he disclosed to federal district judge Richard Peters what his aims were and what material he was interested in collecting. Watson said that he had been collecting "ancient facts" on Philadelphia of a "curious and entertaining" kind: "My aim is to lay hold of all such facts as do not belong to the dignity and gravity of history . . . but which shall nevertheless furnish the materials for raising works of the imagination [i.e., fiction]."(5)

Watson's concern was for the "curious" and "entertaining." He wanted anecdotes to be collected as material that could serve as the basis for fictional writing, which markedly differed from the aims of the New England antiquarians, with their passion for accuracy and fact. Whereas Watson typically relied on the memory of the elderly, New Englanders characteristically sought "runs" of town and church records. For Watson, the recapture of the past through anecdote made history closely akin to fictional story telling. For Lewis, Felt, Coffin, Willis, Williamson, Moore, and others in New England, history was a precise reconstruction, sharply contrasting in form and substance with myth, legend, and tales – linked instead to the gazetteer, to topographical and statistical accounts.

However, Watson's interest in recording the man-made physical setting and in describing the old houses and street layouts, went far beyond that of most of his contemporaries in New England, as did his accumulation of information on the social life of his community, on the groups, activities, and behavior of those who had inhabited early America's leading population center. And though he brought a "literary" cast of mind to his effort at recovering Philadelphia's past and placed great emphasis on the entertainment and amusement of what he found, Watson was also concerned about accuracy. He clearly sought truthful recollections, and, indeed, utilized other, written evidence, such as the Philadelphia newspapers, the minutes of the Philadelphia Common Council, surveys, reports, and archival material from the state capitol at Harrisburg.(6) In other words, Watson's aim or purpose differed from the New Englanders'. Whereas they sought to honor their ancestors by means of filiopietistic, written memorials, Watson wanted to collect anecdotes in order to amuse and entertain. His coverage also differed from theirs in that he attempted to recapture the full range of life in an urban society, whereas they tried above all else to portray towns whose civil and ecclesiastical history constituted the priceless legacy of the founders. But Watson and the New Englanders shared a particular method: gathering all available material and being as accurate in the use of it as possible.

In 1823, Watson worked out a "List of Questions to Aged People," which reveals a great deal about his method and coverage. Many of Watson's questions concerned recreational/entertainment/leisure time activity. ("1. What plays of boys and girls can you remember[?]. 2. Where were your chief Field- Playgrounds and where nearest to the city, and describe the scenery, if surprising to us now? . . . 39. What objects can you remember of recreation and amusement. . . . What of boxing, wrestling – horse racing – cock fighting – bull baiting – *Fairs* – Shows, etc. . . . 41. What seemed to be the feelings of the People who visited the first plays?").

Other questions involved food, clothing, and shelter.

> 3. Notice anything remarkable, if any, in change of diet or cookery. . . . 4. Describe minutely wherein the *Dresses* of boys and girls, of men and women where most different from our own day – anything that would surprise us. . . . Describe the dresses of those who were the Fops and Dandies of your youth of either sex. . . . 5. Have you not any small scraps to give as specimens of any curious or expensive old dresses[?] . . . 9. Were there any remarkable houses either for meanness or grandeur, before or in your day, and since gone down[?]. . . 37. Think of any remarkable alterations in living and in furniture since your youth and think of society when families set at them down in their Porches – under Sheds and Porticoes, etc.

Other queries involved crime and violence. ("22. What degree of interest did the Public take in Pillorings and whipping, etc., of culprits — What kind of people made the crowd when following the cart and where was the nearest gallows[?]. . . 26. Was drunkenness and gambling as frequent as now[?]. 27. Were not low bawdry girls, and sailor-trulls, more *conspicuous* then than in any *present* reputable place — Are not *genteel* lend-women a *modern* luxury among us[?]").

There were many questions about the man-made physical layout and the topographical setting of the city, as remembered. But, of other dimensions of life he provided either one, well focused query or exhibited only a fleeting interest: the family ("38. Was early marriage and courtship better conducted then than now and were young ladies better wives, more useful[?]"); famous people ("7. Think of remarkable men either for good or bad actions and any anecdotes of them."); social class ("34. What remarkable changes of persons from Wealth to Poverty and from Poverty to Wealth and who in your youth chiefly[?]"; economic life ("45. Have the prices of Fresh Shad and herrings — and of oyster, Lobsters, and Sea Fish much raised and how much[?]"); political life ("30. Speak of Elections and of the places held. . . . Was their character ever as virulent as now — and what Parties[?]. . . 12. Were Governors or other officers in authority (magistrates) much more reverenced than now — and were they statelier?); religion ("36. Were there any remarkable facts about Whitefield or Rowland or Gilbert's [evangelist] preaching, or of their converts — and did they generally abide long, devout, and zealous, etc.[?]"); settlement ("42. Did you ever hear your grandparents or others describe their feelings on their voyage or their return views of things as they found them at the first settlement[?] 43. Did any of them ever tell you any anecdotes of Penn [the founder of Pennsylvania] — of his personality — or any of the first remarkable men[?]").

Watson also sought stories ("8. Were there any popular stories[?]), anecdotes ("35. Try and remember and set down all the ancient anecdotes about the first settlers you have heard — especially from your old relatives"), and source material ("44. Do you know of any ancient papers printed or [manuscripts] or familiar letters in families — which I could get to see and use[?]").(7)

As Watson copied and arranged material gathered by himself and others, he began to wonder whether or not such information ought to be published.(8) In the summer of 1824, Robert Vaux wrote that Watson's growing manuscript should, in fact, be published.(9) During the fall of 1824, Vaux wrote again, urging Watson, as he had others, to support his plan for the creation of a historical society "which can devote itself exclusively to this too long neglected subject."(10) Watson responded favorably almost immediately.(11)

When the Historical Society of Pennsylvania was in fact founded by Vaux and six others on December 2, 1824, Watson remained aloof, pleading that his bank's directors might object to him — as their cashier — becoming involved in such an activity. But, within a year, he proposed to William Rawle, president of the society, a scheme for the gathering of local history involving the society's members as special agents who would" ascertain throughout the state all the remarkable incidents of the Revolution known to individual soldiers—also the remarkable facts observed by those Pioneers, who first settled towns and counties in the interior—and . . . the same things to be recommended to all other historical societies in the Union."(12) In this way, Watson hoped to turn the focus of state historical societies away from national history toward local history, though his interest in "remarkable incidents" of the Revolution alongside "remarkable facts" concerning the settlement of towns and counties, reveals a lingering attention on the event that had led to the creation of the nation.

In any case, Watson wrote to Edward Everett of the Massachusetts Historical Society about his scheme, stressing that "my aim has been to gather data which might serve for future exercise in poetry, printing, and works of the imagination."(13) Everett showed it to "several Antiquarian friends" and said: "[It] will gratify me to be able hereafter to inform you that it has had proper effect in stimulating our Antiquarians to new efforts and researches."(14) Watson clearly wanted antiquarians elsewhere to devote their research to the accumulation of material to be used for "literary" purposes, as he himself was doing.  Everett could at least hope that Watson's plea would be heeded because local historical writing was just beginning to assume its earliest book-length forms in the Boston area, and there was as yet little evidence whether that writing would have a "literary" or some other cast.

It is not clear whether Watson had seen the historiographical and topographical sketches that had been appearing since the 1790s in the Massachusetts Historical Society *Collections*, but those sketches certainly contained material of the kind he was calling for.  Snow's *History of Boston* was published in 1825, but as the publisher was a local firm, and, as the subscribers were from the Boston area, it is not very likely that copies of the book circulated as far away as Philadelphia.  Nor is there evidence that Watson was aware of any press notices of Snow's history.  Watson's perception of himself as the pioneer local antiquarian may have derived in part from his ignorance of the situation in Massachusetts.  Not until 1831, after the publication of his own work on Philadelphia, is it indisputable that he was aware of the early book-length publications of the Massachusetts group.(15)

Watson continued to publicize his work during the late 1820s, hoping to stimulate others.  On November 4, 1826, he wrote a letter to the *Chester Upland Union* on the early history of the area.  On November 30, Doylestown's *Bucks County Patriot* included a piece entitled "Antiquities of Pennsylvania" and indicated that "Mr. Watson, of Germantown, has been idefatigable in collecting and preserving whatever related to the early history of our state."(16) In 1827 Watson still saw himself basically as a compiler, hoping to awaken in others a similar passion, and was even unsure of the propriety of his own writing style.(17) Watson welcomed the assistance of his friend J. Jay Smith, at one point disclosing: "You are a true Disciple to have ferreted out such rarities.  My mantle shall fall upon you."(18)

In September 1829, Watson began discussing the actual publication of his material, something Robert Vaux had urged him to do five years before. He wrote to Smith that "I propose only the smallest edition—say of 1,000 copies." Watson hoped to induce a particular firm to serve as publisher "*after* I have shown them 50 to 70 names or the subscription book procured personally by myself of dignitaries." And, in order "to catch the eye and confidence—I shall procure a recommendation . . . from the Historical Society," something that Watson actually drafted for Smith to present to the officers. Although Watson had the officers indulging "the hope that there is not one of sufficient ability to purchase who will not possess it for his own information and as a useful and entertaining behest to his children [or as] a proper present to Philadelphians dwelling in distant places,"(19) the actual endorsement was shorter and less commendatory.(20)

In December 1829, Watson told Vaux that "[the] Annals of Philadelphia are actually in press—and will be got through during the winter—Almost everything wrote out anew under better arrangement and classification—In due time I must try to procure some brief 'Recommendation' of it to the citizens, so as to facilitate its sale—to be done by the Historical Society officially."(21)

In a section of the published *Annals*, entitled "Olden Time Affections and Researches", Watson tried to explain why he had developed his strong and durable curiosity about Philadelphia's past. He believed that, as a middle-aged man, he was more apt to ask good questions than old men. To him, the subject was "all new and unexplored, and . . . with the eagerness of a child which asks questions about everything, I felt constantly awake to inquiries on topics which would not affect the minds of old persons; things in which they had long ceased to be curious."(22)

Watson's *Annals* begins with a "general introductory history" in which he describes the early years of Pennsylvania's and Philadelphia's past.(23) What Watson found was the rapid and progressive attainment of "riches, independence, and renown," coupled with "numerous and successive disastrous events," a lot of "struggling with what they deemed adverse circumstances, such as, low markets, want of currency, slow returns for debt, and loud contentions about deficiencies of public funds for national purposes."(24) He often noticed not the heroism and persistence that his antiquarian brethren in New England found in their Puritan forbearers but a kind of despondency of tone in which the early settlers of Philadelphia were accustomed to speak of their condition and prospects.(25)

What follows are "fragments of our primitive history," "several items of a miscellaneous character, illustrative" of Philadelphia's early past, taken from the materials collected by a Mrs. Logan, which were mostly "confidential letter correspondence" of the first leaders of the city and colony.(26) In "The Primitive Settlement," Watson describes the geographical setting and the physical shape of the first village.(27) In "facts and occurrences" of the earliest settlement, he mixes letters of Penn, reminiscences of pioneer settlers, minutes of the city council, and early published descriptive accounts of the city to produce a mosaic of events and physical developments throughout the colonial period.(28) Sections on the Penn family(29) and on Penn's descendants(30) are based on letters written by various members of that family.

There follows a number of sections on particular places and buildings: Penn's early landings, inns, churches, houses, bridges, riverbanks, caves.

And then, suddenly, Watson turns to "habits and state of society." He found that "[n]umerous traditionary accounts attest to the fact that there was always among the early settlers a frank and generous hospitality,"(31) adding "I have often heard aged citizens say that decent citizens had a universal speaking acquaintance with each other, and everybody promptly recognized a stranger in the streets. A simple or idiot person was known to the whole population."(32)

Groups of different rank dressed differently and did not put on the appearance of a gentleman by "dressing up," as they had come to by Watson's time.(33)    Descriptions of dress follow in a section entitled "Apparel,"(34) which is, in turn, succeeded by another called "Furniture and Equipage."(35) Unlike dress, furnishings in early Philadelphia "descended acceptably unchanged from father to son and son's son," "simple articles which contented," in sharp contrast to the time since about 1750, when "the introduction of foreign luxury, caused by the influx of wealth, has been yearly effecting successive changes in those articles."(36)

In a series of sections involving change and modernization in the material world, Watson describes the development of wells and pumps, pavements and lamps, bridges, balconies and window glass and porches, cellar kitchens and ice houses, shade trees, the changing locations of retail and craft shops, the new modes of conducting business and producing goods, the rising prices of scarcer land and food, and the procedures for electing officials.(37) He took particular notice of the shift from craft to factory production,(38) emphasizing the dangers of bankruptcy and monopoly,(39) both of which had accompanied the rise of industrial capitalism during the early and middle nineteenth century in Eastern urban centers such as Philadelphia.

In a section on "superstitions and popular credulity," Watson observed that "our forefathers (the ruder part) brought with them much of the superstition of their 'father-land,' and here it found much to cherish and sustain it, in the credulity of the Dutch and Swedes, nor less from the Indians, who always abounded in marvellous relations, much incited by their conjurers and pow-wows."(40) For Watson, chief among the superstitions of his forefathers was a belief in witchcraft, but he also found evidence of conjuring and hexing: that is, people going to those with special powers to find stolen goods, water, precious minerals, or money.(41) In "Sports and Amusements," Watson described such leisure activities as dancing, fox-hunting, horseracing, skating, and sledding.(42)

"Education" was restricted to reading, writing, and arithmetic.    All else "[came] as a matter of course, by more readings at home, when the mind was matured and the school-acquirements were finished.    They then learned to read on purpose to be able to pursue such branches of inquiry for themselves; and having the means in possession, the end as certainly followed without the school-bill charge as with it," — unlike their offspring, who in Watson's day learned through painful lessons.(43)

In a section on "courts and trials" and "crimes and punishments," Watson describes criminal behaviour and the punishments for it, observing that "[we] have been so long happily delivered from the former exhibitions of the pillory, whipping-post, ducking-stool, wheelbarrow-men, and even hanging itself, that it may serve to show the aspect of quite another age to expose the facts in the days of our forefathers."(44) He proceeds to cull from court records references to many whippings, some hangings, and one instance of a woman "to be *burned alive*, for the murder of her husband."(45) Watson's view of Pennsylvania's laws is summed up in the section entitled "the excellencies of Penn's laws":(46) "Everything in our laws has been popularly constituted, even from the beginning," in Penn's early republic, where there was "a general adherence to equality not seen among the other colonies."(47) Watson was quite unsuccessful in his efforts to compile a list of the early Philadelphia bar, though he was able to amass some evidence on the colony's defence force, the militia, and, to his shame, on duelling, that is, the settlement of personal grievances in a private, extra-legal manner.(48)

There follows a long series of sections giving specific information on such physical structures and features of the city as bridges, courthouses, prisons, markets, churches, halls, coffee-houses and taverns, the state-house, barracks, forts, academies, mansions, hospitals, poor-houses, libraries, theaters, banks, custom-houses, gardens, springs, and ponds — many of which were accompanied by illustrations.   A brief segment on fires — or the destruction of physical structures — and the development of fire-fighting equipment ends with the observation that "[the] present manner of subduing fires presents an aspect quite different from former doings in such cases. When there were no hoses in use and no hydrants, but only pumps and buckets to keep the engines supplied, the scene was much more busy than now.   Few or no idlers could be seen as onlookers.   They made long lines of people to attend to pass, the cry was passed along the line — 'fall in! fall in!' If disregarded, a bucket of water was discharged upon them."(49)

Watson then considers the place of various racial, ethnic, and religious groups in Philadelphia's past.    Of the Indians: "What can be more melancholoy than their history! By a law of their nature, they seem destined to show but sure extinction.   Everywhere at the approach of the white man, they fade away."(50) The Indians around Philadelphia — the Delawares — were, by the time Watson wrote, greatly reduced and scattered and the subject of missionary activity.(51) After a brief account of the pirates — such as Captain Kidd and Bluebeard — who were active along the Atlantic coast in the late seventeenth and early eighteenth centuries, Watson provides information on the Swedes, the Germans, the Irish, Negroes and slaves, indentured servants, and the Quakers.   The Swedes, it was observed, "were a plain, strong, industrious people, but had made no great improvements."(52) The Germans, Watson called "[this] hardy, frugal, and industrious portion of our population," but added that at first "it is manifest there was a fear they would not be acceptable inhabitants" because of a belief that (as early Pennsylvania leaders put it) "foreigners do not so well among us as our people."(53)

Similar views concerning the Irish were also expressed.(54) Of blacks, Watson tells his readers: "[We] have happily been so long relieved from the curse of slavery." But, he did not like the conduct of the freed "coloured" population of Philadelphia.   Separated into their own churches, blacks had become "dressy and dandy *colour'd* beaux and belles," with aspirations and "little vanities," insisting on being called coloured people and, instead of servants or blacks or Negroes, gentlemen and ladies.   They used to be "much humbler, more esteemed in their place, and more useful to themselves and others."  Regretting that "they show an overwhelming fondness for display and vainglory," Watson admonished that "[with] the kindest feelings for their race, judicious men wish them wiser conduct, and a better use of the benevolent feelings which induced their emancipation among us."(55) Indentured servants were those "[numerous] persons [who] used to arrive every year from Germany and Ireland, [and] engaged themselves for a term of years to pay their passages.   Some of them turned out frugal and industrious, and became in time a part of our wealthy citizens."(56) The segment on the Quakers is a compendium of the practices that set the sect apart from others, but Watson in no way reveals their preeminence in early Philadelphia.(57)

In a section entitled "Seasons and Climate," Watson includes "only such notable changes of the temperature in the extremes of *heat and cold*, as was a matter of surprise or remark at the time of the occurrence, and therefore most likely to arrest our attention in the present day—as a wonder of the past,"(58) such things as snow storms, mild winters, especially hot summers.   He quotes from diaries, provides charts of temperature comparing various years, includes a long annual listing of when navigation of the Delaware was obstructed by ice.(59)

In "Medical Subjects," he presents an annalistic compilation of the incidence and variety of diseases, especially small-pox and yellow fever, and describes some plants used as remedies.   He observes that "[t]he people were accustomed [in 'olden times'] to the use of plants and herbs in cases of sickness, and then chief resort to physicians was in calls of surgery or difficult cases of childbirth."(60) Doctors homes were the drugshops that have since become separate establishments.   Doctors were usually trained in Britain, and, indeed, the earliest physicians of any prominence and influence were from Britain.(61)

Watson had succeeded in gathering some vivid accounts of epidemics, particularly yellow fever ravages of 1793, but refers his readers to his unpublished manuscript for the details, awakening curiosity with such comments as: "Look then, in which way you would, through the street, you saw exposed coffins on chair-wheels, either in quick motion, or you saw the wheels drawn before horses to receive their pestilential charges."(62)

Scattered through the remainder of the *Annals of Philadelphia* Watson includes brief sections on such economic activities as silk-manufacture, shipping and ship-building, "whales and whalery," "grapes and vineyards," "beasts of prey and game," and anthracite coal.   Paper money and lotteries are also given separate treatment.   Watson asserts that "[in] the first introduction of paper money, there was much difference of opinion concerning its eventual benefit to trade and to the community"(63) —something that had continued to be the case, he believed.   Of lotteries, he asserts that they wore in colonial times a "fairly conducted" "ways and means" of finding revenue for public purposes,(64) but since independence, had degenerated into the hands of "wily traffickers" who had turned them into a "notorious". . . "waste of treasure and morals."(65)

Aside from a few short section on the resistance to British policy during the 1760s and 1770s on "occurrences of the War of Independence"(66) and several more on vacation spots and the rivers of the area, the last portion of Watson's *Annals* are given over to "Remarkable Incidents and Things," "Curiosities and Discoveries," "Statistical Facts," and "Miscellaneous Facts," petering out with "Relics and Remembrances," which ends with references to pages in Watson's unpublished, longer manuscript. The sections contain, like those that appeared in contemporary local histories in New England, references to the unusual or bizarre (unfamiliar animals, floods, storms, earthquakes, strange deaths, amusing incidents); statistical computations involving taxation, trade, and population; or just bits of fact not easily classifiable.

Watson's *Annals of Philadelphia* is a vast, sprawling compendia of information — as he thought it was, but it does have some form and structure and about some subjects reveals a sense of change over time. For Watson, early Philadelphia was both superior and inferior to the Philadelphia of his day. Change produced an ambivalent reaction in him, more openly so than was the case among his New England brethren, some of whom indicated that it was worthwhile noting the material progress that had been made since the founding of the Puritan towns, and others of whom wondered if later New Englanders had sustained the founders' high level of moral and religious strivings. But underneath these occasional references was a generally shared belief that the Puritan town had survived and flourished within the original mold.

How different was Watson's perception! As annalist of the largest population center of colonial America, he was confronted with variety and change, and he revelled in it. The vitality and excitement of living in such a community is communicated in his pages, even when he simply quotes from sources similar to those the New England antiquarians used. For Watson, the growth of Philadelphia was not a simple story of progress; with each gain, something was lost. In this sense, he was a more sophisticated observer and memorialist than those urban antiquarians who, after the Civil War, would present histories as civic testimonials whose overriding aim was to celebrate the progress these authors and editors believed had accompanied the mushrooming growth they chronicled.

Adopting the annalistic format, Watson organized his history chronologically, in the same fashion as Felt in his *Annals of Salem*, which appeared three years earlier. But, though Watson adopted a format like some of the earliest antiquarians in Massachusetts, his sales method was novel. He explained to G. N. Barker that he had sent him a free, autographed copy as one "whose affections have been so strong for olden time enquiries." But in order that Barker not feel any sense of obligation, Watson also sent him "two other copies which as occasion serves among your visiting Guests, you may oblige them and me, by their sale at $3 each[!]"(67)

The *Annals'* press run of one thousand copies sold rapidly, with six hundred copies sold before book-agent Uriah Hunt took the remainder. The reviews or "notices" in the local press were favorable except for that of the *Philadelphia Gazette*. Watson explained away the less-than-favorable comments in the *Gazette* in a note (written years later) following his clipping of the review: "The above . . . has been the only one to 'hang a doubt' upon the Annals—It springs from pique for the Editors formerly solicited my pages for their paper. . . .     George had once been my Apprentice, and liked this chance to look big over his former Master."(68)

What the *Gazette* said in its original notice was that "Mr. Watson has been living in spirit with those who lived on earth some fifty or a hundred years ago, that he has imbibed a strong affection for ancient modes and customs, and seems to think the former state of society preferable to the present, [to which Watson added in the margin: "No!"]. The *Gazette's* reviewer went on to refer to material progress, improvements in the arts, discoveries in the sciences, and the development of steam power and machinery. The reviewer believed that honest industry was more respected and speculation was not so rampant in the past as in the present, but whether society was presently ahead of or behind the past he would not try to determine.(69)

Watson's *Annals* was also honored—as Watson's marginal note indicates—with a long, thirty-seven page "notice" in Boston's *North American Review*, in April 1833, which meant that his work was brought to the attention of subscribers and readers of the nation's most prestigious journal of criticism, and, more particularly, New Englanders with a developed interest in writing of all kinds. It is clear that the reviewer made his assessment from the perspective of the New England antiquarians. Asserting that "[the] work is certainly rather long.", he accepted Watson's contention that the Annals "may be deemed *sui generis* in its execution," adding that crediting the industrious author for the mass of information he had collected. "Much of it no doubt appears trifling," the reviewer added, "but a great part of that which seems unimportant throws light upon the manners, fashions, tastes, and feelings of the day,"(70) and that such revelations give "a 'local habitation' and reality to recollections, which would otherwise soon die away."(71) Most of the review was an extended summary of the book's contents. It is quite likely that this review was the chief means by which antiquarians in New England learned of Watson's work and the ways in which it contrasted with their own.

In other, shorter reviews, the *Saturday Bulletin* indicated in its notice that "the *Annals* presents a mass of interesting facts respecting the early settlement, to which every descendent of the original inhabitants may turn with interest and profit. The contents are as various as can be conceived. Indeed, we find it impossible to give even a general idea of the huge volume; *we defy anybody to do it*." The *National Gazette* found it to be "an encyclopedia of reminiscences, a panopticon of our antiquities. Mr. John F. Watson is the compiler and annalist; and in archaeology *will be acknowledged* peerless. He will be the Homer of his class." The *Norristown Free Press* exclaimed that "[no] one can read the book without being astonished at the singular industry which could collect the vast fund of information exhibited. The author, who is a cashier of a bank, is remarkable for fondness to explore the traditions of the 'Olden Time,' and to preserve recollections of the things that were."(72)

It is not clear when Watson decided to have a second edition of the *Annals* published, but in his "Prospectus and Testimonials" for that edition, he indicated that the original edition had been out of print for several years, "and has been repeatedly sought for since, at advanced prices." Watson and his publisher proposed to publish a second, two-volume edition "*by subscription*," and at "the lowest possible price." The author proclaimed that "the object is not so much to profit by the publication, as to circulate and diffuse to the greatest possible extent among our city and country population." In the "Advertisement" for the 1844 edition, it was revealed that "[many] of our distant subscribers are [former] Philadelphians [who] retain an affection for their early home." Watson' *Annals* was offered as a "work full of entertainment and instruction, [abounding] in attractive information, the undercurrent of history – too often rejected by the more formal chronicler, as inconsistent with the stately dignity of his subject."(73)

George Lippard, later author of the popular, myth-laden *Washington & His Generals or Legends of the American Revolution* (1847) wrote a favorable two-part review of the 1844 edition in the *Philadelphia Daily Chronicle*. Lippard asserted that the *Annals* "is a book that will be read, quoted, and treasured, when nine-tenths of the publications of the present age are dead, buried, and forgotten. It will live with the volumes of history, science, or philosophy. It will live though petty critics may carp at it." Lippard admitted that while the "style of the *Annals*, it is true, is not Johnsonian, . . . still the book accomplished the object which the author designed. . . . The future historian, novelist, or poet will bless his memory and the patriots of generations yet unborn hold his name in reverence."(74)

It is revealing that a nationally known writer of a myth-laden account of a great national event, the Revolution, should have assessed a work of local history so favorably. That those who wrote national history paid attention to those who wrote local history indicates a broadening impact for local historical writing. That someone with Parson Weems' approach to writing about national heroes should find the anecdotal, story-telling preoccupation of Watson congenial and attractive, places Watson's brand of local historical writing somewhere between myth and fact, between fictional renderings and gazetteer-like objectivity.

Watson added to his copy of Lippard's review that "the composer of the foregoing, tho' cordial in his commendation, was but a shabby fellow in his morals! and did what he could to cheat me out of money he received for my Annals."(75) To a friend, he later wrote: "George Lippard gave a capital review of the Annals in the Daily Chronicle. . . . He has written me also, as a *disciple*, with as much enthusiasm as yourself. For our encouragement, there are men enough, whose course is in unison with our stimulating pursuits." But Watson insisted that he had done enough work as an antiquarian, and disclosed to his friend: "I have jealous lookers on, who do not like to hear of my being further engaged in such inquiries. . . . [T]he field is therefore fully open to others, like yourself."(76)

Watson's "jealous lookers on" – at least in Pennsylvania – were not numerous during the remainder of his life – in fact, there were only two who actually wrote other local histories: Neville B. Craig, whose history of Pittsburgh appeared in 1851,(77) and George H. Morgan, whose annals of Harrisburg were published in 1858.(78)

In the "Prospectus and Testimonials" for the third edition of Watson's *Annals*, which came out in 1856; the language used simply assumed fame and popularity: "The merits and character. . . have secured for it universal commendation, and entitle it a place in every household."(79) On September 18, 1860, a short time before his death, Watson summed up his long career in a letter to Howard Jenkins, who had sought his "opinion and advice" in preparing a history of Pennsylvania. He wrote, with some bitterness, that "[W]hat the public should know is very different from what they will read and *pay for*." Local history does "not realize any adequate *Profit*, for the time and labor employed. Romance and fictions, have the rule of men's minds." Watson told Jenkins: "It is not in my heart to offer you any encouragement. What I did was a grateful homage to God, to mark the way of his Providence to my country. . . . I care not for recompense."(80)

These keenly felt revelations of a devoted, pioneering antiquarian show the deeply mixed feelings Watson experienced as he reflected on an enterprise that spanned nearly forty years. Proud of his pioneer status, he remained disappointed over the initial lack of public response to factual historical writing, even hinting that his "anecdotal style" was a concession to the popularity of fictional writing. Far from seeking out followers, his parting advice to one who sought guidance came close to outright discouragement.

Watson's status as a pioneer was enhanced by the fact that his *Annals of New York* (1832),(81) patterned after the earlier *Annals of Philadelphia*, was the first local history of a New York community. Watson did not seek out the honor, admitting in 1825 that two years earlier "I endeavored to prompt the New York Historical Society to institute some such researches for their city. Dr. Hosack was commissioned to inform me that it was received with great cordiality, and that my principles of enquiry would be adopted for New York."(82)

In fact, New Yorkers were slow to respond, and, when they did, it was not in slavish emulation of Watson's literary, anecdotal style. However, the earliest effort by a native New Yorker was the *Chronicles of Cooperstown* (1838),(83) whose unacknowledged author was the most famous novelist of the time, James Fenimore Cooper, after whose family the village was named. Whether Watson's earlier histories in any way influenced Cooper is not known, but Watson's format for his history, the chronicling of local incidents, was congenial to a writer of stories.

Nevertheless, Cooper was concerned to establish accuracy and authenticity.(84) Yet, it is notable that other writers of fiction did not heed Watson's plea and did not move, as did Cooper, from the novel to history. Given the immense popularity of fictional "romances"(85) and the concurrent growing interest in local historical writing during the 1830s, 1840s, and 1850s, it is surprising that those who wrote novels and short stories did not also write histories. Watson believed both factual and fictional writing—properly composed—shared a focus on detail, description, incident, and particularities in all their concreteness and specificity. Perhaps Watson's life-end brooding had its source in his awareness that so few writers of talent had actually followed his advice. In any case, even Cooper's *Chronicles of Cooperstown* was revised by the Rev. S. T. Livermore in 1862. Livermore's revisions and additions reveal a concern for fullness and accuracy that the great storyteller had not exhibited in his random renderings of a quarter-century before.(86)

Most of the other early local histories in New York were of communities in and around what had become the nation's leading metropolis, New York City: Thomas Strong's Flatbush (Brooklyn) (1842), James Riker's Newtown (Queen's) (1852), Daniel Curry's New York City (1853), Mary Booth's New York City (1859), Giles Mandeville's Flushing (Queen's) (1860). In none of these was outsider Watson's early "Annals" pointed to as a model.

Only a very few of the early settlements upstate were made the subject of an early local history. When an obscure schoolteacher, John B. Wilkinson, presented his *Annals of Binghamton* in 1840, he revealed "[that] which suggested the present enterprise, and which has resulted in the production of the following history, was the reading of the little volume entitled "The Chronicles of Cooperstown."(87)

When E. M. Ruttenber published his *History of the Town of Newburgh* in 1859, he wrote about local history with a confidence that reflected its growing popularity: "The necessity of Local History is unquestionable; it is, to a large extent, the material of history in its highest sense and scope." Ruttenber called upon the descendants of the pioneers to write down their family history, to found local historical associations in every town, and to educate the public upon the importance of preserving old records.(88)

Ruttenber's summoning had little immediate effect, but is of significance in that it reveals a growing awareness among early antiquarians in the Midatlantic area of the importance of local historical preservation, research, and writing of a kind that Massachusetts antiquarians and Watson and his colleagues in Philadelphia had come to a generation before.

With the notable exception of Watson, most local historical writing in the United States before the Civil War was confined to communities founded by the Puritans in New England. With very few exceptions, the early settlements along the Atlantic coast from New York to Florida did not contain antiquarians willing to devote themselves to the production of a full-length history of their town or city. Those who wrote the early local histories of the Puritan-founded villages and seaports enlarged upon an old and firm conviction that these communities were extraordinary, special, and worth writing about. Nowhere else in the United States during these decades were there numbers of antiquarians who perceived the local past with as much seriousness.

It did not matter that William Penn, as the original proprietor of Pennsylvania colony, had planned, not only Philadelphia, but several county seats in the earliest-settled south-eastern part of his colony.(89) Nor did it matter that Southern colonial capitals such as Annapolis, Williamsburg, and Savannah were planned or that Southern seaports were also.(90) The planned community in colonial British North America did not in itself generate an early propensity to record and preserve the past. The Puritans planned their settlements, but they also invested them with a transcendent purpose: a religious utopia or model community that was from its inception meant to be out of the ordinary.

Even less did the antiquarian impulse reveal itself in ordinary places, whether in villages located at the fall-lines of rivers around mill sites inland from the Atlantic coast, or in the cross-road villages that served governmental, market, and social centers for the surrounding rural population.(91) In the early South the impulse was at its very weakest because, in the large areas over which a dispersed rural population was spread, plantations, churches, and courthouses constituted a shredded community, serving as scattered focal points for farming, religion, and politics.(92)

Local historical writing in its early phases was, thus, largely a New England phenomenon.  It was factual, not fictional, or even anecdotal, as Watson hoped it would be.  And it was largely about small communities, only rarely about the early metropolises whose chronicler Watson tried to be.  This writing was usually the product of very ordinary people who were not accomplished writers and had no theory or even prevailing model to serve as a guide.  Their histories were mixtures of description, listings of facts, quotations, authenticated records, and reminiscences.

Unlike writers of fiction, biography and national history, there were no prescriptions for what ought to be done, no learned debates in journals on proper form and content.  When Hermann E. Ludewig presented his pioneering *The Literature of American Local History: A Bibliographic Essay* in 1846, he was silent on such matters.  Not as popular, in terms of sales, as fiction, biography, or national history, local histories were more closely linked to the oral tradition their authors scorned than they were to these other, more developed forms of writing, which commanded a large, national circulation.  Generally bought and read only by people in or from the locality, often dependent upon subscribers for publication of any kind, introduced in the early years with statements indicating doubt as to their efficacy or even the desirability of a printed version, the first local histories were a truly popular form of writing in another sense of the term, in that they were based on the recollections and record-gathering capacities of people who were not primarily writers.

What the Massachusetts group developed in their idiosyncratic way was picked up by others elsewhere, who worked on in "beachheads" of antiquarian activity from Maine to Philadelphia.  As settlement spread westward and as communities elsewhere aged, the antiquarian impulse possessed others after the Civil War. In the decades that followed, local historical writing evolved and spread, becoming more popular in both senses of the term.

# PART II
# The Later Antiquarians

# CHAPTER 5
# The Later Setting

The American Civil War had the paradoxical effect of heightening both nationalism and localism, the identification with and loyalty to both nation and locality of those engaged in the bloodiest of modern fraticidal conflicts. In villages and cities all over the old, divided union, citizens of the United States and the Confederate States turned their attention outward, toward the national crisis at the same time they became concerned about the contribution of their local community to the larger cause.(1)

Historical writing was affected by the war in two ways. At the local level, some who wrote about their towns, cities, counties, or even states turned their "histories" into accounts of their regiments' wartime experiences. As Van Tassel puts it: "In the strictest sense, every state, county, and town was represented by its male citizens in military units which served on the battlefield as extensions of the local community. . . . Histories of towns or states published during and shortly after the war were simply histories of regiments."(2)

And, at the national level, the political division during the war years greatly increased the difficulty those who wrote national histories had in attaining a genuinely national perspective. Even Bancroft's *History* was criticized for reflecting a New Englander's bias toward other parts of the Union. James Schouler, another Northerner, embarked on a Bancroft-like multivolume project and produced seven volumes between 1880 and 1913, covering the period from 1783 to 1877.(3) Schouler attempted to be fair to both sides, even though he had an anti-Southern bias. But: "He wrote as if a representative of the federal government, using as his primary sources government documents and the personal papers of Presidents."(4)

The reemergence of nationalism after the war was enhanced by the centennial celebrations of 1876, which linked patriotism to history in the marking of the one-hundredth anniversary of the Declaration of Independence, the birthdate of the nation. Those who wrote or spoke about the past were naturally encouraged to play a major role. In 1871,

Congress authorized a national exposition to be held at Philadelphia, and, in 1872, created the United States Centennial Commission. But, like the Civil War, the centennial had the effect of heightening both national and local consciousness. The director general of the exposition sent out a circular to all the governors "urging them to have historical studies written" so that the country might display "a correct history of the birth and progress of the several communities that have contributed during the century of growth and strength of the Union of States." With this kind of official approval, some states did authorize or encourage the writing of such histories.(5)

Indeed, Congress recommended in a joint resolution "that the people of the several States assemble in their several counties and towns on the approaching centennial anniversary of our national independence, and that they cause to have delivered on said day a historical sketch of such county or town from its formation."(6) That such requests and recommendations acted as a spur to the production of full-fledged local histories can be seen in a number of prefatory comments in volumes that appeared in the years after 1876, and nowhere in such detail as in John S. Hittell's *A History of the City of San Francisco* (1878):(7) "This book was written at the request of the committee appointed to manage the celebration in San Francisco of the Centennial Anniversary of the Declaration of our National Independence, in accordance with a resolution adopted by Congress on the thirteenth of March, 1876."(8)

Those who commanded a national perspective – congressmen, centennial officials – found it natural to have the citizens of the nation celebrate the nation's one-hundredth birthday along with a celebration of their local community's place in that nation. The decentralized, federated character of American life dictated such an approach. Nationalism and localism were not seen as antithetical, even though regional attachments and national loyalties had become so – devastatingly so in the case of the Civil War. National officials recognized the force of localism by calling on all citizens everywhere to create an outburst of patriotic celebration in their own communities. In local ceremonies, the meaning of the past of both nation and town or city would be recalled simultaneously.

This complementary conjunction of nationalism and localism can also be seen in the successful attempt of Joseph R. Hawley, President of the Philadelphia Centennial Commission and an owner of the *Hartford* (Connecticut) *Courant*, to persuade the firm that published *Rowell's Newspaper Directory* to manage a display of all 8,129 American newspapers at the centennial exhibition. A pigeonhole was provided for each publication within the building, designed especially for the occasion. A sign reading "Come in and see a paper from home" was an effective lure for passersby, and the Rowell exhibit was well attended.(9)

As white settlement moved westward across the continent, historical societies proliferated at the local, county, and state levels. These organizations provided the same kinds of support for those who wrote local histories as their predecessors along the Atlantic Coast had in the decades before the Civil War. Some of the state societies, especially those in the midwest, were directly funded by state governments. Others, particularly in the South, were actual state agencies, typically called the "Department of History and Archives."  County and local societies were founded with names of "Pioneer Societies (or Associations)," "Genealogical and Biographical Societies," "Memorial (or Monument) Associations," or "Old Settlers Societies (or Associations)."  Such organizations collected artifacts and documents, sponsored research and writing through the publication of papers, addresses, and collections of source material, and held elaborate commemorative meetings in memory of important historical events.  Some of these meetings took place outside and, with an atmosphere akin to an outing or a revival meeting, consisted of long programs, including such things as hymns, prayers, dedicatory and historical addresses, chorales, dirges, audience marches, basket lunches, music by a band, open singing, and odes or other poems.(10)

The state historical societies continued to be in the forefront of these efforts to promote state and local history, though none matched the Wisconsin State Historical Society in the scope and scale of its director's activities.(11)  In a pamphlet issued in 1874 entitled "The Importance of Local History", the librarian of the Wisconsin society made a plea for those in every locality with an interest in the past to collect materials and publish them either in book form or, serially, in the area's newspaper.  The librarian also hoped the "custom in some places to have annual gatherings of the old settlers to reconstruct their experiences . . .   could become universal and a printed account of the same preserved."(12)

Farther west, in the lead article of the first volume of *Papers* of the California Historical Society, in 1887, Martin Kellogg, in a piece entitled "The Local Units of History", argued that the current style of writing history "is minute and exacting.   . . .    The daily life of men must be understood and pictured." To understand the history of nations or states, those who study the past "must descend to particulars." Why? because "[t]he greatest sums are made up *of units*." Kellogg asked: "How shall we best find the *units of history* for a State like ours? By *localizing* our studies." Making a plea for fullness and range, that materials be gathered for not just the pioneer years, but for "[e]very decade since the first settlement," Kellogg went on to implore historically minded Californians not to be "discouraged because our townships lack the cohesiveness and individuality of New England towns."(13)

Older state historical societies made similar efforts.  In New Jersey, the corresponding secretary of the state's historical society " was an ardent believer in local societies as adjuncts to [the state] Society, and securing the endorsement of the Executive Committee, vigorously pushed the project during his encumbency in that office, issuing circulars and corresponding with gentlemen in all parts of the State."(14)

Further south, in Mississippi, Franklin J. Ripley presented, in 1898, "Suggestions to Local Historians" in the first volume of the *Publications* of the recently formed state historical society.  Ripley admitted that in 1876, there were centennial celebrations held in many of the state's counties at which historical addresses were given in accordance with the Congressional resolution of that year.  Unfortunately, many of these addresses had been lost, with the exception of some that the state's historical society had gathered into its archives.   As its charter gave the historical society the authority to establish branches in the various counties of the state, Ripley went on to urge all local organizations to affiliate with the state society with the aim of encouraging research through the presentation of papers and through their subsequent publication and distribution, thus furthering cooperation and avoiding duplication of effort.   He ended his piece with "suggestions" for sources and topics to be dealt with.(15)

In March, 1924 an "Outline for a Survey of Local History and Historical Material" appeared in the *Indiana History Bulletin*, whose author similarly presented "a guide . . .   to any locality for the study of its history," consisting of a list of topics.(16) Likewise, in 1933, Harlow Lindley, Curator of History at the Ohio State Archaeological and Historical Society in Columbus, Ohio, wrote a piece entitled "A Systematic Study of Local History," which appeared in the *Michigan Historical Magazine*. Lindley presented an "outline for the study of local history," which was largely an unacknowledged list of topics copied from the earlier article.(17)

These varied efforts by officials of (and others connected with) state historical societies to persuade active local antiquarians to collect and perserve materials and then to write in comprehensive and orderly fashion about their communities are clear indications that historical societies continued, after the Civil War, to perform an important supporting role for the actual production of local historical writing.

So too with newspapers.   By the 1860s and 1870s, the daily and weekly press — both urban and rural — had developed formal local news columns and thus had become community journals with regular factual, descriptive items delineating the ongoing life of village or city.

During the 1830s and 1840s, the "penny press" of the eastern urban centers introduced local news items for readers living in communities too large for the inhabitants to grasp what was happening through the traditional mode of oral communication.   In the decades that followed, the press in smaller urban centers, and then in villages and towns, emulated the big urban dailies, sometimes goaded into change by the appearance of weekly or semiweekly "country editions" of the New York or Boston papers, editions that featured local news columns.

The result was that printed "news" no longer referred to something that happened in places far from where one lived, that is, from one's state, nation, or the world beyond.   The contents of newspapers in the United States came to bear a significant relationship to the communities in which they were printed.   Whether paid reporters, as in urban dailies, or unpaid volunteers, as in rural weeklies, local news correspondents were observers, but also to some extent "boosters" of their villages, towns, and cities, occasionally moralizing on, praising, or chastizing those around them, but also with a promoter's concern to enhance the reputation of their community, which they identified with and loved and whose basic arrangements and goals were beyond questioning.(18)

It was natural for the editors of such journals to be hospitable to antiquarians who sought to recapture the past.   "News" and "history" were similar in nature.   Just as the reporter sought to observe and accurately record the contemporary life of his community, so too, the historian attempted to recover and present a factual account of the community's past. Both journalist and antiquarian believed they reported on a village or a city of which they could be proud, whether in recounting its noble beginnings and progressive development or in relating its successful present or optimistic future. Both did so as accurately and as descriptively and as concretely as observation or research allowed.

It became a common practice during the decades after the Civil War for newspapers in communities of all sizes to serialize local histories-in-the-making. The relationship between local history and newspapers was probed in a thoughtful paper by Carl C. Weicht, "read at the twelfth annual conference on local history work in Minnesota, held in connection with the eighty-third annual meeting of the Minnesota Historical Society in the Historical Building, St. Paul, January 11, 1932." Weicht began by saying that "[because] of the newspaper's strategic position as a chronicler of events, as an historian of the contemporary scene, it is interesting to examine the relationship between the local historian and this agency." He then made the point that in areas of the United States (west of the Appalachians, mainly) where newspapers existed at the time of white settlement, they constitute an important historical source: "It would be next to impossible to find a Minnesota community that has not had the service and advantage of its own organ of expression, its own agency for the printing of news and of advertisements, its own recorder of local history."(19)

Weicht went on to say,"[that] newspapers would contain exhaustive historical material on every subject is not to be expected. Yet surely they are worthy of examination, for they yield [as a member of the Minnesota Historical Society put it] 'the type of record invaluable in piecing together the story of the normal life of the past.'" Weicht believed that historians should seek "the normal life of the past, . . . not merely a chronicle of wars, elections, the brief hour of prominence of the leaders, and the curious or unusual departures from the normal life. . . . How did they live and how did they make their living? What did they think and what did they believe? What were their economic and social problems?"(20)

But the relationship between the local historian and the newspaper went beyond the former using the latter as an important historical source, Weicht argued. A newspaper with only "straight news, editorials, and advertising" could not build or maintain its circulation. Such a publication had to have more varied contents, chief among which were its "features." Weicht found that "[p]robably the most frequently used types of feature is the historical and reminiscent article." Historical anniversaries of all kinds are occasions "for the publication of historical material that serves the dual purpose of recording valuable material in somewhat more permanent form than would ordinarily be possible and of awakening increased interest in things historical."(21) Weicht believed that both historian and journalist were "boosters": "The local historian and the newspaper, working together, may well provide such a stimulus to community spirit."(22)

Whatever the precise forms of the connection between reporters and historians in particular communities, the newspaper was unquestionably a major outlet for local historical writing and constituted a single source for readers interested in accounts of both the past and the present. The newspaper contributed significantly to the popularization of local historical writing. The past was as much the community's as the present. The same readers who followed the local news columns also noticed historical commemorations, anniversary celebrations, even serialized histories or — less ambitious in scope and scale — addresses and papers and notes.

The study of local history also became a matter of concern to educators in the decades after the Civil War. Though the number of schools that actually included courses on the subject is unknown, the frequency with which contributors to journals of education wrote about the matter suggests that adding local history to national history as part of a child's civic education was something under serious consideration at various times and places.

Winfield S. Nevins, in a piece entitled "The Study of Local History," which appeared in 1893, asked: " [W]hat is being done to educate people to acknowledge of their own immediate surroundings?." "Every city and town," Nevins argued, "should have its history written with some detail for use in the schools of that town." He insisted that "[t]he child loves to read and talk about places and things with which he is familiar. . . . The local history and geography are the easiest for the child to grasp." Nevins went on to include a suggested list of topics to be covered in "local text books" that looked much like those suggested by officials of state historical societies.(23)

In 1907, Claude S. Larzelerle of Mt. Pleasant, Michigan, wrote a piece he also called "The Study of Local History," which appeared in the *Journal of Education*. Larzelerle was disappointed to find that "in the public schools of Michigan . . . very little has been done so far with local history." Larzelerle argued that pupils get "the notion that events which took place near at hand and in more recent times are not of historical importance." Instead, such pupils "should be brought to see that history is being made all the time, and all about [them]. . . . In no other way can the pupil so well be brought to have the historical sense, to think historically." Larzelerle urged teachers to set "the children to ransacking their homes for old letters, old newspapers, old relics, old costumes, old weapons, etc. Get some of the earliest inhabitants to come to the school and tell the children about the early times. . . . Get up appropriate exercises with costumes and relics of olden times." But Larzelerle warned that "The gathering of material is not enough. . . . The facts gathered from various sources should be criticized, compared, corroborated, or correctly discarded. This gives the pupil a valuable exercise in historical criticism." Finally, Larzelerle advised: "The results of the work may be written up for the local papers, which are always glad to publish such articles if put in suitable form."(24)

In 1910, as part of a "How to Teach" series featured in the journal, *Education*, Charles A. Ellwood, Professor of Sociology at the University of Missouri, submitted an essay entitled "How History Can Be Taught from a Sociological Point of View." Though not concerned with *local* history in particular, what he wrote concerning the proper relationship of sociology and history could only have come from an awareness of the way local, rather than national, history had in fact been written since the early nineteenth century.  Ellwood argued that history as a subject taught in high schools should be taught as "a broad history of all phases of a people's life, not of one phase, such as internal government and international relations . . . [, but giving] due weight to all factors evident in the historical process . . . [thus providing] a sane and balanced view of the social life as the outcome of many forces working together in a complex process of evolution."(25)  Ellwood believed high schools trained students for citizenship.   He urged history teachers to train themselves in such a way that they would be able to apply abstract sociological concepts to history and thus aid students to seek an understanding of the society they were to enter.(26)

The study of local history became, in some instances, a matter of community concern, something involving the adult population in a broadly educational undertaking.  In the largest of the urban centers – New York – a "City History Club" flourished in the early years of the twentieth century with "its constant object the training of good citizens."   The unknown author of "Local History and the Civic Renaissance in New York," which appeared in 1897,(27) indicated that the City History Club believed teaching local history "would most appreciably stimulate local consciousness and neighborhood pride,"(28) and so had devised a two-year course, replete with "pamphlet monographs," and "excursions" around the city.   The Club offered courses in institutions as varied as the Hebrew Institute on the East Side, Columbia College, private schools, and the industrial schools of the Children's Aid Society.   The author of the article thought that most people "would be surprised to know with what great avidity the children of humble immigrants will enter upon local historical study if they are properly guided . . .  [indeed,] with as much thoroughness and with even keener delight than is likely to be shown by the young men of Columbia College or the young ladies of the best private boarding schools." The author believed that "this is a most encouraging discovery,"(29) so encouraging that it "would seem to us that there are many cities and towns in the United States in which there might well be undertaken a like study of local history."(30)

The involvement of a whole community in the commemoration of its past more typically took the form of a pageant, a phenomenon that, by the early years of the twentieth century, was sufficiently common for Herbert T. Wade to write "What the Pageant Does for Local History," in September 1913.(31) Wade opened his piece with the comment that "[were] testimony needed to show that in many cities and towns of the United States people look back upon local history and traditions with quite as much interest and fondness as do the inhabitants of older nations of Europe, it is to be found in the continuous succession of pageants recently held for purpose of local celebration." Referring to a recent revival of interest in locally planned pageants in Britain, Wade thought "it was not strange that the pageant should prove an attractive vehicle of expression" in the United States as well, given the number of local anniversary celebrations and "the aroused interest in local history and increased civic pride."(32)

Wade went on to describe the typical pageant, which "shown forth by appropriately costumed actors stimulates the civic pride of the citizen and arouses in him the desire to make still more illustrious the good name of his town, of which, perhaps, until now he has had little understanding or appreciation."(33) Wade referred specifically to such "illustrated [stories] of development" in New Rochelle, New York; Meriden, New Hampshire; St. Johnsbury, Vermont; Easton, Pennsylvania; Saratoga Springs, New York; adding, "[indeed], one could make an extensive list of the various pageants held within the last decade throughout the United States." Praising the "distinct individuality of treatment" and the "immediate and noteworthy . . . results and lessons," Wade concluded that the underlying cause of "our civic ills is ignorance," which such knowledge of local history can dispel: "[T]hen the citizens of today, proud in their knowledge of what their forerunners have done, will endeavor to prove themselves equally alive to present day problems."(34)

Indeed, pursuing local history became so popular after the Civil War that by the turn of the century it became the subject of editorial comment in national magazines. In the August 1910, issue of *Scribner's Magazine,* "The Point of View" column featured a piece entitled "On Local History" in which the editor advised readers how to give vent to their natural proclivity to recapture the past: "In choosing some nucleus for a study of local history, one cannot do better than begin with one's house or yard. . . . [Y]our facts form layer after layer around your center . . . [and] grow and crystallize into a shapely, lasting concretion of local history."(35)

What began as a small-scale enterprise in the environs of Boston and Philadelphia in the decades after the American Revolution thus became a large-scale undertaking of many dimensions in the decades after the American Civil War. As white settlement spread westward from the Atlantic Coast, beyond the Appalachian Mountains, as the number of local communities grew from hundreds to thousands, the writing of local history burgeoned, and the impulse to preserve and record the past manifested itself in celebrations, newspapers, historical societies, and educational systems, becoming in the process an activity of importance in communities all over a vast continental nation.

Similarly, genealogical investigation became widespread during the decades following the Civil War, to the point that national associations catering to the interests of "old" American families developed around the turn of the century: the Sons of the American Revolution (1889), the Daughters of the American Revolution (1890), the General Society of Mayflower Descendants (1897), the National Genealogical Society (1903). Professional genealogists, like J. R. Trumbull of Northampton, Massachusetts, combined their much-sought-after services with an avocational interest in collecting and preserving historical materials and writing local histories, thus directly linking genealogical and historical inquiry.(36)

But linkage of a broader kind did not develop. In England, local historical research and writing became dominated by the "Victoria History of the Counties of England," privately funded in 1899 (in the words of a later editor) to be "in the realm of local history a standard work of reference comparable in quality and comprehensiveness . . . to the *Dictionary of National Biography* and the *Oxford English Dictionary*. It was to be a cooperative enterprise, in which the leading scholars of the day were to engage, and it was to rest upon original research."(37)

The "chief architect" of the county histories was William Page, who retained the division between "topographical" (physical features) and "general" (human features), subjects that had characterized local and regional studies in Britain from their inception in the late sixteenth century. This equal emphasis upon inquiry into physical and human features of local life did not serve as a guide to antiquarians in America.

Indeed, even though paid and amateur genealogists regularly traced family trees to their British roots, local historians seemed either unaware of or unconcerned with what their counterparts in Britain were doing at the turn of the century. Local historical writing in America thus developed in a self-imposed isolation, a vast enterprise little guided by agreed-upon procedures, the product of individuals concerned about their own family and locality, and not about proper British form.

It was one thing to do research on your own family or local history; it was quite another to write and publish local history. Only in New England was there a sufficient number of individuals with the inclination or the capacity to produce book-length histories of their local communities for the actual writing of local history to become both an individualized effort and a widespread one involving villages, towns, and cities in a virtually unbroken linkage across the landscape. And, not surprisingly, only in New England did the authors of local histories take time on occasion to present accounts of what they thought a serious effort entailed. Local historical writing after the Civil War developed into an identifiable "New England Way," based upon a tradition stretching back to the early nineteenth century, nourished by antiquarians who kept watch over the past of the colonial towns and cities bequeathed to Americans by their forbears, those religious utopians, the Puritans.

This manner of writing local history was well sketched by the Rev. Wilson Waters who presented a paper entitled "The Writing of Local History" on October 12, 1910. In a note appended to the printed version, which appeared some years later,(38) it was indicated that Waters was in the process of writing a history of Chelmsford, Massachusetts, when he delivered the paper. The members of the class of 1911 were invited to attend, having entered a contest sponsored by the area's historical society for the best essay on the history of Chelmsford (the "mother" town of Lowell).(39)

Waters was, like a substantial number of other New England antiquarians in the decades after the Civil War, a Protestant minister. What made him distinctive was his reflective cast of mind. Many clergymen wrote local history; very few had an inclination to philosophize about its nature. An active writer of local history, Waters was also aware of the overall character of historical inquiry of all kinds. In all the years between the Civil War and the Great Depression, his "talk" was the most skilled and best-crafted statement on what local historical writing should be. From it, we learn that the amateur should attempt to present a descriptive narrative based upon all remaining evidence, both documentary and artifactual, rigorously tested for its accuracy. The narrative should deal with all aspects of a community's life, without bias, or prejudice, or partisanship.

Waters' comments are not different in kind from those made earlier by such similarly reflective pioneering antiquarians as Alonzo Lewis, Joseph Felt, or John F. Watson. The difference is in tone: Waters' conception of local historical writing was fuller, more comprehensive than that of his predecessors. Local history, in Waters' view, should not be simply an annals, based upon public or church records, or simply a compendium of snippets of life from bygone days. The local history Waters called for was, in fact, being written with varying degrees of success all over the United States at the turn of the century.

In the same year Waters spoke, another reflective New England antiquarian, James O. Lyford, addressed the New Hampshire Historical Society on the practical difficulties and problems in writing town histories.(40) "In what I shall present to you today," Lyford began, "I have drawn from my observations and experience in the preparation of two town histories, those of Concord and Canterbury." What prompted him to write? "My work on them has been my gift to the communities, prompted by my sense of public duty. . . . The writing of town histories is a labor of love, for there is no compensation to be offered commensurate to the work involved. Obligation to the public, calling for personal sacrifice, must be the moving incentive to the writer."(41)

This financially precarious situation created dangers, which if unattended, could undermine the integrity of the writer's account. Lyford was concerned that the local historian was forced to focus on "certain families to the detriment of his narrative, because they have contributed directly or indirectly to the financial side of the history." Lyford believed that for "a town history to be of real value, [it] should portray the life of the average citizen." For him, there was a danger "[w]here the cost of a history is met in part by families able to pay for the pictures of ancestors or of living representatives, [in that] there is often a discrimination against those more worthy of consideration but less able to meet the requirements."(42)

What could be done to avoid the dangers posed by a reliance on the financial assistance of prominent people, either through advanced subscription or prearranged biographies and portraits?: "If the genealogy is looked after by a committee," Lyford suggested, "the writer of town history will be relieved of a most wearisome task, thus enabling him to give his whole thought and time to his narrative."(43)

More importantly, Lyford suggested that "future efforts . . . should be the business of the community."(44) He urged that all town libraries in the state automatically purchase a copy of each new town history: "Two hundred subscriptions from the town libraries of New Hampshire would almost guarantee the cost of publication of a town history, leaving the other sales to care for the expense of preparing the manuscript. Upon such terms any town could afford to have its history prepared, for the work would entail little or no ultimate expense to the taxpayers."(45)

This scheme would eliminate the need to rely on individual subscribers and would make the community bear the major responsibility for the expense of such projects, especially since Lyford had found "only a limited demand for these local histories at the present time. To the people at large they are merely reference books to be sought in libraries." Why was this so? — because, Lyford argued, the geographic mobility of much of the population, "in our rural towns especially," meant that "only part of the inhabitants . . . by family connections are interested in the story of their past," though he admitted that "[s]ome of the scattered descendants of former residences, if found, may be induced to purchase copies." But, "[i]n the main," he believed, "the outside subscribers must be the library, whose trustees are seeking to supply their patrons instructive as well as entertaining reading."(46)

What concerned Lyford above all was that the subscription system, upon which the pioneer antiquarians before the Civil War had typically relied, could generate pressure upon the local historian to give unfair prominence and uncritical or partisan reference to those who provided financial support for the enterprise. In Lyford's view, a community's history should be supported by the community-at-large: in a sense, family and community should not be allowed to blur together, with one a mere extension of the other.

Lyford's plea that local history be a community-wide project mirrored perfectly the kind of range and fairness that Waters called for in his reflections on the proper nature of historical writing. What Waters and Lyford presented as models for antiquarian endeavor were sometimes approximated in the town histories that appeared in great profusion during the decades surrounding the turn of the century, even though such publishing adventures were, as Lyford said, always financially precarious.

Some of the histories — especially in New England, but scattered elsewhere as well — were as thorough and comprehensive as Lyford and Waters would have wanted or were community-sponsored projects of the kind these two theorists envisioned. But, more typically, antiquarians found only scattered records to base what turned out to be their fragmentary accounts upon, or they felt compelled to rely upon the subscription payments and research contributions offered by the prominent, successful, and durable element of their community's population — the very people Lyford believed would compromise the integrity and fairness of the serious amateur. But, other antiquarians did not live in Lyford's ideal setting: they needed the kinds of support local elites provided, and, even when community sponsorship obviated such a need, the antiquarians perceived the past the way their usual supporters did. For, what they wrote invariably represented an elitist view of local history.

# CHAPTER 6
# Town Historians

As before the Civil War, only in Massachusetts was the production of local histories so pervasive and uniform that by the 1930s such publications had appeared town-by-town, approaching a contiguous basis across the state, with some communities the subject of a second or even a third book-length history during the century from the 1820s to the 1920s.

But, even in Massachusetts, the impact of the national centennial on local historical writing was very evident. Except for a two-year period right after the Civil War (as if certain antiquarians took time to finish tasks interrupted by the war), the publication of such histories was virtually nonexistent until 1877, directly after the national centennial, with three in 1877, six in 1878, four in 1879, seven in 1880, and so on, never thereafter losing momentum until the late 1920s.

Those who wrote local history in Massachusetts during these decades were a varied group, not reducible to a sharply defined social profile and were without much awareness of each other, conscious only that they, as antiquarians, attempted to do for their community what other like-minded individuals were doing for theirs. Variation came in many forms: they were by principle occupation ministers, doctors, lawyers, businessmen, politicians, journalists, professors, and teachers; they presented themselves as individuals so unused to writing for publication that they occasionally apologized in prefatory remarks for their verbal inaccuracies and inelegances, but also sometimes introduced themselves as individuals whose income actually derived from their writing. Some graduated from Harvard or another college, whereas others were apprentices to printers, lawyers, doctors, scientists, merchants or bankers. Some meekly claimed the title of compiler, but others proclaimed the importance of local historical writing and perceived themselves as historians like Hubert H. Bancroft and James Schouler, only with a smaller purview.

Rarely did those of genuine prominence, that is, those whose fame stretched beyond their own community, owe that fame to antiquarian activity. Samuel Francis Smith (1808-1895) was a Baptist clergyman whose translations, poems, and hymns (the most famous of which was "My Country Tis of Thee"), professorship of modern languages at what became Colby College, editorship of the *Christian Review*, and long-time presidency of a Baptist theological seminary made him famous.   His history of Newton, Massachusetts produced in 1880 during his pastorate there, was only one of a number of varied writings.(1) Adin Ballou (1803-1890) was a Universalist clergyman who founded the Hopedale Community in Milford, Massachusetts, in 1841 as a utopian, communal experiment.  His history of Milford, in 1882, was one of a number of prose works that included an autobiography, a family genealogy, and several studies of Christian socialism.(2) Elias Nason (1811-1887) was a peripatetic school principal and Congregational clergyman among whose thirty-nine books and pamphlets was a history of Dunstable, in 1877.(3)

Prominent or not, all the local historians of these years stressed the importance in historical writing of fact over myth, distortion, or outright fiction, as had the earlier, ante-bellum antiquarians.  What distinguished the post-Civil War local historians from their predecessors was a tendency to broaden the subjects dealt with and the sources used: nothing seemed too unimportant or inappropriate for inclusion in a community's history, as long as accurate information existed.

This broadening of the scope of local historical writing was not the result of a conscious design for what history ought to be, but a consequence of increasingly intense efforts to find and preserve sources — both documentary and artifactual — by local and state historical societies. History that was born of curiosity and nourished by familiarity did not assume a form determined by some philosophical view of the past. Amateur local history was an accumulation of facts about the place and people the author knew best.   What those facts showed was that the communities the Puritans founded had survived and flourished.   They were successful, progressive, and something to be proud of, to commemorate. Local history was of the successful, by the successful, and for the successful. That is all the antiquarians needed to know, cared to know.

The preface remained the favored form for whatever reflections the writers chose to make on their time-consuming labors of love.   In 1883, Lucius Paige indicated at the outset of his history of Hardwick, Massachusetts,(4) that he had long been "deeply interested" in the history of the town as well as in the genealogy of its inhabitants, especially since "my own ancestors were among the early pioneers, were actively engaged in the management of public affairs and by numerous intermarriages wee connected with so many of its families." Paige admitted that he had "been a non-resident and comparative stranger for more than fifty-six years," but he also insisted that "my attachment to my native town has never grown cold." During all those years, "[a]s I had opportunity, from time to time, I have gathered and preserved historical materials, intending to embody them in a permanent form."(5) The associations, the delays, the persistence: all are typical, as are Paige's comments on the skewing of both his genealogical and historical material toward the early years of the town's past: "   I desired to revive and perpetuate the memory of what might otherwise fade entirely from remembrance and pass into oblivion.   The current events of the day are fresh in the minds of the living, and not liable to be soon forgotten."(6)

Even the manner of publication contained elements of the usual arrangements, though Paige and the town were unusually well balanced in what each was prepared to do. Paige referred to his "willingness to furnish the manuscript without any compensation whatever." Nevertheless the town voted to publish four hundred copies of Paige's history "at an expense not exceeding sixteen hundred dollars, and that Mr. Paige retain fifty copies for his own use, for his labor of love in writing the History of his native town, and that the expense of publishing the above History be paid out of any money belonging to the Town . . . [and] that the Selectmen be instructed to sell copies of this History, when published, to any who desire them, at four dollars per copy."(7)

When James F. Hunnewell wrote a history of Charlestown (annexed to Boston) from 1775 to 1887,(8) he began his text with a notably personal account of how he became aware of the local past. Hunnewell's "first lessons in local history" were at what were called "old ladies' parties" at his father's house. He remembered these old relatives "in their black dresses and quaint white caps, chatting." He insisted that "[w]hat the old ladies said was undoubtedly quite as true as a good deal that we call history, and it was certainly much more interesting, — especially than some of the matter we compose from dry bits of record." These old women "knew all the people, too, and could make them seem living if they were not." Hunnewell believed "[t]heir talk of them was far different from the poor little strings of items and dates, some dubious, that forms what is called genealogy." But he also cautioned: "[t]here is a good deal to be gleaned from written or printed statements or records, that, when sifted, and facts are used, and safe deductions made, will help to [create] a pretty full and true story."(9) Hunnewell here displays his sensitivity to the varied sources the antiquarians of his time drew on. He clearly prefers the reminiscences of old people for their story value to the impersonal information to be garnered from records of various kinds, but like his contemporaries in general, he was unable to equate true history with reminiscence.

Alfred S. Hudson's history of Sudbury, Massachusetts, published by the town in 1889, was notable for the planning that went into its organization. Facing directly the question of whether local history was to be a chronology or a topical survey, Hudson informed his readers that his arrangement had been to combine the chronological with the topical, to consider the town's history "in successive periods of a quarter century each, taking topically, in the main, the events which each contained." Hudson believed that the "advantage" of such a system was that "the reader will be able to take a general view of the town in all its relations — civil, social, religious — *at any period of its history*."(10) Most of the local historians from Massachusetts during these years were content to present a loose mixture of incident, information, and particular subjects determined by available sources or personal interest, rather than to express any concern for a systematic coverage of the various dimensions of their community's history presented in a full, chronological sequence.

Rare too was Hudson's "Conclusion," his conscious effort to sum up what the history of Sudbury had meant overall. He was led inexorably to the view that God had blessed him and his fellow townsmen "by bringing us safely forth from the vicissitudes and exposures and peril of two hundred and fifty years, and by the benign influences of the institutions that our ancestors established and maintained." Next to God, "we should bear in grateful remembrance the privations and hardships endured by our ancestors," from whose faith "has come the prosperity, the integrity, the worth of our town."(11) Hudson's rare summing up articulated what his contemporaries probably felt, but usually left unsaid. Though each community varied in the particularities of its past, all the early Puritan towns shared the larger historical pattern that Hudson had the peculiar disposition to try to depict in his concluding section.

That local historical writing in Massachusetts was a cooperative enterprise is abundantly clear. On occasion, what was started by one antiquarian was finished by another, a fact vividly revealed in the introduction to Henry S. Nourse's history of Harvard University, published by the initiator, Warren Hapgood, in 1894.(12) The partnership of Hapgood and Nourse was an unusual, exaggerated instance of age giving way to youth, of the uncertain amateur deferring to and financially supporting the authorship of one more confident and educated.

Most of the local histories written in Massachusetts between the Civil War and the Great Depression were on the towns of the state, on small communities of, at most, several thousand inhabitants at the time of writing. The antiquarians who wrote these histories dealt with a vast array of subjects, with many dimensions of town life, through description, dramatic narrative, or the mere listing of information. There was rarely any effort to explain, interpret, analyze, or sum up. The sources available and the particular interests of the author determined what appeared in print; there is little evidence these writers tried to shape or mold the documents they relied on.

Nevertheless, "ordinary" antiquarians – those notable for their lack of extended education, prominent occupation, obvious wealth, or for anything, indeed, except their family's long-term association with the community whose past was, therefore, an extension of their own – sometimes produced huge tomes, large compendia of information on such topics as: (1) the town's origins (land grants, proprietors); (2) its physical aspects (topography, street and road layout, bridges, meeting houses, town clock and bell, family houses, graveyards, common fields and fences, farmlands, mills and general topography); (3) its relations with the Indians (wars, treaties, and artifactual remains of the native popultion); (4) its economic life (agriculture, crafts, and milling activities); (5) its religious life (various ministries, churches, and controversies); (6) its political life (town officials, town meetings, local controversies, the military, the Revolution, the Civil War); (7) its social-cultural-intellectual life (sermons, lectures, newspapers, cultural events, various associations and institutions, schools, libraries, holidays, reform movements); and (8) the establishment of new towns out of the original township. Biographical and genealogical sketches on particular individuals and families indicated the interdependent character between individual, family, and community that these writers perceived.

Such antiquarians tried to be more systematic in their examination of sources than the ante-bellum pioneers had usually been. Town and church records and the reminiscences of the oldest inhabitants were no longer sufficient. The ideal came to be a comprehensive and systematic examination of all pertinent evidence. For example, George Sheldon and his mentor, the peripatetic Rev. J. H. Temple, explained in their preface to their history of Northfield, Massachusetts, (1875): "The field of these researches is to a great extent new ground." Theirs was a work based consistently on manuscript documents. In addition to town and church records and the memories of aged persons, the two authors had utilized family papers, county records, and the state archives.(13)

For his own history of Deerfield, Massachusetts, (1895 and 1896), Sheldon read family papers, thanking "the owners of the hundreds of garrets, closets, and trunks which I have ransacked at will ";(14) traveled to and did research at the Massachusetts State House as well as at historical societies and various libraries in Boston, Cambridge, and Springfield; looked at registries of deeds and of probate in the Connecticut River Valley counties; and examined town records at the town clerk's office in Deerfield and surrounding towns. His aim was "to write as far as may be from original sources of information; where this was possible I have taken nobody's say for it." He concluded that "[the] amount of manuscript matter available have been found to be surprisingly large. Old letters, diaries, records, are coming to light every year, giving the later student that advantage over all others."(15) Unusually assiduous, Sheldon tried to accomplish what his contemporaries valued highly: a local history based upon comprehensive sources, accurately used.

George Sheldon was in some respects a typical antiquarian town historian of the late nineteenth century. He certainly looked the part of a patriarch of antiquarian endeavors. He was a "handsome, tall, and large man, with brilliant eyes deep set under bushy brows, a hawk nose," and a long, pointed white beard. His head was bald and he often wore either a skull cap or a round wire screen bound with metal, the latter for protecting his head from flies or for ventilation.(16) Long-time president of the local historical society, curator of its museum, and author of a two-volume history of Deerfield, he dominated the historical activities of his fellow townsmen to an unusual extent. These were impressive achievements for a man who had no education beyond that of the local academy, who had no long-term occupation other than that of a farmer, and whose only public office beyond one term was that of justice of the peace.

Though largely self educated, and initially without economic or social prominence, Sheldon recognized his own family as every bit as prominent as any other, if viewed historically. It may have been the Rev. John Williams who was the most prominent survivor and captive at the time of Deerfield's early massacre, but it was a Sheldon who led the hostages out of captivity. The story was incomplete without either; Sheldon made sure it was complete. In his *History*, he wrote of his ancestor: "In the efforts for the recovery and redemption of the captives from Canada, Ensign John Sheldon was a central figure. To his tenderness of heart, to his unflagging faith, is due in large measure, the success which followed."(17) It was Ensign Sheldon who built the "Old Indian House," where the stiffest defense against the attackers during the massacre had been made.

Sheldon's dedication through half of his ninety-eight year life to the task of preserving the past of family and town was what one associate called simply, "a labor of love."(18) His second wife, Jennie Arms, had a more elaborate explanation. Sheldon, she thought, had been driven on by a vision. In one word, it was a "Memorial": "A memorial of the men, women, and children of early New England, especially of the valley of the Pocumtuck." Sheldon believed that "lives and deeds of these people should not perish from the earth, but should live on in their records of stone and iron, of wood and manuscript page." To him it was important that "[t]hese records should be snatched from destruction, gathered together and reverently preserved." How had Sheldon come to his vision: Raised on stories of Deerfield's early times, as a man "he had lived, in thought, with the white pioneers until . . . he had become one of them, not only in blood but in spirit. Loyalty had changed to love—then the vision was born."(19)

Sheldon's account of Deerfield's version of the birth trauma of colonial frontier villages—an Indian massacre and ensuing captivity—shows him off at his best. Still the most important event in the history of the town, in his judgment, the incident receives one hundred pages of detailed investigation. All the relevant sources—town records, correspondence of commanders and ministers and government officials, the legislature, and the Rev. John Williams' contemporary account—are examined separately for their authenticity and accuracy and the information they reveal. Only then is the reader given an account of the incident as understood by Sheldon himself. It is a thorough treatment presented in Sheldon's typically amateur, rather fact-laden prose, which he vitalized, nevertheless, to sketch word pictures and create vivid, dramatic situations when he forced it to. To Sheldon, the story had little religious significance. To him, it was the supreme example of the essential heroism of the original settlers of the town.(20)

The past as reverence toward one's heroic ancestors and local history as the extension of the lives of old, prominent families never found precise definition in Sheldon's writings. This is not surprising, for that definition of the past was an assumption, something almost beyond articulation. Still, he comes close to giving it all away when he allows himself the freedom to reflect on an event, as he did at the end of his description of an even earlier massacre in Deerfield, that at Bloody Brook, in the outskirts of the town, when sixty-four soldiers were ambushed and killed by Indians in 1675 on "a day memorable in [our] annals." The scene was too much for Sheldon to handle in his usually prosaic way. Steeped as he was in the lore of his town's past, he could not confront the incident as a writer without letting his imagination run wild and his prose to inflate to the point that he almost lost control: "[We] may be sure all nature was in sympathy [with the slain]; that pitying pines sighed and moaned, as they stretched out their protecting arms above the spot that the conscious brook crept softly over its broken banks to lap the sanguine stain; that the birds sang sweetly on the swaying vine; that the crimson leaves fell lightly on the bare, brown earth, and the soft September sun struggled to send bright beams to fleck the swelling mound." Then came the real point of it all: "So we leave its tenants behind the dim mists of two centuries, to the resurrection at the last day, to receive their crowns among the rest of the martyrs, that have laid down and ventured their lives, as a testimony to the truth of their religion as well as love to their own country."(21)

What Sheldon did not like about his ancestors came out in an introduction he wrote to a 1908 reprint of the Rev. John Williams' account of the massacre. What alienated Sheldon from Williams, who was "a striking example of the Puritan life in thought and action," was his infernal Puritan theology: "hard and narrow enough in our eyes, and utterly lacking in charity. . . . To modern minds the deity worshipped under this theology seems a tangled mass of contradictions. . . . [Rev. Williams] believed that the scripture with all its contradictions and crudities was the language of God, from the first word to the last." Then there was Williams' profoundly debilitating Calvinist theology: "He might have known . . . that the 'revelation' has been read a thousand ways, and that the disagreements have filled the Christian world with misery and woe; that millions of men, women, and children have been butchered, and their homes turned to ashes in consequence of this disagreement."(22) In short, Sheldon was thankful he lived in the nineteenth and not the eighteenth century, but he was also grateful to his ancestors for creating and nourishing a town like Deerfield, even though they had acted to further their abominable brand of Protestantism, which, happily had been stripped of its Calvinist sheathing by the penetrating power of scientific inquiry.

Appropriately enough, Sheldon's own, most balanced statement on the meaning of Deerfield's past came in an address on the bicentennial of the massacre: "We honor our ancestors for their bravery and their steadfastness; we sympathize with them in their sufferings, and are grateful to them for the results—which are ours. They filled that measure which the world of today demands as the pride of its homage—they were successful. . . . We meet today in vain if we are not stronger for their strength, and more faithful, persevering, industrious and economical for their example." Sheldon readily admitted the Puritans were bigoted, self-centered, superstitious, and intolerant, "but speaking broadly in the perspective of the centuries, this other fact remains: we see in them a people sifted out from the deeper darkness and despotism which they left behind them in Old England: we see them as the pioneers and the vanguard of civil and religious freedom for the nations."(23)

Sheldon's *History* was often praised by those who shared his view of the past with such words as, a "triumphant model of local historical writing."(24) Even Professor Grosvernor of nearby Amherst College, who had studied "many histories of New England towns . . . did not know one that showed the broad, comprehensive research that characterized the work of Mr. Sheldon."(25) Some simply threw up their hands with comments like: "No more complete, well-balanced and trustworthy record can be conceived."(26)

Sheldon's *History* was, in fact, a good example of late nineteenth century town history, and, as such, represented a great expansion of the earlier efforts. The result was not the comprehensive history we expect to find, given the means adopted. Sheldon did add considerably to the scope of what had been included in earlier town histories. A great array of subjects receive at least brief attention. But there is no attempt at analysis and interpretation. Great chunks of information are lifted, in undigested from, from the mass of material he examined so closely. The result is a catalogue or chronicle. Thus, Sheldon failed to develop historical writing beyond the mere listing of information. Mesmerized by the sources he labored over for so long, he did not have the capacity to analyze them. Local historical writing, in his hands, thus expanded in length and scope, but did not significantly alter in character.

Sheldon's interest in Deerfield's past all but ends with the Revolution. The short portion of his *History* dealing with the nineteenth century is highly fragmentary. At times, in the last section, he almost seems bored with it all, as if fulfilling some obligation to bring the story into his own time. The account does not end; it just stops; the reader does not know where he has been left. For Sheldon, the drama and adventure of his heroic ancestors ended with the great triumph of liberty over tyranny, the Revolution. Thereafter, his view of historical time became vague and misty. The New England town had been established through strenuous effort during the colonial period and had placed itself under a national government dedicated to human freedom as a result of a successful revolution. That was all one really needed to know; that is all George Sheldon cared to know. Real "history" was something that happened long ago, before the revolution. Everything else was a description of contemporary life and its setting. There was nothing in between. The nineteenth century, even when it was eighty or ninety years old, did not have a past. Its pattern of life was listed, put in to descriptive categories, but not made the subject of sweeping human drama. For, that was the stuff colonial history was made of, when Sheldon's ancestors stalked the earth, when life was more dangerous and, above all, more heroic.

Though broad in scope both as to its coverage of town life and the sources on which the account relied, local history as written by Sheldon and others in Massachusetts during these years was narrow in its definition of who was in or of the town whose past the author so lovingly uncovered. The "people" of the town were those who descended from the settlers, that is, those who persisted through the generations. These antiquarians thus gave to their town a sociological-psychological definition, even though it ostensibly had a political-territorial one. Recent immigrants from Ireland or Southern or Eastern Europe, living in "Tough End" or whatever their part of town was called, were not full members of the community, even though they clearly lived within its political-territorial boundaries. The consequence of the antiquarians' identifying a particular kind of individual and family with the community was that those who were transient, different, or recent were more easily perceived by those who were prominent, who persisted, or who were already successful, as "outsiders," as "them," and not "us." This sociological-psychological definition of community was a narrower construct than the town as a political-territorial entity.

The antiquarians do not appear to have been aware of the inconsistency of writing about the history of a township as community, when the political town did not equate with the social community. Theirs was a success story: the toil of their Puritan ancestors yielded the presumably flourishing towns of late nineteenth and early twentieth century Massachusetts. This perception of the past could not accommodate the contemporary stresses and strains created by the influx of alien immigrants or the change from an agricultural, craft-oriented village society to an increasingly industrialized, urbanized one. The antiquarians and their subscribers and readers took refuge in a past that was important to their identity and were thus able to partially deflect their attention from the problems of their own time.

Local historical writing of the kinds produced in New England from the 1820s to the 1930s was also written in other regions of the United States, but much more sporadically. The New England towns, with their utopian religious origins, were unlike those formed in other parts of the nation. The utopian impulse lived on, resulting in a sprinkling of special communities whose founders, like the Puritans, dedicated themselves to the furtherance of some special purpose.(27) Most communities grew in response to mundane economic or political circumstances — at fall-lines, rivers, cross-roads, harbors, mountain passes, accessible central locations in counties and states — and thus lacked the sense of purpose that animated those who participated in the varied utopian ventures.

The township system of New England, whereby all territory in a state was divided into townships, was copied in the Midatlantic area and through much of the Midwest; but only in New England was the local level of government clearly primary. In the Midatlantic and Midwest, county goverment predominated or shared power with town and city governments, and in other parts of the United States — in the South, the Plains, the Rocky Mountains, the Pacific coast — the township system was not established at all, meaning that rural areas outside incorporated towns and cities were directly under county governments. In all parts of the nation, especially in the huge central plains and mountains, there were vast areas with no established communities at all, with rural populations living largely outside the boundaries of locally organized communal life. So, "community" in its political and territorial definition, varied in importance, from area to area, across the vast landscape of America.

In this setting, what was "local" also varied. One's "community" might be a town or a village, more rarely a city, but just as likely a whole county, or even, in its early phases of settlement, an entire territory or state. In fact, the earliest "local" historical writing to the west and south of the Northeastern coastal region was state history. Extending a tradition that began in the colonial period in the form of provincial histories, and continued after the Revolution in the new states along the eastern seaboard, the pioneering "local" antiquarians in states to the west typically chose the entire territory (recently admitted into the Union) as their subject.(28)

There were many specific reasons why a local antiquarian decided it was time to present a history of his town, city, or county in the areas west and south of the northeastern seaboard.   What was shared with their earlier counterparts to the east or north was a sense that their community was in jeopardy of losing an accurate record of its early life, as the first settlers died, as records were lost and destroyed.   But, why one community contained someone who cared enough to act and another of comparable age and size did not is a question with many, largely unrecoverable answers.

There were, here and there, local histories with the fullness and coverage of those regularly written in New England during the decades between the Civil War and the Great Depression.   Andrew Young's history of Warsaw, New York (1869),(29) is clearly divided into civil history, ecclesiastical history, war history, and family sketches, with the civil history section subdivided into settlement, village layout, post office, agriculture, trade, manufacture, roads, railroads, cemeteries, libraries, schools, physicians, lawyers, banks, newspapers, societies, festivals, meetings, and reform. Across the continent, George H. Tinkham's history of Stockton, California (1880),(30) was also especially well organized by topic. "The history," Tinkham indicated in his preface, "is taken up by topics, and each subject is complete in itself. . . . In each division there are single examples of many which have taken place."

By the 1920s, such examples were more numerous.  J. Marmus Jensen's history of Provo, Utah (1924),(31) is neatly organized into a series of chapters in chronological sequence, dealing with different periods, followed by another series arranged topically.    Frederick Davis' history of Jacksonville, Florida (1925),(32) deals neatly with topics of a wide range. Isabella Brayton (her town's historian) mixed, in consistent fashion, chronological and topical treatments with her history of Hartford, New York (1929).(33) The incidence and geographic location of these unusually well organized town histories defies rational explanation.

Even the less notable, more typical histories, those with a fullness of sources and content that makes them considerably more than sketches or "bits and pieces" of scattered information and incidents, are sporadic in time and place.(34) Indeed, so individualized were local histories outside of the Northeastern seaboard that it is impossible to generalize about them beyond making the statement that all were accounts of a given community's past, as factually accurate as the author could make them and based on as many sources as the author had access to.   The sources used, the way in which they were utilized, the organization of the writing, and the range of subjects covered all differed widely from one local history to another.

Some town histories were little more than a series of short essays appearing originally in serialized form in a local newspaper, a practice most in evidence in the South.(35) Others were brief sketches accompanying what were mainly biographical and genealogical compilations.(36) Other histories were confined to special subjects that happened to interest the authors or were organized on the basis of the older chronicles, annals, or gazetteer forms, or even on a new form invented for the purpose. Rev. Philias Garand's *Historical Sketch of the Village of Clayton* (New York)(37) was based on the records of the village's Catholic Church and consisted of chronologically arranged narratives on the pastorates of the various priests of the church. Rev. Uzal W. Condit's *The History of Easton* (Pennsylvania)(38) featured an interweaving of biographical sketches and topical units on various institutions of the town. James Hadden's *A History of Uniontown* (Pennsylvania)(39) featured a descriptive tour of the town's streets. John J. McLaurin's *The Story of Johnstown* (Pennsylvania)(40) is mainly about the most famous incident in the town's history: a flood. James Helman's *History of Emmitsburg* (Maryland)(41) is organized in the appearance of a newspaper, with headings on various subjects, followed by a bit of information on each. Natalie Cooper's *History of Prospect Valley* (West Virginia)(42) is mainly a printed scrapbook of random items based on various documents. Maude Hearn-O'Pry's *Chronicles of Shreveport* (Louisiana)(43) is in the form of an old gazetteer, with listings of information. Wallace A. Bruce's *History of Fort Wayne* (Indiana)(44) is in reality a chronological narrative consisting largely of military incidents. Richard Cordley's *A History of Lawrence, Kansas*(45) is an account focused entirely on the turmoil of the town's early years, during the Kansas "Civil War" of the 1850s and 1860s, and presents nothing on the normal life of Lawrence.

The looseness and variety of form, content, and sources exhibited in such local histories indicate that these writers were unaware of what the more organized antiquarians in New England and those in larger cities all over the United States were doing during these years, or lacked the concern or capacity to emulate these contemporaries, or were frustrated over a dearth of sources that would have made it possible for them to try. What is clear is that the number of towns outside of New England with an inhabitant sharing a New England antiquarian's thoroughness, dedication, interest, and ability was relatively small and scattered. The inhabitants of towns beyond the Hudson River (with the exception of those of a utopian or communal character) did not have, like the descendants of the Puritans, a long tradition of preserving their records and recovering the past of a special community.

John Hill Martin was one of the post-Civil War, beyond-New England town historians. He was neither exceptional nor remarkable. Indeed, his histories of Bethlehem (1872) and Chester (1877) Pennsylvania are sketches, bits and pieces of information first appearing in print in serialized form in newspapers of the area.(46) In the late 1860s, Martin contributed a series of "Sketches of Bethlehem" to the *Philadelphia Intelligencer*. Urged on by acquaintances,(47) Martin signed a contract with B. Lippincott on March 30, 1872, in which the Philadelphia publishing firm agreed to print 350 copies for a sum not to exceed $225.(48)

As the book was being prepared for publication, H. J. Milchsack came forth to serve as Martin's agent. On January 14, 1872, he wrote to Martin that "I will most cheerfully take hold of your book and think I can get about as many subscribers as any one can to it." On January 24: "How I would like to be a canvasser for the city of Philadelphia. I am acquainted with a good many Moravians [the dominant religious group in Bethlehem] in P. and know some of the prominent business men who would undoubtedly subscribe for it and from our party could get good many names of others and so on, that I think a great many subscribers might be obtained."(49)

Once the book was published, Martin in fact sent out the usual complimentary copies. Reactions varied. One wrote with candor: "I do not promise to read all of it with great pleasure. As a book of reference it must be very valuable."(50) But another indicated: "I will read it with much pleasure and always think kindly of the author to whom I hope may come much profit and great fame."(51) Martin knew other antiquarians, such as Thompson Westcott, a journalist with the *Philadelphia Dispatch* who was working on a history of Philadelphia during this time, and Samuel Pennypacker, a Senator from Pennsylvania who wrote several local histories. Westcott also wrote with candor: "Please send me the *title* and *publisher* or your book. I have laid it away so carefully in my library that I can't find it — this has delayed a notice which it should have had weeks ago."(52) Pennypacker's response, by contrast, showed gratitude and involvement: he esteemed the book "very highly not only for its own inherent value but as an evidence of your high regard — I send you herewith a copy of "Phoenixville" which I hope may prove worthy of your acceptance."(53)

*Historical Sketch of Bethlehem* (1872)(54) was focused on the Moravians and their town's institutions and contains long passages directly quoted from journals and other descriptive accounts. Martin introduced his *Sketch* with a brief overview.(55) The *Sketch* was as much a guide for visitors as it was an attempt at historical writing.

He was encouraged to go right on and provide an account of Chester's past as well and chose the same format, serialization in a local newspaper. In a spirit of encouragement, J. Smith Futhley wrote: "I have been very much interested in the history, as it has progressed — the materials when thrown into a volume will be very valuable."(56) Futhley must have thought he himself lacked the capacity to prepare a full historical account, and perhaps that Martin, by contrast, would be able to, for Futhley revealed that he had contributed about one-third of the sketches in the earlier "Notices of Chester County Men and Events."(57) Futhley then aided Martin to take account of even earlier efforts at uncovering Chester's past.(58)

When Martin prepared his own sketches for the *Delaware County Republican*, his correspondence clearly reveals the extent to which even antiquarians who were concerned with bits and pieces, or with particular subjects, and not with breadth and thoroughness of coverage, relied on others for information. Certainly this was true of genealogical information. When Charles J. Davis sent Martin a simple list of his children's names, Martin was not satisfied. He wanted to know: "Are any of your children married? To whom? Names of the parents of the children they married? And where did such persons live before marriage?" And then came the enticement: "As soon as you give me this information I will send the *Republican* sketch of the Davis branch of the Morton family, with an account of ancient Morton tract in Amesland."(59) Martin encountered many problems as he sought genealogical information, as contributors referred to tragedy,(60) business,(61) or less specific excuses(62) in order to explain delays or failures. Others demanded anonymity(63) or displayed their concern about the proper length for a submission,(64) deletions,(65) digressions,(66) referrals to others,(67) and mistakes.(68) Martin also had difficulty in attempting to gather information for other aspects of Chester's past. Some correspondents tried to explain or justify their delay in responding.(69) Others acted quickly, though briefly. Ellwood Harvey admitted: "This is a very slim sketch, but is as full as anybody wants to read. Even the members of the profession do not care much about the past history of the society I think."(70)

Martin was not always successful in obtaining the information he sought. J. Smith Futhley reported that: "I have received yours of the 16th instant and have made search in the clerk's office for the documents referred to, but without success." Futhley told Martin the court's early records "have not been properly cared for or arranged. On one occasion, I called the attention of the court to the matter, but nothing was done."(71) On another occasion, Martin requested information from the Recorder of Deeds, adding: "[Let] me know what an uncertified copy thereof will cost — I enclose 50 cents to pay for the search and 3 postage for reply. . . . I am writing a History of Chester. The information is therefore important."(72) The Recorder responded that: "I am unable from the data you gave me to furnish you with any information of any value [. If] you could ascertain by inquiries made among the old inhabitants of Chester the names of any parties to the conveyence either — grantor or grantee — we might be able to hunt the matter up."(73) A correspondent's outright refusal to contribute was sometimes accompanied by the suggestion that Martin ask another proposed individual.(74)

But several contributors were eager to assist, to the point of welcoming Martin into their homes. F. A. Dick said: "Do come by and take dinner with us today 4 o'clock. Only my wife and children make our party so you need make no preparations whatever and we will all give you a welcome."(75) James Miller indicated: "I am generally at home to meet you."(76) Thompson Westcott, the historian of Philadelphia, said that "[it] is much easier to talk to you than to write you a letter when you consider that my eyes are very poor. If you will come and see me, I think many of your troubles will be dispelled. I will be at home on Friday night."(77) C. Justis was anxious to provide Martin with his reminiscences, saying: "I remember many circumstances connected with the town that took place in my boyish days 50 to 55 years ago. They seem as fresh as though it were only yesterday that they happened."(78)

Others tried to encourage Martin in his endeavor at the same time as they assisted him. H. G. Ashmead wrote: "I desire to see your history — one worthy of the subject — correct, chatty, and interesting. Such I am sure you will make it. Publish it by subscription and it will sell, and *pay too*."(79) Even voluntary, unsolicited contributions came in at a steady pace.(80) Martin relied on others for information for every subject he dealt with in his serialized sketches: politics,(81) judges,(82) the military,(83) lawyers,(84) bankers,(85) railroads,(86) library,(87) churches,(88) schools,(89) and lodges.(90) What Martin's correspondence reveals is the great extent to which the antiquarian of even a small community could rely on others for research and information. Martin's collaborators were usually extremely cooperative and even those, like Futhley, who had previously assembled material or even published sketches of their own were eager to have Martin utilize their earlier efforts and hoped he could build upon them. Though many who assisted desired anonymity, all seemed anxious that an enterprise of the sort Martin embarked upon be a successful one.

Martin's editor at the *Republican* was also supportive, but candid about the difficulty in achieving total accuracy in such an undertaking. He wrote that he had been making "slight alterations" in Martin's sketches, and indeed that "[s]ometimes I am called to look upon your errors. I merely say: 'Could you do it better?' and if yes, why didn't you do it." In an effort to reassure Martin, he added: "You have things singularly correct, and the sketches show the immense amount of labor required to collect them. There is scarce a day that we have not applications for back numbers."(91) And, indeed, readers did on occasion write to Martin, pointing out errors of fact in his submissions.(92) Someone corrected a small error, adding: "If history is worth anything, it is prized for its accuracy."(93)

Another antiquarian, Gilbert Cope, advised Martin on the difficulties and problems of turning serialized sketches into a history in book form. In April, 1874, he promised Martin that he would "look over" his sketches of Chester and comment on them, adding that "from my own experience correctness is not to be expected in newspaper articles. I wrote some . . . for our newspaper here [West Chester] but the printers made so many errors that I became disgusted."(94) In November, 1874, Cope became more specific and more candid. With respect to the publication of Martin's sketches in book form, "I will speak plainly and say that I should be sorry to see it done without much correction." Cope admitted that he did not know "where the errors have crept in or whether you have the facts by which to correct them," but supposed that "the printers have been like myself, unable to decipher all your writing with certainty, [though] this will not account for all the mistakes." Cope felt that there was "a large amount of interesting and valuable information in the sketches but in their present condition I cannot feel confident in their correctness which would be desirable in works of reference."(95)

Martin must have indicated that, in spite of these difficulties, he intended to publish the sketches, for Cope wrote two weeks later that with respect to the proposed publication "I will offer some suggestions and won't charge anything for them either." Cope still found that the sketches contained much "repetition and there is no order either as to date or subject." He added: "Of course I know it would require considerable trouble to digest the material thoroughly but it would also add much to its value."(96)

But others were anxious for Martin to publish his sketches,(97) and some put in orders as subscribers as soon as they learned of Martin's intention to publish. One wrote that "[y]our well known qualifications for the task which you have taken upon yourself is a sufficient guarantee that it will be well performed and I am therefore very desirous of obtaining a copy of the work as soon as it shall be given to the world."(98)

Some of Martin's correspondents indicated that his serialization in the Republican was quite popular. One "felt so much interest that I obtained all the back numbers and secured the regular receipt of all future ones."(99) Another reported: "There is quite a desire in the community for sketches of ancestral generations—and yours is much read here."(100) And yet another, in somewhat more detail: "The historical sketches of which I received another installment today are beginning to attract attention, and any irregularities are freely talked about by those who are unable to write with sufficient intelligence to make themselves understood."(101)

Martin occasionally asked Thompson Westcott (the historian of Philadelphia) for assistance. As early as April, 1871, Westcott wrote that "[your] conundrums require a good deal of time to answer. Can't you come up some evening next week and see me? I have books and can easily, I think, work out your problems."(102) Two years later, Martin submitted a list of questions, with the ending: "You can answer on this and return it—I have searched all my books . . . or would not trouble you."(103) Though the friendship of Martin and Westcott is an indication that town historians sometimes knew city historians and were thus connected to a wider world of antiquarian endeavor, Westcott—as he was in the case of Martin's earlier history of Bethlehem—seemed badly informed about just what his fellow local historian was doing out in the countryside. He wrote that he had heard "last week for the first time" that Martin was publishing his history of Chester "in some paper." Westcott added that "I am very sorry that I did not know it before," but that the "exchange" that had been arranged between Martin's Philadelphia newspaper and the one in which Martin's sketches had likely been appearing had recently ended, "otherwise I would have known about the sketches."(104)

Martin's publisher was W. H. Pile of Philadelphia, and the history was entitled *Chester and Its Vicinity* and did not appear until 1877. Eschewing fellow antiquarian Gilbert Cope's advice, the history Martin published consisted of bits and pieces of information on a selected series of incidents, individuals, and subjects, and was, therefore, typical in its formless, random quality of the less organized efforts of these decades. Certain subjects received a prominent position in the reworked sketches and, through the haze of disorganized writing, many dimensions of Chester's past are described.

In his treatment of various subjects, Martin reflects the concerns of many other unsophisticated town historians of these years. For example, amidst his accounts of crime and criminals, he presented a detailed description of John Hill Martin, an individual so unusual and adventurous that his life leaps out of the records into folklore.(105) Like many others, Martin ironically took up a disproportionate amount of space recounting something that was so extraordinary as to be a natural subject for story telling, tall tales, folkloric, and anecdotal renderings, all of which worked against the "facts" of the unadorned records. In short, the temptation to be a good dramatist sometimes overwhelmed the passion for accuracy. In his account of health and disease,(106) Martin includes the reports of a medical doctor with personal memories of folk medicine, well illustrating the coexistence of professional and lay explanations for the state of a community's health — or, more broadly, the blending of document and reminiscence as evidence.    As for Chester's physical layout and population,(107) Martin attempted to perform the common task of providing accurate information on what the town looked like and how many people lived in it, and found, as did many others, that such information was scattered and uneven.

In his segment on inns,(108) Martin relied, as did others, on description derived from personal memory when other sources failed to provide the detail he sought.    And on schools, "I regret exceedingly," he wrote, "that the records of Chester schools cannot be found,"(109) forcing him to rely on bits and scraps of documents, and not the continuous source all local antiquarians prized.    As for the library,(110) Martin's account displays the rather common familial connection between these same antiquarians and key figures out of the past (that is, Martin's father was the librarian).    In his treatment of public facilities, in particular of the water system, Martin, like others, interjects his view on the question of what the proper place and extent of government or community-wide activity should be:

> The question of proper water supply was, therefore, one that rose above mere considerations of revenue, or private profit to stockholders in corporations, and that appealed to the public authorities as a sanitary and police regulation that should be inaugurated and conducted for the health and convenience of the people, and the protection of their property in times of fire, without regard to the question of profit and loss, that the safety and comfort of the community, rich or poor, were considerations superior to the matter of pecuniary returns.(111)

As for his account of the professions, and the law in particular, Martin relied on others, as did all the antiquarians, but made unusually explicit that reliance and the extent to which he found such assistance in need of correction and elaboration.    The basic lists of those who practiced law were provided by a collaborator, J. Smith Futhley, but Martin disclosed that: "I have added to Mr.    Futhley's list  . . .   names   . . .   he overlooked," and even altered Futhley's information when he believed him to be in error.(112)

In contrast to Martin, Charles C. Jones(113) was a good example of a prominent citizen and an experienced author who also happened to have an interest in local history.    Jones wrote a history of Georgia in the early 1880s.    By the time he dealt with D. Mason, a publishing firm, in 1888, he was as active a participant in the making of the contract as Mason was. Jones wrote on January 14, 1888: "I will expect to see and read proofs after they have received the careful attention of your proofreaders.    They will, when sent to me, be promptly read and returned." He added: "As compensation for this labor I will expect the sum of three hundred dollars."(114)

Jones overestimated the amount of time it would take him to prepare the manuscript, for, by February 22, he had already received his payment from Mason and mailed the firm his manuscript. In subsequent letters, he indicated with precision what he would do and what he expected Mason to do during the process of publication: "Pray let your compositors follow copy strictly. I will expect to read the proofs after they have passed the revisions of your proofreaders. There will be no delay in their return. Apart from the general title page of the work, I would suggest a special title page for that portion of the history which I have written. Such a title page you will find in the MS. . . . I would be glad to have a copy of this early history of Augusta in sheets, folded, but uncut and unbound, which I may preserve in my library."(115)

Indeed, Jones apparently had made another agreement with Mason, because in a postscript to his letter of February 22, he indicated that "[upon] the preparation of the history of Savannah during the Eighteenth Century I am busily engaged, and I hope to have it completed before long." Jones in fact completed the second piece by February 29. Mason then told Jones to keep the manuscript until April, at which time the firm would send him a check for $100. On April 2, an apprehensive Jones wrote: "My arrangements have been made based upon the receipt of this remittance at the time thus promised, and I hope there will be no delay in responding to the engagement."(116) A week later, a relieved Jones received a note "at one month" for $400, "which, when paid, will be in full of amount due me, as per contract for preparing a history of Savannah, Georgia during the eighteenth century. . . . The MS is entirely ready for the compositor and embraces a complete history of that city during the period indicated."(117) Jones sent the manuscript on to Mason in May and, after some delay, by December of the following year, had finished reading proofs of both volumes.(118)

When a prominent citizen of Savannah, General A. R. Lawton, asked Jones through Mason for a personal sketch, Jones was at first reluctant, saying Lawton "should make the request of me, and communicate such dates and memoranda as are necessary to the suggested labor. My time is at present so much occupied that I shrink from undertaking a matter of this sort in which I may be considered as acting the part of a volunteer."(119) Relenting, he wrote to Mason asking the firm to "advise me of the number of words of which the sketch should consist. I desire to be advised in a general way before entering upon its composition."(120) When Jones submitted the sketch, he admitted that Lawton was "the leading citizen of Savannah. I think [the sketch] will work its influence in enlarging the sale of your memorial history of that city."(121) Similarly, Jones asked the co-author of the history of Augusta to prepare a sketch from material Jones gave him of ex-Governor Jenkins as the city's most distinguished citizen and sent Mason an illustration of the ex-Governor for inclusion in the volume.(122)

Jones wanted an engraved portrait of himself included in the history of Augusta, and, when Mason sent him the impression to be used, he revealed: "I will take the latter home with me this evening and will invoke the judgment of the family in regard to the truthfulness of the portrait."(123) They must have approved, for Jones later asked: "Will you use my portrait in illustrating both of the History of Augusta and of the History of Savannah? . . . As I am a native of Savannah, was at one time a Mayor of the City, and am the author of the history of that place during the eighteenth century as run in press by you, it occurred to me that the use of my portrait in connection with the History of Savannah also might be deemed appropriate."(124) When Mason asked Jones to prepare a biographical sketch of himself, he wrote: "I will give attention to the matter," and, after sending the sketch to the publisher the same day that he received the request, he added: "I will read [the proofs] and promptly return [them]."(125)

Jones' concern that a sketch and a portrait of himself as author and as prominent citizen be included in his own histories is an indication that some antiquarians could not distinguish themselves from those whose prominence they confirmed: his life was as worthy of notice as theirs. The observer/author was also a full-fledged participant.

John Hill Martin's sketches of Chester contain in a loosely integrated format the array of sources and styles of writing that characterized town histories during the decades after the Civil War.  The fact that Martin's historical writing appeared in the *Delaware County Republican* and that many subscribers, inquirers, and collaborators regularly referred to his work on a "county" history is indicative of a kind of ambiguity or confusion town historians in rural areas labored under.  In parts of the Midatlantic, in large areas of the South and Midwest, practically everywhere in the Plains and mountains, and in significant portions of the Pacific coast region, rural settlements predominated, and often the only towns of significance were county seats (or shire towns, in an older terminology).  County and town were, therefore, closely related.  In such areas, the county was the most significant level of "local government." For a large rural population, one's locality, one's community, was the county.(126) In this context, histories of counties were the local history for people inhabiting large areas of the United States.(127) And yet, the county histories that proliferated in the decades after the Civil War were very rarely the result of efforts by indigenous local antiquarians dedicated over long periods to a genuine labor of love of the kind that animated amateur town historians.  County history in these areas of the United States with large, far-flung rural populations, were usually produced under the auspices of publishers and authors with primarily commercial objectives.

# CHAPTER 7
# City Historians

Local historical writing on cities during the decades from the Civil War through the Great Depression contained the same range and variety as that on towns: mixtures of chronological and topical treatments, of sources, of information, listings, descriptions, and quotations. There was no strict standard, no ready-made model that authors everywhere knew about and copied, just as there was none for towns. City histories were apt to be more widely distributed than town histories, with regional agents seeking subscribers from all over the nation, that is, former inhabitants scattered as a result of the continuous flow of people in and out of urban communities. City histories were also more likely to be exchanged with various state and local historical societies and libraries.

Awareness of what others had written did not lead to slavish imitation, however, and there were unusual, bizarre examples of historical writing on cities, just as there were for smaller communities. But there were also geographically scattered and temporally random typical or outstanding examples of city history, again, just as there were for towns.(1) What separated city history from town history was its greater range of subjects, reflecting the more complex nature of urban life, the greater variety of both governmental or public as well as private institutions, groups, and activities. And what distinguished a history of a city west of the original states along the Atlantic coast was the author's access to still-living pioneers for their reminiscences and to newspapers containing bits of local information dating from the inception of the community.

Melrose, Massachusetts, is a good example of the making of an urban history in that, at the time Elbridge H. Goss' history was published in 1902, "Melrose [was] the youngest city in the Commonwealth of Massachusetts." Goss asserted that "from a small, sparsely settled town, it has grown, during more than half century, to be an influential city of more than thirteen thousand inhabitants."(2)

How Goss' history came to be written is a revealing instance of how increasing size affected the way an antiquarian constructed a history. Goss first became involved right after the Civil War, when he prepared *The Melrose Memorial: The Annals of Melrose*, in the Great Rebellion of 1861-65. In 1880 and again in 1890, he contributed a short history of the town to histories of Middlesex county, in which the town was located. In 1898, when Melrose was still a town, fifty-five citizens petitioned for a full history to be written. At the town meeting, Goss was invited and authorized to write such a history and was granted unrestricted use of the town's records. The city (as of 1900) went on to appropriate $1500 for the printing of one thousand copies of Goss' completed history.

What is striking about the history is its organization, which is fully topical and includes chapters dealing with specifically urban developments, such as the water and sewerage systems, parks, hospitals, and fire and police departments. Goss' treatment of the newly emergent city took account of a range of urban life so wide that a wholly topical approach seemed the most effective way to embrace the past of this urbanized community, a conclusion shared by many other contemporaneous city historians, who similarly shunned chronology as the mode for organizing their writing.

Others, like Rev. Samuel A. Eliot, in his history of a small city like Cambridge, chose periodization by rubric — "The Foundations," "The Founders," "The Colony," "The Community," "The Village," "The Town," "The City," "The Outlook"(3) — ordering incidents and developments within periods chronologically arranged and described by cover terms like those just listed.

For the largest urban centers, like Boston, accounts were sometimes partial, like Nathaniel Shurtleff's *A Topographical and Historical Description of Boston* (1871), or impressionistic, like Horace Scudder's *Boston Town* (1881), and Mark A. D. Howe's *Boston: The Place and the People* (1903).(4) Nathaniel Shurtleff (1810-1874), though mayor of Boston from 1868 through 1870, became famous as an antiquarian, editing the records of Massachusetts Bay and Plymouth colonies, holding an office in the Massachusetts Historical Society nearly all the years from 1847 until his death, and presenting a series of articles gathered under the title *A Topographical and Historical Description of Boston*.(5) Similarly, Samuel A. Green (1830-1918) achieved fame as Boston's city physician, a trustee of the public library, and mayor in 1882, but was also well known as a member of the Massachusetts Historical Society Council from 1860 to 1918, its librarian from 1868 to 1918, and its vice president from 1895 to 1914. In addition, during the 1880s and 1890s, he gathered and published papers relating to the history of Groton, Massachusetts, his hometown.(6) Only in major cities like Boston did antiquarian endeavors typically attract public figures of state or national prominence.

In spite of their typically wide-ranging treatment of metropolitan life, historians of major cities usually did not deal with those aspects of community life that the individual historians who wrote on towns and smaller cities avoided. Such authors presented their city's past from the perspective of its elite. The past for them involved a range of activities, institutions, and groups that were greater in number and complexity than those of which their antiquarian brethren in the towns could take account. Small communities did not have municipal governments with police, fire, streets, and parks departments, did not have water and sewer lines, parks systems, wide-ranging educational structures, multiple financial institutions, varied commercial activity, or a many faceted cultural and intellectual life. The sheer size of a metropolis broadened the range of subjects urban antiquarians found suitable to treat historically.

But they generally avoided what those in smaller communities avoided unless the past of a particular city was marred by "famous" incidents that a particular writer felt could not be ignored: evidences of class, of divisions between owners of manufacturing and commercial firms and those they employed, of tensions between the native population and recent immigrants. All amateur historians shared a view of the past that emphasized its unity, its progressive nature, the growth of communities of which they were the successful inheritors. Division and strife were usually examined only if they contributed to that growth and development: wars with Indians, the revolution against Britain, the Civil War against the slaveholders – all were important episodes in the establishment of towns and cities characterized by freedom and prosperity. Even the long term religious antagonisms of the numerous Christian churches seemed by the late nineteenth century to be giving way to a strengthening spirit of interdenominational brotherhood and tolerance.

What the prominent and successful inhabitants of America's cities could not perceive was the character of life of others in their own communities: of laborers in factories or offices, of poor immigrants, of those who failed to fit into their portrait of the historical dimension of local life. In this fundamental sense, a history of a major urban center was like a history of a town: the antagonisms and divisions of the recent past were ignored as unfit for history as a success story.

A good example of a strictly chronological history of a city is J. Fletcher Williams' *A History of the City of St. Paul and of the County of Ramsey*, Minnesota, published in 1876 as volume four of the Minnesota Historical Society's *Collections*. Williams was the secretary of the society as well as of the state's Old Settler's Association. He indicated in his preface that his history was produced because a number of his friends believed that he "had the material at hand and the opportunity to prepare it, better than anyone else who was likely to undertake it." Williams visited and interviewed "every living pioneer of our city" and sent out letters and circulars, "asking information." The labor, the travel, the research, the writing, the expense were all done "solely from a taste for historical research, a feeling of pride in the subject and an endeavor to honor the memory of our pioneers and pioneer days, and without the slightest desire of profit."(7)

Williams chose the older, annalistic form of organization to present a nonetheless multi-faceted historical account of a young, rapidly growing city. The earliest white settlers in the area were French, a basic fact that Williams, like other English speaking antiquarians, had to accommodate. Over vast areas of the North American continent inland from the British coastal colonies of the seventeenth and eighteenth centuries, the pioneers were either French or Spanish. This meant that the Americans, or new

European immigrants, who moved westward as the United States expanded territorially in 1803, 1819, 1845, and 1848, overlaid an even earlier strata of white settlers who descended from the French and Spanish explorers. Those antiquarians along with their contributors, supporters, and readers whose ancestors were among the American pioneers, had to defer to an even earlier group of whites: non-British, non-Protestant, alien, and Catholic, but with a stronger claim as originators of the very communities whose past Williams and others sought to recover. The antiquarians of the east coast did not have to share their claim of a direct linkage to the source; in their case, the oldest white settlers were their own ancestors.

Williams accommodated by praising the French Catholic Jesuits: "Here the Jesuits assume the role assigned the British colonists in local histories of eastern communities." By contrast, Williams characterized Captain Jonathan Carver, who first explored the area around St. Paul as "a keen Yankee from Connecticut. . . . History must record him as the progenitor and founder of the noble order of real estate speculators who have flourished here since,"(8) this in spite of Carver's professions in his own account that he was a dedicated explorer with the welfare of all future settlers in mind.(9)

Williams' account of St. Paul is better written, more systematically organized, and more often reflective than most early city histories of communities west of the Appalachians, but it shares with them a focus on rapid growth, on the swift transformation of a small pioneer settlement into a modern city. Drawing especially on personal memory, the reminiscences of living pioneers, city directories, and early newspapers, the first historians of transappalachian cities celebrated progress. The celebration was most graphic in the older, annalistic, chronological format, which in the service of an antiquarian as able as Williams yielded a great array of evidence of urban development.

As for the native population, the Indians, Williams wrote that "[they] seemed doomed to disappear before the settlement of the white man, and, however lightly they may be regarded by those who have mingled with them on the frontier, there is something sad in the way they have been dispossessed of their ancestral heritage by the pale-faced intruder." Sad but no more so than the effect of "civilization" on the land itself. Though civilization had come "with its burning force, changing and moving the natural face of creation," it had also instituted "new forms of beauty planting in the solitude a busy, populous city, with its dust and noise, and smoke and clang of factory and mill, and the scream of engine and steamer."(10)

The domination of both a native population and the land, while each had regrettable effects, were clearly of secondary importance to the sheer growth of the community the white settlers implanted along the Mississippi River. Williams' prose conveys his continued astonishment as he provides an account of that rapid growth: "The record of these wonderful changes which have transformed this wilderness of yesterday, comparatively, into a garden of fruitful fields and busy cities, with railroads and factories, and churches and colleges which have built up a prosperous empire, populous with civilized and educated people, where were only the few wandering bands of a pagan and savage race before seems more like a tale of enchantment than sober history."(11)

For Williams, the superiority of what the white settlers built was beyond question. Where animals and Indians lived, now stand homes "built in the highest style of elegance, and furnished with every appliance of comfort that human ingenuity and taste and desire, or wealth procure." Where "medicine man performed his barbarous incantations," now exist colleges "in which a science more profound is taught." Where the "rude worship" of the Indians occurred, "now rise stately temples dedicated to the true God." In brief: "[U]pon the spot so recently wrested from the savage, . . . a great, opulent, prosperous, populous city, with its wharves, shipping, railroads, factories, granaries, and business warehouses, schools, churches, and all the institutions of the highest civilization of the age [is situated]."(12)

All urban historians in these decades wrote about their community to demonstrate that local history revealed progress, which they assumed would continue indefinitely into the future, and they did so at a time when American urban centers were growing at an astonishingly high rate.(13) But historians of the larger cities in this period typically chose the topical format to embrace the past of an increasingly complex urban community. J. M. Guinn explained why he arranged his history of Los Angeles (1901) in this manner. Guinn believed that the "topical plan" was preferable to a "Chronological presentation" because "it presents in a consecutive narrative all that has been said on some certain topic," and allows any reader seeking information on a certain topic "to find what has been said, without reading over pages of matter foreign to the subject he is investigating."(14)

Indeed, when big city historians tried to retain the older chronological format, they encountered serious obstacles. Charles Greve, whose history of Cincinnati appeared in 1904, explained that "[t]he effort to present the subject . . . to some extent in a chronological form rather than according to a topical arrrangement has involved much more labor than the writer anticipated, and also has necessitated many repetitions and no doubt a number of apparent contradictions." Greve admitted that "[a]s the work developed it became more apparent that even a chronological arrangement must fall more or less under topical headings." Greve nevertheless defended his effort, which "has resulted in some measure at least, in giving a more comprehensive view of each period under discussion than could possibly be obtained by the treatment of various phases of the city's development each by itself."

Greve went on to justify his particular mix of sources and contents and coverage, a mix not unlike that of many other urban historians of these years, though few bothered to comment as Greve did. He believed that the history of a city "should be neither a directory, a guide book, nor a chronological table, and yet it is hard to avoid giving to it some of the qualities of all these valuable methods of treatment." He thought the most interesting and revealing part of a city's development was its "formative period," because, after a city has grown into a metropolis, "its history, in the main, is similar to that of all the other cities of its class." A city in this class has such varied interests and numberless institutions "that it is impossible to give more than a mere suggestion of its many features."(15)

Other city historians agreed upon the importance of what Greve called the "formative period," giving it a fuller account than they gave to the more recent past.  But there was no fixed formula for such local histories during these decades, and the contents, coverage, and sources varied considerably: from histories emphasizing the early years to those emphasizing the growth and recent past of the urban center; from Williams' strictly chronological format to Guinn's strictly topical one; from extensive to sparing use of quotations, listings, and descriptions; from reliance on one to another source, whether directories, newspapers, reminiscences, municipal records, or the files of private associations and institutions; from a single author, like Williams, to a team of writers presided over by an editor over whose name the history was published.  Most of the urban antiquarians tried to present full, general histories of their cities, however.  Zoeth Eldredge's history of the beginnings of San Francisco,(16) William Griffith's history of the rise of Kansas City, Missouri,(17) and Benjamin Lossing's(18) (on New York City) and Charles Dahlinger's(19) (on Pittsburgh) avowedly social histories were all unusual in this respect.

It was standard for these local historians to give as their motivation and purpose for writing a desire to reveal the historical perspective on their progressive, successful urban community.  William Griffith, in his history of Kansas City (1900), was unusually direct in "boosting" his city, arguing throughout that the circumstances were propitious for Kansas City to become the greatest of America's urban centers.  Similarly, Frank Moss, in his history of New York City (1897), was distinctive in linking his project to the movement for civic revival and urban reform that flourished around the turn of the century.(20)

What distinguished a small minority of other city histories was their authors' effort to be analytical, to comment on why particular communities became cities.  This mode of thinking was alien to the antiquarians in towns and to most of those in cities as well.  But the obvious fact that so few communities underwent the process of urbanization to a significant extent induced a few to generalize about those factors that allowed Los Angeles, Chicago, and New York to build up rapidly and most other communities to grow slowly or even to diminish in population.

Two of Kansas City, Missouri's historians made this effort.  W. H. Miller, Secretary of the Board of Trade, explained in the preface of his history (1881) that it had been his aim "to trace the causes that have led to the almost phenomenal growth of Kansas City.  . . .    The writer believes that the causes leading to the development of the city in any one epoch of her history were but the development of causes in a preceding epoch, and that the causes of future development exist at this time, which are as much the outgrowth of past causes as the present large city is the outgrowth of past events."(21) The most basic factor determining which communities became cities (at least west of the Appalachians, after the Revolution) was, according to Miller, the existence of transportation facilities, which, he insisted, "have exerted a very great and controlling interest." Miller believed that America was a country "of wonderful and varied productiveness" and that "Americans are, of necessity, a producing and trading people." Because this was so, "[t]he chief consideration of such a people is transportation, and the city or the proposed city, possessing this feature in the highest degree . . . will be the most prosperous." And, more particularly, "the one that by such means . . . has accommodated the country furthest into the interior has commanded the widest extent of trade." In brief: "the history of interior cities is but a history of transportation in its different forms."(22)

Miller thought Kansas City's growth was attributable to the fact that it "from the first . . . held the advantage over all rivals in all phases of transportation development."(23) Kansas City had the best natural position for transportation facilities along the entire Missouri River.(24) Miller believed that Kansas City's future preeminence was thus assured. Two decades later, William Griffith, in his history of the same city, copied without acknowledgment Miller's introduction and made it his concluding chapter.(25)

But the great inland cities of America were not the only urban centers whose mushrooming growth prompted such analysis. Historians of certain cities on the Pacific Coast also tried to explain urban growth. Frederic Grant's edited history of "American"-settled Seattle (1891) contains in its introductory chapter sections entitled "Causes Tending to Growth and Development of the Pacific Coast — Geographical Position and Topography of Seattle — Commercial Advantages — Value of Puget Sound — How Seattle Satisfies the Requirements of a Commercial City."(26)

William E. Smythe, in his history of "Spanish"-settled San Diego, asserted the historical importance of his city lay in the fact that civilization on the west coast began at San Diego: "What Plymouth is to New England and the region facing the Atlantic, San Diego is to the great empire which faces the Pacific." Smythe was struck by the comparison that could be drawn between these earliest lasting presences of Spanish Catholicism and British Protestantism: "Plymouth and San Diego! Each the scene of the first enduring settlement on its own side of the continent; each the offspring of religious zeal." But, Smythe continued, "mere priority of settlement, even when this priority is a matter of large historical consequence, does not guarantee the growth, nor even the permanence of a community," citing Jamestown, Virginia, and Plymouth itself as examples. "There can be little question," Smythe added, "that priority of settlement and its resulting historical preeminence are assets of extraordinary value when joined to the possession of great natural advantages. . . . Boston and New York enjoyed strategic locations and were thus able to reap the benefits of their early settlement and the fame which it brought them. It is to [this] class that San Diego belongs. Hence its historical pre-eminence ought to count heavily as a factor in its future growth and ultimate greatness."(27)

The contents of city histories varied considerably, though most of the urban historians attempted to include at least a brief reference to all the subjects their sources dealt with. Some excelled at narrative, descriptive accounts. Such writers usually did not engage in serious research and were at their best in dealing with unusual incidents or personalities. For example, Joseph Kirkland, whose history of Chicago appeared in 1892 and 1894,(28) presented a pen portrait of the city's great "booster" businessman and city official, William B. Ogden,(29) and described the "Great Fire" of 1871 at length, taking up a whole chapter.

Natural disasters like fires and epidemics were calamities, sometimes involving the entire community, and urban historians like Kirkland admired the communal spirit they awakened. Such disasters, though tragic, bound communities together and hopefully led to further progress and growth and a greater capacity to overcome or prevent similar ones in the future. Incidents that divided the inhabitants of a city were more difficult to place in an account whose purpose was to illustrate the on-going development of an urban community. The chief source of urban discontent in the late nineteenth and early twentieth centuries was the antagonism within industrial corporations between the owners and managers on one side and the wage laborers on the other. At its most extreme this antagonism assumed the form of strikes and riots.

During this period, Chicago contained many corporations of this kind, and its life was disrupted by rioting as much as was the case in any other large American city. No historian, especially one whose mode was narration, could ignore such incidents. Kirkland devoted a whole chapter to them, entitling it "Riots and Their Suppression." Kirkland accepted the economy, as it had evolved to that time, from the perspective of the owners and managers. He believed combinations of wage earners and of employers were natural, with employers not raising wages except when necessary and employees not accepting a reduction of wages except when all employers refused to pay more: "Both seem to be as necessary as are two parties in national politics. Their contests and clashings are inevitable and lawful (so long as peacefully carried on) and from them comes the 'market rate,' the meeting point of supply and demand."(30)

Kirkland was highly critical of the violence caused by riots, whatever the cause. Violence impaired the unity of the community and interrupted its progress. The greatest deterrent to such violence is for a city to have widespread home ownership. Kirkland insisted that "[h]e who has much to lose is a sure defender of law and order." For him, "[t]he dangerous classes are nomadic, rovers, 'foot-loose', dwellers in tents, figuratively if not literally."(31)

In Kirkland's reckoning, the "Railroad Riots" of July, 1877, were "in reality a combined and premeditated effort on the part of wage-earners all over the Union to force down the hours of labor and force up the rate of wages, the railroads being chosen as the point of attack. In many Eastern cities there were great riots, with bloody results."(32) In Chicago, police, state militia, and U.S. infantry joined forces to disperse mobs and stop their destruction of property and violence against laborers and the armed forces themselves.(33) "The Anarchist Riot" of 1876, Kirkland declared, occurred when lawbreakers "(all of foreign birth) tried to bring the masses of American workingmen to the principles or sentiments entertained by certain European theorists who hold . . . that 'property is robbery', that law is oppression, and that order is slavery." Kirkland thought it was fortunate that, "[r]ight or wrong, the American public disagrees with them, and they are in a minority so hopeless as to be trivial. They are neither loved, hated, nor feared; they are only laughed at."(34)

Kirkland, though exhibiting a fondness for dramatic narrative, also presented overall assessments of Chicago's place as an urban community. He enumerated the reasons his city had attained its preeminent position in central America. First and foremost, "[from] the earliest times her position was conspicuously favorable. She stands just where water-travel and marine freightage intrude furthest into the bosom of the continent. All men may sail to her, no man can sail past her."(35)

But Kirkland was not an uncritical "booster." He admitted that Chicago's marshy prairie setting meant its streets were hard to drain;(36) that the city was smoky, dusty, and muddy;(37) that its people still exhibited "village-like characteristics" out of place in a modern city;(38) that its streets were overcrowded, its buildings too large.(39) Nevertheless, Kirkland loved Chicago, offered advice on how it could overcome its shortcomings and problems, and concluded with a defense of himself as a narrative chronologist: "Fortunately this is not a report, a compendium, or a guidebook; it is merely a story, and at best can only, by a touch here or there, indicate the ascending steps, leaps, and bounds by which the fair city has advanced."(40)

Similarly, Charles P. Willard's history of Los Angeles (1901) consisted of a smoothly flowing chronological narrative. As Willard put it: "The writer lays no claim to any amount of original research, his work being chiefly that of collecting, arranging, and presenting in logical order the established facts."(41) Willard confronted the fact faced by many other urban antiquarians throughout considerable areas of the United States that the original white settlers were not British colonists, or, later, "Americans," but Spanish (or, in other cases, French or Dutch). He contrasted the Spanish and Americans as community builders: "An important point of difference between the Spanish made-to-order city and the American accidental city is that the former possesses all of its site on a communal basis, while the latter has no land of its own except such as it may purchase." The Spanish pueblo owned all the land – like the early Puritan settlers of New England, except for what officials gave to the original inhabitants. Willard asked his readers to "contrast this situation with that of the average American city," which usually had its origins at a place that naturally drew people together because the location was "favorable for local business." In such cities, the inhabitants owned all the land, the city nothing, "until it has attained a size that makes the purchase of land for municipal use a neccesity."(42) Thus, the Puritans' planned, utopian, religiously oriented community shared important features with the Spanish colonial pueblo and in some respects was more like a Spanish settlement than a typical "American" town or city.

Los Angeles' transformation from a Spanish pueblo, with its Puritan-like communal orientation, to a frontier American town characterized by its disorder, lawlessness, and violence, and finally into a sprawling, modern American metropolis was swift. At the time Willard wrote, the inhabitants of Los Angeles looked back on pioneers whose character contrasted sharply with the noble ancestors easterners extolled in their local histories. Still, having traced the city's astonishing growth, Willard confidently predicted "that [Los Angeles] should some day become one of the great metropolitan centers of the nation is not a dream, but the natural outgrowth of existing conditions."(43)

The chronological narratives of Williams, Kirkland, Willard, and others was a format well suited to reveal massive growth and its attendant problems and progress. But many of the urban antiquarians chose the topical format as the most appropriate means for conveying the multifarious categories of life within these growing communities. Notable in this regard is "City Historiographer" Silas Farmer's history of Detroit (1884).(44) Farmer was candid about the importance of someone who was native born preparing such a history: "I am compelled to believe that no stranger or resident of a few years could have accomplished what I have attempted. Without an intimate knowledge of the city, continuing through many years, various obscure and buried facts could not have been unearthed, and historic problems that have eluded all previous research would have remained unsolved."(45)

Farmer disclosed that his method was to treat each subject entirely by itself. He added that this "plan, in the fullness with which it has been attempted, is believed to be original."(46) Farmer also revealed how systematically he garnered material, first searching "everywhere for everything of interest on every subject," then classifying all the facts by subjects that were thereupon arranged chronologically, and finally writing up each subject separately.(47) He concluded: "My aim has been to offer so complete a list of subjects, such fullness of information, and such thoroughness of classification, as to make the volume a model of its kind."(48)

And, indeed, the layout of the *History* suggests that Farmer in fact attempted to present Detroit's past in all its significant dimensions or, at least, all of those for which there was adequate evidence. "Part I LOCALITY" is a topographical, that is geographical, physical, and territorial description of the city, replete with early maps and surveys and land grants. "Part II HYGIENIC" is a cleverly designed rubric containing sections on climate, diseases, doctors and medical societies, cemeteries, burials and coroners, health officers, drains and sewers, water and water works, parks and boulevards. Observation blends with promotion in Farmer's general comment on disease:

Detroit cannot be recommended as the paradise of physicians. The general mildness of the climate, the pure breezes from the river and the lake, the complete system of drainage, for which there are exceptional facilities, the inexhaustible supply of superior water, the abundance and variety of fish, meat, fruits, and vegetables in its markets, the favorable sanitary conditions, resulting from our wide and well-kept streets, the enlighted and efficient efforts of the Health Officers and Sanitary Police, the almost entire absence of tenement houses, and the fact that a large majority of the inhabitants own their homes, are all to be taken into account in explaining its fortunate condition as one of the most healthy cities in the world.(49)

Even "ordinary epidemic and contagious disease . . . are exceptionally mild in type."(50) However, the earliest epidemics (involving cholera) of the 1830s produced the crisis situation that confronted other cities at this time: "Business was hardly thought of and the air appeared unusually oppressive, and to purify it large kettles of pitch were burned at night in front of various houses, and at intervals along the streets, the burial rite was shortened; and persons were not allowed to enter or leave the city without inspection and due delay. It had been the custom to toll the bell on the occasion of a death, but the tolling became so frequent that it increased the panic, and was therefore discontinued."(51)

Farmer found that, though an act of 1824 gave the city council "power to provide for the construction of sewers, . . . the desirability of building them seems to have been for many years an unsettled question."(52) Similarly, "[the] subject of waterworks continued to be agitated,"(53) and not until the 1870s did the city build its own works.(54) A committee on parks was established in 1854, but the "park question" did not become a major public issue until 1870 to 1873, and it was 1880 before agreement on the establishment of a large park was reached.(55) In these instances, Farmer uncovered a significant lack of consensus on the desirability of extending the dimensions of municipal government.

"Part III GOVERNMENTAL" conveniently goes on to examine that institution, to a considerable extent from the perspective of its structure. That is, Farmer provides a description of the powers of county officers; city councillors and alderman; the mayor; the city clerk, attorney, counsellor, even historiographer (Farmer's own position); boards, auditors, comptrollers, accountants, treasurers, and collectors. Information on territorial and state governments; lists of state, county, and surrounding township officials; references to the state's constitution and the city's incorporation; rules on elections at all levels; and a delineation of the types of taxation at each level of government reveal Farmer's sensitivity to the interconnected uses of a federal political system. Similarly, "Part IV JUDICIAL" describes the court system at its national, territorial, state, district, county, and city levels, along with the jails and the city's law enforcement agencies. A police force was created during the Civil War in response to race riots and the fear of rebel raids from Canada, over the opposition of an older constellation of marshalls, constables, and sheriffs.(56)

"Part V MILITARY" suggests the importance Farmer attached to the fact that Detroit began as a military fort, first under the French, in order to secure control of the western fur trade with the Indians of that area; later, the British; and, finally, the Americans.(57) There are sections on the forts, their military commanders, and, later, under U.S. jurisdiction, the militia. But most of all there are accounts of all the major wars Detroiters were involved in: the Seven Years War, the Revolution, various Indian Wars, the War of 1812 (with Hull's ignominious surrender to the British), the Mexican War, and the Civil War.

Under the rubric "Part VI SOCIAL," Farmer deals with the arts, recreation and amusements, manners and customs, and clubs, together with the original inhabitants (the Indians) and the blacks (as slaves), as well as a biographical sketch of the founder, Lamonthe Cadillac. His treatment of these subjects is sketchy in some cases, and chronologically incomplete. Of the blacks, he writes: "One of the darkest pages in the history of Detroit is the [race riot] of March 6, 1863. . . . The war with the South was then in progress; a draft was feared, and the ignorant and the vicious were glad of an opportunity to vent their ill-nature on a race which was claimed to be the cause of the war."(58)

"Part VII ARCHITECTURAL" embraces the city in its physical manifestations: descriptions of houses, stores and business buildings, court and municipal buildings, cultural halls, taverns and hotels, and, in a clever coupling, fires (or the destruction of these structures) and the development of the fire department as a means of dealing with such calamities. This section is profusely illustrated, with a portfolio of the homes of prominant citizens running for eighty pages.(59) By 1849, the City of Detroit Gaslight Company was incorporated for street lighting.(60)

Farmer's chronological listing of major fires is introduced with a comment that reveals how central these catastrophes were as events demarcating a city's past: "Many of the fires which have occurred at Detroit are vitally connected with important historical facts. Some of them affected all the future of the city. The mention of many will recall collateral circumstances, locate various events, and suggest items of interest."(61) Farmer's long list goes on and on with almost annual conflagrations occurring throughout the nineteenth century. The first company was organized in 1825,(62) with others added from time to time thereafter, apparently without the division of opinion that marked the enlargement of other municipal services,(63) though the companies themselves often engaged in rivalries of various kinds. Farmer observed that "[the] loud cries, the hoarse shouting, the rattling thud of the breaks, and the picturesque dress of the firemen, were in marked contrast with the quiet and system of the present day"(64) with its well organized steam-driven fire-fighting equipment.(65)

Farmer introduces "Part VIII RELIGIOUS" with the statement made in various ways by various city historians in the transappalachian area of the nation that "[the] first settlements of the West differed from nearly all the eastern colonies, in that settlers were not Puritans, but members of the Roman Catholic Church. Long before the first posts were established, the Jesuit and Sulptitian missionaries, with unsurpassed skill and courage that no difficulties could overcome, traversed the entire West, exploring, studying, and planning for the future of their Church."(66) In sections on the Catholics, Mormons, Methodists, Episcopals, Presbyterians, Baptists, Congregationalists, Lutherans, Unitarians, Universalists, and Jews, Farmer presents illustrations, facts about the founding, and lists of ministers and rabbis of each of the churches and synagogues in the city—eighty in all.(67) He then presents information on Sunday schools and mission schools, the YMCA, and bible societies.

And, in another surprising but sensible coupling, he goes on to deal with the poor and with charitable or benevolent societies, the latter linked in many ways to the churches.   In a homily on the absence of poverty at the outset of settlement, he writes: "The first settlers were mostly poor, but for many years pauperism was unknown.   The pluck that inspired the coming to a wilderness, and the vigilance which a residence in such wilds demanded, precluded that supineness of which poverty is born."  And, then, in an effective turn of phrase: "Not until the Yankees came did 'beggars come to town', and then not because the Yankees set the example of begging, but because upon their advent the population increased, and as towns grow, beggars multiply."(68) The office of Superintendent of the Poor was created in 1833 and was replaced by a Poor Commission in 1879, both of which bought and gave supplies to those determined by officials to be paupers.(69) A poorhouse opened in 1832 (but was replaced by a farm in 1839) and an insane asylum began in 1869, but both were under the county's jurisdiction.(70)

Farmer found that the year 1817, when the first newspaper, public library, and charitable institution were founded, was the beginning of an era in Detroit: "Prior to that date individuals had not associated themselves into public societies of any sort, but in this year the Yankee element began to assert itself, and very soon institutions of almost every kind were organized or projected for Detroit." Here Farmer expresses the widely held view that it was transplanted Yankees or New Englanders – heirs of the Puritan tradition – who took the lead in the establishment of such social institutions as communities developed westward.   He goes on to catalogue and illustrate a profusion of benevolent societies: orphanages, hospitals, ethnic clubs, industrial schools, insane asylums, working women and female moral reform institutes, homes for the aged poor, nurseries and kindergartens, and a more general "Detroit Association of Charities" formed to assist other charitable organizations but more specifically to "repress street begging, and to better the condition of the honest and deserving poor."(71)

Under the rubric "Part IX LITERARY" Farmer brings together accounts of newspapers and magazines and books; literary, historical, and scientific societies; private and church schools; colleges and universities; public schools; and the public library.   Brief reference to a larger number of short-lived newspapers and magazines under the heading "Newspaper Graveyard"(72) illustrates Farmer's point that from 1809 to 1884 (the time of his writing) 181 different publications came and went in this precarious undertaking.   Brief references to almanacs, gazetteers, directories, and maps indicate the range of popular publications turned out by the city's printers. Farmer goes on to provide information on such intellectually oriented groups as young men's societies, lyceums, historical societies, mechanics' societies, pioneer societies, and scientific associations and then proceeds to offer additional illustrated sketches of the varied private educational institutions, with somewhat longer accounts of the university, colleges, and public-school system.

"Part XI COMMERCIAL" is introduced with the observation: "Detroit was founded as a commercial colony.   . . .   Those who organized the colony in the wilderness of the lakes, came not because of religious persecution, nor in order to live under a government of their choice: money and adventure were the objects they sought."(73) Farmer describes the early city as a trading post and goes on to provide sketches and illustrations of the wholesalers and retailers who emerged during the course of the nineteenth century.   Of the produce markets which flourished and whose regulation by the city he describes, Farmer observes: "In the market the rich and poor met together; it was common ground, and the poorest were sure of a good morning from the richest in town."(74)

Farmer goes on to provide a rather familiar statement on his city's relationship to manufacturing (a statement of the kind found in many histories of the largest cities published in the decades after the Civil War): "The advantages of Detroit as a manufacturing center have never received the attention that their number and importance demand.   No city in America is more favorably situated, and few cities possess so many necessary and desirable conditions for successful manufacturing.  . . .  It is well-known that iron, copper, lead, and wood enter largely into the composition of all articles manufactured, and the location of Detroit in the midst of the chief sources of supply of these materials gives it unequalled manufacturing facilites."(75) There follows the usual illustrated sketches of a wide array of manufacturing establishments, followed by a similar coverage of banks and insurance companies.

Farmer's final "Part XI COMMUNICATION" links descriptions of the post office and mail, telegraph and telephone, horses and wagons, boats and ships, railroads, navigation facilities, streets and roads, and city street officials dating from the 1830s.   Compendia of information on Detroit's past ends with "The Annals of Detroit," a checklist of important events placed in chronological order.

Whether using a chronological or a topical format, whether concentrating on the early years or employing a more balanced coverage of all periods, including the recent past — at least some urban antiquarians were aware that their city represented a certain type of community, a special breed that had quickly grown into population centers of great size and complexity.   This awareness is what distinguished these antiquarians from those in villages and rural areas.   City historians did not write a different kind of history from town historians — except to take account of the greater range of urban life. But some city historians were conscious of the rarity of the metropolis and instinctively sought to explain why, say, Chicago became a great center and Cairo, Illinois, did not. Why their communities were the most spectacularly successful, progressive, large, and fast growing. This search for an explanation forced some of the urban antiquarians to become analytical, to probe and discover the rare combination of factors, which together produced the big communities whose past they described.   In this they were unlike antiquarians in the towns and counties whose concern almost never went beyond their own small community, beyond what made, for example, Deerfield, Massachusetts, what it was, unlike any other place in the world.   Whereas town historians usually sought the particularity and distinctiveness of an unduplicated entity, *their* hometown.   Some city historians, while sharing in that search, looked beyond their birthplace or adopted home, to a wider world of urban centers that were both distinctive and alike. What made New York, Chicago, and Los Angeles what they were in their entirety was unrepeatable, but there were common factors that resulted in their all becoming great regional centers while hundreds of other communities did not. It is in this context that a primitive, but notable, form of analysis first appeared in local historical writing.

Some city historians were unwilling and unable to encompass the many dimensions of urban life, either as single authors or as editors supervising a group of contributors. Instead, they presented serialized accounts of selected subjects from their city's past. These accounts usually appeared in a local newspaper, and some grew into series lasting for several years. Thompson Westcott's articles on Philadelphia's history appeared in the Philadelphia *Sunday Dispatch* from 1867 to the mid-1870s and constituted one of the longest efforts of this kind.

It is clear that others wanted Westcott to publish his writing in book form. As early as December 3, 1867, a reader wrote: "As your history [of Philadelphia] progresses it becomes more interesting and I feel that you must in the end put it in book form.(76) Later, another used a further enticement: "I beg you whenever you publish your 'History of Philadelphia' in book form, please place me on your subscription list for a copy."(77) Still later, at greater length, William J. Egle indicated that "I have your history of Philadelphia from the commencement cut out and pasted properly in eleven scrapbooks. I propose taking them to the book-binder's and have them properly labelled."(78)

When, in 1874, J. T. Scharf, one of the best known antiquarians of the time, asked Westcott to gather his articles together in book form, Westcott responded that he hoped to continue his weekly "Chapters" until his chronological survey reached the year 1854, something he thought he could accomplish by 1876: "After that time, if I live, I shall try to make arrangements for its publication in book form, but until that time such a proposition as you make, will be beyond my ability to consider."(79)

Westcott was sensitive to the charge of being "diffuse" and "loose," which was natural for those who presented history in serialized, episodic fashion, but what such a presentation made possible was a close, bit-by-bit assessment of subjects quite circumscribed in range by the thousands whom Westcott claimed as week-by-week readers. In Westcott's submissions the great complexities of life in an urban community were chopped into accounts with a narrow focus, allowing readers to react to description and fact within a small compass — and they did react.

Westcott was pleased when fellow antiquarians commented favorably upon his work, writing to one: "I am obliged to you for your favorable opinion of my book, and this opinion is more esteemed as coming from one who from the continuing study of kindred subjects is so well calculated to form a first estimate. I would rather have your good opinion than 99/100 of ordinary readers."(80) As Westcott's weekly contributions came out over the late 1860s and well into the 1870s, his reputation as an antiquarian grew among "ordinary readers" as well, and he received continuous requests for information about particular subjects that readers and others were investigating.(81) One wrote: "Your example and your help has been a stimulus to me in my particular line of historical investigation."(82)

Westcott's "Chapters" were based on a lot of information contributed by others and were thus the product of many researchers, even though Westcott did research of his own and actually wrote all that appeared in the *Sunday Dispatch*. Some sent documents to him.(83) Most were glad to be of assistance, pleased that Westcott could do more than they could with the information.(84) Others sent information on theaters,(85) churches,(86) the military,(87) Indians,(88) and genealogy.(89) Still others provided material of a physical kind, artifactual evidence: on burial grounds,(90) monuments,(91)       coins,(92)     calling     cards,(93)     songs,(94)     maps,(95) drawings,(96) and photographs.(97) Westcott's readers, in addition to being contributors, were also critics, noticing mistakes and informing Westcott of his errors.(98)

Westcott went beyond his readers and contributors in his capacity to deal with the past of a large community, but he was like other urban antiquarians in his extreme reluctance to summarize, to encompass the entire past of his city. For a full history he, in turn, became a contributor to the work of another local historian, one who lacked his inhibitions.(99)

# CHAPTER 8
# Repeaters

An indication of the growing popularity of local historical writing after the Civil War was the presence of antiquarians who wrote or served as compilers for a number of different local histories antiquarians who can suitably be called "repeaters." In New England, the work of Dr. William B. Lapham in Maine, Rev. Josiah Temple in Massachusetts, and Rev. Samuel Orcutt in Connecticut was a consequence of the desire of those with a personal and remunerative interest in producing local history to do so on a continuing basis. Officials of some towns decided to hire outsiders when inhabitants did not undertake the task. Even though outsiders, Lapham, Temple, and Orcutt respected the individuality of New England towns and resisted the temptation to reduce local historical writing to a set formula, sometimes, indeed, drawing on the earlier or on-going antiquarian endeavors of the inhabitants themselves.

Dr. William B. Lapham launched his career as a local historian with his history of Woodstock, Maine, in 1882.(1) "Though reared elsewhere, . . . [and] having labored under the disadvantage of living at a distance from the town while the work was going on," Lapham was anxious to display his connections with the place: his wife and mother were both natives, and his maternal grandfather was among the earliest settlers. Lapham found that Woodstock was a typical, or at least unexceptional town in that it was founded after the period of Indian warfare, was without resources for manufacturing, and thus remained a peaceful, agricultural village.(2) In Lapham's hands, local history served the same purpose as it had before the Civil War. Lapham arranged the contents of his history into a brief, annalistic treatment, followed by topical accounts of the churches, schools, military, post office, hotels, traders, physicians, lawyers, mills, family sketches, and so on a combination like those that appeared in the more comprehensive local histories written before the Civil War.

Lapham's antiquarian efforts started in a typical manner, notable only in that he was not a native of the community whose history he wrote.

Within the next two years, however, Lapham joined with Silas P. Maxim to produce another local history, that of Paris, Maine.(3) "Of the compilers," they wrote in their preface, "one [Maxim] is a native born of Paris, and has ever lived in the town, and also his father before him, his grandparents being among the early settlers." As for Lapham: "The other, though born in a neighboring town, spent his boyhood days upon the banks of the Little Androsgoggin river in Paris, his grandparents and great grandparents were early here, and his near kindred have always lived in the town; as that while one is a native the other is no stranger to Paris and its people." Prompted by the same desire to preserve the written and unwritten sources of the past before they were lost, Lapham and Maxim admitted that "mercenary motives had no part in our undertaking, for no money is ever made in publishing a town history; it is generally a labor of love and quite frequently a thankless task."(4) For this volume, Lapham and Maxim have interwoven the annalistic or chronological treatment — year-by-year — with topical coverage.

Two years later, in 1886, Lapham's *Centennial History of Norway* (Maine) appeared, sponsored by a special town committee, which indicated in its preface that "[at] the annual meeting of the town of Norway, held March 3, 1884, it was voted that there be written and published a history of the town, in view, not only of the fact that it was nearing its one hundredth anniversary, but to meet the desire for a more complete history than that which had been written a long time previous, and which contained but a partial record of its earlier period." The committee, "authorized to arrange for, and superintend the writing and publication of the work," hired Lapham, "whose services they were fortunately able to secure, and whose ability as a local historian is too well known to here require any encomiums."(5) Lapham actually revised an earlier history of Norway, published in 1852, and written by David Noyes. Lapham's comments on how his effort differed from Noyes' is a concrete illustration of the distinction between the less developed forms of pre-Civil War local history and what an experienced antiquarian of the late nineteenth century understood to be acceptable form for his time.

Lapham praised Noyes for his assiduity in gathering materials for his history. With a mixture of condescension and sincerity, Lapham indicated that Noyes had "compiled a very good history, as town histories were then considered." Noyes' history was the first for a town in Oxford county, and, at the time of publication, "less than half dozen Maine towns had had their histories written." Lapham conceded that at that time "[t]his field of Literature . . . had been but little worked." Still, Lapham felt compelled to add that "all the early town histories were very defective." From Lapham's perspective, Noyes' earlier history "was certainly not now up with the times, either in the arrangement of matter or in the matter itself." The material "is loosely thrown together [and] in many instances not chronologically arranged." There were no genealogical records, no chapter divisions, no indexes. Lapham was particularly critical of Noyes' failure to include a genealogical section: "A town history in these days without genealogical records is of comparatively little value. There is a popular demand for them, and the demand is a just and proper one."(6)

Lapham's own arrangement started with chapters on grants, purchases, and physical features, continued with a series of chapters on the early settlers and then the annals of the town, and concluded with topical treatments of the churches, charities, schools, the military, newspapers, reform, post offices, the agricultural society, public houses, the professions, early industries, personal notices, and anecdotes.

As the doyen of Maine's antiquarians, Lapham wrote histories of Rumford (1890) and Bethel (1891), Maine, both published in Augusta by the *Maine Farmer*. Some current and former inhabitants of Rumford sought out Lapham and persisted until he agreed to prepare a history. Lapham admitted he did not receive the cooperation of everyone, "[but] I was pledged to the work and went immediately about it, and the result, such as it is, will be found in the following pages."(7)

What is found is indeed more episodic, certainly less comprehensive and systematic than his earlier efforts. Different too is the inclusion of a list of patrons and subscribers from Rumford residents and from former inhabitants living elsewhere. Practically all the patrons (contributing $5 to $50) were accorded biographical sketches, though regular subscribers usually were not, something that did not bother Lapham at all. His prefatory comments did not have the tone of someone who was concerned about the possibility of a conflict of interest. In Lapham's mind, the patrons deserved their prominence: "[To] those natives of Rumford residing elsewhere who have shown their interest in the work by contributing eleven twelfths of the sum pledged to ensure its writing, I feel under just a deep felt obligation as though I had solicited the task, and had received a compensation commensurate with its performance."(8)

In Massachusetts, the Rev. Josiah H. Temple of Framingham became the author of five town histories during the years from 1872 to 1889: Whately (1872), Northfield (1875), North Brookfield (1887), Framingham (1887), and Palmer (1889). Temple's first effort, on Whately, "grew out of an invitation from the citizens of Whately, to deliver an Address at the celebration of the centennial anniversary of the Incorporation of the Town," and was published under the sponsorship of the town. Temple built on the "Family Registers of the first settlers of the town, including two generations, [which] were collected and published by the author, in 1849. Those records have been enlarged so as to embrace all the permanent inhabitants; and the families have been traced down to the present time [by others]." Temple then provided an unusually full account of the sources used and the contributions of others, emphasizing particularly "the abundant material furnished the writer while a resident of the town" of four inhabitants "who were eye-witnesses of events for the ninety years following 1760."(9)

In 1875, Temple joined with George Sheldon, who was researching the past of nearby Deerfield, to present a history of Northfield. Temple praised the earlier work on Hadley, another western Massachusetts town, by Sylvester Judd (published in 1863),(10) and served as a kind of tutor for the less experienced Sheldon. All three were as interested in the Indian tribes and their territories as they were in the New England towns founded by the Puritans:    Hadley was also the territory of the Norwottocks, Northfield, the Squakheags, and Deerfield, the Pocumtucks.(11) The Temple-Sheldon scheme interested a well-known publisher in Albany, Joel Munsell, who published the history.    Temple's work also interested current and former inhabitants of Northfield: 361 subscribed, and Munsell included a list of all their names in the back of the volume.

Temple was also interested in his own town.    In 1881, the town of Framingham appointed a committee to "consider and report on the matter of the publication of a history of the town." In 1882, the committee reported that many inhabitants of the town had known that Temple had long been gathering material for a history of the town.    Temple's credentials for actually undertaking the preparation of a history were "exceptionally good," in that he was "a native of this place, and familiar with its localities and traditions." The committee recommended that the town appropriate up to $4,000 to publish the history he prepared and that a further committee be appointed to make the "necessary contracts, and advise Mr. Temple as to the details of publication."(12) At about the same time, Brookfield made the same sort of arrangements with Temple.    As the Town History Committee explained:    "In 1882, after due inquiry and personal interviews, the committee voted unanimously to employ Rev. J. H. Temple of Framingham to write the history. . . .    The committee believe they secured the best man they could have found."(13)

When the town of Palmer appointed a committee on town history in 1883 and appropriated a sum adequate to the support of a sponsored history, the committee chose Temple "as a competent man to do the work, as he had extensive experience in this line of literature.    In the judgment of the committee, the result has justified the choice made.    Mr. Temple has been able to gather more valuable material from archives outside of the town records than would probably have been done by others less conversant with such work."(14)

Temple's histories in general were characterized by an undistinguished mixture of the chronological and topical approaches.    In his later histories, written as an outsider hired by town committees, he understandably allowed local inhabitants to prepare the genealogies.    But, by his own accounts, he delved through the available source material with care, and, in the case of at least one of the towns (North Brookfield) he "made a personal exploration of the entire tract embraced in the original township of eight miles square, with a view to determine important matters relating to topography, boundaries, mill-seats, early land grants.    In comparing with experts, he traversed this and the adjacent territory of 20 miles in extent, in order to fix upon the points occupied by Indian villages and trace Indian trails and early English bridle-paths."(15)

In Connecticut, the Rev. Samuel Orcutt wrote histories of Wolcott (1874), Torrington (1878), Derby (1880), New Milford and Bridgewater (1882), and Stratford and Bridgeport (1886), and was thus active during the same time Temple was. Orcutt's history of Wolcott started out as a history of the Congregational Church written while he was its preacher, which happened to coincide with the church's centennary (1873).    He added to this

"Ecclesiastical History" a "Civil History" of the town, thus retaining one of the characteristic organizational schemes of the earliest local histories in New England.(16) Four years later, in 1878, Joel Munsell of Albany published Orcutt's history of Torrington. In 1880, Orcutt joined Dr. Ambrose Beardsley to present a history of Derby.(17) In 1882, Orcutt alone wrote a history of the towns of New Milford and Bridgewater, and, in his prefatory comments, called attention to the special assistance of "Rev. Dr. Porter, President of Yale College, and for six years a pastor in this town, who first urged upon the author the undertaking, and afterwards aided much with his pen, and his most intelligent wife . . . who . . . came to the aid of the author somewhat with her pen, but largely by suggestions as to sources of information."(18) Finally, in 1886, the Fairfield County Historical Society, sponsored Orcutt's history of the town of Stratford and the city of Bridgeport.(19)

These five projects must have indeed been labors of love for Orcutt and his collaborators, because, as was the case before the Civil War, local support for such undertakings was not as forthcoming in Connecticut as in central and northern New England. Of his history of Wolcott, Orcutt pointedly commented: "It will be observed that the genealogy of a few families is wanting. The cause of this, in every case, is the want of a sufficient information to make a respectable representation of the family. . . . The limited numbers of subscribers and hence of copies printed has compelled the laying aside of all illustrations, after considerable preparation had been made for their publication. This has been to myself and others a source of great regret."(20) Of his history of Torrington, he confessed: "It is but justice to say that but for the prompt encouragement at a certain time, by substantial aid, by one of the citizens of the town, although some collections for the work had been previously made, the further prosecution would not have been attempted, and the book would not have been written by the present author. It is also true that but for the price paid for one of the books by the town, the amount of matter printed must have been far less or the price of the book considerably increased."(21)

Orcutt's co-authored history of Derby was buttressed with a statement by Noah Porter, president of Yale, who went on record as having "looked with much interest [on the work]. . . . It seems to me to have been prepared with great fidelity and thoroughness, and to rank with the best town histories."(22) Of his history of Stratford and Bridgeport he disclosed: "The only regret the author has concerning it is that the income from the sale of the work would not pay for another year's labor, by which a degree of completeness might have been attained. This is especially applicable to the genealogies, which in their present state are only the beginning of what might have been secured." He admitted that the financial support of members of the Fairfield County Historical Society was "not only greatly helpful to the work but without [it], the enterprise would have gone no further than the publication of the first one hundred and eighty pages."(23)

It is not always clear why Orcutt undertook those projects, or more importantly, why he persisted in his work when he encountered such difficulties. His sheer love of the labor is revealed in a prefatory comment to his first history: "A shade of sadness has touched my mind as I have taken leave of one and another, individuals and families, when they passed from study and research; for, after so much thought expended upon them, it seemed as if they were friends and neighbors among whom I had spent my days, and I was at last attending their funeral services.  The summing up of life, for each one of them, has seemed written in great characters before the mind, in the proverbial expression: 'Born, lived, and died.' "(24)

Joel Munsell may have provided the incentive for Orcutt to work on Torrington, as publisher of the history that ensued.  The project on Derby stemmed from a chance meeting with George W. Beach, superintendent of the Naugatuck railroad, who urged Orcutt to write a history of the town, having just seen Orcutt's history of Torrington: "He then recommended a call on Doctor A. Beardsley as being the service most likely to furnish proper information as to anything already done or likely to be done in the matter." After some delay, "a proposition was made which was at once accepted and the next day the work was commenced."(25) Or, as the Doctor recalled: "[Naturally] fond of reviewing the historic past, I had gathered interesting reminiscences at the suggestion of many friends for twenty years, with a view, some day, of publishing them in book form, but had nearly abandoned the project when the Rev. Samuel Orcutt called upon me and offered to join in the undertaking, and soon the work was commenced."(26) Orcutt added: "Whatever the Doctor has furnished, being written necessarily in a great hurry, has been carefully rewritten but designedly left in the Doctor's style, which has hitherto been so agreeable to the community."(27)

Noah Porter not only endorsed Orcutt's history of Derby but actually collaborated on his history of New Milford and Bridgewater. And finally came group support with the sponsorship of the Fairfield County Historical Society for Orcutt's history of Stratford and Bridgeport.   So, Orcutt labored away with the limited encouragement of others.

Lapham's, Temple's, and Orcutt's love of antiquarian researches and talent for compiling and writing local history was so extensive that they came to regard such endeavors as more than a purely amateur undertaking, the kind of pursuit that most local historians were content to apply only to their hometowns.   In other words, these three repeaters exemplify how important, absorbing, and encompassing historical research and writing could become in the life of an antiquarian.   Responding to the desire of the inhabitants of certain New England towns for a history at a time when native antiquarians seemed incapable of producing one, Lapham, Temple, and Orcutt accepted payments to come in and supervise the enterprise, assuring its completion.   Inhabiting a shadowy world between the amateur and the professional, these hired compilers and authors nevertheless presented their publications as histories written with a sensitivity to what was distinctively local.   All three were aware of what it meant to live in the older New England towns; as ministers or doctors, they were still in a good position to perceive the overall pattern of life in those communities.   Nevertheless, though outsiders, all drew heavily upon the researches of local investigators and actively sought the advice of prominent inhabitants of each town.   The resultant histories of Lapham, Temple, and Orcutt were offered as histories tailored to fit the varied past of individual towns, not as histories written to some formula and presented as mere examples of a common Puritan heritage.

Indeed, the mix of topical and chronological treatments these authors developed was as ranging as the contents in the works of the pioneer antiquarians of the antebellum period. And though hired to write these histories, none of the three professed to making a profit, any more than ordinary local antiquarians would have. Payments from town committees usually covered expenses only. Like others, these unusual hired historians depended upon subscription sales for the financial success of projects entered into for what they stated publicly as having been a passionate concern for preserving the past. Their work can thus be seen as evidence of the great popularity, and financial uncertainty, of local historical writing in New England during the decades after the Civil War and not as illustrative of a swift development of formulaic history, that is, history easily and simply reproduced from town to town, city to city, county to county.

The most influential antiquarian in New England between the Civil War and the Great Depression was Abby Maria Hemenway, whose *Vermont Historical Gazetteer: A Magazine Embracing a History of Each Town, Civil, Ecclesiastical, Biographical, and Military* (five volumes, 1867-1891) included historical sketches of almost every town in Vermont. The *Gazetteer* was the result of the efforts of an impresario of historical inquiry. With fierce and single-minded determination, Abby Hemenway cajoled, badgered, persuaded, persisted, and endured, wresting sketches from those active in historical research in towns all over her state.

What she brought together was aptly named. Her *Gazetteer* was an enlargement but also continuation of Zadock Thompson's efforts during the 1830s and 1840s. Under her supervision, the historical sketch was enlarged to embrace the various dimensions of local historical writing that became commonplace after the Civil War. Hemenway's decision to start with Addison County was apt, because that county not only came first in the alphabet among Vermont's counties, but was also the only county with an established historical society. It was the Addison County Historical Society that tried, in the 1850s, to persuade individuals around the county to write book-length histories of individual towns. The lack of response was undoubtedly a factor in Hemenway's decision to build upon Thompson's sketches, county by county in alphabetized fashion, rather than to continue the largely futile effort to find those with a capacity to produce full histories. Vermont, unlike some of the longer-settled New England states, had not yet provided the proper kind of setting for the maturing of such home-grown antiquarians. Her choice of Addison county was shrewd: fortuitously first in the alphabet, it was also the only county whose inhabitants had developed any sort of tradition of historical investigation. Unassisted, Addisonians floundered; with Hemenway's leadership they might point the way.

Abby Maria Hemenway's dogged determination, tenacity of purpose, and persistent labor were all in abundant evidence from the beginning of the more than thirty years of her life she devoted to the project. Having published an anthology of poetry of Vermonters, she noticed sometime in the late 1850s an appeal in a newspaper by Rev. Pliny White of Coventry (later the president of the Vermont Historical Society) to the inhabitants of St. Johnsbury, "urging them to take some measures toward the gathering up and preserving of their local history."(28) She consulted with Philip Battell, Secretary of the Addison County Historical Society, who (according to Hemenway's biographer) "gave her the names of the members of the society who had been chosen to write up the histories of their towns, and suggested that she interview them to find out at first hand how Vermonters already historically minded would respond to her idea [to edit a gazetteer]."(29) She ordered a thousand circulars explaining her proposal and wrote a hundred accompanying letters.

But then she received a letter from the Middlebury College faculty (Middlebury being the County seat), in which the faculty indicated they favored another edited anthology of historical pieces, to which some of them would contribute: "They argued that the project was unpractical and unsuitable for a woman. No woman could accomplish what the forty men of the Addison County Historical Society had failed to accomplish in the sixteen years of the society's existence." Undaunted, she travelled around the county: "Everywhere she was entertained with the most generous hospitality, and the list of those who opened their homes to her read like an ecclesiastical directory of that section of the state."(30) In other words, the opposition of professors was countered by the sympathy of clergymen.

The support of the clergy for women who contributed to particular facets of American cultural life was a fairly common occurrence during the mid- and late nineteenth century. There is evidence that liberal Protestant clergymen believed that an appropriate role for women in American life included that of culture-bearer in addition to the traditional ones of guardian of morality and family nurturer. This was in sharp contrast to the male professors who, typical of the wider male society, had a much narrower perception of what was suitable for women. Still, Hemenway's skill as an historical impresario was impressive, because – even with expressions of clerical support – few women actually became antiquarians, much less managers of multifaceted enterprises, at any time before the 1930s, a fact that makes Hemenway's achievement quite remarkable in scale and durability.(31)

In any case, Hemenway had continuous financial problems throughout her thirty-year effort. She hoped to sell enough of her anthology of Vermont poetry to pay for travel expenses, but the actual cost of publication had to be met by advanced subscriptions. For the first volume, or *Quarterly*,(32) on July 4, 1860, she listed twenty-one historians and twenty-four others who had gathered subscriptions. She admitted in the second issue of the *Quarterly* that she had received voluntary loans from friends and relatives. Her biographer adds: "This was the beginning of a long series of financial troubles which extended beyond her death. Her relatives on many occasions assisted her financially with her work, but even with their contributions, it was a physical impossibility for her to keep out of debt."(33)

On June 28, 1877, Hemenway wrote "a leading member of the State Historical Society [to] ... bring our Publication cause before you," explaining the varied and complicated arrangements she had made up to that point.(34) Hemenway went on in 1878 to ask the Vermont State Legislature for assistance.   In a follow-up letter to the *Burlington Free Press and Times* (which ended up publishing the first two volumes), Hemenway asked "[what would] become of all this mass of historical material we have been so many years gathering—so many persons have expended so much labor." Hemenway pleaded with the legislature to act, arguing that the work "is equally for every town in the state, and we have brought it to the Legislature and it dies or lives with them."(35) The result, according to Hemenway's biographer, was that the state made no out-and-out grant: it agreed simply to buy five copies of each of volumes I, IV, and V, the price not to exceed four dollars a volume, and to set aside $1500 to pay for subscriptions for any towns in the state that wished to have the *Gazetteer* for their libraries.(36)

When, in 1882, the long-awaited fourth volume appeared, Joseph Poland, whose Montpelier *Watchman and State Journal* Press published it, brought suit against Hemenway "to satisfy the debt incurred by the printing" by attaching the edition, which already had a mortgage placed on it by her brother-in-law! In an out-of-court settlement, a committee of arbitration determined the amount of debt she owed Poland, who retained a lien on volume IV.  Samuel L.  Forman, owner of the *Burlington Free Press and Times* had already established ownership over the second and third volumes.  In 1884, Hemenway decided to become her own publisher, first in Ludlow, Vermont, and then in Chicago, where she moved in 1886, possibly to escape further litigation.(37)

Through all these financial and publishing difficulties, Abby Hemenway remained an indefatigable, and, in the last years of her life, obsessive worker.  She wrote in a memoir that when she first returned to Ludlow, in 1859, her assistants sent out letters soliciting subscribers.  They worked "14 hours a day" to assemble material and write historical sketches.   Her workplace was her own room, and she discloses in her memoir that "mother always had much company and callers below, but, usually they expected nothing from me but a few good natured words through the room, down from my chamber, or up to it.  It would have irked me to try to entertain them; mother did better."(38)

When Hemenway became her own publisher in 1884, once again in Ludlow, her biographer relates that she displayed "an amazing amount of eccentricity and ingenuity in the setting up of her living and working quarters." She divided her room into three different sections, using "deep turkey-red draperies" as partititions.  The main room was the workshop and kitchen, the reception room "was furnished with several beautiful pieces of furniture," and her bedroom featured "a pineapple mahogony four-poster."(39) Later, in Chicago, she rented the second floor of "a little brick cottage at 29 Newberry Avenue," and turned the front room into a printing office, where "she worked at her case, setting up type and putting it into forms for "her printers, located downtown." Struggling against time and limited resources, she set during the day material that she edited at night."(40)

Hemenway encountered a variety of difficulties in the midst of her unremitting labors. She was involved in a protracted court case involving some property bequeathed to her, which she — a convert to Catholicism — promptly sold to the nearest Catholic bishop, and lost much in litigation fees. She suffered a broken collar bone "when she was run over by a sleigh driven by George Bridges, proprietor of the local restaurant; Bridges at least paid her doctor's bills. A fire burned the Donahue and Henneberry printing firm in Chicago and she lost sixty-seven pages of the fifth volume. Near the end, she supported herself by writing memoirs about her struggles in publishing the Gazetteer, memoirs that she tried to sell as pamphlets along with bound copies of the histories of individual towns."(41)

Her biographer believes that at end "her life became increasingly narrow and her purpose grew sharpened to an obsession. Her mind, once clear and decisive, betrayed an erratic instability of expression in her [memoirs]. . . . On February 24, 1890, she died of apoplexy, unattended and alone. . . ."(42) She did not finish: Windsor, the last county, remained undone.

The obituary in the *Burlington Free Press and Times* (one of her publishers) stressed that she "was a very eccentric character. . . . Her work is as unique as was its author, and perhaps has not been better described than by one who said that it was a great mass of valuable matter 'shovelled into book form.' Without any particular regard to arrangement, articles by the best informed of men of the state are here brought together with historical facts, incidents of pioneer experiences, stories, etc., constituting altogether what has been styled a historical monument for the Green Mountain State such as no other State has."(43)

Combining the tasks of editing, financing, publishing, compiling, and rewriting, Hemenway dominated local historical writing in Vermont from the Civil War to the 1890s. Her influence over the historically minded of a whole state extended beyond that of anyone else in the United States during these decades. Nevertheless her efforts were based upon the work of unknown researchers, writers, canvassers, and agents throughout Vermont. Perhaps the most notable of these was the Rev. William G. Brown of Chicopee, Massachusetts, who had been editor of the *Chicopee Journal* and whose poem "Vermont" was the first selection in Hemenway's anthology of Vermont poetry. Brown became general agent for four counties and at least proposed that he become an associate in the editing and publishing when he gathered a thousand subscribers, taking a one-third commission from the actual sales. Though it is not known whether Hemenway agreed to this proposal, her biographer says that "[the] winter was rough, with the snow piled high, but Mr. Brown trudged through the mountains of Bennington County, appointing local agents to complete the list in each place."(44)

Hemenway's *Gazetteers* stimulated others to pursue antiquarian research and writing independent of her, and during the same years she worked on her state-wide series of historical sketches, book-length histories of individual Vermont towns appeared: two in 1867, one in 1870, one in

1872, one in 1874, two in 1875, one in 1878, one in 1885, two in 1886, and three in 1889.

As had been Israel Daniel Rapp in Pennsylvania during the 1840s and 1850s and Franklin Hough in New York in the 1850s, Oren Morton was a repeater for county history, writing on several western Virginia and West Virginia counties between 1910 and 1923: Pendleton, West Virginia (1910); Highland, Virginia (1911); Preston, West Virginia (1914); Monroe, West Virginia (1916); Bath, Virginia (1917); Rockbridge, Virginia (1920); Alleghany, Virginia (1923). Morton moved around a lot, amassed material, and wrote quickly. He depended on the income he received for his genealogical and historical research and writing, except for income from occasional teaching positions.

In his prefatory statements, Morton revealed with exceptional clarity his methods and purposes. A stranger rather than a native of the counties whose histories he wrote, Morton was sensitive to both the advantages and disadvantages of his postition: "To a person thus situated there is the possibility of keeping free from bias and treating all persons and all interests with fairness. Yet on the other hand his unfamiliarity with his field at the start places him at a disadvantage."(45) "He is very much in need of live cooperation on the part of the inhabitants. This cooperation needs to be active and not passive."(46)

Morton's ability as a county historian was evident to others. As early as 1907, Horatio S. Whetsell of the *Preston County Journal* asked Morton to prepare sketches on the county's history and "a series of articles on the group—families which have sprung from the pioneer settlers. . . . [However,] there were repeated requests that the published matter appear in book form, and not in fugitive articles only."(47) Similarly, in 1912, Joseph McAllister of Hot Springs in Bath County, Virginia, who had been collecting material for a history of the county, asked Morton because of "his favorable opinion [of him] . . . to use his collections to write the history himself."(48)

Morton had definite views of what a county history should consist of. A county history, he believed was either "general" or "genealogic." A genealogic history "is little else than a dry network of names and dates" unless someone has done something "a good deal out of the ordinary." A general history contains an account of the times in which such families lived: "how they dressed, labored, and housed themselves; and what was the environment, physical, civil, and social, in which they were placed." Then, Morton argued, we "have begun to put flesh and blood into the skeleton of names and dates."(49)

Such a history correctly begins with a geographic survey, and "then explains whence pioneer families came and why they came, and in what manner they established themselves in the wilderness." A good history "attempts to trace the civic, social, religious, educational, and industrial unfolding that has since taken place." But, it also "tells of the steady growth of the centers of population, and of the steady outflow of people that has been true of this region from the start."(50)

In this context, elaborate biographical sketches "were out of the question and they could not be inserted gratuitously." "Biographic mention" appears "where it is plainly called for," but was usually a simple statement of fact.(51) Morton's method was to trace a family "forward from the pioneer ancestor, thus giving a comprehensive outline of the entire connection," rather than "tracing backward the subject of a special sketch." Morton thought the result was that "the appearance of partiality is avoided and the interest of the whole community awakened."(52) In this way, Morton gave adequate but not in his judgment, excessive attention to biographical and genealogical sketches for a population whose forbears in the colonial South had given priority to family connections over the development of community.(53)

Morton believed "that if every well-informed American should know his country's history, he should also know his county's history. Patriotism begins at home, after the same principle that geography is best taught by beginning with the school district. If this view is correct, local history should be presented with a fullness comparable to that of national history."(54) To Morton, both the size and price of a county history should be limited: "What has been attempted is to put as much local history as possible into a book that could be offered at a reasonable price, and thus circulate generally among the families of the county."(55) Or, put another way: "The true purpose of local history is educational. This purpose is defeated if the price is beyond the reach of the average man, and if the book is designed and used as a parlor ornament. But if the book is to be reasonable the book cannot be large."(56)

In organizing his writing, Morton consciously "followed a topical method, as that the reader will not have to look through the whole book to find what properly belongs under a single caption. . . . (57) [He] intentionally dwelt more on the pioneer than on the recent period. The knowledge of the former is fast slipping away, and as much is already lost beyond recovery. A knowledge of the latter will remain for a while on much firmer ground."(58) Morton was notably thorough in his research. For his history of Highland County he visited nearly all parts of the county, including various courthouses, travelling "about 547 miles on foot and 266 by conveyance." Morton figured that he had "been entertained in the homes of seventy-two of the citizens" and had "interviewed 168 persons, besides receiving written communications which would raise the number to nearly 200." He thought "[a] warm and helpful interest in his undertaking has everywhere been expressed."(59)

But Morton was not always satisfied. Of his research in Rockbridge County he wrote: "The compiler hoped thus to come in touch with many persons who could supplement the data he was gleaning from the public documentary sources. The responses were few and not all promised [were] forthcoming."(60) But, Morton persevered. His history of Alleghany (1923) was, with his customary thoroughness, "based upon the documentary records of [the county and its parent counties]; on archives in the capitol and state library of Virginia; . . . on questionnaires kindly filled out by several citizens; on personal interviews with residents of the county."(61)

His attitude toward his work was most revealingly summed up in a prefatory statement on his history of Rockbridge in which he states that this, the first history of the county, "represents eighteen months of hard work. No statement has gone into these pages without a careful scrutiny." But Morton cautioned that "there is no claim for immunity from error in statements of fact or in the spelling or proper names," adding that "[t]he man or woman who can write a local history and escape censure is not to be found on this side of the millennium."(62)

In Morton's surviving correspondence with the Joseph Ruebush Publishing Company of Dayton, Virginia (which published his history of Alleghany County in 1923), there are detailed descriptions of many facets of Morton's work as an antiquarian. It is clear that Morton's researches and writings were a major source of income for him, and in his dealings with Ruebush, he revealed his interest in and awareness of every facet of the preparation, writing, publishing, and sale of local history.

In December, 1922, Morton indicated that his history of Alleghany County would be ready for a printer in January, 1923, and that the book would be ready for sale in March of the same year.(63) In January, Morton reported that the "News-Record terms are rather tight and I find that the office cannot work speedily enough. . . . The printing has to be done elsewhere, that is all."(64) In March, Morton sent seventeen copies of the printed history of Alleghany to Ruebush from Schultz, the printer he found, adding: "J. F. McAllister says it is my best history. Our Canvasser here uses a sampler and finds people well pleased." Always open to new opportunities, Morton also told Ruebush: "[It] is possible that a Greenbrier history on a medium scale will be 'started' next month, a lady genealogist taking the family history section. If so, it will be like Alleghany, only having about 320 pages. Price probably .75. We could put your imprint on this also. Greenbrier is larger game than Alleghany."(65)

Morton's "history" of Greenbrier turned out to be a collection of documents only, for in May 1923, Morton advised Ruebush on how to make certain alterations and additions in order to "help the book a good deal commercially. It would then have an appeal to genealogic friends."(66) As for his "lady genealogist": "I don't think there is a paragraph of Mrs. White's own matter fit to go into print as it stands, so I am typing all of that." To his dismay, Morton found that "[i]t is worse than I thought from my cursory examination. Every page swarms with bad grammar and spelling and mistakes of [typing] machine." Worse still: "She made no effort to correct them. Her diction is loose, often foggy and contradictory, and too diffuse." But: "[I]t will all be all right when I get done with it, and will make a very good thing."(67)

In June, 1923, Morton sketched out the proposed contents of a book of documents on Greenbrier County, suggested the size of the press run, the printer's cost, the book's price, and the sales arrangements with the publisher: "The entire book would be a good local history, *all* of it excepting the introduction, being by Greenbrier parties. With an efficient agent sent to work it would have a very respectable sale in Greenbrier, and as it would be 'lousy' with family history data, it would appeal to the genealogical workers."(68)

In other correspondence, Morton conveyed a sense of the hard work,
low income, frustration, and hope of a full-time antiquarian: His work on
the history of Alleghany County "has been annoying. On the whole, it is a
very unappreciative community."(69) "I work from 6 a.m. till 9 p.m. but the
days are not long enough for all I need to do, and I cannot subdivide
myself."(70) "I am in ideal working order, though of course I cannot help
feeling my status, and no change in it is to be expected. I get up between
5 and 6 and hammer away all day."(71) "Please make me an offer on the
[history of] Alleghany stock [of unsold books]. . . . You would have full
control of what is left of the edition."(72) "The suggestion has been made
to me that I go ahead and get out a history on my own account. . . . I
cannot work on any such basis myself, nor assume any responsibility of
personally selling an edition. I have always worked on some sort of
cooperative basis."(73) By the mid-1920s, Morton ran out of momentum,
though he considered compiling another collection on Botetourt County.(74)

What emerges in Morton's letters to Ruebush over a four-year period
is a portrait of an extremely busy local historian, one who tried to derive
his principal income from his labors. Morton was constantly thinking about
new projects—of both a documentary and a historical character—and often
worked on several at the same time. He was thoroughly familiar with all
aspects of an antiquarian's endeavors, believed that what he did was well
done, and that the array of collectors, contributors, genealogists,
subscribers, and well-wishers who surrounded him as a serious historical
writer simply did not have his capacity and commitment to do research and
to write history. Morton pursued his objectives in spite of uncertain sales
and the indifference of many of the local inhabitants whose prominence
made them natural benefactors. He did so in a close symbiotic relationship
with Ruebush, a small local publishing firm. Morton sought Ruebush's
advice and financial support by continuously proposing imaginative, clever
schemes, some of which worked, some of which did not. Their relationship
had many facets. Some of Morton's letters even contain information on
individual orders placed directly with him; others include requests for the
kinds of supplies a publishing firm had in stock.

Morton's own history of Alleghany County, published by Ruebush in
1923, contains a familiar mix of descriptions, quotations, and listings, and
of chapters organized as chronological narratives or as topical accounts.
Segments on geography, pioneers, Indians, and the early annals interlace
with others on transportation, industry, government, wars, families, and
"Alleghany as Seen in a Tour." Morton's writing is also on occasion
interpretive, analytical, or in the form of generalizations when he focused
on the patterns of life the inhabitants of the county shared with other
Virginians or the British colonists more generally.(75)

That Ruebush, as a small publisher of local history, was successful in
widely publicizing and generating sales for the books he published in the
1920s is illustrated in a letter written by Kate White, another writer whose
work Ruebush published, in which White refers to individuals having used
her book in such scattered libraries as the New York and Cincinnati Public
Libraries, adding: "I have received letters from everywhere, asking for more
information, showing how widely you have advertised the book: Texas,

California, Minnesota, New England — all southern, middle, and western."(76) Another added: "I feel that an establishment of your sort is a real service to those people interested in the history of Virginia."(77)

J. Thomas Scharf was more active on all levels of subnational or local historical writing state, county, city, biographical collections — than anyone else in the United States during the decades following the Civil War. His histories of the cities of Baltimore, Philadelphia, and St. Louis; of Baltimore, western Maryland, and Westchester (New York) counties; of the states of Maryland and Delaware; along with other proposals and published writings are all evidence that he was the most enterprising of all the antiquarians with the possible exception of Hubert H. Bancroft, who prepared histories of all the Rocky Mountain and Pacific Coast states. Like Bancroft, Scharf hired assistants and published historical writings that were the product of an organization presided over by a commander concerned about every facet of the operation. But, unlike Bancroft, Scharf had no grand design, no guiding mission. The Marylander cast about for workable projects and was often dealing simultaneously with several in various stages of development.(78) As Scharf labored on through the 1870s and 1880s, usually out of Baltimore, he built up a reputation as an antiquarian that was referred to unhesitatingly by those he asked to write on his behalf when he applied in 1879 and 1880 for such positions as Maryland's Commissioner of Land Office and State Librarian.(79)

Other letters of praise were obviously unsolicited. Boyd Crunvime wrote that he had received from Scharf's publisher a copy of Scharf's history of Baltimore County "and have examined it with great interest. I am now engaged in doing editorial work, and in writing a part of a similar history of Washington County, Penna, and if our work shall come only approximately near to yours I shall be proud of it."(80) O. H. Bruch wrote "to say that the holding of the entertainment was suggested by your 'School History' of Maryland, which we use in our classes and which has given us both pleasure and satisfaction relative to the early history of our grand old state."(81)

Others were certain of the success of any project Scharf undertook. George Childs of the Philadelphia *Public Ledger* disclosed that "I had about made up my mind not to be placed in any more publications of the kind suggested, but I know that anything you are connected with must be good and command attention."(82)

When Scharf extended his operations beyond Maryland, he either sought the opinions or accepted the advice of qualified people on the scene. Scharf's proposal for a history of St. Louis brought a favorable response from Jonathan Cockneel: "I believe there is a good field for you here though, of course, a personal survey would be necessary to secure a correct idea."(83) Scharf also expressed an interest in Philadelphia's history, when he urged Thompson Westcott to gather his serialized segments of such a history into book form.(84) Westcott's response, written after he had bought a copy of Scharf's *Chronicles of Baltimore*, was that "[if], in future labors, you should require any information about matters connected with the history of the Quaker City, I shall be pleased to help you if I can."(85) By

1881, Scharf explored the possibility of preparing a history of the city.
George Childs, his contact, wrote that he could "hardly give an opinion."
Childs believed that "Watson had a very large sale," but, if Scharf's
publishers "feel confidence," Childs would assist in every way he could.
Childs cautioned that "[t]hey should consider the undertaking in all its
bearings before going into it."(86) When Scharf decided to go ahead with
the project, Westcott actively assisted him and, indeed, became his co-
author.(87)

John Shea commented on still another proposal made by Scharf, that
Scharf prepare a history of New York City. Shea thought that a good
history of the city was "sadly needed by general readers. Every history of
New York that he ever appeared," Shea thought, "has been more or less an
imposition." He believed that the latest, by Martha Lamb, was "perhaps the
worst of all," in that a great deal of her volume focussed on colonial
history, while "the [political, economic, and religious] growth and
development of the city . . . cannot be traced at all; and it is completely
useless as showing changes in social life."(88) Shea's assessment of Lamb's
history reveals the wide variation in the contents of local historical writing
in the decades after the Civil War. Shea found Lamb's narrative, episodic
treatment of New York's past out of date in its lack of systematic coverage
of the many dimensions of urban life. Perhaps himself daunted by the
complexity of life in the nation's largest metropolis, Scharf never went
ahead to present his own version of that city's past.

In preparing his histories, Scharf or his assistants sometimes solicited
information directly from public officials.(89) It is also clear that Scharf
paid for contributions to his histories.(90) Fred Billon indicated that "as [a
particularly complicated subject] would involve a labor of some little time, I
would expect a somewhat more remunerative compensation for it than you
propose to give me for miscellaneous matters."(91) Others asked Scharf for
employment. One disclosed: "It occurred to me to ask if there is any of
that left unfinished by [Spenser who] has been doing some work in aid of
certain literary projects that you have in hand . . . which you might be
inclined to assign me. I have had, as perhaps you are aware, some
experience in . . . historical writing, and should like employment
again."(92) Another wrote: "If you have any extra writing in your office my
contiguity to it would enable me to do it at my office, and return daily if
need be.(93)

Scharf's own labor in the research phase of his operations involved
sending form letters and queries to those institutions or groups he believed
were in a position to provide information.(94) Another kind of form was
sent to individuals, with the request that they respond to a list of
biographical inquiries.(95) He also relied on paid assistants who interviewed
various individuals in a continuing search for information.(96) But many
others who actively assisted Scharf were voluntary contributors with whom
he corresponded. Some whom he asked refused outright.(97) Others greatly
limited their aid.(98) Some contributors, following their initial agreement
with him, asked further questions about the size and desired contents of
their segments.(99) On some occasions, Scharf actively aided his
contributors. William Perine wrote that "[the] matter which you send me is

fragmentary and undigested, but will help serve me in the way of references."(100) Similarly, J. W. Forney indicated: "I would be glad if you would send us at your earliest convenience the data you referred to. My sister is waiting to arrange the matter and begin the article."(101)

But Scharf's assistance was not always welcomed. An irate paid assistant, Malcolm H. Johnston, exclaimed: "I am utterly at a loss to know why you will have to rewrite all my manuscript, as you say in your telegram. . . . I must say I cannot see why it should be *necessary*." In an effort to understand Scharf's decision, Johnston tried to explain what he had done and to show that his writing was acceptable. He had "attempted but few rhetorical flourishes." He insisted that "[t]he history must necessarily [consist] of masses of details." But, with melting resolve, Johnston added that Scharf was, after all, "the proper judge as to what you desire. I have tried to do faithful and conscientious work for you." And then: "I will be much obliged if you will send me a cheque for the manuscript I send."(102)

In this frank, revealing letter, Johnston displayed the difficulty contributors and antiquarians could have in arriving at a mutually satisfying submission. Johnston also disclosed how extensively reworked older accounts of certain subjects sometimes were. Fresh research was not a feature of every historical project; certainly Scharf did not insist upon it for his varied enterprises. Johnston also defended the stylistic mode, favored by Scharf, of listing facts rather than making a dramatic presentation.

Even when Scharf and his contributors worked in harmony, the sheer difficulty of preparing a finished segment was sometimes evident. Charles Lindulry wrote to Scharf about his "manuscript chapter" on Pelham. Lindulry told Scharf that he was "conscious of its deficiencies, but it was the best I could do under the circumstances." What really concerned Lindulry was his belief that "[n]o town in the United States of the same age as Pelham has had a less eventful history. To follow all the Pells and other families down to the tenth generation is a tedious task to both writer and reader."(103) Here Lindulry was unable to hide from Scharf what doubtless troubled many contributors to local historical projects: the gnawing anxiety that what they did research and wrote was of interest only to the particular family or community — and to nobody else in the world.

The most sophisticated of all Scharf's assistants was Henry B. Dawson, editor of the acclaimed *Historical Journal* and a leader in the movement to make local historical writing attain exacting standards of reliability and accuracy.(104) When Scharf decided not to prepare another history of New York City, but chose instead to survey the towns of suburban Westchester County, Dawson became his chief advisor. Not surprisingly, Dawson advised Scharf that "[the] more I think abut the matter, the more I am convinced that some general guide should be given to writers of town sketches, in order to ensure not only some degree of uniformity of treatment of the several towns, but to prevent the omission of what may be important, either through ignorance or negligence." Dawson also enclosed copies of "their agreement" and asked Scharf to write a "note of acceptance" on each copy.(105)

Dawson also gave quite specific advice and observations.(106) However, what turned into a harmonious relationship between Scharf and Dawson did not last.    Four years later, Dawson thanked Scharf for writing, "notwithstanding what have been grounds of our discontent. . . .    I shall be pleased to hear from you, at any time, *bygones being bygones*."(107) The nature of their estrangement is unclear.

As the only repeater who operated at all levels of subnational historical inquiry—city, county, parts of a state, state—Scharf was in a position to know other antiquarians and to be known by them.    Thompson Westcott ended his long-term serialized history of Philadelphia to aid Scharf in the preparation of a book-length history of the city.    Westcott obviously admired Scharf.(108) T.J.C. Williams wrote to Scharf, "You have collected so great an amount of material in your History of Western Maryland that it leaves but little room for me.    My design is not to touch what you have given but to get up a gossippy account of ordinary affairs written exclusively from the newspapers."(109) Both Westcott and Williams deferred to what they considered to be Scharf's greater capacity to present a full history, contenting themselves with serialized snippets of "gossippy accounts." In their view, there was a hierarchy of antiquarian endeavor: Scharf represented the pinnacle; he was the serious historian; theirs were more modest achievements.

But Scharf also deferred to others, to national historians—like Francis Parkman—upon whose mastery of sources and range of inquiry Scharf sought to draw.    While preparing his history of St. Louis and its county in the early 1880s, Scharf asked Parkman for information.(110) Parkman's response was in the form of a short note in which he said he was "unable to throw any light upon the points concerning which you inquire." Parkman referred Scharf to Lyman Draper of the Wisconsin Historical Society, "who has given special attention to the period in question."(111) It is clear that Scharf knew of the work of national historians like Parkman, but Parkman's response to his inquiry indicates that Scharf was not especially knowledgeable of the work of other local historians, at least in other parts of the country.    As the best-known local historian of the Midatlantic states in the decades after John F. Watson's death, Scharf undoubtedly made himself familiar with local historical writing within that region, particularly for those places about which he chose to write.

But even with his scope, scale of operations, and persistent labor, Scharf seemed unaware of developments in New England.    In 1884, one of those Scharf asked to assist him complained about his assignment and lectured him on the desirability of using Winsor's *Memorial History of Boston* as a model for setting up an appropriate division of labor, but insisted that it be used in an accurate manner: "The principle on which [it] is based is a doublefaced one.    It is not merely to assign to a given writer the subject with which he is most familiar.    It is also to assign a given subject to the writer who is most familiar with it."(112) Indeed, when Scharf wrote to Winsor, seeking his advice about a proposed history of railroads, the letter was misdirected.    Winsor in responding, explained that the letter, sent to the Boston Public Library, was fowarded to the Harvard University Library, since Winsor had "left the Public Library three years and more ago." Winsor added crustily that, in any case, he found "it difficult at present to see where I can come in, as I know nothing especially of railroads."(113) When Scharf wrote to Samuel Drake, an earlier historian of Boston, Drake's acerbic response was: "I am not, as you seem to suppose, a member of the Massachusetts Historical Society, and do not think of any way in which I might forward your wishes."(114)

It is not clear from such scraps of evidence whether the reserved and correct tone of Winsor's and Drake's responses to Scharf's requests for assistance indicates that those at the heart of the New England antiquarian enterprise thought of Scharf as a disreputable operator, a wandering impresario, gathering together material for histories whose purpose was personal profit rather than for a community's benefit — or whether Winsor and Drake were simply ruffled over the fact that Scharf did not know enough about them to address them properly. In any case, well known antiquarians like Winsor and Scharf did not exhibit an easy familiarity with each other's work. In this sense, the world local antiquarians inhabited was still very narrow in its geographic parameters.

Scharf's histories mirror the shifts in the ways antiquarians arranged the printed contents of their work during the 1870s and 1880s. *The Chronicles of Baltimore* (1874) adhered to the older annalistic approach, with Scharf informing his readers that "the only plan in the work that has been followed has been to chronicle events through the years in their order; beginning with the earliest in which any knowledge on the subject is embraced, and running on down to the present."(115) Written by a "native here and to the manor born," the *Chronicles* were "a labor of love, of pride, of sympathy, of ambition," prepared as "a public necessity and a benefaction, nothing of a similar character having been placed before the public since 1829, when Griffith's 'Annals of Baltimore' was published," and to which *Chronicles* were an enlargement.(116)

When *The History of Baltimore City and County* appeared in 1881, Scharf disclosed that the work was undertaken at the request of Major Louis H. Everts, an "enterprising publisher in Philadelphia." Scharf went on to catalogue with presumed precision the extent of his research. He consulted "the most reliable records and authorities"; addressed 2,500 "communications" to persons "supposed to be in possession of facts or information calculated to add value to the work"; traveled with "his agents" throughout the entire county, "examining ancient newspapers and musty manuscripts, conversing with aged inhabitants"; and consulted over 5,000 pamphlets, "consisting of town and city documents, reports of societies, corporations, associations."(117) Supported by a publisher and buttressed by assistants, Scharf shifted over to a more voguish topical approach in his 1881 history.(118)

In 1883, Scharf's *History of Saint Louis City and County* was published, once again by Everts. The lengthy preface reveals Scharf's sensitivity in moving far from his own area. Having made inquiries and surveyed the field, the author admitted he was "discouraged at first by the magnitude of the task," but "his generous and thoroughgoing publishers held out to him every possible inducement."(119) Scharf arranged and used the materials already collected by a local antiquarian, Frederic Billon, and added others to produce what he called "the most complete and satisfactory record, in its every department, which has ever been prepared and published in the United States of the growth, development, and expansion of a municipality." Scharf made this claim even with what he exaggeratedly called a "thorough knowledge of what has been done in New England and the East since the revival of public interest in and enthusiasm for local details."(120) He pointed to his linkage of St. Louis' local history to wider developments in the region and the nation, to the fullness of the materials on which his history was based, and to the range of institutions and activities dealt with as proof of his assertion.(121) Scharf thanked individual contributors for preparing particular segments of the history(122) and the subscribers for "consenting to take it unseen on the author's own recommendation and the strength of his and the publisher's reputation."(123) Of a history organized far more topically than chronologically, Scharf commented: "In no sense of the word is this work founded upon, built up out of, or repeated from any previous one on the same subject, or any of its branches. It is a new book, treating its theme in a new, comprehensive, and original manner."(124)

The following year, Everts published Scharf's *History of Philadelphia*, co-authored with Thompson Westcott, and Scharf used some of the same language to describe the preparation of this work. But he was far more specific on who contributed to the writing, admitting that "[several] of the themes or chapters . . . have been treated by those who have some particular association or long acquaintance with the subject."(125) Scharf named the contributors who had written specific portions of the text and singled out his co-author for special commendation. Scharf called Westcott's aid "indispensible" and referred to his "invaluable stores of material" diligently collected for thirty years and "used in every department of this work." Westcott also contributed "drawings, portraits, maps, plans, etc."; was "constantly consulted by all engaged in the preparation of the special chapters"; furnished "important suggestions, facts, and items"; and "read and corrected all the proofs, from the first page to the last."(126)

In preparing his histories of both St. Louis and Philadelphia, Scharf therefore relied on the materials gathered by local antiquarians, Frederic A. Billon and Thompson Westcott, who consented to his guidance and overall supervision. Their deference indicates that Scharf had a capacity to direct that others lacked. And though he appears to have been the sole author of the first state history to have been published under his name — that of his own state of Maryland, in 1879 (127) — by the time histories of western Maryland (i.e., its counties) (1882) and Westchester County, New York (1886), appeared, Scharf clearly relied on others for the preparation of sketches of the counties, as was also his final history, that of Delaware (1888), which consisted of sketches of counties as well and whose title page indicated that the author was "assisted by a staff of able assistants."(128) Like Winsor in *Memorial History of Boston*, Scharf, in his history of Westchester, assigned various chapters to writers, "most of them well known in their respective spheres, and some of them of national reputation," who are identified with their subjects "from study and association."(129)

Scharf's own writing reveals that he shared an awareness with other urban antiquarians of those factors that produced a modern city.(130) With good rail and water transportation, located between North and South, with an enterprising yet stable business community, Baltimore's ascendancy, Scharf believed, was assured.(131) Again, like other urban antiquarians, Scharf could not ignore the chief threat to urban progress: communal division that took the form of "mobs" and "riots,"(132) and he devoted an entire chapter to the rioting that occurred in Baltimore, as in other east coast cities, from the 1830s to the Civil War.

In the sheer variety of his projects and the persistence of his labors, Scharf stood out as an impresario of antiquarian endeavor. He was undoubtedly one of the most widely known local historians during the late nineteenth century. In him, the antiquarian impulse found its most frenzied outlet. His wide-ranging interests and great energy induced others, publishers and more modest antiquarians alike, to defer to him as one who could manage. City, county, and state histories were becoming vast enterprises requiring the contributions and assistance of many interested and knowledgeable individuals. Those who could direct such an undertaking came to be much sought after. J. Thomas Scharf was the earliest and most notable of a new breed of antiquarian: the editor.

# PART III
# Formulaic Local History

# CHAPTER 9
# Local History as a Publishing Venture

From its inception, local historical writing was published by subscription, as well as sold through bookstores. That is, individuals agreed to buy in advance one or more copies of the completed volume or volumes. In this way, antiquarians proceeded with some assurance that, at least, the cost of publication would be covered. Actual profit was more likely to accrue to those who found an aggressive publisher or who were favored with the financial support—either in the form of subscriptions or direct subsidies—of libraries, historical societies, or a government, whether at the town, city, county, or state level.

One of the problems confronted by the local antiquarians who wrote histories was how to retain their independence, their sense of objectivity and fairness in a context in which the financial success of their project depended on the support of particular individuals, institutions, or governments. This problem was one shared by all who wrote with advanced subscribers instead of unknown buyers, but was particularly acute for a group whose writings were focused on the same people who supported them. Antiquarians were intent on being factual and accurate, on describing individuals, institutions, and activities in a manner and to an extent that seemed appropriate, given their knowledge of the entire history of their community. What if this treatment was in any way unsatisfactory to their financial supporters? How could an antiquarian favor their benefactors through unmerited—that is, unfairly enlarged or favorable—coverage of their subscribers' lives or historical interests without undermining their sense of themselves as local historians of integrity and worth. Antiquarians struggled with this irresolvable problem through all the decades from the 1820s to the 1930s; to confront it was a natural part of their endeavors.

What limited the problem, and acted as a powerful countervailing force, was the natural rapport between the antiquarians and their subscribers: all were interested in the past and belonged to families with a sense of place and continuity and prominence, which itself derived partly from adherence to a particular community. The distinctions among subscriber, reader, contributor, and writer frequently were not clear.   When a person urged a fellow townsman or urbanite to write a history, pledged his financial support through an advanced subscription, provided information and materials, did research, made a contribution, and urged others to do the same, how separate was he from the actual writer — other than the writer's additional capacity and willingness to write for publication? All those who were in any way connected with the production of a local history shared a perception of their community's past and a willingness to work together for the preservation of a common heritage.

The problem local historians regularly confronted was how to reconcile their publicly stated commitment to accuracy and objectivity with the natural desire of all those who took part in their recapturing of the past to appear as model citizens of model families in a model community — all of which embodied those virtues esteemed by successful Americans.   Most antiquarians failed to arrive at a position as explicit and unambiguous as Augustus Gould and Frederic Kidder, who proclaimed that "to 'say nothing of the dead except what is good,' is an ancient and most charitable maxim; but it is by no means one which can be admitted in impartial history."(1) Or as William Boyd, who asserted (with stylistic crudity) that "it has been my intention not to give anything in this work, to reflect upon the character of persons, or hurt the feelings of their descendants.   Should there be an instance of that kind in the book, I humbly ask their pardon from unintentionally doing them an injury."(2)

As local historical writing steadily increased in popularity after the Civil War, several subscription book publishing firms were organized that specialized in presenting historical works.   These firms were primarily interested in profit, and so devised formulas that would appeal to large numbers of subscribers at a lucrative price and, in the process, reduced the writing of local history to simple sketches and flattering portraits, to that which did not offend the sensibilities of those with prominence and power — to what critics called the "mug book."   Local history so produced escaped altogether the problem of attaining fairness and proper proportions that plagued serious antiquarians.

George S. Cottman, in an article entitled "History to Order" (1911), assessed this phenomenon while it was at its height.(3)   Cottman noted that there were "at least two large publishing companies, each with an organized corps of men in the field."   The state (Indiana in Cottman's case) was divided into counties, and those selected were "those richest not in historical interest but in well-to-do farmers and hustling booming businessmen." Cottman found that the historical portion of the published work was secondary, "its chief value being its service in giving title and pretence to the book." Occasionally, these publishers selected "an old time resident" to write the history, but when such a person was not available, "a stock man or professional compiler is put in the field who has a happy faculty for scraping together fragments and rounding them into readable form in the expeditious style of one who can make good as a space-filler." These "histories" were in reality "loose, unconfirmed local traditions compiled in undigested form with a "view to readableness and flattering appeals to prospective purchasers of the work." Such compilers have "no idea whatever of what a local history ought to be, or the exact relation between its value and its truthfulness, and of the difficulties in getting at the truth." But, in any case, Cottman found that "the biographies are, from the publishers viewpoint, the all-important part of the work and the history merely a floater." For Cottman, "[t]he foundation of the whole publishing scheme is a certain pitiful human vanity" out of which these publishers make profit.  Local elites, "for the sake of a page or so about themselves," are persuaded to subscribe to the work for ten to twenty dollars.  Cottman added: "How adequately a community is represented by a discrimination so determined may be imagined." But he also believed that these publishers were skilled psychologists in their recognition that "what his patrons hunger and thirst for first of all is something flattering – something  . . . that will make him feel good while he is alive and look well after he is dead." Cottman discovered that the "corps of workers is trained accordingly." Interviewers collect "all the nice things" they can; sketch writers create word portraits "with the touch of an artist." Cottman concluded with statements showing his awareness of the larger social value of this kind of work: "Stock virtues and horrors are tacked onto the subject whenever possible.  He must by all means be a 'prominent citizen' and the merits monotonously attributed to him are such as folks on a certain plain think everyone ought to have."(4)

Oscar Lewis, who himself wrote a narrative history of San Francisco in 1931,(5) assessed mug books when the phenomenon was in decline, during the Great Depression.(6) Lewis wrote in a "muckraking" style, in prose exaggerated for effect.  He called the "mug book racket," in its "heyday," during the 1870s, 1880s, and 1890s, one of the largest and most profitable phases of American publishing.  He claimed that the "larger companies often had a score of crews in the field at the same time, and hence that many histories in active preparation." Those who wrote the "histories" – perhaps a "dispirited    ex-newspaperman,"    or    "some    bright    college    youth    on vacation" – remained "a week or two" in a county and "threw together" their text.  If there were preexisting histories to draw on, the writer "merely adapted that and added a paragraph here and there to bring it down to date." But, if he had the misfortune of being himself the pioneer historian," he interviewed a few old timers, cribbed from the state histories, and ran through the files of the local newspaper." The resulting "histories" commonly took up the first fifty pages of the book to be published, the remaining four or five hundred pages consisted of portraits and biographies of the county's "leading citizens." Who were the leading citizens?: "[T]here was but one gauge of prominence.  The man who subscribed for the book passed the test; the skinflint who refused to subscribe, even though he owned three-quarters of the county and had served in the State Legislature was left out."

Lewis attributed the decline of the mug book business after the turn of the century to "excessive competition." So many publishers tried to compete that "the ground began to be covered at too frequent intervals." Lewis thought that the mug book publishers had been "hit hard by the depression" of the 1930s.  But he found they were still optimistic, "and for an excellent reason." For, these publishers offered more than mere books:

they offered a man "a chance to inflate his ego in public, the opportunity to read . . . the stirring chronicle of his life, and to know that others, including his enemies, are reading it too." Lewis had already observed several modifications in practice as evidence that these publishers would likely survive the depression. They had sometimes increased the size of the territory covered, to include several counties or a section of a state. They had at times persuaded a local person of some prominence to serve as overall editor, "thus giving [the work] the appearance of a purely local enterprise." And they had also exhibited a "growing tendency" to include biographies not only of luring notables, "but of those recently deceased." Lewis noticed that "[b]ereaved widows, if they are approached soon enough, can very often be persuaded that no memorial to the departed is quite so fitting as a eulogistic account of his life in the new county history." Lewis added: "Moreover, recent widows often have substantial cash balances in the bank."(7)

On the positive side, Marjorie Stafford, in *Subscription Book Publishing in the United States, 1865-1930*,(8) observed that "[in] many cases these books represent the first important effort toward the preservation of local history by publication. No one looks to them, however, for literary or historical scholarship."(9) L. B. Hill in his privately printed history of the Lewis Publishing Company (1938) — one of the two largest of these firms — indicated that the value of this type of publication "is measured directly in proportion as they contain local chronicles written from the standpoint of the participants." Hill conceded that the "historians who set down these impressions may have erred as to proportion and perspective but they were quite diligent and faithful in drawing the picture as the patrons of the book believed it to be."(10) In other words, this kind of historical writing did not involve the inclusion of conscious or deliberate inaccuracies or falsehoods. The agents and writers hired to perform certain functions in a standardized way tried to be truthful, but were dependent upon information taken from subscribers and so presented accounts that were congenial to those who paid, accounts written from the perspective of the patrons and not out of sensitivity to proper emphasis and proportion.

These subscription firms were centered in Chicago, and the kind of history Cottman, Lewis, and Stafford assessed was largely, though not exclusively, a Midwestern phenomenon. The largest of these publishers were S. J. Clarke and Lewis, but others were prominent in particular states. The mix of the most active firms varied from state to state. In Michigan, Lewis, Clarke, and Chapman (Chicago) were about equally involved. In Ohio, W. H. Beers (Chicago) and Lewis were especially busy, Clarke less so. In Indiana, Lewis and a local publisher, Bowen of Indianapolis, dominated. In Illinois, Munsell (Chicago) was particularly active, hiring Newton Bateman to serve as editor for many of its histories; Clarke was less so, and Lewis was scarcely in evidence. In Wisconsin, Western History Company (Chicago) was the leader, along with Clarke, and, to a lesser extent, Lewis. In Minnesota, two different companies stood out: Bowen (Indianapolis) and H. C. Cooper (Chicago). In Iowa, Clarke was most prominent, followed by Bowen and Western. In Missouri, Clarke and Lewis shared the field with Goodspeed (Chicago) and the local National History Company (St. Louis). In Texas, Lewis was practically alone. In the Northeast, Clarke and Lewis shared the market with such regional firms as J. W. Lewis of Philadelphia, which hired Duane Hamilton Hurd in the 1880s to compile and edit county histories in parts of New England (particularly in Massachusetts, Connecticut, and New Hampshire), and D. Mason of Syracuse, which hired Lewis Cass Aldrich in the 1890s to do the same thing in the same area (particularly in Vermont).

Actually, the county histories that Lewis and Clarke and the other, smaller firms produced varied considerably in format. Some were accounts that balanced a general history of the county, histories of towns and cities within the county, and biographical sketches of prominent individuals. Others were primarily biographical records, with briefer historical sections added. It was the second type that Cottman, Lewis, Stafford, and Hill, as well as John Tebbel, in *A History of Book Publishing in the United States*,(11) all dwell upon. In either format, the publishers involved explain and defend their work in the way Hill did in his study of the Lewis Publishing Company, carefully avoiding any indication that they were primarily motivated by the expectation of profit, as Cottman and Lewis argued.

The Goodspeed Publishing Company indicated in the preface to one of its county histories that "this volume has been prepared in response to the prevailing and popular demand for the preservation of local history and biography." The publisher asserted that the "method of preparation followed is the most successful and the most satisfactory yet devised."(12) B. F. Bowen explained in a preface to one of its county histories that a "sincere purpose to preserve facts and personal memoirs that are deserving of perpetuation . . . is the motive for the present publication." Bowen insisted that the work was prepared by "able writers who have, after much patient study and research, produced here the most complete biographical memoirs . . . ever offered to the public." The publisher pointed with pride to "the sketches of representative citizens of this county whose records deserve publication because of their worth, effort, and accomplishment." Bowen revealed that "[e]very biographical sketch . . . has been submitted to the party interested, for correction, and therefore any error of fact, if there be any, is solely due to the person for whom the sketch was prepared." The publisher was "confident that our efforts to please will fully meet the approbation of the public."(13)

Chapman Brothers, in their biographically oriented *Portrait and Biographical Record of Buchanan and Clinton Counties, Missouri*,(14) disclosed that "instead of going to musty records, and taking therefrom dry statistical matter that can be appreciated by but a few, our corps of writers have gone to the people, the men and women who have, by their enterprise and industry, brought the county to rank second to none." Aware of the larger significance of what they were doing, the Chapmans announced that in "this volume will be found a record of many whose lives are worthy [of] the imitation of coming generations. . . . It tells of those in every walk of life who have striven to succeed, and records how that success has usually crowned their efforts."(15)

One of the two largest of these firms, the Lewis Publishing Company, was founded by Benjamin and Samuel Lewis in 1886. At first, they decided to publish histories of counties in the Midwest in conjunction with the Chapman Brothers and the histories of three counties in Illinois — Knox (1878), Tazewell (1879), and Pike (1880) — were published by the Chapmans, having been worked on by the Lewises in addition to their regular duties for different publishing firms. The Lewis brothers established their own firm — the Interstate Publishing Company — in 1880 and published histories of counties in Michigan, Ohio, Indiana, Illinois, Kentucky, and Iowa before assuming the name of Lewis Publishing Company in 1886, and moving farther afield with histories of counties in California (1888), Texas (1892), New Jersey (1897), and New York and Pennsylvania thereafter.(16)

An important figure in this kind of publishing was the book agent. As Marjorie Stafford explains: "[It] was the custom for publishers to send agents into certain counties, where, through interviews with citizens, they obtained facts for their biographies and at the same time secured orders for the publication.(17) Downing P. O'Harra, in *Book Publishing in the United States, 1860 to 1901*, described the "instructed book agent."(18) The publishing house prepared "[a]ll his speeches" and prescribed "[t]he manner in which he approached a door, the distance he stepped back from the screen door when the lady appeared, the way he presented his speech, how he handled his order blank, the manner in which he closed a sale." Agents were even instructed to study "[a]ll the possible ways in which maids could be induced to let an agent in a house." O'Harra described this "new type of book agent" at the turn of the century "as one who was well-dressed, carried his stock in his suitcase (or carried only a prospectus), was above the average in education, and whose earnings varied from $3,000 to $12,000 a year."(19)

Nathan Wilson was a book agent for the Lewises in the 1890s, a rather successful independent agent, who acted as a canvasser in various counties all over the central third of the nation. In voluminous surviving correspondence between Wilson and his publishers, as well as other agents, every facet of an agent's work is described. The Lewises carefully explained each arrangement made with Wilson. For example, in Kansas City, Missouri: "If you are willing to undertake the work there on $3.75 per order on your weekly reports, and $5.00 per order on cash collections on delivered orders, we shall be glad to have you do so."(20) Or, for Texas: "We are advancing you in Texas on a $20.00 book a commission of 25% or $5.00 per order, and will give you credit upon cash collections for one-third of cash receipts, which equals 33 1/3% on collected orders, less the amount advanced."(21) The Lewises tried to maintain the income of their favored canvassers in the lull between active periods, and, on occasion, allowed Wilson cash advances on orders for volumes planned, but not yet written: "As we have no fresh territory for you at this time, we will concede the advance, in order that you may keep employed, and at the same time receive fair compensation for your labors."(22) Sometimes the advances were not based on orders at all: "Eight dollars seems to be a small remittance, so with your permission we will make it $15, which you will be able to cover during the present work."(23)

Much time and energy went into setting up new and profitable territory for canvassers like Wilson.(24) But, sometimes the Lewises simply did not have any territory to assign Wilson: "The territory we now have open is pretty well covered or provided for, and just at present we cannot say what new field we can give you, until new territory is opened, and the canvass started."(25) The Lewises even on occasion asked Wilson to decide: "So after thinking the matter over and looking over these maps . . . we leave the question with you as to whether you go into Ross County, or into Pike."(26) Others provided Wilson with information on whether a territory was good or bad for canvassing: Michigan, no; Minnesota, yes;(27) Texas, probably.(28)

Lewis could be quite specific about the prospects for canvassing in particular areas, both encouraging(29) and discouraging.(30) Canvassers sometimes found new territory to have been already overworked.(31) By contrast, other areas, especially urban ones, were continuously fruitful: "My opinion of Chicago work is that there are still lots of good men to write in the city and county, and that is about as good territory as one can find anywhere."(32)

Wilson's correspondence is full of information about the various facets of canvassing.  Canvassers needed equipment: "We send you by American express today to Jackson, Minnesota, prospectus, contracts, scratch pads, and envelopes."(33) They needed atlases by which to plot territory.(34) They sought out prominent persons to write letters of introduction.  A fellow canvasser wrote to Wilson that he was enclosing "a letter from Mr. Todd addressed to a leading man in that town [Montpelier, Indiana].  . . .  I have not seen Mr. Dougherty yet, but will call on him today and see if he knows of anyone he can give me a letter to for you.  Let me know how you make out."(35) Wilson at one point carried around such a letter signed by John F. Dayton and L. W. Hersey of Wauken, Allamakee County, Iowa, dated November 9, 1895:

> This is to introduce Mr. N. H. Wilson representing the Lewis Publishing Company of Chicago, who is engaged in gathering data for the compilation of the "Memorial and Biographical Record of Iowa" which will be a work of undoubted value for future reference, and I desire to recommend him to the favorable consideration of all in encouragement of his work.(36)

The canvasser's first task was to take orders, to find subscribers. Wilson used an order form for signatures:

NUMBER _____          _____1894
               THE LEWIS PUBLISHING COMPANY

Please enter my name as a subscriber to your forthcoming work,
entitled "Portrait and Biographical Record of Scioto Valley,
embracing the Counties of Ross, Pike, Scioto, Highland and
Adams, for which I promise to pay to your order Fifteen Dollars,
when delivered at my residence or place of business. I base this
order on what is promised in your prospectus, a copy of which I
have.


               Name _____


               County _____ Address _____(37)

     Lewis asked its canvassers to prepare weekly reports(38) as well as to
provide biographies of the subscribers. The Lewises asked Wilson: "Will you
kindly send to us by express the biographi[ies] for the 27 orders you have
reported from Highland County."(39) The Lewises provided their canvassers
a "memorandum of instructions" put together by the in-house biographers
who wrote the finished sketches, "giving some points the writer of these
sketches wishes to impress upon your mind, and which no doubt will enable
you to prepare your notes so that they will be more acceptable to the
writer of your sketches."(40) Lewis told Wilson that "[it] is the custom of
our men usually and we think preferable, that they keep their original
notes, and copy their sketches each week, upon other pads, very
carefully."(41)
     The procedure Lewis favored was for Wilson "to forward the sketches
here and let us put them in type-written form and return to you, and then
when you get back to see the party you can say to them that you return
to revise and complete the biography which you have prepared."(42) The
Lewises even agreed to publish biographies prepared by Wilson of persons
from whom he was unable to obtain a subscription, "providing we are short
on matter for that county,"(43) though ordinarily "there is too great an
element of uncertainty with unsigned orders to pay [a commission] on them
or to even publish the sketches."(44)
     There was no objection to canvassers' taking information from existing
sketches: "It would be well for you to secure [a] sketch of Wells from [the]
State Biographical sketch as you suggest[ed] when passing through
Cin[cinatti --] as we have no sketch of him."(45) But the Lewises were
uneasy about extensive copying: "We do not recommend that you take data
from the old book, but had much rather you would get new data for a
sketch and where occasion requires, weave in such interesting matter as
may be necessary from the old work."(46)
     Subscriptions and biographies were closely linked. The Lewises told
Wilson: "An order isn't worth the paper on which it is printed unless the
sketch is obtained."(47) It is evident that Wilson took the preparation of
biographies seriously and even criticized the work of those in the
publisher's office who rewrote what canvassers like himself submitted. The

Lewises admitted that "[we] think your points are well taken, and it may serve as a guide in writing the biographies of your patrons."(48)

Wilson regularly submitted a form on his sketches:

DAILY REPORT OF SKETCHES WRITTEN
SOLICITOR  SKETCH NO.   SUBJECT'S NAME  NO. PAGES
EDITION


TOTAL

SIGNED(49)


The Lewises were willing to use sketches and portraits of famous individuals as an inducement for others to subscribe.(50) A fellow canvasser, working in close proximity, told Wilson: "I have taken three of [your orders] to use in my order book. . . .   I wanted the names of your prominent subs[cribers] to put in my order book."(51) As Wilson moved into a new territory, Lewis reminded him "that but two orders have been taken at the county seat and they were complimentary.   We send the orders herein so that you can put them in your order book to quote."(52)

But, beyond this concession, Lewis hoped that their canvassers would collect the subscription fee as indicated on the order forms.   The publisher opposed "time cards," or delayed payment schemes, calling them "poor property," hoping "you will give us just as few of them as possible and under no condition let them exceed 15% of the orders taken."(53) The Lewises were far more adamant about their canvassers' avoiding "conditional orders."   Wilson wrote on one agreement: "Privilege of cancelling contract when sketch is returned to house – N. H. Wilson, Biographer."(54) The Lewises emphatically informed Wilson "that not one of your conditional orders were worth the paper upon which they were written."(55)

The canvasser-biographer was only one member of a two-man operation.   Lewis sent "portrait men" around the territory the canvassers had already covered.   The "portrait men" tried to persuade subscribers to pay for photographic portraits as a further indication of prominence beyond that provided by the brief biographies. At one point the Lewises wrote to Wilson that "[our] idea now is for the portrait man to call on every subscriber and submit his sketch and endeavor to portrait those who are able and proper subjects.   This plan we believe will give the largest profit to both solicitor and company."(56)

First the canvasser-biographers and then the portrait men worked over a common territory, with the Lewises trying to keep the whole operation going with efficiency and without confusion.(57) The other members of the team were the "deliverers," those who handed over the published volumes to the subscribers.   The Lewises instructed Wilson to "kindly mark on the map the location of the residents from whom orders are taken, so that it can be preserved to aid the deliverers."(58)

Nathan Wilson was a peripatetic but persistent canvasser who over a three or more year period became one of the Lewis firm's more experienced field workers.   But Wilson was independent in his ways and rather frequently tried out new procedures and sometimes exasperated his publisher in the process.   In his early days with the Lewises, the publishers gave him regular pep talks in an effort to boost his morale: "We wish you to be in good cheer and not throw up the sponge, even if you have a few weeks of temporary adversity, it will average up all right in the end."(59) Or: "We however believe a turn in the tide of your affairs will set in and doubtless that change will come during the present week. . . .   We sincerely hope Mr. Wilson that you will be able to do some paying work.   We will gladly do all in our power to render you assistance."(60) Or: "It goes by streaks in both book and portrait work.   It will be better with you later."(61)

As time went on, the Lewises recognized Wilson's experience.(62) And Wilson's fellow canvassers also praised his work.   Said D. F. Smith: "I hope you will make a go of it among the hoosiers and think with your industry, pluck, and intelligence you will make it win."(63) Theodore B. Du Bois, the canvasser Wilson was closest to, wrote: "I think your list of orders last week is remarkable considering the territory in which you are working.   I hope you will do as well this week.   B. F. Lewis spoke very highly of you when he was in Auburn with me."(64) As Wilson became a seasoned canvasser, his publisher even on occasion indulged in friendly banter.(65)

And yet, the business relationship between Wilson and the Lewises was strained at times as well.   Wilson's very ability and independence – his success – worked against smoothly functioning arrangements.   The most persistent problem, one that produced flurries of notes and letters from the Lewises, was Wilson's habit of tardily submitting his biographical sketches: "[Please] forward them at once that they may be put in shape for submitting. . . .   Please don't neglect to forward them."(66) The Lewises explained the importance of Wilson's sending biographies on time: "If you fall into the habit of leaving these things until a convenient time, there will be no end of trouble, and there will always be a certain percentage of your orders for which you will have no sketch."(67) Even with this explanation, Wilson failed to change his practice, and the Lewises badgered him for sketches again and again.(68) Sometimes the publishers showed their exasperation openly: "[We] are sadly disappointed to find that you did not enclose biograph[ies] for the orders you have already reported and about which there has been so much correspondence ....   Now Mr. Wilson please don't write us that you will send them at a given time, but just make a package of them and send to us at once, please."(69)

Another source of friction was Wilson's practice of making new or special arrangements with prospective subscribers.   The Lewises were particularly upset by contracts with time-delayed payments: "If one gets in the habit of making concessions it becomes an easy matter to do and a difficult matter to take an order without some form of concession.   Our experience is that the man who sticks closest to the contract succeeds best in the long run."(70) The Lewises later complained to Wilson that 20 per cent of his contracts involved time-delayed payments, which was much too high, something "that has always been a source of disatisfaction and annoyance. . . .   With 30 or 40 men in the field you can readily see that if each one gave that number of extensions our credit business would be larger than any firm could carry. . . .   We refer to this pleasantly and would not mention it at all if our business interests did not absolutely demand it." The Lewises asked Wilson that in the future "in giving time it would be well if you could make the payment at some definite time from the date of the order in place of making it from date of delivery and always specify that it is to be settled by note with interest."(71)

The most serious disagreement between Lewis and Wilson was over territory for Wilson to canvass, a disagreement so serious that Wilson stopped working for the Lewises in the summer of 1896, though he returned in 1899.   Wilson wanted to canvass in Canton, Ohio, after finishing his work in Akron, but his publishers refused to agree with his proposal, arguing that they were not yet ready to assign Wilson to that city, having already sent others there.(72)  Wison argued that he had instructions from the firm to go to Canton, something the firm denied.(73)  As the dispute escalated, Theodore Du Bois, Wilson's closest friend among the Lewises' canvassers, wrote in alarm: "Now, old boy, don't let your angry passions rise, but hold them down and you will be better off.   The tone of both your letters [is] somewhat [worrisome] and I am fearful lest you do or say something that may injure you with the company."(74) But Du Bois' admonition went unheeded, for Wilson submitted his resignation.   The Lewises regretted "very much that you have taken the ill-advised and hasty action. . . .   You have a mistaken idea about your assignment in Ohio. The territory in question was never assigned to you, and we cannot see from the conversation held with you in this office, how you could have supposed that you were to go to Canton."(75)

Du Bois wrote: "I am sorry you have quit the Lewis Pub[lishing] Co[mpany] and hope that something will turn up between you and them that will again place you in the field. . . .   Now that B. F. [Lewis] has returned I should think that you could go to work without lowering dignity."   But when it became clear to Du Bois that Wilson had in fact resigned, Wilson's friend said "[it] seems strange to me that you and the Lewis' do not get along well together.   They are losing money all the time by sending green men into the field and for this reason I should think that they would appreciate a man that they knew they could trust."(76) Still hopeful, Du Bois added that B. F. Lewis would be seeing him soon, and "I will not be slow to tell him what I think of the way you have been treated." Du Bois promised Wilson that "I will use my influence with him to see if things can be made right between you and the co[mpany], and I hope that something I may say will be the means of bringing you back into the fold."(77)

In the aftermath of Wilson's resignation, other difficulties arose. When Du Bois talked to B. F. Lewis, the publisher argued that Wilson was "unjust" in claims for compensation he made on work done.   Lewis was upset about an "itemized bill" containing charges "for which you are in no way entitled to compensation." Nevertheless, Du Bois felt Lewis "will settle with you if you are reasonable in your demands," rather than "have a lawsuit." So, Du Bois urged Wilson to "act judiciously" and "bring about a settlement that will be agreeable all around." Du Bois acted as Wilson's friend in this matter, but he asked that he not quote me in any reference to your trouble, because it would injure my standing with the company if you did."(78)

Wilson and Lewis doubtless resolved their disagreements, because Wilson returned a few years later. But the difficulties between the publisher and the canvasser indicate how unsettled and precarious the publishing of local history by formula was. The mid-1890s were depressed years economically and though at one point the Lewises reported to Wilson that "[our] business seems to be improving all along the line and we hope that a new era of prosperity is beginning to dawn on this depressed people," news of the state of the publishing business was usually of a negative character. At first Lewis tried to explain Wilson's lack of success. Perhaps a previous canvasser soliciting for an earlier history "was a little crooked and took too many orders." Or perhaps that canvasser's "work may have been only in the township you are now working and when you enter another township you may find entirely different results."(79) The Lewises also noticed "with regret that you have encountered some opposition in your work because of previous publications at that point."(80) But, before long Wilson received reports from co-workers about the Lewises' laying off canvassers and abandoning territories.(81) The Lewises themselves had to admit that "[all] hands have to hustle for everything they get."(82) Even political campaigns seemed to effect sales adversely. As one canvasser put it: "There is so much politics in the air now that it makes it more difficult to do business."(83)

The Lewis brothers had a clear view of who their most likely subscribers were: "People that are out of debt will most of them survive financially and are good subjects for our work."(84) The publishing firm was equally clear on who constituted a bad prospect: "You certainly did the wise thing by not taking orders from those young and irresponsible business and professional men who have only recently come to town. No one should be called on for an order unless he is in law collectible. Irresponsible subscribers are by far worse than none at all."(85)

The firm sometimes received cancellations from signed subscribers if canvassers like Wilson made such an action part of the agreement. As one wrote: "I hereby notify you to drop my name from your list of patrons. As I don't feel that I am able to pay for the history under the present pressure of hard times. Your biographer Wilson gave the right to withdraw my name."(86) Hoped-for subscribers sometimes died. A fellow canvasser — D. F. Smith — wrote Wilson that "[the] sick widow Ward whom I hoped to sell a [steel plate] for her deceased husband died yesterday, and now when the proper time comes I will have to try the family for something."(87)

The Lewises sometimes gave specific advice on the sort of people Wilson would do well to solicit: "If you can't get them started in town would it not be well to feel of the farmers. They are as a rule well to do and may come down hands only."(88) Fellow canvasser Theodore B. Du Bois provided additional advice, writing that he enclosed "the name of the only [doctor] on my list so far. He is a good one and may help you."(89) D. F. Smith "found Judge Granger a very pleasant old gentleman and offered him a [steel plate for a portrait] at a low price, but failed to get him as he wanted to do about as the other members of the bench did in this and as only one of the others was sub[scriber] I let the matter drop."(90)

Nathan Wilson was, of course, only one of many canvassers who worked for Lewis.    There were many sources of tension, many sorts of problems between the firm and its army of field workers, given the complex set of procedures that defined the kind of publishing the Lewises engaged in.    Sometimes a complete break between the Lewises and a particular canvasser ocurred: "I am led to believe [Townsend] to be anything but an honorable and fair minded man and I want no more of him in any line of work.   This is the third time he has served us in a similar manner."(91) The Lewises told Wilson what the firm expected of its canvassers: "[It] is very unsatisfactory to ourselves and the deliverers to have any unpaid bills left by the canvassers.   We expect all bills for board and livery to be paid each week, as certified to in the weekly reports. You see how essential this is in order that we may keep good faith with the public."(92)

Wilson's surviving correspondence reveals the many ways the Lewises' canvassers related to one another in the course of their work for the firm. They assisted each other in a prescribed manner by passing on subscription lists to others who were assigned to contiguous territories.   Du Bois told Wilson: "I enclose a list of my subs[cribers] to use as reference and I think they will help you as they are all prominent men."(93) The list could be used as an inducement for others to subscribe.   Sometimes they wanted to "know by return mail what the outlook is in that town."(94) On occasion, they confided in each other, relating information about the publishing firm, other canvassers, or advice on the best arrangments with the Lewises concerning a particular assignment.   Smith wrote Wilson that "I prefer . . . you say nothing about this information or the source of it to the house [the Lewises]."(95)

Some of the Lewises' canvassers not only knew one another, but became friends, to the point that they sought out each others' company, wrote to each other frequently, and visited as often as they could arrange to do so.   "If you pass through here on your way to a new field, could you drop off the train and stay all night with me?" Smith asked Wilson.(96) Du Bois appreciated Wilson's "kind invitation to visit [on] Sunday but I will have to decline with thanks as our son has just got a tooth through and I am devoting all my leisure time watching for another to come.   As you are not encumbered with a large family I would like to have you come and spend Sunday with me.  I will expect you without fail."(97)

Wilson's fellow canvassers, Smith and Du Bois, appear to have genuinely admired him and his efforts and hoped he was comfortable and successful, that (as Smith put it) "they will come your way in paying numbers and that you are 'domiciled' in comfortable quarters."(98) On one occasion, Smith referred to Wilson's getting "as many [subscribers] as any person could have gotten" and to Wilson's "industry, perseverance, and excellent tact."(99) Du Bois reported that "I am living in your old rooms in Dr. Lyon's house and eating with Mrs.  Deverma.   Everyone has a good word for Wilson in Huntington.   They say you were such a genteel nice sweet pretty young man."(100)

Smith and Du Bois sometimes went further and actively assisted Wilson. Smith said that "I would like to talk over your work with you . . and shall be glad if you will come and spend the day here."(101) Du Bois even "wrote to the Lewis Co. last week asking them if you [were] not employed in other territory to send you to this city [Kansas City]."(102) Du Bois sent out another request in March(103) and in June was still hoping Wilson could join him.(104) Persisting, Du Bois asked in July that Wilson be sent to Akron.(105)

The friendship of Wilson, Du Bois, and Smith was not unique. The Lewises' canvassers were generally companionable, out of the circumstances of their work if not by inclination. They regularly reported news of each other in their letters. Du Bois praised Wilson as a correspondent: "[How] do you find time to write so often and such long letters?"(106) Du Bois himself wrote: "It is now past 11 o'clock p.m. and owing to a three hour snooze I had after supper I am unable to go to sleep so I decided to drop you a line and let you know how the work is going among your subs[cribers] in this town."(107)

Wilson's friends even assessed each other. Smith thought "Du Bois must be a hurricane. Bly told me he was a very strong man and his work certainly shows it." But, he added: "I doubt if he could make such a record in this state among the scattered lists I have had to work."(108) At times, the canvassers revealed deeply felt concern for one another. Du Bois asked Wilson: "What's the matter with Bly[?] [Has] he lost his grip again or is his health poor again.[?]"(109) At another point, Smith said: "I am sorry to hear that Bly is in such hard luck. I will write to him next week and see if he will allow me to return a favor he rendered me when I was almost an entire stranger to him."(110)

The Lewises' canvassers relied on each other for companionship during stints sometimes lasting for months, and if without a wife or children (as Wilson was during his first years with the company), depended upon visits from fellow workers as the only means of interrupting their isolation. Smith told Wilson: "You will not be so lonesome now that you can enjoy the good fellowhip of those two good fellows [Caldwell and Ward]." He added: "If you folks were not so far away I would run up some night and visit you. Give my regards to Vriet and Hilliard."(111)

But the Lewises' canvassers were sometimes critical of one another and noted in detail what they regarded as the failings or improper business practices of each other.(112) Smith reported that "Bertram was still there sucking whiskey, smoking cigarettes and working a little."(113) Du Bois wrote that "[my] opinion of Dunbar has gone down. [In] fact I am so mad at the way you say he treated Bly that I would like to tell him what I think of him."(114) On another occasion, Du Bois revealed: "I know Ward has played me for a sucker and I don't expect to ever get a cent I loaned him."(115) He later added: "Ward has not paid me a dollar of what he borrowed."(116) Du Bois found others to criticize: "Poor Teeple is gone to the dogs sure. He was drunk the whole time Mr. B. F. Lewis was in Cleveland, and I never saw a more disgusted man than B. F. was."(117)

The correspondence between Wilson and other canvassers also reveals how it felt to be alone when assigned to an area apart from the rest of the Lewises' crew.   Smith wrote: "I wish you had remained here and helped me finish.   I was awful lonesome Friday night, and wandered about here like a 'cat in a strange garret.'"(118) Smith was delighted that Wilson had "the society of a 'charming young lady,' [She] will doubtless help you to while away some of the otherwise long and lonesome hours."(119) In addition to confessions about lonesomeness, there were also disclosures about hard work and the discouragement that came from a lack of sales. Du Bois wrote: "I worked hard all day today and did not do a *darn* thing."(120) But some reports were of a positive character, especially at those times when all the elements of a canvasser's life seemed to be in balance or harmony.(121) What sustained a canvasser, Du Bois thought, was hope: "I am each day expecting better results, but you know how it goes. If it were not for hope what would a fellow do in this world; I hope more than any other man on earth, but I rarely have my hopes realized."(122)

Wilson and the canvassers with whom he corresponded were well aware of the wider world of subscription publishing within which the Lewis Publishing Company operated and sometimes commented on the Lewises and their rivals. Smith thought that "Lewis is the best house.   I have no use for Goodspeed's and not much for Chapman, but Beers is a good fellow. Like you, I prefer to stick to Lewis unless I am quite sure of bettering myself."(123) Awareness of other firms was important in case a canvasser wanted to change jobs.   For instance, when Smith got restless and considered leaving the Lewises, he disclosed that "I think Bowen and Co. are all right financially.   Charles Ellis worked for them and liked them very well.   I may go and portrait a county in Ohio for them if they accept my terms unless something better shows up."(124) However, after opening negotiations, Smith changed his opinion: "I have not heard from Bowen and begin to think he is not much of a business man."(125) Dealings with other firms were no more reassuring.   Du Bois reported that Ward "will quit working for [S. J.] Clark at the end of this week if he can get enough money to pay RR fare to Chicago to look for another job.   He don't tell me the reason he don't get his pay, but he says he is broke, and that Clark will not give him enough money to pay his own expenses."(126)

The life of Wilson and his fellow canvassers at Lewis Publishing Company was transitory, nomadic, competitive, restless, sometimes satisfactory, but often lonely and depressing.   It was, in sum, the life of a salesman, of gatherers and sellers, of book peddlers who were the front men in the commercial enterprise that local historical writing often became during the late nineteenth and early twentieth centuries.

The commercialized nature of much, though never all, local historical writing from the Civil War to the Great Depression clearly mirrored wider developments in American life during this period.   There was in these decades increasing evidence of the standardization, commercialization, bureaucratization, and nationalization of products and activities of many kinds.(127) What had been local in character became regional and national in scope.   Something as highly idiosyncratic as the production of a local history could not remain wholly apart from these pervasive tendencies. When various publishers located in Chicago perceived themselves to be a profitable vehicle for the preservation of innumerable local pasts covering many cities and rural-dominated counties fanning out over vast stretches of the continent from their mid-American focal point, the ironic result was a formulaic, standardized local history, scorned by true antiquarians.

These developments in local historical writing were almost exactly duplicated in the production of wall maps and published atlases (of towns, cities, counties, and states) both of which were also reduced to a formula and made commercially successful by Midwestern firms after the Civil War. Paid-for illustrations of houses, farms, and businesses to establish prominence; teams of itinerant artists, lithographers, and salesmen working to a predetermined standard; and the uneasy blending of rather idealized visual depictions for promotional purposes with a concomittant concern for accuracy(128) all found their counterpart in the kind of local history published by such firms as Lewis and Clark.

However, both the serious amateur and the profit-minded publisher shared a need to awaken and nurture the interest, historical contributions, and financial support of those who were prominent in a given locality. Serious amateurs chose advance subscription pledges and unpaid, voluntary contributions to their research. Commercial publishers used paid staff for research and writing and reduced the role of the established inhabitants to the payment of a subscription fee in return for the creation of an immediate kind of personal, historical stature. Contemporary prominence was, in this way, meshed with historical noteworthiness to produce for future generations a lasting fame based upon an ability to pay, or at least an interest in doing so. The result was, nevertheless, a fairly accurate portrait gallery of who was in fact important in a particular community, since a person's power and influence were so closely linked to wealth in these years.

# CHAPTER 10
# Local History as an Editorial Project

A more developed and sophisticated version of local history by formula occurred when publishing firms appointed a locally prominent general editor to supervise the preparation of a city's history, an editor who, in turn, persuaded the most knowledgeable persons on particular aspects of a community life either to provide information or a finished piece of writing. Such publishing ventures were confined to cities or, occasionally, urbanized counties, that is, to areas with the population and range to warrant such an investment on the part of a publisher. For these, like the more simplistic, formulaic county histories of the same period, were basically commercial undertakings, with the objective an assured profit, though the firms involved did not always rely on advanced subscription sales.

Larger, more populated communities had a more complicated past. The simple formulas that served in rural county histories as companion pieces for the paid-for biographical sketches were not appropriate to urban areas, which required more substantive accounts if interested publishers were to give the appearance of dealing historically with the various dimensions of city life. Oscar Lewis, in his assessment of the 1930s, referred to the practice of these publishers "persuading some local man, or judge or a superintendent of schools or state senator, to place his name on the title-page as author, thus giving it the appearance of a purely local enterprise."(1) Indeed, one of the most active of the publishing firms, S. J. Clarke, established the practice of indicating the location of the firm as being in Chicago *and* wherever the history was about. But, though local people supervised and wrote these histories, the projects themselves were initiated, financed, planned, and designed by the publishers, not urban antiquarians.

In 1879, Harvard's librarian, Justin Winsor (who as a young man, in 1849, had produced a history of Duxbury, his hometown), worked out a plan with publisher Clarence Jewett of C. F. Jewett and Company and several others whereby the history of Boston would be done by a team of established writers, each of whom was particularly knowledgeable of the subject he was assigned to write on, all of whom would work under the supervision of an editor, according to a carefully devised arrangement. Winsor became the editor, under contract first to Jewett and later to James R. Osgood, who retained the original agreement.    Winsor was as commanding, persistent, and indefatigible an editor as he was a librarian (at the Boston Public Library before moving to Harvard).    His four-volume history (1880-81) became a model for others who attempted to encompass the past of other American metropolises during the decades that followed.

Forming a committee with Edward Hale and Samuel Green, Winsor sent out a letter to prospective "collaborators" to meet with the committee and the publisher on January 3, 1880.(2) In the letter, Winsor indicated that Boston would celebrate the two hundred and fiftieth anniversary of its settlement in September 1880, something that prompted C. F. Jewett and Company to plan a memorial history.    The proposal was for a work to be written in four volumes, "of at least five hundred pages each, to cost $40,000 in the production, and they expect to pay contributors." The organization of the volumes had already been determined, "and the wish is to have its various sections committed for preparation to those gentlemen best fitted from associations and from study" to write on particular facets of the city's history.    The committee "annexed" a list of collaborators: "You will find your name among them; and you are invited to meet with them for private conference."(3) In a circular written to be used to promote the sale of the history, Winsor summed up that his objective was to present an account of "the principal historical phases" of Boston's past, along with sections on the Indians and on the "natural history of the locality." The writers of all the sections "are in a measure identified with their subjects" and Winsor boasted that their treatments "may be taken as the best comprehensive expression of existing knowledge." He asserted that the "plan of the work is to a large extent novel."(4)

Winsor organized the proposed multiauthored history chronologically, but each epoch was subdivided into various subjects and the work's final section was entitled "Special Topics" that for some reason could not be as easily subdivided.    Winsor drew upon Boston's large "literary community" to be authors of the various sections and was quite successful in evoking positive responses.    Among those who responded were Brook Adams, Henry Adams, Charles Francis Adams, Jr., Oliver Wendell Holmes, Henry Cabot Lodge, and Thomas Wigglesworth Higginson. However, most of those whom Winsor persuaded to be contributors were not especially prominent either locally or nationally and lacked the independence of an Adams or the contrariness of a Higginson.    It is in the voluminous correspondence between the editor and these ordinary contributors that the complications and complexities of a multiauthored project on the scale of Winsor's come clearly into view.

Displaying the critical reaction contributors sometimes felt in response to Winsor's incessant stylistic revisions, E. L. Bynner returned the first proofs of his piece "in some points pretty well cut up.  I have rephrased several of the opening sentences as your vigorous cutting away had left them in a very bob-tailed condition that set my teeth on edge."(5) Bynner, tiring of the effort, returned the galley proofs with the message, echoed by others: "I have not had time to go over and verify the corrections you have made in my mss. but have let them go and shall fall back on you to 'rise and explain' if I am attacked by some zealous and savage antiquarian."(6)

At times, Winsor himself was overzealous, as when he made an agreement with Bynner concerning another segment of the volumes, but went on to make so many comments about Bynner's notes that Bynner felt Winsor had done his work for him.(7) Characteristically, Winsor instructed Bynner to continue as arranged, and, on January 13, 1881, Bynner mailed "the last few pages of my copy with a feeling of joy and relief which you know already too well by experience and which I could not describe if I would."(8)

Winsor's dealings with Henry Edes, treasurer of the New England Mutual Life Insurance Company, reveal the difficulties the editor had in keeping the submissions of contributors within established boundaries. Edes agreed to provide several sections on Charlestown, one of the established communities annexed by Boston as it became a metropolis during the nineteenth century. The relationship between Winsor and Edes began in a congenial way, with Edes writing "I will, with pleasure, write the sketch assigned me and will gladly do anything in my power to help on an enterprise so auspiciously .begun and in which I take a great interest."(9) But when Edes sent his first segment (on Charlestown from 1629 to 1696), Winsor discovered that it exceeded his page limit. Edes explained that since Frotheringham's earlier history and Drake's earlier sketch of the town in a history of Middlesex County were inadequate, he wanted to present a freshly written history based directly upon source material.(10) Apparently, Winsor was sufficiently impressed to revise his rule.

On December 14, 1880, Edes submitted his second segment on Charlestown. Once again, it was too long; once again he compiled reasons for its acceptance, unaltered. He obviously felt strongly about his work, writing that "[i]f you do not feel free to accede to some of my proposals, will you be kind enough to refer the matter with this letter to the publishers?"(11) Once again, Winsor and Edes must have reached an agreement, because by January 1, 1881, Edes was at work on the third segment about Charlestown and submitted his final piece on June 15, with the estimation that it would not exceed the length of the last one and also with the by-now-expected defense.(12) George Ellis, one of Winsor's committee members or assistant editors wrote Winsor on July 22 that "I am reading Edes' chapter on Charlestown, which is thorough and very good."(13)

But this time Edes had gone too far for Winsor, whose response was saved in draft form in his letterbooks, indicating he thought what he said was noteworthy in some way. Winsor told Edes that his chapter was "much too long," was "not cast in the scale of the book," and was "quite apart from its mates in the book, in the extent of its personal and genealogical detail." There was only one solution for Winsor: "[R]ewrite it, bringing out the prominent points, and giving them relief. Now[,] all is a mass of details — quite at variance with literary expression."(14) Though associates like Ellis approved of Edes' work, Winsor was fully supported by his publisher."(15)

Edes was upset by Winsor's curt, peremptory tone. Just because others had dealt with their subjects "in what appears to me a superficial manner," why should Edes not "be permitted to print a chapter filled with details drawn from original sources [?]"(16) But, on August 13, 1881, a repentent Edes submitted a revised draft, which, as he put it, "I have pruned to the extent of at least fifty per cent, and I think more than that. It does not appear to me to be possible to throw out more without omitting important facts; but when the paper reaches your hands be good enough to do with it whatever seems to you to be proper. I have striven to adhere in this chapter as closely as possible to the plan on which the other two were cast."(17)

The antagonism expressed in the correspondence between Winsor and Edes was partially a result of the tension of two active, busy, strong-willed men working under short deadlines, but was also attributable to contrasting perceptions the two men had of what was proper content for a multiauthored history. Edes felt previous antiquarians had not written about Charlestown's past in sufficient detail or accuracy, and he was willing to spend considerable energy and time to do research in sources and to write out detailed accounts. Unlike many other contributors, Edes was willing to present a fresh version, and not simply a gloss on his own or some one else's earlier writings. Winsor, by contrast, saw the segments on Charlestown as fitting in an exact way into a large mosaic of accounts, which, because of their brevity, had to be general, succinct, covering highlights, and not the detailed, heavily noted submissions of Edes.

These conflicting views revealed a more fundamental distinction. Edes was typical of those antiquarians who labored close to their sources, whose talent extended to the establishment of accuracy and the careful transcription of sources little altered to the printed page. Winsor, by contrast, was in a position, as editor, to see the overall texture of the historical development of Boston, to perceive relationships and the relative significance of specific elements of urban life. To his eye, a wordy, formless, sprawling, detailed account was not appropriate to the general history he tried to assemble as editor-impresario. The distance between Edes and Winsor over what constituted good historical writing indicates the wide range in perception among the antiquarians of the late nineteenth and early twentieth centuries.

A further dimension of the relationship between editor and contributors was how Winsor dealt with subjects that were controversial, historical matters on which there were several, conflicting views, specifically religion. On no other subject was there so apt to be division because of the existence of many different churches and theological viewpoints. Winsor and his associates were sensitive to the matter. One thought, for example, that "the non-unitarians should have a chance to see [the section on unitarians] in proof perhaps – that no insidious or careless phrase might slide in by accident."(18)

When Winsor assigned "Witchcraft in Boston" to W. F. Poole, who had moved to Chicago to become the librarian of its public library, Poole agreed, calling it "a new subject, for it has never been treated historically except in an incidental way."(19) When Poole submitted his piece, he indicated he had treated the subject "in a purely historical and not controversial spirit. I have no idea that what I have written will conform with your opinion in every instance . . . but it will be no less true and historical on that account. If my paper has any value it will be because I have gone out off the old beaten track, and have investigated the subject from original sources."(20)

But when Winsor passed Poole's piece on to his committee and other associates, they remarked on its controversial character. One thought that "this article requires a strong editorial note, stating that it is not to be viewed as a judicial dealing with the subject. . . . It is throughout a partisan plea designed to exculpate C. Mather [a leading Puritan clergyman who was involved in the matter]. Every qualifying passage quoted from him might be offset by another of a directly opposite one."(21) But another wrote that "it is a very interesting and well written paper. The concluding part of the article deals with a controversy into which Mr. Poole throws himself with all his force. I wish he had dealt with the subject a little more judiciously. But, of course, each contributor is alone responsible for his opinions or his treatment of his theme."(22)

When Winsor indicated that he and his fellow committee member Charles Deane had certain suggestions to make concerning the content of Poole's piece, Poole responded by saying "I am certainly desirous of meeting your wishes and those of Mr. Deane, and shall do it so far as is possible and maintain my own integrity in setting forth what I regard as historical truth: I never supposed that I should write a paper in which my opinions and conclusions on the witchcraft theme would accord with your opinions or Mr. Deane's."(23) In the meantime, Henry D. Dexter's piece on the "Mathers in Boston" presented the Mathers in the same favorable manner as Poole had. Poole thought Dexter's submission to be "admirable, fair, and impartial. . . . What a stupid blunder I should have made if I had taken the old conservative ground and run my head against Dr. Dexter's human and charitable estimate of the Mathers in the witchcraft business! As it is there is not a hint of conflict between us. I confess I did not expect such an outspoken, flat-footed defence of the Mathers' on the witchcraft."(24) Perhaps because Poole and Dexter both treated the Mathers favorably, there is no indication that Winsor and his associates insisted that Poole redraft his account in order to avoid controversy.

After the volume containing his piece on witchcraft appeared, a mystified Poole wrote Winsor: "I have not seen a single critical notice in the eastern journals of my chapter on witchcraft. . . . Unless my chapter is answered, you Boston men must let C M and the other church fathers alone in the future."(25) Though Winsor and his close collaborators sought to avoid controversial treatments of controversial subjects and believed the subject of the Mathers and witchcraft to fit that category, they miscalculated: there was no reaction to the favorable accounts of Poole and Dexter.

It is apparent that Winsor pursued goals that, if pursued rigorously, were antithetical. If his overriding aim was to allow each contributor to write about his subject from his own perspective on it and understanding of it, then those same contributors could not with consistency be asked to avoid taking controversial positions. If the primary objective was not to upset any group or individual when opinions on a subject varied, then Winsor would not have asked that certain subjects be written on at all. If the history were to have a consistent tone, style, and overall view of Boston's past, then Winsor would have had to write it himself and would not have sought the best qualified or knowledgeable individuals to write on the subjects he and his committee chose. Winsor's success as an editor was based on his capacity to balance these conflicting objectives, and not to be fanatical in the pursuit of any one of them. This restraint was in contrast to his persistence in drawing out of his contributors pieces that were of a certain level of accuracy and stylistic competence.

His collaborators or committee members – Edward Hale, Charles Deane, and (unofficially) George Ellis – gave advice on who the most suitable and available individuals would be to prepare pieces on the great array of subjects to be included in the projected volumes. Edward Hale was the most active of Winsor's associates in the task of giving advice on who should be contacted as potential contributors. Hale's outpouring of advice started at the beginning of the project and continued until contributors for all segments were found. Hale wrote Winsor that "my object is interesting writing by first rate men. A book must not only be true – it must be *interesting*."(26) Hale was sometimes critical of suggested names: "I do *not* think much of Woodward's knowledge, judgement, or pen."(27) Or: "[Elbridge Smith] is very light metal--I would not let him in."(28)

Winsor's associates were keenly aware of the difficulties of writing a good piece for a multi-authored history. Deane wrote that "in preparing my paper I avoided as much as I could putting into it any matter or references to kindred themes, feeling that I ought to confine myself as nearly as possible to the subject in hand – I had constantly to resist the temptation to make notes relating to such matters."(29) Hale disclosed his personal involvement in an actual case in which contributors writing on overlapping subjects presented conflicting accounts – an ever-present danger. Hale, after reading such a submission by another contributor, concluded: "It is so full of errors that I must allude to them – or correct my own work – in any case where he is right and I am wrong."(30) Winsor and his committee developed a formal procedure with their contributors revealed in a "Memo to Collaborators," presumably sent to each one as an agreement was made. The publishers agreed to pay $2 per page. The writers were obliged to hand their copy to either the editor or the publishers at the agreed upon time. Proofs would then be sent to the writers.(31)

Clarence Jewett, the original publisher, tried to establish at the outset a clear understanding of the overall relationship he hoped would be sustained between Winsor, as editor, and himself: "I don't propose to coerce you in any sense during our association in this work, yet there are points under consideration in the commencement of an enterprise of this magnitude, in which the party taking the entire financial risk, feels a deep interest. . . . *I shall never expect* to *advise* you in your capacity as *editor*."(32) In the weeks that followed, publisher and editor did in fact establish a generally effective operation on the matter of allowing contributors to republish their articles,(33) on canvassing for subscribers,(34) on press notices,(35) on contributors,(36) on their reliability,(37) and on contents.(38)

For reasons that are unclear, Jewett decided not to remain as publisher beyond the first few months of the project. As early as January 16, 1880, J. R. Osgood, of Houghton, Osgood, and Company wrote to Winsor: "I have heard whisperings of your great new undertaking. . . . I hope you will not regard it as impertinent or ill-timed if I ask you whether you have made or considered any publishing arrangements respecting it as yet. If not would you like to."(39)

Without explanation, Jewett indicated on May 5 that he thought an agreement would be reached with J. R. Osgood Co. and "that the work will go forward without delay."(40) On May 10, Osgood sent out a form letter to the contributors, indicating "[we] shall publish the work in exact accordance with the terms of the prospectus issued by them. Mr. Jewett will remain connected with the work as a business superintendent under our direction, until completed."(41) An accompanying note from Winsor assured the contributors that "The conditions of editorial supervision and literary contributions" were to remain "unchanged."(42) Osgood later wrote to Winsor that "I am desirous to meet Mr. Jewett's wishes as to his name appearing there in some form. The idea being his, and the work having been carried along by him to such a point, any suitable and consistent recognition of his relation to it would seem to be a proper act of courtesy." Osgood suggested something like: "The work projected and superintended by Clarence F. Jewett."(43)

Whatever the precise division of labor, the command structure was effective. After the changeover, Winsor dealt continuously with Jewett, Osgood's representative B. H. Ticknor, and the printer of the Riverside Press in Cambridge, J. Wilson. There were difficulties with the arrangements for the illustrations; contributors were late with their submissions or prepared segments that were too long; the press was ahead of (or behind) the proofs ready for printing. Through it all, the steady hand and inexhaustible energy of Winsor provided the needed guidance, even to the point that the publisher's assistant apologized "for the way the book shatters your vacation."(44)

Winsor was not wholly above criticism in his dealings with the other key figures in the enterprise, however. A. W. Stevens of the Riverside Press wrote: "[Your] copy, never clear, has been particularly obscure and complicated in your notes on Mr. Scudder's chapter—a markedly unhappy circumstance taken in connection with the haste with which you have demanded of us just now."(45) Several contributors complained of being confused about submission deadlines, with the implication that Winsor had not kept them fully informed, or had been arbitrary in establishing them, perhaps in response to pressure from the publisher or the press.

Winsor was, no doubt, under immense pressure. He was, after all, still, at least nominally, Harvard's librarian. His letterbooks reveal a daily pace that must have been extremely hectic: writing several notes and letters; arranging or going to meetings with the publisher, the press, or contributors; maintaining his duties at the college. It is evident that most involved in the undertaking admired him as an editor. The tone of much of the correspondence suggests this. There were several requests for assistance on source material and many for advice on what to include or exclude in order to avoid overlapping with what other contributors would submit. Some even invited him to salvage what he could or to rewrite at will. Winsor's fellow committeeman Edward Hale called him "an editor of learning and genius and matchless industry."(46)

Winsor divided the four volumes into parts: The Prehistoric Period and Natural History, Early History, The Colonial Period, The Provincial Period, The Revolutionary Period, The Last Hundred Years, and Special Topics. Education, libraries, philosophic thought, women, drama, fine arts, music, architecture, science, medicine, law, horticulture, and charity were thought to be subjects most suitably treated apart from particular periods, whereas towns later annexed to the city, literature, "life in Boston," topography and landmarks, Boston families, religion, and — later — industry, capital, canals and railroads, finance, insurance, trade, commerce, and navigation were all treated several times within particular time frames. Winsor did not explain how and why he and his committee and his publisher decided upon this scheme. In any case, neither the format — with its mixture of chronology and topics, nor the writing — with its blend of narrative, description, and the listing of information, is what Winsor believed was distinctive about *The Memorial History of Boston*.

In the preface, Winsor indicated that his "novel plan" consisted of having each section prepared by someone with "a particular association [and] long acquaintance with the subject."(47) It was in this regard that editor, committee, and publisher alike thought the four-volume history, as published, was a great achievement in local historical writing, one with national significance. To Winsor and his associates the history was an advancement because of the independence each contributor had to deal with his subject in the way his knowledge indicated was best. As Edward Hale put it: "The variation of method and style is no disadvantage but a positive benefit. This would not be so had the book been *unedited*. But with . . . [Winsor] to edit it — it makes a better book. It is far more of an authority and it is more entertaining."(48)

Animated by this conviction, Winsor and the others emphasized the work's importance in the publicity they controlled or influenced in a widespread effort to enhance subscriptions and sales. Osgood asked contributors "to favor us with the names of persons of your acquaintance in different parts of the United States, and particularly New York City, who in your opinion would be likely to feel an interest in the book, that we may send them circulars and notices explaining its scope."(49) Publishers, authors, and editor all tried to exert influence over the content of press notices of new books, which were little more than advertisements. A loss of control, that is, the appearance of a critical notice by someone not already involved with or sympathetic to the book just published might adversely affect sales and was to be avoided if possible.

Jewett wrote to Winsor (concerning the publication of one of the four volumes): Of the *Advertiser*: "I suppose this was printed with your consent." Of the *Sunday Herald*: "The Rev. Julius Ward has been in this P.M. and wants to write an article for [it]. . . . I asked him to come in here tomorrow morning and see you." Of the *New York Times*: "Meantime [Rev. Ward] wants to send off a general editorial tonight to [it]. I told him he could do so *based on the Advertiser article*." Of the *New York Tribune*: "Now is there any objection sending a copy of the circular to [it] tonight? I should like to have Reid [the editor] feel that I had given him as early information as possible."(50)

In Chicago, the librarian (and contributor) W. F. Poole wrote that "I shall prepare the notices of [one of the volumes] for several of our Chicago journals, The Dial and The Tribune — perhaps others."(51) Poole later confirmed: "I have written the one for The Dial and have seen that the right persons are to treat it in the 'Times,' 'Tribune,' and 'Inter-Ocean' — How much Janson McClung and Co. [Osgood's Midwestern agent] will push it remains to be seen. I shall look after them and give them *points*."(52) And still later: "Tomorrow our city papers will have notices of 'the Memorial History' and as I have taken some trouble to see that they have been entrusted to good hands and have posted up the writers, I believe they will be good. I will send them to you."(53) And, after the notices appeared: "The book is taking here splendidly. It will be a great literary and financial success."(54) But, Poole thought Janson McClung did "not seem to me to be doing anything to push or even advertise [the volumes]. They publish 'The Dial' where I have a notice, but they have no advertisement. I have dropped a line on the subject confidentially stating this point."(55)

The genuine review in *Poole's*, one of the most highly regarded review journals of the time and therefore presumably beyond the direct control of Winsor and the others, focused on the long-term importance of the project. The reviewer thought it was possible that "general history in the future is to be written in this way — by allotting chapters or topics or periods to the specialists who are most competent to do it. This is an age of specialties and specialists."(56)

And Winsor did have imitators. Of similar format or coverage was the history of Milwaukee, edited by Howard L. Conrad (1896) and written by a team of contributors on the model established by Winsor. Conrad believed "that the cooperative plan of writing histories subdivided into topics is productive of the best results attainable in the preparation of historical works." And so Conrad "appealed to leading citizens of Milwaukee specially well qualified to deal with certain phases of the city's history, to become contributors to this work." Conrad was pleased to announce that the "response to this appeal was prompt and generous."(57) The most active publishers for this particular kind of city history were located in Chicago. The Lewis Publishing Company selected cities in every region of the United States, from 1900 to 1930, as did the S. J. Clarke Company, which was active in the same period.(58) The pioneer of the group was D. Mason and Company of Syracuse, New York, over the period from 1884 to 1895, but whether Clarke and Lewis were consciously continuing a publishing venture first developed by Mason is unclear.

Clarence Bagley of Seattle, Washington, was active as a printer and a writer as well as a long-term city official (from 1890 to 1930) and was thus personally aware of the city's past from its earliest days.  Bagley was also president of the Washington Historical Society from 1906 until his death in 1932.  Bagley also saw himself as a pioneer.  As he wrote to two friends, Ezra Meeker and George H. Hines "Do you two realize that we three are practically all who are left in the Northwest . . . who have witnessed the birth of more than one Commonwealth between the Rockies and the Pacific?" Bagley was proud of the fact that they "were of a pioneer race as far back as the records show and we have done our full share of pioneering."(59)

In 1911, the S. J. Clarke Company chose Bagley to be its editor for a history of Seattle.  The arrangements and ensuing problems are revealed with rare clarity in Bagley's carefully preserved correspondence.  In 1913, Bagley told a friend that two years earlier he and S. J. Clarke had made an arrangement for a history of Seattle "to be prepared under my direction." He disclosed that "[m]uch of the work I shall do personally, but there will be a larger part that will be done by others." In particular, most of the "formative period was under my daily observation and I shall not have to appeal to persons or to authorities for its history."(60)

As for the financial aspects of the project, Bagley indicated: "The historical work I am superintending is of no financial interest to me – that is the concern of the publishers; however, I feel that all the newspapers of the city should encourage the enterprise.  The outlay will be large and the returns slow to come in.  I believe the work will be a credit to the publishers and of value to the reading public."(61)

In June 1914, Bagley wrote to a friend about the frustrations he was encountering: "The work of editing the History of Seattle, that I took up some time ago, has proved burdensome and vastly annoying.  So much so that I cannot tell what the outcome is to be.  Thus far, I have had to cut and slash in every direction." The matter presented by the writer provided by Clarke to "write out" all sections of the book that Bagley himself was to prepare "is the foundation for a history but in no sense 'History.' I have notified the home office that unless it is rewritten I shall not father it. . . .  This morning I started in on an eighty page lot of it, and after cutting twelve pages all to pieces I threw it aside and shall require it be again rewritten."(62)

A week later, a concerned Bagley wrote to S. J. Clarke Company about disagreements he had had with Goodspeed, the man the publisher had sent to assist the editor.  Bagley disclosed that, when Goodspeed arrived, "much discussion between him and me was had about the plan and scope of the work." Bagley told Goodspeed "that I wanted [the history] written in plain narrative style." At first, all seemed well, as Bagley passed on to Goodspeed various materials, which Goodspeed said "he was reading . . . with care, noting facts and observations for future use." But then "a good natured disagreement arose between us" about the overall "plan" of the work. Bagley believed that the history "should, so far as possible, be carried as a whole, chronologically." But Goodspeed's "plan was to take each main subdivision of the work and dispose of it.  . . . [That is, the topical plan]." The crux of their disagreement was over Bagley's assertion that "it would be impossible to prepare a good history upon this plan, that it would result in too much duplication of names, incidents, etc."(63)

Bagley's friends also became concerned. One of them — Curator and Assistant Secretary of the Oregon Historical Society, George H. Hines — talked to another, Scholefield, about Bagley's making a formal contract with Clarke: "Unfortunately, as matter of record, the class of publication the Clarkes issue, as well as all others of the same class, pretending to be 'Histories,' are governed by the profit to be gained rather than the real history they contain. That, of course, is to be expected, as it takes a good many thousand dollars, to float an enterprise of this kind."(64) There is here, once again, an example of the differing perceptions of what historical writing should be. As publisher, Clarke's primary interest was in profit. The appearance of providing a good local history would be maintained if someone of Bagley's competence would agree to be editor-supervisor. But, Clarke's writers or "historians," sent to assist editors like Bagley, were hacks, men whose research and writing were not up to the standards genuine antiquarians set for themselves. Antiquarians shared the belief that real "history" had to pass their critical review.

Bagley's response to Hines' observation was to say that "I have received a very satisfactory letter from the house [Clarke], acknowledging that I am right about the almost worthlessness of the work done here by their men and asking me to suggest some one to do it over and also to suggest his compensation."(65) In October, 1914, Bagley reported to a friend: "Interest in historical matters is at the extreme ebb flow over here. I have done nothing on the Seattle history lately. The man the company had at work here [Goodspeed] made a complete botch of it and he was recalled. I advised them to drop matters while the war is in progress, and as I have not heard from them since then, they have undoubtedly taken my advice."(66) But, by the winter of 1914-15, there was a marked change: "That history of Seattle has indeed been vexations of spirit," he confided to the same friend, "but within the past few weeks has taken on new life and is now progressing finely. M. M. Clarke came out here, and acting on my advice engaged Mr. Wilford Beaton to do the writing. I like his style very much and he is a glutton for work. I believe the book will be all in hand by May 1."(67) It is not clear when Bagley and S. J. Clarke Company actually signed a formal contract. Despite the hiring of a writer Bagley felt he could work with, it was May, 1916, not 1915, before Bagley could report that he had "just returned from a four-week trip to Chicago, where I went to read proofs and attend to the makeup of a History of Seattle that I prepared during the past winter for the S. J. Clarke Company of Chicago,"(68) and even then the actual writing remained incomplete.(69)

The difficulties of a publisher finding a writer-for-hire who would satisfy their hand-picked, prominent editor who himself had well developed antiquarian interests contrasted sharply with Bagley's unstinting search for the best critical evaluations he could find of what he had prepared. For example, he relied on the knowledge of Judge Thomas Burke and on Judge Roger S. Greene,(70) to whom he wrote: "The best of my appreciation of your aid is the fact that I have embodied in my papers all of your marginal notations and the three separate sheets of additions. These were just what

I hoped you might furnish to me."(71) Bagley, a good antiquarian, tried to render truthful accounts of historic incidents by a search of all pertinent available records and by a subsequent evaluation of those records by the leading participants.    However, those who wrote the records, those who culled evidence from them, and those who evaluated them all shared one perspective on the event, that of the prominent citizens of the city.

In the preface of the completed history, Bagley confessed that at the outset, "his connection with [the history] should be that of editor only; to give aid and counsel in its preparation and to read and approve it in advance of its publication" — presumably not a very onerous task.    But, in reality and to his surprise, he and "his co-workers" have put in "long hours of unremitting toil." Bagley thanked in a vague way the writers S. J. Clarke provided — Wilford Beaton, Floyd C. Kaylor, and Victor F. Farrar — for "much work in [the history's] preparation," as well as assistance from prominent figures such as Judge Roger S. Greene.

As for material: "His own recollections cover nearly all the years since Seattle's founding and he has not deemed it necessary, excepting on rare occasions, to quote authorities regarding matters within the range of his personal knowledge." That an antiquarian wrote largely from personal recollection was noteworthy, as was Bagley's proclaimed and justified disassociation from the biographical portion of the published results.    Clarke divided the three volumes equally between history and biography.    Bagley chose to make a sharp distinction between the two,(72) thus distancing himself from the biographical sketches of hoped-for subscribers, so central to the book-making of commercial publishers like Clarke.    In doing so, he indicated indirectly that a self-respecting antiquarian such as himself did not accept the lives of the living as a fit subject for historical investigation.

Ironically, the organization of Bagley's history of Seattle is thoroughly topical, even though his own predilection was for a chronological narrative account.    This question, should a local history be chronological or topical, is what divided him and Goodspeed (Clarke's original writer-for-hire) and what led to Goodspeed's dismissal.    Why Bagley later decided to adhere to the departed Goodspeed's plan is not known.    But Clarke's hack writers were probably more aware than local antiquarians like Bagley of the popularity of the topical approach: like the biographies or mugs, topical treatments were what hacks like Goodspeed believed the buyers of local history wanted.    In any case, Bagley's history deals with a pioneer period, an Indian wars period, mining, lumbering, fisheries, shipping, harbors and canals, railroads, industry, banking, education, churches, the press, libraries, lawyers and law, doctors and health and medicine, clubs and associations, women, and fires and riots.    In its coverage of city life it is a model local history.

Like other urban antiquarians, Bagley thought he knew the primary basis for Seattle's growth: its location at a fine harbor.(73) The city became an industrial center, according to Bagley, because of the conjunction of "the four cornerstones upon which manufacturing is built. . . . Just as raw material, labor, power, and transportation are necessary to the building of a manufacturing industry, so is that industry necessary to the building of a city."(74) In short, Bagley's assessment of why Seattle quickly grew into a major city is thoroughly economic in character: the community's location provided the proper combination of factors for the swift development of a capitalist economy, flawed only to the extent that the areas' inhabitants relied on outsiders for capital. Bagley was, thus, an avowed apologist for urban growth's being linked to capitalistic economic expansion — as were other antiquarians whose histories explained the emergence of other population centers.

These antiquarians shared the perspective of those prominent in the political, economic, and social-cultural life of their communities. None questioned the centrality of commercial growth even though that growth led to extremes of wealth and poverty unimaginable to the pioneers whose lives and contributions occupied a significant place in their histories. Bagley displayed a certain ambivalence toward this situation, arguing that "profits" should have accrued to pioneers "as compensation for [their] struggle under adverse conditions" instead of to later entrepreneurs.(75) Bagley admitted that the pioneers lacked "business ability," as currently defined, but were men "living close to nature . . . [and] therefore out of harmony with the extreme selfishness and dishonesty of modern business tactics."(76)

By contrast, Bagley was unequivocally certain that "orderly progress" was a basic requirement for a heterogeneous, fast-growing urban center resulting from untrammelled commercial expansion. He and other urban antiquarians shared with those prominent in their city's civic life the conviction that order and obedience to law were of fundamental importance to the continuance of their community's existence. For Bagley, the maintenance of law and order was more basic, even, than the exclusion of an unwanted minority by any means. Bagley's explanation for the prejudice against the Chinese on the Pacific Coast was that even though large landowners and early railroad builders wanted "increased immigration," practically everybody else "soon became convinced" that their interests would be best served by the exclusion of such immigrants, "who could never be assimilated and whose only object in coming" was to earn money and to return to China with it. Bagley thought that "[u]nlike the immigrants from Europe they neither sought an asylum from oppression nor the enjoyment of the blessings of a free government."76 For Bagley, the clear lesson to be learned from "the Anti-Chinese Agitation and Riots" and their containment was that "organized order is mightier than disorder, that martial law . . . is a mighty beneficial and constitutional resource, within easy . . . reach of a community oppressed or menaced by invasive or insurrectionary lawlessness."(77)

Similarly, the greatest challenge to the physical growth of the city, the natural disaster of a great fire, led to renewed and improved growth. Nothing attested to the vaulting, indomitable commercial spirit of the city's business community than the astonishing speed with which they rebuilt the center after one such conflagration.(78) In other words, Bagley found progressive growth in his city's past, even with the challenges posed by social and physical calamity.

Bagley found that physical, moral, social, and intellectual improvements were brought both by a reformist Christian social gospel movement and by

public action.  The municipal government built a school system and provided
other services, in the case of electric power and street railways, through
direct   public   ownership.(79)   In   Bagley's   view,   these   controversial
experiments in local socialism had mixed results: city-wide services at the
price of a sizeable city debt.  From the vantage point of a long-term city
official, Bagley exhibited an ambivalent attitude toward growth and progress
in Seattle.  He was an urban antiquarian who knew and admired the
businessmen whose fortunes mirrored the fast growth of the city, but he
wrote his history at a time when reform involved Christian agitation and
the exercise of municipal power in ways that were not always harmonious
to the interests of those businessmen.

Change could divide as well as unify.  And when a fast-growing
community like Seattle was divided, as it was over the question of
municipal ownership, antiquarians like Bagley were anxious because they
could not make their histories convey what they wanted their readers to
find:  that urban America consisted of progressive communities whose
hallmarks were ever greater material prosperity, intellectual acumen, and
moral rectitude and whose growth was accompanied by harmony and order.

Sometimes, the leading publishers in local history combined a history
of a particular city with that of its surrounding county, or even group of
counties. Between 1931 and 1933, the S. J. Clarke Company published, not
only a *History of Milwaukee*, but also *Southeastern Wisconsin: A History of
Old Milwaukee County*, *Southwestern Wisconsin: A History of Old Crawford
County*, and *West-Central Wisconsin: A History*.  As editor for the 'county'
volumes, the firm selected John G. Gregory, a retired newspaper reporter
and editor, who also wrote the history of the city.

Gregory's prominence is revealed in a letter he wrote to a former
mayor of Milwaukee, Sherburn Becker: "Your cordial letter, suggesting a
conference on the subject of the work relating to the history of Milwaukee
on which I am now engaged recalls pleasant memories at a time when both
of us were younger, and when it was my fortune to be associated with you
and other earnest promoters of Milwaukee's public interests."(80) Gregory
was responding to an earlier letter from Becker, in which the former Mayor
indicated he had been solicited to subscribe to Gregory's forthcoming
history: "I feel there is no one more competent or more able to do this
work and as I have a most friendly feeling for you personally in as much
as you were always kind to me during my political activity in Milwaukee,"
Becker became a subscriber, but not without qualms.  He wrote, "I do wish
to state positively, however, that the list of subscribers submitted to me
was not a representative one and did not comprise enough men who were
really builders of Milwaukee.  It appeared to me more like a list of
politicians and people who simply wanted to take this opportunity to have
their names appear in print.  Of course I do not blame the publishing
company for getting anybody that they can in order to swell the subscrition
list and make money for themselves, but as I said above, I do not think it
is a representative list."(81)

Becker's concern was shared by any urban antiquarian who wanted his
history to embrace who and what was important to the making of his city,

and not those currently of prominence who were willing to pay for mugs. The way publishers like Clarke assuaged the qualms of amateur historians like Gregory was to absolve them from the responsibility of preparing the biographical segment of their multivolume histories.    This arrangement did not mean that those who wrote the historical sections were wholly disconnected from the process, however, as the following note to Gregory from V. B. Miller of the Biographical Department of the S. J. Clarke Company reveals: "Enclosed please find the newspaper clipping you loaned our representative, Mr. H. E. Cutter, for use in preparing the sketch of Allen J. Roberts."(82)

     After the publication of Gregory's history of Milwaukee in 1931, Clarke appointed him to serve as editor for further volumes on clusters of counties fanning out from the city.    Gregory's associate was Harry A. Preston, another journalist in Milwaukee and, at that time, vice president of the Wisconsin State Historical Association.    The surviving correspondence relating to these regional projects is quite revealing about the ways ordinary, paid contributors prepared portions of the published volumes. One contributor, Craig Rice, sent Preston the segment she wrote with the assertion that she had tried to keep them "as brief and concise as possible," though "[i]f you want any additions I will try to make them." Rice was, in fact, extremely accommodating, offering her sources "in any other venture you may engage upon," in furthering "publicity and sales," in devoting her "weekly book-review column to a description and review" of the history when it appeared.    Rice's enthusiasm to be involved with all aspects of the project derived in part from her eagerness to be paid during the onset of the Great Depression: "P.S. I hate to mention such a mundane subject as money, alas, with me . . . an important one. I wonder if I could be paid for my work before the 10th of December? It is rather important to me and my plans." Preston wrote across Rice's letter: "[send her $100 as per agreement – H.A.P.]"(83)

     Contributors like Craig Rice were paid by Clarke to prepare the historical segments in the multivolume project and were undoubtedly like those hired in the 1890s, at the time when Clarke, and Lewis and other firms first developed formulaic local history.    But, in the 1890s, when men like Nathan Wilson served as canvassers and writers of biographical sketches, those who prepared the historical segments tended to be "staffers," people regularly employed by the firms involved.    Preston's correspondence with Clarke during the latter part of February 1931, reveals that Clarke was, by the Depression at least, hiring out such tasks to field workers.(84)    Much   of   Preston's   time   was   taken   up   with   making arrangements   with   individuals   to   prepare   the   histories   of   particular counties, as well as with canvassers and portrait-men.

     Clarke, at one point, was frank about the practice to which Oscar Lewis referred in his piece on "Mug Books:" "[Davidson, a portrait-man] thinks, and rightly so, that he should get started very soon in Cleveland [and not Wisconsin] so that the widow women can open up by the first of April.    You know the golden months for widow work are April, May, and June.    July and August find women gone and they generally remain until the middle of September."(85)

The system by which formulaic local history was produced was, by the depression of the 1930s, even more elaborate than it had been in the 1890s. There were supervisors of groups of field workers, positions attractive enough to be avidly sought.    A. D. Bolens wrote to Clarke that "it has occurred to me that you might be interested to have my services, at proper compensation, as a supervisor of your Corps of workers . . .  to direct these workers whom to call upon and how to approach them."  Bolens insisted that he was widely acquainted with the region and its history, probably as much so as Gregory himself.    Concerned that he might be considered too old, Bolens added: "In spite of my age, I am healthy, vigorous, and active, physically and mentally; most persons whom I meet think I am much younger than I really am, guessing me to be somewhere between 55 and 60, and some guess around 50.    My hair is still almost wholly black and there are few marks of advanced years on my features. Best of all, my mind seems to be as keen and alert as ever."(86)  Clarke wrote Preston that "[naturally] we can't use him in any such capacity but I don't want to write him anything that may cause him to withold any support for West so have written him putting the proposition up to you . . .    [to]  tell him that the work is so far advanced now that there wouldn't be any place we could use him."(87)  Bolens was mollified.    He reported to Gregory that "Mr. West is a fine chap.   He calls frequently. Had a letter from Mr.  Clarke, notifying me in appreciation with Mr. West [that] I am to receive a complimentary set. Fine!"(88)

In a further development of the procedures used, Clarke decided that one of the supervisor's tasks was to find advisors for the history.   As West indicated to Clarke: "I have arranged with the following men to act as advisors to Mr.  Gregory and have their consent to add their names to the advisory board with the understanding that they are to review the chapters pertaining to their respective positions or edit same on La Crosse County."(89) Next in the chain of command in the system evolved by firms like Clarke for the publication of formulaic local history was the editor, a person of unquestioned local prominence.   The fact that all contributors had to gain the approval of Gregory meant that the paid writers had a certain standard to aim for, just as Gregory's name as editor aided canvassers in their search for subscribers.   As one contributor put it: "Praise from Mr. Gregory is high praise indeed."(90)

Those who worked directly with Gregory deferred completely to his presumed authority.   William E. Brown wrote: "As far as form and general content are concerned, this is the final draft.    Minor additions and alterations will undoubtedly have to be made, and any criticisms and suggestions which you make will be gladly considered.   You may note a missing link, a slight mistake, an ambiguity, or a missing date which I, being too familiar with the premises, might have overlooked.  If you do run across anything of the kind, let me know, and I shall send you the necessary material to patch it up."(91) A. O. Burton indicated: "You will perhaps want to rearrange the chapters somewhat in better sequence."(92) One B. Earll hoped her contribution "will meet your expectations in most things though we know it might be improved."(93) L. J.  Murphey enclosed ". . . the first seven pages . . . and ask that you criticize them in every particular if necessary as your criticism will be a guide to me in [the] future."(94)

Helen B. Derthick wrote: "I am enclosing a copy of chapter headings, with outline of contents, dates covered, and approximate number of words in each. This sort of work is entirely new to me and any suggestion which you can give as to the sequence of chapters or other details of handling material will be much appreciated."(95) And later: "I am glad to know you are untangling some of my involved sentences.(96) . . . Thank you for your suggestion concerning the division of the last two chapters, which I shall be glad to follow. I certainly appreciated your encouraging word. It helps when one feels such a novice. . . . If you do your own proofreading I am glad I am out of hearing when my copy is being gone over."(97) Finally: "Thank you for your encouragement and help, and wishing you every success in the completed work."(98)

A friend of Gregory's summed up the way those who worked with Gregory perceived him as an antiquarian: "I am amazed that you accomplish so much. This is particularly remarkable when the quality of your output is taken into consideration, for I well know that you could not bring yourself to do slipshod work, even with an irate publisher prodding you for copy."(99)

In the history of Old Milwaukee County (1932), Gregory did not impose a uniform format on the contributors; each one was allowed to devise whatever chapter divisions seemed suitable. Gregory himself prepared many of the sections on counties in this, the first of Clarke's three projects, but there were also sections by those Gregory corresponded with, such as William E. Brown (on Racine County), Helen B. Derthick (on Walworth County), and Craig Rice (on Jefferson County). These sections took on a variety of concrete forms. Brown's sketch of Racine was strictly chronological; Derthick's on Walworth was selectively topical; Rice's on Jefferson combined chronology and topical treatments. Similarly, in Gregory's history of Old Crawford County (1932), many of the chapters were written by contributors, most notably Loyola J. Murphy, but also Mrs. J. W. Earll and Mrs. J. P. Evans — all of whom Gregory corresponded with. By contrast, in the last of the trilogy — dealing with west central Wisconsin or the "Old Carver Tract" — Gregory not only provided an overall historical account, but a series of very brief historical sketches on the cities of the region, relying on Thomas J. Cunningham for a long segment, topically arranged on the Chippewa area.

In sum, the local histories published by firms such as Clarke and Lewis were, by the 1930s, more respectable, more the product of knowledgeable local editors and caring local contributors than were the in-house publications of the 1890s, even though the biographical sections continued to be the mug books Oscar Lewis critically described.

# CHAPTER 11
# Local History as Literature

In the decades after the Civil War, local historical writing became a large-scale enterprise in every sense: in the materials used as sources, in the number of people involved in the preparation, in the array of subjects treated and in the sheer size and bulk of the published volumes.Such history became encyclopedic, as exhaustive as those who produced it could make it. The antiquarians had no doubt that their ceaseless quest for facts accurately recorded would result in an account showing their ancestors' admirable and successful efforts at community building, of which they were the proud inheritors.

But a question arose in the minds of some as to whether the lengthy or multivolume history was the only way to portray their community's past.Who read such huge tomes, beyond subscribers and library users? Was history meant to be something that appeared only in a reference book, in volumes perused and checked, but not widely read? How popular, how financially successful were published histories of hundreds or, if in several volumes, thousands of pages?

As early as 1887, Robison and Cockett, the local publishers of a history of Cleveland introduced their 510-page single volume work with the comment that "[in] endeavoring to profit by the experiences of the publishers of the histories of other cities, it was deemed most judicious to produce a book that could be sold at a price considerably less than that of the average local work of this kind.Voluminous and elaborate local histories, with their proportionately high cost, have not proved commercial successes.So large is the amount that you must read in these days to keep up with the times, that the majority of people find it necessary to select condensed treatments of subjects."(1) Though sensitive to the problem, Robison and Cockett did not choose a format that differed, except in its somewhat briefer treatment, from the prevailing mode: that is, a combination of chapters organized chronologically or topically and written by knowledgeable individuals.

After 1900, however, a growing number of authors set aside the encyclopedic approach in favor of an episodic, narrative account, "literary" in the way that John Watson hoped the earliest antiquarians would present the past: through vivid description, memorable anecdote, famous incident.From 1900 through the 1930s, these writers mined the past for stories that anyone would be interested in reading, not just those who lived in or near the town or city written about, but anyone who could respond to true historical stories about real people in real communities.In doing so, such authors usually disclaimed having done original research and admitted that they relied on older, fuller, encyclopedic histories.

In 1900, T. J. Chapman, in *Old Pittsburgh Days*(2) told his readers that "in the following pages we have attempted an outline of the story of Pittsburgh. Within the compass of a small single volume it has been impossible to relate all the details of that story; but we have tried to preserve the thread of the narrative and to embody the more striking events." Chapman went on to say that "[w]e have not aimed to make a book of Indian stories.We have not aimed to make a book of industrial and social statistics.What we have aimed to do has been to present a sketch of the origin and early development of our city that should be correct as to matters of fact and as attractive as possible." He concluded: "We trust the reader will find entertainment and profit in contemplating the old days of Pittsburgh."(3)

A year later, in 1901, Charles D. Willard, in his history of Los Angeles,(4) provided his readers with a frank and critical assessment of the standard local history of urban centers, at the same time that he presented a justification for a brief, narrative treatment.Willard believed that a city's history "contains as much good material, out of which an entertaining history may be constructed" as the life of an individual or of a nation.Willard thought it was unfortunate that local history had "fallen into the hands of schemers who exploit the prominent citizen for his biography and throw in something of a narrative, merely as an apology for the book's existence." Such histories are "huge unwieldy affair[s], that [circulate] only among the hundred or two victims." Willard guessed that these volumes were "not read even by them, except as to the pages where each one finds the story of his life set forth in a flamboyant and patronizing style." It was sad that the history portion often represented "careful, conscientious work on the part of the (usually anonymous) writer" but was "buried under such a mass of rubbish." Willard thought earlier histories of Los Angeles were "considerably above the average standard." The most recent, "published by the Chapman Company in 1900 contains a history written by that conscientious and devoted searcher in the local field, J. M. Guinn, Secretary of the Los Angeles Historical Society.Mr. Guinn's portion of the volume is an admirable piece of work, but the 780 pages of biography that accompany it contribute to the document a weight of ten pounds – and very little else."

What of Willard's effort? "The present book is an attempt to supply in convenient and portable shape the material facts in the history of Los Angeles City.It contains nothing in the form of paid or biographical matter (strange that such a statement should be needed!) and it is offered for sale at bookshops on its merits as a book [that is, there were no subscribers.]"

Willard told his readers that he laid "no claim to any great amount of original research, his work being chiefly that of collecting, arranging and presenting in logical order the established facts.As the volume employs only 80,000 words to cover a period of nearly a century and a half, there is not much opportunity for detail[ed] work.It is, however, carefully indexed."(5)

In 1917, Ralph Birdsall, in *The Story of Cooperstown* (New York), explained the new, shortened, narrative account as applied to a town: "The ensuing narrative is a faithful record of life in Cooperstown from the earliest times, except that the persons and events to be described have been selected for their story interest, to the exclusion of much that a history is expected to contain."(6) In Birdsall's history, "[t]he dull thread of village history has been followed only in such direction as served for stringing upon it and holding to the light the more shining gems of incident and personality to which it led." In sum, "[t]he effort has been made to exclude everything that seemed unlikely to be of interest to the general reader."(7) Or, as an established writer, James Truslow Adams put it by way of introducing his history of Southampton (New York) (1918): "It will . . . be noted that I have endeavored to obstruct the narrative as little as possible with purely genealogical or antiquarian detail. . . . The task I set myself was a different one, and was simply to tell the general reader the story of the town from its founding, to the present day, to picture the continuing life of an American community from its beginning."(8)

In 1930, Henry K. Rowe gave the same message with even greater confidence in his history of Newton, Massachusetts: "The story is told as a connected narrative against the background of the times.The older method of writing history in a succession of topical paragraphs or chapters, in which each subject occupied a separate compartment," he announced, "is no longer good form.It is being succeeded by an attempt to recreate the life of a period as it was lived in all its complexity and variety, to bring all the factors into synthesis and see all phases of life as a single whole, even as it is lived." Rowe admitted that "[t]his method may not satisfy the antiquarian who will miss some of the old landmarks, or one who is interested almost exclusively in his own village, church, or club.But it has been selected after due deliberation and seems preferable."(9)

By the 1930s and the great economic depression, abbreviated, narrative histories of cities were not uncommon.Maria Letila Stockett, in her *Baltimore: A Not Too Serious History* (1928),(10) disclosed that "[the] writing of this book has been sheer joy.Foreign travel is exciting, but travel in one's hometown is even more thrilling, and the life and adventures of Baltimore Town are romantic and rich to a degree." Openly acknowledging that her history was based upon older work involving original research, Stockett thanked "my chief and support — J. Thomas Scharf.He, certainly, has written the best and biggest book on Baltimore and to him I am deeply grateful."(11) Part tour guide, part story, her history comprised such chapters as "A Battle and a Monument," "The Rich Array of Market Street," "Inns, Priests, and Merchants," "Old Town," "Charles Street Long Ago," "Red Brick Houses — White Front Steps," "From Federal Hill," and "The Green Chain of Parks."

Similarly, Roberta Frye Watt, in her *The Story of Seattle*,(12) admitted that "I have not tried to write a formal history; that has already been done, but I have tried to write of romance and of the heart throbs that mingle with the sterner facts.May it be an inspiration to all when life presses hard." Once again, the open acknowledgement: "I am further indebted to Mr. Bagley for his kindly interest and approval, and for the inestimable privilege that it has been to draw from his remarkable memory for reference and verification."(13)

Henry R. Hamilton introduced his *The Epic of Chicago*(14) with the frank admission that "I am not a historian and should not think of attempting to write a history of Chicago.I have simply taken those incidents in the life of Chicago which seemed to me the most romantic and interesting and set them down in chronological order, avoiding as much as possible statistics and other matter which might prove uninteresting to the general reader." Hamilton added that he hoped "my readers will also find these incidents interesting and, if in reading the book they acquire a working knowledge of Chicago's history, this will be a by product and not the main purpose."(15) William G. Bruce summed up the case for the short narrative treatment in his *A Short History of Milwaukee* (1936):(16) "The general public is not inclined to delve exhaustively into local history. . . . [Elaborate] studies serve the research student and statesman, rather than the average reader. . . . [The present volume] is intended for popular reading rather than for extensive study."(17)

These brief, derivative histories of cities were a consequence of a reaction against the lengthy tomes favored by publishers such as Lewis and Clarke.Some writers felt that the history of cities in America deserved a wider audience than the prominent people who subscribed and had their biographies included in multivolume histories.The way to gain that wider audience was to present the past as a popularly appealing and more affordable brief narrative of dramatic incidents or vivid descriptions, rather than as an expensive historical encyclopedia for those with genealogical interests.

The communities most favored with the newer kind of account were famous cities or towns that were unusual or distinctive and thus had the advantage of broad public recognition.Certain publishing firms in New York found accomplished writers to prepare what were, in part, factual romances or stories, and in part, travel or visitor guides.As early as 1881, G. P.Putnam's Sons published William W. Dewhurst's *History of St. Augustine, Florida*, which Dewhurst subtitled "Sketches of Events and Objects of Interest connected with the Oldest town in the United States, to which is added A Short Description of the Climate and Advantages of Saint Augustine as a Health Resort." Dewhurst proclaimed that St. Augustine was "famous throughout the world," and hoped that his history "may supply the desire, felt by an ever-increasing number of its citizens and visitors, to be better informed as to the early history of a place so justly celebrated. . . . Dewhurst's aim was "to condense and render to the general reader the very interesting but elaborate accounts of the early writer concerning some of the more notable events connected with the early settlement and defense of St. Augustine." He added: "Copious quotations have been borrowed, and the quaint language of the early historians has been retained as peculiarly appropriate to the subject and locality described."(18)

Similarly, J. B. Lippincott (in Philadelphia) published Harriette K.Leiding's *Charleston: Historic and Romantic* (1931); E. P. Dutton published Henry C. Brown's *The Story of Old New York* (1934); Doubleday published Walter Noble Burns' *Tombstone* (Arizona) (1927), Oliver R. Pilat's *Sodom By the Sea* (Coney Island) (1941), and Archie Binns' *Northwest Gateway: The Story of the Port of Seattle* (1941); and Dodd, Mead published Max Miller's *Reno* (Nevada) (1941).

Local histories as brief narratives or stories never prevailed over encyclopedic versions; not even during the 1930s; but, after the turn of the century, there was clearly another way of treating the past of local communities, a way that certain publishers believed would be more popular, easier to read, and cheaper: local history for everyone, not just elites.The great size and abundant detail of the multivolume histories of the post-Civil War decades were excessive to some publishers, writers, and readers.The growth of a more literary history, in the manner of John Watson, brought local historical writing closer to the conventions of fiction, to storytelling unencumbered by lists, data, statistics, and sources.

## PART IV
# The Coming of the Academics

# CHAPTER 12
# Amateurs and Academics

The great outpouring of amateur local historical writing between the Civil War and the Great Depression coincided with, indeed was intricately connected with, the swift development of academic historical study at the turn of the century. It is important to recognize that, until at least the 1930s, academic historians in the United States were connected in important ways to the much older and popular world of antiquarian activity. Academic history did not develop in isolation from amateur history, even though academic historians from the beginning tended to concentrate on the nation's past.

This connectedness was clearly evident in the manner that local, state, and national historical societies developed during these years. In the 1870s and 1880s, historical study patterned after German scholarship was introduced to American colleges and universities by those who received advanced training in Germany, most notably by Herbert Baxter Adams at Johns Hopkins University in Baltimore. In 1884, a group of forty met in Saratoga, New York, at the annual meeting of the American Social Science Association (founded in 1865) and decided to form an American Historical Association(AHA). J. Franklin Jameson, a member of that group, later explained the timing of this action by referring to the "heightened sense of national importance and unity" following the Civil War, the training of advanced students in Germany who were eager, upon their return, to raise the level of historical writing in America, and a general "impulse toward the formation of national societies of specialists," already much in evidence.(1)

Among that founding group, Jameson later believed the two most influential men to have been Adams, who served as secretary until his death in 1900, and an amateur historian, Dr. Clarence W. Bowen, who served as the original treasurer. Indeed, Adams, as perhaps the most influential scholar in the United States during these years, focused the attention of his graduate students at Johns Hopkins on the study of local history, hoping that the interests of amateurs and academics within the AHA would continue to converge.(2) Justin Winsor, Harvard's Librarian and editor of the influential *Memorial History of Boston* (1880-1881), was also active. He was elected President in 1887, and, as chairman of the committee "to test opinion and consult the government on the establishment of a national commission for the collection, preservation, and utilization of historic manuscripts," he announced that in 1888 Congress incorporated the association "for the promotion of historical studies, the collection and preservation of historical manuscripts, and for kindred purposes in the interest of American history and of history in America."(3)

George Bancroft (1800-1891) was chosen President of the AHA in 1886. The "scholarly" Senator Hoar, who sponsored the incorporation act, praised Bancroft at the 1886 meeting held in Washington, D.C., where the venerable Bancroft lived in the winter.(4) Jameson later remembered that the octogenarian Bancroft was "so vigorous that when Herbert Adams, secretary, went to his house on H Street to see if he felt equal to the duties of the Presidency, he showed the young man, with sprightly complacency, that he could still go up stairs two at a time." The academically trained Jameson added: "We looked upon him as the personal embodiment of the historic spirit in the United States."(5) The near deification of Bancroft, the most famous of the amateur national historians by members of the newly formed American Historical Association is perhaps the most vivid evidence that the earliest academic historians in the United States did not perceive themselves as separate from those amateurs who, like Bancroft, had, until recently, written the only history there was.

Indeed, the American Historical Association became directly involved with the state and local historical societies, which amateurs continued to dominate until the 1930s. In 1904, Henry E. Bourne presented a paper on the development and activities of the country's historical societies, stressing the need for cooperation among them. A year later, the council of the American Historical Association appointed a committee, with a prominent amateur state historian — Reuben Thwaites of Wisconsin — as one of its members, to suggest a plan of coordination for the four or five hundred societies. The committee prepared and fowarded an elaborate questionnaire to all the societies. Also, in 1904, the Association instituted an annual Conference of Historical Societies as a semi-autonomous body, but one whose proceedings and papers were reported in detail in the Association's Annual Reports until 1914.(6)

Another indication of the linkage between academics and amateurs was that certain state historical societies. . . . those in Minnesota, Wisconsin, Illinois, and Indiana. . . . established "a close alliance" between themselves and their state university's department of history.(7) Furthermore, such academically- trained historians as Benjamin Shambaugh in Iowa, Solon Buck in Minnesota, Dixon Ryan Fox in New York, and Julian Boyd in Pennsylvania gave long-term leadership to particular state historical societies.(8)

In 1907, the Conference on Historical Societies appointed a committee, consisting partly of amateurs such as Thomas Owen, Dunbar Rowland, and Reuben Thwaites, for the purpose of devising a plan for the cooperation of history departments and historical societies in securing and publishing

transcripts of archival material.   The committee decided, in May 1908, to
begin the "work of cooperation" with a publishing project that would appeal
to "the entire Mississippi Basin" and appointed Clarence Alvord of the
Univeristy of Illinois to supervise the project.(9)

The founding of the Mississippi Valley Historical Association, which
resulted from these collaborative efforts between amateurs and academics,
nevertheless produced a dilemma for Reuben Thwaites, a well known and
respected amateur.   To Clarence Alvord, Thwaites wrote in a positive tone,
lauding the new organization's objective, which was "to preserve and make
available for future use material that would not otherwise be accessible.
. . . I am very much interested and should be glad to cooperate to make it
a success, or to become the publishers for the Association." Thwaites
offered to meet with Alvord to discuss plans for publications if the
executive committee so desired.(10)

But Thwaites' tone changed abruptly when he wrote to a friend(11)
concerning his correspondence with Alvord, clearly revealing the profound
uneasiness and embarrassment accomplished amateurs like Thwaites felt
when faced with the prospect of associating with those they considered
casual or inept amateurs.   To Alvord, he wrote: "You have a good
executive committee, with all of whom I am acquainted by correspondence
except Mr. Paine, which is a new name to me."(12) But, to A. H. Clarke, his
friend, he confessed in a "purely" and "intensely" confidential letter that he
did not "quite have the same faith in the future of the *Mississippi Valley
Historical Association* that my good friend Mr. Alvord seems to have."
Why? — because of Mr. Paine, who some on the committee believed joined
"largely for the purpose of self-glorification." Thwaites pronounced that
Paine was "not a historian" and arrives "with only the mental and scholarly
preparation of an insurance agent." The only way the new Association would
succeed, Thwaites insisted, would be "by eliminating the Paine element." As
long as men like Paine manage historical societies, Thwaites believed, "we
shall have more bluster than scholarship." Thwaites confessed: "I sometimes
get woefully disheartened and pessimistic."(13)

The "unknown" Mr. Paine was, in fact, Secretary of the Nebraska
Historical Society and editor of a history of that state.   At the meeting at
which the Mississippi Valley Historical Association was formed, Paine was
chosen as its secretary-treasurer, a position he occupied until his death.
According to a historian of the Association, Paine "had in mind an
extensive program of activities to popularize the study of history. . . .   He
. . . hoped to build a broad popular foundation for the support of historical
study and research."(14) Thwaites, by contrast, favored calling the new
organization a "section" of the American Historical Association and hoped to
confine its membership to historical societies.(15) Alvord succeeded in
eliminating Paine's phrase "and popularize" from a draft constitution. As
altered, the purpose of the Mississippi Valley Historical Association was "to
promote historical study and research and secure cooperation between the
historical societies and the departments of history of the Mississippi
Valley."(16) Thus, from its inception, the MVHA was oriented toward
academic endeavors.(17)

Nevertheless, in the Association's earliest years, the most evident stresses and strains were produced by the antagonisms generated by seasoned amateurs, like Thwaites, who were convinced that what they did was far closer to what academic scholars were doing than to what ordinary antiquarians like Paine could accomplish.    Influential directors of state historical societies blurred the line between amateur and academic.    Their work turned historical inquiry into a spectrum of enterprise, with shadings from the rankest of antiquarians to the most analytically minded historians — all the way from Thwaite's despised Clarence Paine to Frederick Jackson Turner.

Just as amateurs and scholars joined together to form the American Historical Association, so too did they share in the writing of national history.    George Bancroft (1886) and James Schouler (1897) were both elected to the Presidency of the Association, presumably for their fame and the quality of their writings on American history.(18) And when a full national history became too detailed and ranging for one person to prepare, the so-called cooperative method, by which a number of authors contributed portions of the overall treatment, was obviously adopted from the projects supervized by the well known amateur, Justin Winsor.    As one historian explains: "The method was first employed in America on a local history and then spread to national histories.    The success of a cooperative history of Boston edited by Justin Winsor led him to apply the same method to the history of America.    The result was the *Narrative and Critical History* [of America (1886-1889)]."(19)

When Harvard's Albert Bushnell Hart, president of the Association in 1909, decided to edit a series to be entitled *The American Nation: A History*, his letter announcing the project clearly indicates why he chose the form he did.    Hart thought that the source material and writings on American history had become "so extended" and the field of study itself "so confused" that it was "hardly possible" for a single writer to prepare a history of the United States from its origins to the present. However, he believed such a history was needed "to make available the latest research and to bring out the most well-thought points of view." Hart had decided to edit a series consisting of twenty-five volumes, "to be written upon the associative method," and he hoped the state historical societies would advise him on various aspects of the project.(20)

On February 1, 1902, Hart met with the committee appointed by the Wisconsin State Historical Society, one of the state societies closely linked to a history department at a state university.    All aspects of the venture were discussed.    Hart wanted the contributors to his national history "to take into account as far as possible social and economic factors as well as political."    In volumes dealing with the political, constitutional, legal, economic, commercial, social, religious, diplomatic, and military aspects of American history, the "social and economic background of history," was to be treated in "separate volumes," "separate chapters," or "worked into the narrative."(21) It is clear that Hart was influenced by more than the cooperative method: he also took account of the wide ambit of subjects commonly dealt with in local historical writing when he sketched out his prospectus.

Reuben Thwaites, long-time Secretary of the Wisconsin Society and one of the best known antiquarians in the United States, wrote Hart that "I feel that I am really much better on the narrative than I am on stating underlying principles, and prefer it."(22) Thwaites contrasted himself with Frederick Jackson Turner, whose writings treated the development of the West "on those broad, philosophical lines for which he has won such general admiration, and in which field he stands unapproachable." Thwaites told Hart that he did not want "to venture [preparing] a Western volume, alongside Turner, unless it were chiefly of a narrative character."(23) Here is a particularly concrete example of an experienced amateur contrasting what he did and wanted to do with what he understood the new academic scholars to be doing: narrative treatment versus philosophical or analytical inquiry.

Hart replied that the conference with the committee in Wisconsin had helped "to clear up the very difficult questions of arrangements and subdivisions." Unwilling to share Thwaites' sharp distinction between amateurs and scholars, Hart added: "With regard to [you and Turner], it is more important for the series that you should participate and should participate in such a way as to give you a feeling of working in a unified field, than that we should follow any hard and fast principle of arrangement; and I will go as far as seems humanly possible in meeting the preferences of both of you."(24)

Later, when Hart convinced Thwaites to be a contributor, the general editor wrote that "[in] preparing a circular briefly describing the *American Nation*, for the information of the purchaser, I wish to say something of the personality of each writer, — his place of education, degrees, academic connections, and his previous works. Can you send me a brief statement which will contain the information for which I seek the general form of the enclosed? The statement will be carefully guarded from puffing of any kind."(25) In responding, Thwaites displayed the growing sensitivity of amateurs to the lack of proper education, degrees, academic connections. He confessed that, since "I was obliged to work for my living during the greater part of my early life, my college studies were taken irregularly with a local tutor." Thwaites admitted that "in those days, [I] had something of a contempt for degrees," but that later, living in a university town, "I saw that I had made a mistake in this matter, but it was rather too late to rectify it."(26)

The amateur Thwaites and the scholar Turner remained close friends until Thwaites' death in 1913, a death Turner called "a great loss to all of us." Turner told his friend's wife: "I have promised to give the memorial address in honor of Mr. Thwaites at Madison on Dec. 19. No one knows better than I do how hard it is to give adequate expression to our appreciation of his life and his work in this address."(27)

However, there was an unmistakably progressive domination of academic scholars in such cooperative enterprises as Hart's *American Nation* series. In Winsor's *Narrative and Critical History of America* (1886-1889), two of the thirty-four authors were professors of history and eight others were professors of other subjects, with only one of the other professors having had graduate training in history. In Hart's *American Nation* series

(1904-1907), according to one historian, "twenty one of the twenty four authors were university professors and all but two of them had done graduate work in history." In Arthur Schlesinger, Sr.'s and Dixon Ryan Fox's *History of American Life* series (1927-1948) "only two of the twelve authors [were] not university professors."(28)

But this increasingly apparent ascendancy did not result in a sudden shift away from national history as a chronological narrative filled with description.    Hart's *American Nation* series was arranged in a strictly sequential fashion and dealt (in spite of Hart's projections) largely with political developments.    Schlesinger's and Fox's *History of American Life* series was also arranged chronologically, but its authors were instructed to deal with all aspects of American life that they could find information on, not just politics.    In neither case did analysis and new methods obliterate the older form of writing history devised by amateurs.    Contributors to these series included "Critical Notes on Sources," that is, bibliographic notes on previous writings and documentary material examined, and the title pages of Hart's series indicated the volumes were based on original research.

But the transition from an amateur to an academic way of writing American history was a messy, overlapping, and ambiguous one.    In the decades after the 1890s increasing numbers of academic monographs were produced by young historians trained in graduate schools to perceive their work as a contribution to knowledge, not as an end in itself, which was the manner in which amateurs viewed their histories.    The theses of, first, Turner and, later, Beard gave a larger meaning to the studies of trained historians, but the form or content of this monographic literature did not shift suddenly to a scientific mode of writing.    As Richard Hofstadter put it:

> To some [academic historians] . . . the language of science . . . seemed to mean only zeal in collecting facts and the critical use of sources. . . .    To others it might mean striving for objectivity, avoiding judgments. . . .    To some it meant concentrating on answering questions about events rather than retelling a narrative, to others systematic and quantitative work.    In its most demanding form it meant some combination of all of these in order to formulate general laws of historical development.(29)

What the "language of science" did not mean was an arcane, technical, abstract, analytical language with its own terminology.

Amateurs like James Schouler, James Ford Rhodes, and John Bach McMaster continued to write multivolume narrative histories of the United States that appeared alongside the "cooperative series."    By the 1920s, academically trained Edward Channing continued the tradition of presenting multivolume narratives of the American past and was encouraged in his endeavor by prominent amateurs like Dunbar Rowland.(30)

As the American Historical Association became increasingly dominated by scholars at the turn of the century, cooperative efforts with amateurs became progressively more difficult to sustain.(31) For instance, planning for Hart's *American Nation* series began at the Association's meetings in the late 1890s "as a consequence of dissatisfaction" (as one historian put it) with Winsor's earlier effort. In 1914, Dunbar Rowland, an amateur and the director of the Mississippi Department of Archives and History, complained in a public letter that the council of the Association had—for at least ten years—ignored the constitution and appointed a nominating committee that chose the officers, thus ignoring the right of the rank and file to elect by ballot the officers of the convention.(32) In fact, the officers so nominated and automatically approved by the membership were increasingly often scholars, not amateurs. The Conference of Historical Societies went into a rapid decline after 1914. As one observer put it: "Tacked on usually at the end of the annual meetings of the American Historical Association, its sessions sparsely attended, its papers scarcely ever printed, and its officers and policies constantly changing, the conference . . . succeeded chiefly in enlisting the support of the societies of the [Midwest] and of those closely allied with the universities."(33) The problem was that the conference was "a volunteer, advisory body," whereas only an "autonomous national organization," a "central coordinating agency" could deal effectively in a continuous manner with the needs of the great array of state and local agencies.(34)

When, in the late 1930s, the conference appointed a policy committee to study the status of the state and local history in the United States and Canada, the committee recommended that an independent organization be formed. In 1940, the Conference decided to disband and created the American Association for State and Local History. The new society committed itself to assist both academic and amateur endeavors; to cooperate "with patriotic and civic organizations"; to "encourage the writing of good state and local histories, and promote the establishment of adequate courses on these subjects"; and to serve as a clearinghouse for "information on how to conduct historical tours, how to stage historical celebrations and pageants, how to preserve historic buildings, how to prepare and broadcast historical radio programs, and other similar topics."(35)

As the Association developed, however, it focused on the provision of services for those outside of the colleges and universities: preservationists, genealogists, professionals in historical societies, museums, and villages. It established a popular magazine of history, *American Heritage*, in 1949, along with directories, conferences, awards, bulletins, and technical pamphlets to assist state and local historical societies and agencies. In 1970, its director, William T. Alderson, stressed "[its] determination to bring history to a lay public."(36) So, what began as an offshoot of the American Historical Association, with its early mixture of amateur and academic members, became, by the 1950's, a new, separate national organization, catering largely to the needs of nonacademics: those operating state and local historical agencies and those in the larger public they served.

Though amateurs and academics shared a common membership in historical societies, and though both wrote national history, the question of whether these two groups could also agree on what constituted good local historical writing was regularly raised from the 1890s through the 1930s, during the early development of academic scholarship.

In 1897, J. Franklin Jameson presented a paper at a meeting of the still-young AHA "on the function of [state and local historical] societies with respect to research and publication," a pertinent subject in that one reason the AHA was founded "was the desire to promote better cooperation between teachers of history and historical societies." Jameson found that "the essential weakness of the publications of these institutions involved subjects too highly localized with little or no bearing on general American history; too much emphasis upon the colonial and Revolutionary periods; too much concern with genealogy; and too little attention paid to economic history."(37)

In 1921, Dixon Ryan Fox, in an assessment of state history, observed that the local historian "is generally dismissed with something of contempt as an antiquarian, uncritical, and queer, in whose myopic vision perspective has no part, and who painfully works out a futile record of the insignificant." Fox accepted the criticism that the antiquarians' "interest in the past is "incidental to genealogy, which itself grows out of snobbishness and vanity." Fox added: "[Throughout] the east, to join an historical society has too often been a gesture of social aspiration; names were added, but such infusion never stayed the course of dry rot too often, it is true; their historical interests did not come nearer than the eighteenth century."(38) And still later, Fox declared that "[of] all categories of historical writing in America county histories are probably the worst."(39)

Julian Boyd, writing in 1934, thought some of the historical journals sponsored by state and local historical societies "are badly edited, emphasize antiquarian interests, and tend toward highly localized subjects."(40) W. Stull Holt, in a speech delivered a year later, referred to "the contempt for the amateur local historian."(41) Holt found that the bulk of local historical writing "was the work of amateurs with no good models to follow: with no appreciation of the simplest test of scholarship, and with the handicap of misguided local or family pride." He thought that local histories "often resemble a second-hand bookstore operated by a junk man.  The materials are arranged in a haphazard fashion, [and] most of them are worthless." Local historical writing had been "further damaged," Holt believed, "out of sordid motives," out of the discovery "that the rapidly expanding, substantial middle class would repay flattering references in a local history by subscribing to the volume at a fancy price." Library shelves everywhere attested "to the extent of the trade and to the degradation of local history."(42)

But Jameson, Fox, Boyd, and Holt—all academically trained historians with a special interest in amateur historical inquiry—presented somewhat distorted views of the actual range and variety of the history they reviewed.    Jameson (in 1897) ignored the considerable evidence that some local historians did connect their studies to "general" American history, did deal with the nineteenth century, and did pay attention to economic developments.  Holt (in 1935) mistakenly dismissed the period from 1815 to 1875 as "a barren period for American historiography, [with little] history of any kind, good or bad, local or national . . . being written."(43) He equally erroneously indicated that worthwhile local history since then had been written only by scholars.

All of these academic observers believed that amateur local historians were bad historians, antiquarians whose writings were held in contempt by the growing community of academic scholars as well as by themselves, in varying degrees. Finding evidence that substantiated their impressions, they all ignored conflicting indications and certainly exhibited no interest in examining in a systematic fashion the actual writings of the amateurs they criticized or condemned. All agreed, however, that local history was extremely important. As Fox put it: "One may write the history of England from the point of view of London and so perhaps of France from Paris, but one cannot write the history of the United States . . . entirely from Washington."(44) Scholarly local history, Holt insisted, "is studied not for the history of the locality itself but for the light it can throw on the history of the United States. . . . In other words, the history of the whole can only be understood when its parts are known and the history of a locality is lifted from the low level of antiquarianism only when it is used as a contribution to that more worthy end, the history of the United States." Jameson's statement, made in 1897, was echoed in the writings of others: Local history is "American history locally exemplified."(45)

Around the turn of the century, Herbert Baxter Adams' largely inept efforts to focus academic scholarship on local history were eclipsed by Frederick Jackson Turner's formulations of his "frontier" thesis.(46) Both Adams and Turner sought to link the research and writing of their graduate students to an overall conceptual framework, something alien to amateurs, even accomplished ones like Thwaites. Adams, stressing transatlantic continuities, found the origins of American life in the earlier local communities of Europe, whereas Turner believed that America's frontier experience had created important forms of distinctiveness. The greater impact of Turner's persuasively presented views meant that scholarship on America's past increasingly gained a national or regional, but not a local, focus.

Jameson, Fox, Boyd, and Holt all ignored the fact that those academic historians who continued to write local history after the turn of the century did not present a different kind of account from the many amateurs who went on presenting histories of their communities. Just as was the case of scholarly studies of national history, so too with academic local historical writing after 1900: neither was a different or distinctive mode of writing about the past, but were, rather, more thorough, precise, careful histories than most amateur efforts. Shorn of the conceptual framework that Adams had earlier tried to provide, academic local history also came to feature chronology, narrative, description, and a broad-ranging treatment of many aspects of community life, all of which were leading features of the best amateur writing as it had evolved during the course of the nineteenth century. Jameson, Fox, Boyd, and Holt wanted to see a sharp distinction between academic and amateur history, but, after the turn of the century, such a distinction did not exist. Whether a local history was written by an antiquarian or a scholar from the 1900s through the 1930s did not matter in any basic sense.

During these years, there are a number of examples of antiquarians and scholars either working together on state and local history or producing histories indistinguishable from each other in form or content.(47) When academically trained John W. Wayland, who was a Professor of History at the State Normal School in Harrisonburg, Virginia, wrote histories of several counties in Virginia during the 1910s and 1920s, what he wrote was quite similar in character to what his amateur contemporary Oren Morton wrote in his series of county histories published during these same years. When Wayland and the Ruebush Publishing Co. (Morton's publisher as well) agreed in 1910 that Wayland would prepare a history of Rockingham County, Wayland wrote to the company requesting that the publisher delay making their announcement of the project. The reason was that Wayland had told a "Mr Smythe" that "some were wanting me to undertake a history of the county. He took it all right." Wayland added that "[h]e has been very kind to me, and I think the news of the agreement between us should come to him from me personally before it comes as news to his [news]paper."(48) Thus did Wayland reveal his considerable sensitivity toward an amateur historian-newspaper editor who had preceded him as a researcher and compiler.

In the preface of the published volume, Wayland thanked those who had previously written various series of "historical articles," but "at the same time he begs leave to state that the bulk of the matter presented in this volume has been collected and prepared by himself, with the generous aid of many friends, from sources that may in large measure be called original" including, official land, marriage, and court records; statutes; almanacs; newspapers; ledgers and day books; "even personal manuscripts and diaries."(49) Wayland's table of contents are neater than usual, with "Part I — Chronological" and "Part II — Topical" and a "Conclusion". His bibliography is exceptionally well organized, but the contents of his volume are like those of Morton's county histories.

When, in 1927, Wayland's *History of Shenandoah County, Virginia*(50) was published, a poet and literary critic, Allen Tate, wrote to the author: "I have perused with great interest your recently published [history]. It is a model history of its kind; for order and arrangement it is certainly the best local history I have ever seen."(51) The fact that the volume was divided into greatly varied chapters — from incidents and events and particular years to topics and a "genealogical scrap-bag" — suggests that what a literary critic looked for in local historical writing was description and detail, not overall form and coverage.

In any case, Wayland's publisher sold 680 copies of his *History* from September 1927, through May 1931 — most of them in the latter part of 1927.(52) In December 1929, E. E. Keister of the Shenandoah Publishing House wrote to Wayland: "We did not get good results from the Shenandoah County History [advertising] cards as I had expected. We received three orders in October and four only in November. Of course we should get quite a few more from these same cards as many people put off such matters for a considerable length of time."(53) When the predicted resurgence in sales did not occur — partially, no doubt, because of the deepening depression — Wayland wrote to Keister, suggesting they divide up the 750 or more remaining copies "in the same ratio in which you pay me royalties."(54) The facts that an academic scholar had written the history and a literary critic had praised it resulted in no more sales than Wayland and his publisher anticipated and no more than if the author had been an amateur.

The separation of academic and amateur historical writing in the United States has come as the result of a long, complicated process. This has been true for both national and local history. The rise of the historical profession did not result in a different kind of historical inquiry whose findings were couched in a different kind of language until academic historians incorporated the concepts, theories, and methods of other academic disciplines, a development that became unmistakenly evident by the 1960s. Just as Schlesinger's and Fox's multivolume, multiauthored *History of American Life* (1920s through the 1940s) series extended national history beyond the political into the social dimension, so too did Blake McKelvey's multivolume *Rochester* (1940s and 1950s) structure the history of a local community around successive stages of political, economic, social, and cultural development. Whereas Schlesinger and Fox sought to bring to national history the breadth of coverage long standard in local history, McKelvey tried to discern the basic characteristics of Rochester as an American urban center, American cities having been a subject Schlesinger dealt with in a general way in his own contribution to his own series: *The Rise of the City* (1933). McKelvey was "especially grateful to Professor Schlesinger . . . for his thoughtful mentorship over a period of several years in the broader study of urban history,"(55) as well as for his kindly counsel at frequent stages in the progress of this study and for the painstaking care with which he has read the entire manuscript and made innumerable suggestions, all of which have been most helpful."(56)

McKelvey admitted that "thanks to my upbringing in consecutive Methodist parsonages in central Pennsylvania, I early enjoyed a fairly intimate living acquaintance with a half-dozen towns and cities ranging from a small village . . . up through all the successive stages under study."(57) But McKelvey was also an academically trained historian and his "Rochester project" began as a result of the requirement that the towns and cities of New York state appoint official historians. When two academic historians, Dexter Perkins and McKelvey, were appointed city historian and assistant city historian of Rochester, and when Kate Gleason, a prominent citizen, left a fund for the maintenance of a history section in the Rochester Public Library, it was decided to have McKelvey prepare a history "on the basis of careful research, exact scholarship, and expert judgment." Perkins hailed the first volume, produced during World War II and published, as were all but the last of the succeeding three volumes by Harvard University Press, as "a notable landmark in the history of American historical writing." In Perkins' view, McKelvey "has made the story not only interesting in itself, but also a part of the larger story of American history in general. . . . His book deserves to be read not only by those who are interested in Rochester, but also by those who are interested in the growth of urban living in America."(58)

McKelvey rejected the standard topical approach in favor of an organizing principle based on stages of growth, arguing that if particular subjects had "been sorted out and presented as separate strands of the city's history, . . . the resulting picture would have been false, for all the developments were interrelated throughout the period.    To isolate them would be to untie the knots and utterly destroy the pattern." McKelvey tried instead to tell Rochester's history as "a series of natural stages. . . . The overall pattern of economic, civic, social, and cultural activities became progressively more complex as both the city and the civilization of which it was a part matured."(59)    McKelvey thought of his well organized, descriptive narrative as "essentially an urban biography"(60) or "a community biography."(61) He warned his readers that his "successive titles are of course, symbolically descriptive, not analytical.    Readers should not expect to find here a synthetic study of the nature and evolution of a metropolis, but rather a biographical review of the experiences of a particular community in the throes of such a transformation."(62) He added: "A full understanding of urban history will require a broader analysis, encompassing many cities and calling on the techniques of other social sciences, some of which are as yet only in a tentative stage of development."(63)

In 1954, Professor Lewis Atherton presented *Main Street on the Middle Border*, the first scholarly account of a type of American local community, the Midwestern country town.(64)   Like McKelvey, Atherton grew up in the kind of community he was writing about, giving him a feeling for and a rapport with it, but he told his readers that he had attempted "to avoid making this another 'I remember' story by eliminating my own personal experiences in mid-western country towns and oral traditions of my family going back to the Civil War and before." But, Atherton added, "my own interest in research has been determined by family background and I have also felt more competent to judge the records and experiences of others when my own family has participated in so many of the same things."(65)

Atherton "read all the reminiscences, autobiographies, and novels depicting the region and period of which I am writing," in addition to country newspapers and magazine articles, but not town records.   Calling his study "a cultural and economic history of midwestern country towns from 1865 to 1950," defining towns as "service centers" for farmers with a population of less than five thousand, Atherton ignored political activity and the factors producing economic growth or decline.   He provides vivid descriptions that enable his readers to "see" a typical country town and perceive much of its essential character, one device being to take the reader on an imaginary tour of a generalized "Main Street," it being Atherton's assumption that what lines the street should reflect what the town is all about.(66) Atherton believed that "the history of the middle border has been largely the history of its towns,"(67) and, within these fairly isolated communities, life centered on town-wide institutions and activities until developments in transportation and communication broke down this local orientation and propelled towndwellers outward into an ever-widening ambit of awareness and association.   Thus, Atherton was the first scholar to assess the overall place of local communities in "American" history.

The wholesale borrowing of theories, models, concepts, themes, techniques, and methods from other disciplines—such as political science, economics, sociology, anthropology, geography, psychology, philosophy, literary studies, linguistics, and the arts—has led to a fundamental change in the language of history, first notably during the 1960s and increasingly so since that time.   The work of scholars of both national and local history amply demonstrates this important development.   Until the 1960s, amateurs and scholars shared a descriptive language, one without an arcane terminology; it was the language of the journalist, the novelist, the unspecialized or general writer.   Since the 1960s, academic historians have appropriated the procedures of those in other disciplines and, in so doing, have greatly altered the way they write about the past.

Typically, the language of analysis accompanies descriptive prose, giving both an enlarged meaning and significance.   Statistical evidence regularly coexists with verbal illustration, not only describing but measuring historical phenomena.   Academic local historians accept the amateur's concern that all dimensions of life for which there is evidence be dealt with and either utilize or add to the great array of documentary and artifactual materials the amateurs amassed.   But scholars of local communities search for common patterns, shunning the distinctive or unique, and study all inhabitants, not just prominent families.   Urban historians—with their allies in geography, sociology, economics, and political science—focus on the phenomenon of urbanization, examining the whole spectrum of local communities to determine the extent and character of urbanization in given localities. Surveying "Professional Scholarship in America" in the 1960s, John Higham found that "[in] 1925 one-sixth of the contributors to five leading state historical journals were academic people. Thirty years later two-thirds of the contributors to the same journals had academic 'connections.'" Higham's conclusions were "[based] on a tabulation of the contributors to [journals in Massachusetts, North Carolina, Ohio, and Wisconsin] at ten year intervals from 1925 to 1955."(68) These figures graphically depict the shift in the writing of local history from the amateur to the academic.

# Conclusion

Amateur historians still write local history, but those who have been involved since the 1930s have lacked the energy, commitment, purpose, and capacity of the antiquarians whose work spanned the century and more from the 1820s through the 1930s. This change has come as a result of altered circumstances. Until the 1960s, amateurs who wrote local history were generally the only people who wanted to do so. There was no academic group with its own theories, methods, and language. Until recent years, what an amateur did had the authority of something that was virtually unchallenged. Criticism was trivial or nonexistent, with reviews or notices often arranged by the authors themselves. An antiquarian with years of collecting and research to his credit was in a position to assert his authority, to gain the assistance of those who shared his interests, but lacked the ability or interest or time to produce a history on their own. Those who contributed, assisted, and subscribed were extremely grateful that one like them would commit himself to the onerous task of producing a history of their community. The author and those around him shared a view of what the purpose and value of the enterprise were: to preserve the record of the past before it was irretrievably lost, to exhibit pride in their long-term association with their community founded and developed by ancestors worthy of their remembrance, to record the progress of their town's or city's past, and to proclaim the likelihood of a progressive future.

This was local history of the successful, by the successful, for the successful, using the past to display pride of status and accomplishment, as academic observers were quick to point out. When subscription publishers like Lewis and Clarke reduced local history to a formula for commercial profit, those whose counterparts elsewhere supported "genuine" antiquarians brought these firms their desired profits by paying to have laudatory biographical sketches and portraits included, which together comprised half or more of a "history" whose actual historical segment was written by a staff writer in the publisher's office. In short, the antiquarian pursuits that could become the central passion of an amateur historian's life could also be turned into a commercial enterprise that reduced local history to a formula.

The main reason local history could be either the result of the passionate commitment of an antiquarian's lifetime or the quickly fashioned product of a publisher looking for a profit was that in either case the purpose was to find a past that presented the prominent inhabitants of a given community and their forbears in a favorable way. In this sense, local historical writing reflected the belief among many adult white male native-born Americans that theirs was indeed a success story, and more specifically, that America was the setting for a great outpouring of local community-building whose hallmark was progress. In the antiquarians' renderings, the local past revealed continuous improvement in the lives of those who inhabited their towns and cities, that is, both ancestors and contemporaries who, with great and sustained effort, subdued the aboriginal population and fully utilized the abundant resources of a great continent.

The evolution of local historical writing from the 1820s through the 1930s was not a clear, progressive, linear process. In fact, some aspects did not change significantly over the entire period. To focus on towns and cities remained natural for amateur historians because life remained largely, though never completely, organized within local dimensions. To describe a wide array of subjects or dimensions of community life was also natural because, unlike the nation, towns and cities as communities had economic, social, and cultural dimensions, as well as political ones. The sources antiquarians used varied widely in their availability, but not in their basic types: records of the town or city or county and of its organizations and institutions, along with newspapers, family papers, and personal reminiscences, journals, memoirs, or diaries. The amateurs' writing was almost always descriptive and specific and factual and was meant to convey information, not to interpret or generalize about life in local communities. Persons who became antiquarians were usually those with prominence in the locality, those in the professions or in business, or, in any case, with deep roots in the community.

In addition to these unchanging factors, there were other aspects of the antiquarian enterprise that involved change, but change of an overlapping, overlayering kind. The annalistic-chronological treatments favored during the 1820s, 1830s, 1840s, and 1850s, were certainly exceptional in the decades following the Civil War, when a quasi-topical, increasingly encyclopedic format became dominant. But, local historical writing was too loose an enterprise, too much the product of individuals working in isolation from one another, too much a personal, idiosyncratic quest for a local past to become standardized as to form and content. Without printed publication dates, local histories would doubtless elude all efforts to establish any more than an approximate or likely time for their production. Forms, contents, and organizational schemes overlapped, persisted, or reemerged in somewhat different guise.

Similarly, those who produced local history tended to perceive themselves as compilers in the early decades of this period, as historians in the middle decades, and as editors in the late ones, but these were tendencies only. Though the mix varied as to time and place, antiquarian pursuits involved a large range of people: those who were interested in genealogy; who amassed collections of material; who contributed that material or who wrote a section of a history; who had the energy, persistence, and skill to write a whole history; who had the prominence and talent to serve as editors for a number of contributors; or who subscribed beforehand or purchased copies afterwards. In short, the writing of local history was an enterprise that could involve a lone author (and his publisher), but that could also involve interested people in several combinations in various divisions of labor and support. In other words, local histories from one end of this period to the other varied greatly in the quality of the writing, in size, in thoroughness, in organization, and in the evidence actually used.

The antiquarian impulse in its purest and most non-commercial forms was confined largely — though never entirely, to two types of local communities: New England towns and growing cities everywhere. Antiquarians needed to believe that the local past was worth retrieving, that their towns and cities and counties exemplified community-building enterprises whose history was of a kind that the people involved would want to collect and preserve materials on and, above all, to read accounts of. The Puritan towns of early new England exhibited a utopian, religious character that induced their more durable inhabitants to care in just this manner: to care about saving the materials of the past and to support those who took time to write histories of that past. Such New Englanders viewed the Puritan founders as heroic ancestors who had bequeathed to all Americans a priceless legacy of religious and political freedom and whose communities these descendants still proudly inhabited. The best town historians thus looked to the past for the nourishment of an overall purpose for life.

The only other kind of community that generated this kind of allegiance was the fast-growing city whose increasing size displayed dramatic physical and social evidence of material progress. The successful inhabitants of these urban centers were pleased and flattered by antiquarian biographical and historical accounts of their communities, whose hallmark had been increasing material and technical well-being for everyone. Such undoubted material progress generated optimism about America's future and of the city's central role in that future. The best urban historians thus used the past to illustrate the likelihood of a progressive future.

By the Great Depression of the 1930s, this large, loose antiquarian enterprise began to lose momentum. The Depression, which was prolonged and deep, called into question the assumption of continued progress, as local communities throughout the nation experienced marked economic decline. It became difficult to celebrate the progress of a town or a city in such circumstances. And when economic recovery came, the ascendancy of corporations with national dimensions meant that people in the professions and management became highly mobile and were thus often unable to sustain a long association with a given locality. This was the same group who had previously supported antiquarian endeavors during the time when a professional or business person was likely to remain in a particular town or city throughout his career because firms were typically local or regional, not national in scope.

In other words, the very people whose strongly developed sense of place provided essential support for amateur local history until the 1930s, became thereafter increasingly mobile and therefore were less likely to support historical projects involving their birthplaces or hometowns, though, on occasion, some have continued to do so, either as authors or as subscribers.(1) Also, as American life became progressively nationalized, as local communities became less isolated and more influenced by national and international institutions and groups, life lived at the local level seemed less significant, certainly less distinctive, and less worthy of recording. That which is unique about one's community has seemed in recent decades to be less important than what that community shares with other towns or cities of comparable size and character.(2)

Other factors in the decline of amateur local historical writing pertain to developments in the writing itself. Long before the 1930s, some of those active in antiquarian pursuits reacted negatively to the great length of the multivolume histories being regularly produced in the decades between the Civil War and the Great Depression. These people, authors and publishing firms as well, favored shorter accounts, narrative treatments emphasizing unusual or vivid incidents in the pasts of out-of-the-ordinary communities. In their view, local history should not constitute a huge and expensive encyclopedia or reference work, but a short, dramatic narrative history as a story. The writers paid to produce narrative accounts were not notably effective storytellers, however, and did not provide a successful alternative to the encyclopedic treatments of the genuine antiquarians. Nothing reveals how sapped of enterprise and commitment antiquarian endeavors have become since the 1930s than the glaring fact that most recent amateur local historical writing on the older Eastern towns is almost entirely derivative, that is, slavishing based on the research and findings of those who wrote before the 1940s, except for surveys of current community life, offered as updates. This is in marked contrast to those writing a second history, after the Civil War, or even a third history, after the turn of the century, of these early towns, at which times authors often expanded upon the pioneering versions. Today's amateur local historians are in awe of their predecessors' long dedication, massive research, and voluminous writing. All of this, surely, is graphic evidence of the decline of the antiquarian spirit. When academic historians became interested in local history during the 1960s, they quickly came to dominate a field whose erstwhile contributors lacked energy and purpose.

The work of those who participated in the vast, sprawling antiquarian enterprise from the 1820s through the 1930s demonstrated with clarity that, until recently, the predominant popular impulse to investigate the past has been intensely personal in nature. To find meaning for one's own life in history has been a phenomenon involving many literate, successful people, and not one confined to a trained elite. The antiquarians found meaning in a personal, familial, and communal past, not in one involving distant leaders or masses of people or far away events and developments. Now that life has become increasingly global in its patterns, it is appropriate to ask what, if anything, is the lasting legacy of these amateur local historians. Is there any continued validity for such efforts at a time when academic scholars try to understand the complex mass society of the modern world? Is it still of value to believe that one's interest in the past should emanate from simple curiosity about one's own family and community at a time when family and community life are mere reflections of much larger patterns and no longer the controlling influences over an individual's life and personal history?

In spite of current circumstances, the antiquarian impulse has a timeless validity in at least three senses. One is that part of that impulse has been to collect and preserve both the documentary and artifactual evidence of the past. Founders of historical societies, museums, and archives, the amateur local historians have left for future use a priceless legacy, which is much of the source material everyone now uses for the study of the pretwentieth-century past. Some of this material is now lost, and our only record of it is in the form of the long quotations, descriptions, and illustrations the antiquarians had a penchant for including in their local histories. Professional staffs now manage the repositories previously established by such amateurs. But the amateurs' descendants and like-minded successors still possess the impulse to collect and preserve the evidence of their familial and communal past, and our repositories are still dependent upon the generosity of these local elites for many kinds of material.

Another is that, regardless of the scale on which the basic patterns of human life are most insightfully examined, the amateur local historians understood with notable intensity that the only reality in human life is the life of the individual; all else is abstraction and a generality imposed by the human mind. It is, therefore, natural to enter into an investigation of history out of curiosity for one's own past. For the antiquarians, the historical impulse was generated out of a personal quest for meaning. This is something of value at all times and in all places, even in an era when the hallmark of good historical writing is its degree of objectivity and cool detachment. So, too, is the awareness the antiquarians shared that families and communities are interconnected and can be best understood through an account of many, interrelated dimensions of life: economic, social, cultural-intellectual, political. In other words, they instinctively realized that to adequately convey the reality of a human community, of whatever scale, required an awareness of private as well as public life, of perspectives as varied as an individual's or a group's or an entire community's, and of the impossibility of satisfactorily isolating one dimension of life from the others. In this, the antiquarians, through their linked genealogical and historical accounts, serve as a model for academic scholars who only recently have begun to search for ways to construct a history of the "national community" of the United States and of Americans that exhibits the same objectives, that goes beyond the obvious political or "public" sphere.

But there were also shortcomings, weaknesses, and limitations displayed in the work of the antiquarians during the period that their labors dominated the American historical enterprise.   Though many others were involved in what they did, the amateur local historians were usually unconcerned about those who did not persist or become successful in their community.   The self-centeredness of their personal quest for a historical identity precluded their paying attention   (unless forced to do so by obvious and important events or developments) to anybody other than their "own kind."  They were not concerned with those who failed or were transient, in short, with the whole community, as their genealogical, biographical, and communal accounts abundantly reveal.   Their tunnelled view of the past also usually resulted in a lack of interest in the wider patterns of local life, in what made towns and cities alike and not just distinctive, as the particular setting for their particular family. Therefore, the documentary and artifactual evidence they so assiduously collected was also used selectively.   Indian artifacts were described to show an alien, subdued civilization.   Old houses and their furnishing were depicted to provide concrete evidence for the persistence of their own families. Photographs or illustrations and genealogical charts or biographical sketches were the visual and verbal imprints of historical or contemporary prominence in the community.   Public records documented the actions of municipal leaders, just as church records were the basis for an account of successive ministries, and the papers of a great range of organizations and associations were used to show off those who joined prominence with communal undertakings.

Mesmerized by the array of sources at their disposal, the antiquarians lacked both the capacity and the desire to find larger meaning and significance in them.   (The only exceptions were the antiquarians in Massachusetts, who related the past of particular towns to a large "Puritan" culture and a few urban historians, who tried to address the question of why only a small number of communities became large cities.) Great chunks of data were transposed largely unaltered onto their printed pages in the confidence that what was copied would serve as positive testimony to the ancestral families and communities they worked to preserve and praise. Usually lacking the capacity as writers to do more than to list or compile information, their accounts were typically devoid of vivid description or dramatic presentation.   Without the notable writer's innate sense of the larger human significance of the people and communities whose past was being revealed, the antiquarians assured that their histories would be of interest only to those with a direct, palpable connection to a particular town or city or county.   The audience for a given local history, therefore, was generally small and insular, in marked contrast to that for writers of fiction, or even such national historians (and accomplished writers) as George Bancroft and Francis Parkman.   Amateur local histories usually became reference works for genealogists, nostalgic testaments for those of prominence whose roots had been severed through emigration from their hometown, and mug-books for those who stayed on and sought the imprint of historical respectability while still alive.

The domination of local historical writing by academics since the 1960s has brought the study of family and local community life into the same framework that enfolds inquiry into national and regional life. Scholars now seek to establish a meaning and importance beyond that of the amateurs who were interested in recovering and preserving their own past. The objective of academic historians is to find the underlying patterns of life at the local level, to analyze, not what makes a particular community unlike any other on earth, but what that community shares with others of similar size and character. In this search, scholars have unquestionably enhanced our understanding of local history and have given more meaning than amateurs did to the ascertainable facts relating to the past of any given town or city. Through interpretation, analysis, synthesis, conceptualization, and generalization, the same facts that the amateur historians have related gained a significance of a different kind. From the perspective of a time when the patterns of life have become enlarged to a national and international scope, scholars have in a sense broken down the isolation of local communities that amateurs still experienced as they wrote. Academic local history has conquered space, showing how life in one town or city was like that in another.

But these accomplishments have come with problems, and what scholars are achieving could be done with considerably more effectiveness. For instance, the emphasis on urbanization in the field of urban history has distorted the way academic historians study local communities, most of which have remained small and whose history, therefore, is not understood because of a futile search for a process not much in evidence. It would be more effective to examine smaller localities for those characteristics of a political, economic, social, and cultural-intellectual nature associated with smallness. Instead of placing a community along a spectrum from a hamlet to a metropolis, in line with the geographers' hallowed central-place theory or the economists' regional-economic theory, local historians could concentrate on what accounts for the fact that most communities do not become cities, and do not grow rapidly and continuously.

Similarly, these same historians do not appear to be sufficiently aware of the perhaps irreducible complexities that arise when local communities are defined as social, geographic, physical, political, or economic entities with each definition embracing a different size of population or territory. For example, "Deerfield" as a township differs from "Deerfield" as several clusters of settlement, which in turn differs from "Deerfield" as a group of "Yankee" inhabitants who perceived immigrants as outsiders, just as "Boston" is one thing as an economic or cultural region and another as a political entity, which is a fraction of the metropolitan area. That a community has differing meanings depending upon how it is defined is obvious, but scholars have not confronted the problem, or made it central to their work.

Then, too, many urban historians who have studied particular aspects of cities have lost the context of community life by narrowing their inquiry to such subjects as social and geographic mobility, residential patterns, power, wealth, poverty, and class, thereby ignoring the totality of life in the communities studied. These same historians have sometimes focused on particular communities for evidence of general phenomena, without considering the distortions that arise from viewing evidence on one aspect of community life in isolation from other aspects. A similar problem arises when the period chosen for study is far less than the entire history of the community being examined. A phenomenon with a time frame of a quarter or a half a century could take on quite a different appearance if it were interpreted from initial settlement to the present.

Even when scholars do study a community as a whole, they are concerned that it be typed, made to fit into a classification. Communities are not studied for themselves, but for what they share with others with the same overall characteristics. This impulse has led sociologists, if not urban historians, to create fictional names ("Middletown," "Yankee City," "Plainsville") for the particular towns and cities they have probed. One sociologist has written that it does not matter which community is selected, because all exhibit certain characteristics of life in the mass society of this century: "['Jonesville'] . . . is an actual place which we have come to know well because we studied it for several years. Although we chose it above all other places for its particular qualifications for our study, we know that most other places, for purposes of evidence, might have done equally well. The Jonesvilles, Smithtowns, Greenfields, and all other -villes, -towns, and -fields of America are essentially alike."(3)

But how far from fiction, how far from the reality of people who actually lived and died in actual communities is this device? To say that people who actually lived can be subsumed under fictional names is to suggest that human beings are automatons, interchangeable, valued only for their typicality, and not for their uniqueness. And when academic historians write about, for example, urban villages, Puritan towns, cattle towns, mining camps, Midwestern country towns, or the urban frontier, they are creating types of local communities. But types do not exist, except in our minds; only particular communities exist. Similarly, when historians, particularly urban historians, create statistical and descriptive profiles of people, that which they count, measure, and describe is a fiction as well, in the same sense. What was typical was not what was real: only individuals are real. Conclusions about groups or whole populations in towns and cities thus rest on evidence that is used systematically to create statistical averages and generalized descriptions that conjure up fictionalized portraits of a faceless human form, not human beings who really lived.

This has become a fundamental problem for all of academic scholarship as it has swiftly moved away from the empiricism of the amateur to forms, categories, models, laws, and concepts. In a basic sense, the antiquarian was more rooted in reality as he or she pursued the search for his or her own past than the scholar whose study is valued above all for its pertinence to prevailing generalizations.

Academic historians would do well to remember that these antiquarians embarked upon an intensely personal quest as they sought to find their past. What prompted them was a desire to elaborate on their identity, to nurture their self-esteem, to worship their ancestors, and to celebrate progress in their communities as well as their own success or prominence. This was a matrix of motivation and purpose that was self-centered, but greatly animated by that fact. What they did was done out of curiosity, caring, passion, and love. Is academic inquiry, with its objectivity and its dispassionate concern for truth, clearly superior to antiquarian endeavor if scholars lack this sense of personal involvement? Academic historians have added analysis to description, generalizations to particularities, meaning to trivia, awareness of the essential characteristics of human life to simple storytelling.   Why can't they also search in their studies for the past's significance to their *own* lives? In this way, historical inquiry could become "whole" again.

# Notes

## INTRODUCTION

1.　J. H. Plumb, *The Death of the Past* (Boston:　Houghton-Mifflin Co., 1970), p. 25.

2.　*Ibid.*, pp. 30-31.

3.　Alonzo Lewis, *The History of Lynn* (Boston:　J. H. Eastburn, 1829), pp. 4-5.

4.　David J. Russo, *Families and Communities:　A New View of American History* (Nashville, Tenn.:　American Association for State and Local History, 1974).

5.　Peter Laslett, *The World We Have Lost* (London:　Methuen, 1965).

6.　*Daniel J. Boorstin, The Americans:　The National Experience* (New York:　Random House, 1965), pp. 363, 367.

7.　For an account of this phenomenon, see:　Frances Fitzgerald, *America Revised:　History Schoolbooks in the Twentieth Century* (Boston: Little, Brown, and Co., 1979).

8.　Michael Kraus, *The Writing of American History*, rev. ed. (Norman, Okla.:　University of Oklahoma Press, 1985) revised by Davis D. Joyce.

9.　Harvey Wish, *The American Historian:　A Social-Intellectual History of the Writing of the American Past* (New York:　Oxford University Press, 1960).

10.　David Van Tassel, *Recording America's Past:　An Interpretation of the Development of Historical Studies in America, 1607-1884* (Chicago: University of Chicago Press, 1960).

11.　George H. Callcott, *History in the United States, 1800-1860:　Its Practice and Purpose* (Baltimore:　The Johns Hopkins Press, 1970).

## CHAPTER ONE

1.  Van Tassel, pp. 4-5.
2.  *Ibid.*, p. 9.
3.  *Ibid.*, p. 12. Peter Gay, *A Loss of Mastery: Puritan Historians in Colonial America* (Berkeley: University of California Press, 1966).
4.  The historical literature on Puritan towns is abundant. The most notable treatments are: Daniel J. Boorstin, *The Americans: The Colonial Experience* (New York: Random House, 1958), pp. 3-31; Page Smith, *As a City Upon a Hill: The Town in American History* (New York: Alfred A. Knopf, 1966), pp. 3-16; Michael Zuckerman, *Peaceable Kingdoms: New England Towns in the Eighteenth Century* (New York: Alfred A. Knopf, 1970); and Kenneth Lockridge, *A New England Town: The First Hundred Years* (New York: W. W. Norton, 1970).
5.  For a study of one such treatment: David J. Russo, "The Deerfield Massacre of 1704 and Local Historical Writing in the United States," Paul Fritz and David Williams, eds., *The Triumph of Culture: 18th Century Perspectives* (Toronto: A. M. Hakkert, 1972), pp. 315-333. For a recent overall assessment: Alden Vaughan and Edward W. Clark, eds., *Puritans among the Indians: Accounts of Captivity and Redemption* (Cambridge, Mass.: Harvard University Press, 1981), pp. 1-28.
6.  For a general treatment of regional studies in England during the late sixteenth and the entire seventeenth centuries: Stanley G. Mendyk, "'Painting the Landscape': Regional Study in Britain during the Seventeenth Century" (Ph. D. Dissertation, McMaster University, Hamilton, Ontario, 1983).
7.  Farmer to Coffin, April 21, 1824, Coffin Papers, Essex Institute.
8.  "Constitution of the Massachusetts Historical Society," Massachusetts Historical Society, *Collections*, I (Boston, 1792), p. 5; Van Tassel, pp. 60-61.
9.  *Ibid.*, p. 62.
10. New-York Historical Society, *Collections*, II (New York, 1814), Preface; Van Tassel, p. 63.
11. Van Tassel, pp. 65-66.
12. Pennsylvania Historical Society, *Memoirs*, I (Philadelphia, 1826), in the Constitution of the society; Van Tassel, pp. 64-65.
13. For a treatment of the early historical societies: Leslie W. Dunlap, *American Historical Societies, 1790-1860* (Madison, Wis., 1944).
14. Van Tassel, p. 101.
15. *Ibid.*, pp. 101-102.
16. *Ibid.*, p. 76.
17. For an account of Weems: Daniel J. Boorstin, *The Americans: The National Experience* (New York: Random House, 1965), pp. 340-345.
18. *Ibid.*, pp. 357-359.
19. *Ibid.*, pp. 381-382.
20. Quoted in Van Tassel, p. 75 from the July 28, 1832 entry in MS Journal, Sparks Papers, Houghton Library, Harvard University.
21. Van Tassel, p. 109.
22. *Ibid.*

23. J. Hammond Trumbull to Coffin, September 20, 1850, Coffin Papers, Essex Institute.

24. William C. Folger to Coffin, July 1, 1851, *ibid.*

25. Van Tassel, p. 44.

26. *Ibid.*, pp. 87-88.

27. George Bancroft, *The History of the United States of America from the Discovery of the Continent*, abr. and ed. by Russell B. Nye (Chicago: University of Chicago Press, 1966), p. xv. For a discussion of Bancroft's history: *ibid.*, p. xiii-xxvi; also: Russell B. Nye, *George Bancroft* (New York: Alfred A. Knopf, 1945); and Van Tassel, pp. 116-118.

28. *Ibid.*, p. 89.

29. *Ibid.*, pp. 88-90.

30. *Ibid.*, p. 88; also pp. 91-92, 116.

31. *Ibid.*, pp. 139-140.

32. *Ibid.*, pp. 138-139.

33. *Ibid.*, pp. 47-50.

34. *Ibid.*, p. 51.

35. *Ibid.*

36. Thomas Greenleaf, *Geographical Gazetteer of the Towns in the Commonwealth of Massachusetts* (Boston: Greenleaf and Freeman, 1784-85) [issued in parts].

37. Massachusetts Historical Society, *Collections*, 1794, p. 241.

38. Van Tassel, pp. 61-62.

39. Massachusetts Historical Society, *Collections*, 1792, p. 112.

40. Felt Papers, Essex Institute.

41. November 8, 1828, *ibid.*

42. Farmer to Felt, February 26, 1828, *Ibid.*

43. For example: Farmer to Felt, June 17, September 25, October 17, November 8, 1828; January 11, 1829; and August 30, November 17, 1830, *ibid.*

44. Coffin to Farmer, February 8, 1828, Coffin Papers, Essex Institute.

45. Farmer to Felt, August 1, 1833; January 16, 1834; December 7, 1835, Felt Papers, Essex Institute.

46. Farmer to Lewis, September 12, 1826; April 7, May 14, August 27, October 24, 1828, Lewis Papers, Essex Institute.

47. January 7, 1833, Felt Papers, Essex Institute.

48. September 12, 1826, Lewis Papers, Essex Institute.

49. Baldwin to Coffin, n. d., 1832, Coffin Papers, Essex Institute.

50. Baldwin to Coffin, January 21, 1832. Baldwin wrote in a similar vein to Lemuel Shattuck on January 28, 1833, Shattuck Papers, Massachusetts Historical Society.

51. Baldwin to Lewis, March 9, 1832, Lewis Papers, Essex Institute.

52. May 6, 1851, Coffin Papers, Essex Institute.

53. April 21, 1824, *ibid.*

54. September 5, 1829, Lewis Papers, Essex Institute.

55. September 3, 1827, Shattuck Papers, Massachusetts Historical Society.

56. Farmer to Alonzo Lewis, May 3, 1831, Lewis Papers, Essex Institute.

57.    Farmer to Coffin, March 31, 1831, Coffin Papers, Essex Institute.

58.    Watson to Lewis, July, 1831, Lewis Papers, Essex Institute.

59.    Willis to Lewis, April 5, 1830, *ibid.*; Willis to Coffin, August 5, 1851, Coffin Papers, Essex Institute; Coffin to Willis, April 20, August 21, 1855, Willis Papers, vol. A, #52, #53, Maine Historical Society; Shattuck to Willis, July 11, 1856, Willis to Shattuck, July 14, 1856 (copy), *ibid.*, #115.

60.    *Ibid.*, vol. G, #44.

61.    Watson to Willis, March 29, 1852, *ibid.*, #61.

62.    Same to same, April 25, 1852, *ibid.*, #62.

63.    Quoted in: same to same, February 22, 1850, *ibid.*, #44.

64.    January 23, 1833, Shattuck Papers, Massachusetts Historical Society.

65.    Coffin to John Farmer, June 3, 1824, Coffin Papers, Essex Institute.

66.    C. C. Chase to Coffin, February 21, 1848, *ibid.*

67.    J. W. Hanson, *History of Gardiner, Pittson, and West Gardiner* (Gardiner, Maine: William Palmer, 1852), p. iii.

68.    Frances Caulkins, *History of Norwich* (Norwich, Conn.: Thomas Robinson, 1845), p. vi.

69.    Nye, Russell B., *Society and Culture in America, 1830-1860* (New York: Harper and Row, 1974), p. 98. For a discussion of these novels: pp. 97-101.

70.    "Statistics and the State: Changing Social Thought and the Emergence of a Quantitative Mentality in America, 1790-1820," *William and Mary Quarterly*, 28, third series, January, 1981, pp. 36-37. For a book-length treatment: Patricia Cohen, *A Calculating People: The Spread of Numeracy in Early America* (Chicago: University of Chicago Press, 1982).

71.    *Ibid.*, pp. 50-55.

72.    Cohen has a list on pp. 37-38, "Statistics and the State."

73.    John Farmer and Jacob B. Moore, *Gazetteer of the State of New Hampshire* (Concord, N.H.: Jacob B. Moore, 1823), p. iii.

74.    Cohen, p. 39.

75.    *Ibid.*, p. 40.

76.    Hayward to Willis, July 18, 1848, Willis Papers, vol. G., #17, Maine Historical Society.

77.    Van Tassel, pp. 21-23.

78.    Bernard Weisberger, *The American Newspaperman* (Chicago: University of Chicago Press, 1961), p. 18.

79.    Farmer to Felt, May 27, 1829, Felt Papers, Essex Institute.

80.    October 12, 1827, Shattuck Papers, Massachusetts Historical Society.

81.    John S. Champney to Snow, November 22, 1825, Snow Papers, Massachusetts Historical Society.

82.    Rufus C. Torrey, *History of the Town of Fitchburg* (Fitchburg, Mass.: J. Garfield, Printer, 1836), p. iii. For a similar prefatory comment: Emory Washburn, *Topographical and Historical Sketches of the Town of Leicester* (Worcester, Mass.: Rogers and Griffin, 1826), p. 3.

83.    Folsom to Willis, October 31, 1831, vol. E, #17, William Willis Papers, Maine Historical Society.

84.  Edwin M. Stone, *History of Beverly* (Boston:  J. Munroe, 1843), p. iii.

85.  William Barry, *A History of Framingham* (Boston:  J. Munroe, 1847), p. iii.

86.  Caleb Butler, *History of the Town of Groton* (Boston:  T. R. Marvin, 1848), p. v.

87.  John F. Watson, *Annals of Philadelphia*, (Philadelphia:  E. L. Carey and A. Hart, and New York:  G. and C. and H. Carvill, 1830), p. iii.

88.  Caulkins, p. v.

89.  Hermann Ludewigg, *The Literature of American Local History:  A Bibliographical Essay* (New York, 1846), p. xvi.

90.  Van Tassel, pp. 23-24.


**CHAPTER TWO**

1.  Allan Johnson and Dumas Malone, eds.,*Dictionary of American Biography, 21 vols.* (New York:  Charles Scribner's Sons, 1928-1937), vol. 6, pp. 316-317 (Felt), p. 577 (Francis); vol. 18, pp. 387-388 (Thacher).

2.  *Ibid.*, vol. 6, pp. 316-317.

3.  *Ibid.*, vol. 20, p. 403.

4.  American Antiquarian Society, *Proceedings* April, 1898, 12, new series, April, 1898, p. 229.

5.  Massachusetts Historical Society, *Proceedings* 12, second series, November, 1897, p. 460.

6.  John Daggett, *Sketch of the History of Attleborough* (Dedham:  II. Mann, 1834), p. 3.

7.  Lemuel Shattuck, *History of the Town of Concord* (Boston:  Russel, Odiorne, and Co., and Concord:  John Stacey, 1835), p. iii.

8.  Leonard Bliss, *The History of Rehoboth* (Boston:  Otis, Broaders, and Co., 1836), p. iii.

9.  William Lincoln, *History of Worcester* (Worcester, Mass:  Moses D. Phillips and Co., 1837), p. v. A similar statement appears in Nahum Mitchell's *History of the Early Settlement of Bridgewater* (Boston:  Kidder and Wright, 1840), p. 3.

10.  David Willard, *History of Greenfield* (Greenfield, Mass.:  Kneeland and Eastman, 1838), p. iii.

11.  Daggett, p. 3.

12.  Shattuck, p. iii.

13.  James Draper, *History of Spencer* (Worcester, Mass.:  Henry J. Howland, 1841), p. iv.

14.  George F. Clark, *A History of the Town of Norton* (Boston:  Crosby, Nichols and Co., 1859), p. vii.

15.  Coffin Papers, Essex Institute.

16.  Daniel Ricketson, *The History of New Bedford* (New Bedford, Mass.:  author, 1852), p. vii.

17.  *Ibid.*, p. iv.

18.  Lewis, p. 14.

19.  Lincoln, p. vi.

20.   J. W. Hanson, *History of the Town of Danvers* (Danvers, Mass., 1848), p. iv.

21.   Samuel Drake, *The History and Antiquities of the City of Boston* (Boston: Luther Steven, 1854), p. iv.

22.   Coffin Papers, Essex Institute.

23.   Coffin to Lewis, March 23, 1828, Lewis Papers, Essex Institute.

24.   Shattuck to Lewis, May 4, 1828, Shattuck Papers, Massachusetts Historical Society.

25.   Shattuck to Coffin, December 8, 1831, Coffin Papers, Essex Institute.

26.   Lincoln to Shattuck, October 31, 1831, Shattuck Papers, Massachusetts Historical Society.

27.   Felt Papers, Essex Institute.

28.   *Ibid.*

29.   For example:   [?] Jenks to Alonzo Lewis, November 6, 1827, March 28, May 12, 1829, January 12, 1832, Lewis Papers, Essex Institute; General Temple to Joseph Felt, March 3, 1834, Nathaniel Lord to Joseph Felt, February 22, 1834, Felt Papers, Essex Institute.

30.   *Circular* [January 31, 1827], p. 15, Williamson Papers, Maine Historical Society.

31.   Torry [?] to Williamson, March 14, 1823, Blaney [?] to Williamson, September 7, 1824, Little to Williamson, March [?], 1827, *ibid.*

32.   Leavitt to Williamson, April 27, 1821, Ellingwood to Williamson, December 12, 1820, Stonson to Williamson, February 10, 1827, Hobbes to Williamson, April 2, 1823, Blaney [?] to Williamson, September 7, 1824, Coffin to Williamson, November [?] 1822, Cushing to Williamson, March 20, 1828, Giddings to Williamson, November 6, 1826, Gardiner to Williamson, November 13, 1820, Pullen to Williamson, May 12, 1821, Eaton to Williamson, June 5, 1821, Parker to Williamson, March 24, 1821, Sewall to Williamson, March 21, 1820, Francis to Williamson, January 12, 1820, Johnson to Williamson, April 25, 1827, McIntire to Williamson, December 25, 1820, Chandler to Williamson, December 6, 1820, *ibid.*

33.   Wellman to Williamson, May 24, 1825, *ibid.*

34.   Cutler to Williamson, April 4, 1827, Francis to Williamson, January 12, 1820, *ibid.*

35.   Memoranda, in Pamphlet, *ibid.*

36.   William Williamson, *The History of the State of Maine, 2 vols.* (Hallowell, Maine: Glazier, Masters and Co., 1832), vol. 1, p. iii-iv.

37.   *Ibid.*, pp. 712-714.

38.   George Folsom, *History of Saco and Biddeford* (Saco, Maine: Alex C. Putnam, 1830), advertisement.

39.   William Willis, *History of Portland* (Portland, Maine:  Barley and Noyes, 1865) 2nd ed., vol. 1, p. xi.

40.   William Willis, *History of Portland* (Portland, Maine:  Day, Fraser, and Co., 1831), advertisement.

41.   *Dictionary of American Biography*, vol. 20, p. 309; William Willis *The History of Portland* 2 vols. (Portland:  Maine Historical Society, 1972), vol. 1, Foreword.

42. Folsom to Willis, July 16, 1850, vol. G, #48, William Willis Papers, Maine Historical Society.

43. Mitchell to Willis, November 21, 1849, vol. G, #39, *ibid.*

44. Preble to Willis, February 8, 1858, vol. A, #191, *ibid.*

45. William Willis, (1972), vol. 1, Foreword.

46. Willis Diary, vol. 4, Portland Public Library.

47. Johnston to Willis, July 24, 1847, vol. G, #5, William Willis Papers, Maine Historical Society.

48. Folsom to Willis, July 2, 1852, vol. G, #65, *ibid.*

49. Sibley to Willis, August [?], 1851, vol. G, #53, *ibid.*

50. Same to same, September 15, 1851, vol. G, #5[?], *ibid.*

51. Gardiner to Willis, September 8, 1849; March 27, May 1, 1851, vol. G, #68, #69, #72, *ibid.*

52. Norton to Willis, July 22, August 16, 1858, January 4, 10, 28, March 8, 24, 1859, vol. A, #153-160, #261, *ibid.*

53. March 5, 1857, vol. 3, Willis Diary, Portland Public Library. See also: February 2, 1855, vol. 2; March 5, 1857, January 26, 1858, vol. 3, *ibid.*

54. Vol. 4, *ibid.*

55. Jacob B. Moore, *A Topographical and Historical Sketch of the Town of Andover* (Concord, N.H.: Hill and Moore, 1822).

56. *Dictionary of American Biography*, vol. 13, p. 127.

57. Moore thanked Farmer for information on the tribe of Indians who inhabited the area. Farmer occasionally wrote to Moore about their work. Farmer to Moore, October 28, 1822; June 6, 1828, Moore Papers, vol. 2, Harvard University.

58. Nathaniel Adams, *Annals of Portsmouth*, (Exeter, N.H.: Norris, 1825).

59. Charles J. Fox, *History of the Old Township of Dunstable* (Nashua, N. H.: Charles and Gill, 1846), p. 3.

60. *Ibid.*, p. iv.

61. *Ibid.*, p. v.

62. *Ibid.*, p. 3.

63. *Dictionary of American Biography*, vol. 2, pp. 488-489.

64. *Autobiography of Nathaniel Bouton*, John Bell Bouton, editor (New York: Anson D. F. Randolph Co., 1879), p. 57.

65. John Bell Bouton, *Character and Life Work of Rev. Nathaniel Bouton* (Concord, N.H.: Mrs. Arthur E. Clark, 1902), p. 8.

66. *Autobiography of Nathaniel Bouton*, pp. 80-81.

67. Nathaniel Bouton, *History of Concord* (Concord, N.H.: Benning W. Sanborn, 1856), pp. 1-2.

68. *Dictionary of American Biography*, vol. 17, pp. 528-529.

69. William Staples, *Annals of the Town of Providence* (Providence: Knoles and Vose, 1843), pp. iv-v.

70. For evidence: Bruce C. Daniels, *The Connecticut Town: Growth and Development* (Middletown, Conn.: Wesleyan University Press, 1979), p. 75. Also: Bruce C. Daniels, *Dissent and Conformity on Narragansett Bay: The Colonial Rhode Island Town* (Middletown, Conn.: Wesleyan University Press, 1983).

71.   Guy Fessenden, *The History of Warren* (Providence:  H. H. Brown, 1845).

72.   Caulkins, p. v.

73.   *Vermont Gazetteer – Proposal by Josiah Dunham*, Dunham-Thompson Papers, Vermont Historical Society.

74.   [?] to Dunham, August 25, 1814; [?] to Dunham, July 5, 1814; [?] Goodrich to Dunham, July 14,1814; B. Welles to Dunham, October 18, 1814; M. Kenny to Dunham, October 8, 1814, *ibid.*

75.   *Proposals for Publishing a Gazetteer of the State of Vermont* (October, 1823), *ibid.*

76.   For example: Apollos Warner (of Barnard) to Thompson, March 24, 1824; Asabel Stone (of Brillport) to Thompson, May 20, [?]; A. Burington (of Burke) to Thompson, April 24, 1824; Thomas F. Hammond (of Reading) to Thompson, June [?], 1824; James Whitelaw (of Ryegate) to Thompson, February 3, 1824; Samuel Shuttlesworth (of Sharon) to Thompson, August 10, 1824; P. Towner (of Charlotte) to Thompson, December 31, 1823; Ebenezer Wheelock (of Whiting) to Thompson, March 8, 1824; J. A. Mather (of Whiting) to Thompson, December 24, 1823, *ibid.*

77.   Zaddock Thompson, *A Gazetteer of the State of Vermont* (Montpelier, Vermont: E. P. Walton, 1824), pp. v-vi.

78.   Responses: Lamb (of Bridgeport) to Thompson, December 21, 1841; T. S. H. (of Stockbridge) to Thompson, May 6, 1842; N. W. French (of Lunenburg) to Thompson, [?], 1842; Pliny Safford (of Westminster) to Thompson, October 20, 1840; H. T. Keyes (of Vershire) to Thompson, December 6, 1841, Dunham-Thompson Papers, Vermont Historical Society.

79.   For example:   Noyes (of Putney) to Thompson, December 28, 1840, *ibid.*

80.   White (of Washington) to Thompson, March 5, 1842, *ibid.*; Chapman (of Tinmouth) to Thompson, January 13, 1842, *ibid.*

81.   For example:  Lamb (of Bridgeport) to Thompson, December 21, 1841; Perkins (of Castleton) to Thompson, June 1, 1842; Washburn (of Ludlow) to Thompson, [?], 1842, *ibid.*

82.   Zaddock Thompson, *History of Vermont* (Burlington, Vt.: Chauncey Goodrich, 1842), p. i.

83.   Samuel Swift, *History of the Town of Middlebury* (Middlebury, Vt.: A. H. Copeland, 1859), pp. 2-3.

84.   *Ibid.*, notice.

85.   John Weeks, *History of Salisbury, Vermont* (Middlebury, Vt.: A. H. Copeland, 1860), p. 358.

86.   Josiah Goodhue, *History of the Town of Shoreham* (Middlebury, Vt.: A. H. Copeland, 1861), pp. iii-iv.

87.   Lyman Matthews, *History of the Town of Cornwall, Vermont* (Middlebury, Vt.:  Mead and Fuller, 1862), pp. v-vi.


**CHAPTER THREE**

1.   Erastus Worthington, *The History of Dedham* (Boston:   Dutton and  Wentworth,  Printers,  1827),  p.  3.  For  a  statement  of  a  similar  kind:

Solomon Lincoln, *History of the Town of Hingham* (Hingham, Mass.:  Caleb Gill, Jr, and Farmer and Brown, 1827), p. iii.

2.      Daggett, p. 3. For a similar statement:   Charles Hudson, *History of the Town of Westminster* (Mendon, Mass.:  G. W. Stacey, 1832), Preface.

3.      Lewis, pp. 4-5.

4.      [?] to Lewis, September 24, 1829, Lewis Papers, Essex Institute.

5.      Farmer to Coffin, August 29, 1829, *Ibid.*

6.      Farmer to Lewis, September 5, 1829, *Ibid.*

7.      Charles Ellis, *The History of Roxbury Town* (Boston:   Samuel Drake, 1847), p. 6.

8.      Andrew Ward, *History of the Town of Shrewsbury* (Boston: Samuel Drake, 1847), p. 5.

9.      Ricketson, p. vi.

10.     Examples:   James Thacher, *History of the Town of Plymouth* (Boston: Marsh, Capen, and Lyon, 1835), Preface; Herman Mann, *Historical Annals of Dedham* (Dedham:   the author, 1847), pp. 131-134, Conclusion; J. W. Hanson, *History of the Town of Danvers*, pp. v-viii; Edwin Stone, *History of Beverly*, pp. 306-309; Alonzo Lewis, *The History of Lynn*, pp. 7-8.

11.     Fox, p. 6.

12.     Barry, p. iii.

13.     Stone, pp. 301-306. For a similar distinction between material progress and the continued need to emulate the Puritans' character:   John Weeks, *History of Salisbury, Vermont*, p. 349.

14.     Lewis, pp. 8-10.

15.     Joseph Felt, *History of Ipswich, Essex, and Hamilton* (Cambridge, Mass.: C. Folsom, 1834), p. 2.

16.     *Ibid.*, p. 211.

17.     Lewis, p. 60.

18.     Felt, *History of Ipswich, Essex, and Hamilton*, p. 208.

19.     Lewis, p. 141.

20.     Felt, *History of Ipswich, Essex, and Hamilton*, p. 90.

21.     *Ibid.*, pp. 151-152.

22.     *Ibid.*, p. 102.

23.     *Ibid.*, p. 58.

24.     *Ibid.*, p. 114.

25.     *Ibid.*, p. 195

26.     Solomon Lincoln (1827):   "It has been my endeavor to be scrupulously correct" *History of the Town of Hingham*, p. iii; Leonard Bliss (1836):   "Nothing has been inserted which did not bear the stamp of truth," *History of Rehoboth*, p. iv; William Lincoln (1837):   "The primary purpose has been accuracy," *History of Worcester*, p. v; Joshua Coffin (1845): "Throughout the whole of this compilation he has endeavored to make a broad distinction between fact and tradition, and to relate nothing as fact, which he does not believe to be true," *A Sketch of the History of Newbury, Newburyport, and West Newbury* (Boston:   Samuel Drake, 1845), p. iv; Charles J. Fox (1846):   "It would be inconvenient and burdensome to cite the authority for every statement that is made, but the reader may be assured that no fact is stated as such without what is deemed to be good authority. The value of a work like this depends in great measure upon the

accuracy of its details, and to this the writer confidentially lays claim." *History of the Old Township of Dunstable*, p. 3; William Barry (1847): "Suffice it to say that the author has endeavored to be accurate and perspicuous," *A History of Framingham*, p. iv; Herman Mann (1847): "In the following annals but little scope has been given to fancy, or regard paid to traditionary legends, unless accompanied by corroborating circumstances which leave no doubt of their correctness, the design being confined principally to the relation of *facts,*" *Historical Annals of Dedham*, p. vi. See also: David Wilder, *The History of Leominster* (Fitchburg: Reveille Office, 1853), p. 4; Francis Jackson, *History of the Early Settlement of Newton* (Boston: Stacy and Richardson, 1854), p. iv; Daniel Ricketson, *The History of New Bedford*, p. iv; George F. Clark, *A History of the Town of Norton*, p. vi.

27.   Mann, pp. 4-5.

28.   Abiel Abbot, *History of Andover* (Andover, Mass.: Flagg and Gould, 1829), advertisement.

29.   Bouton, p. v.

30.   Caleb Snow, *A History of Boston* (Boston: Abel Bowen, 1825), p. iii.

31.   Drake, p. vi.

32.   Mann, p. 5.

33.   Samuel Deane, *History of Scituate* (Boston: J. Loring, 1831), p. 2.

34.   Hudson, Preface.

35.   Daggett, p. 3.

36.   William Lincoln, p. v.

37.   Stone, p. iii.

38.   Hanson, p. iii.

39.   Coffin, p. iv.

40.   Felt, p. 16.

41.   *Ibid.*, pp, 6-7.

42.   Bouton, p. 1.

43.   Weeks, p. 349.

44.   Josiah Goodhue, *History of the Town of Shoreham* (Middlebury, Vt.: A. H. Copeland, 1861), p. 111.

45.   Johnson to Williamson, December 31, 1819, Williamson Papers, Maine Historical Society. Jacob Moore's gazetteer for New Hampshire was published in 1823 and Zadock Thompson's for Vermont in 1824.

46.   Erastus Worthington's *Dedham* (1827), after chapters on the settlement and a description of the physical setting, settles into an annalistic treatment of the town. William Biglow's *Sherburn* (1830) is part gazetter and part official history. Lemuel Shattuck's *Concord* combined chronology with a topical treatment of "ecclesiastical history," "natural history," "topographical history," and "social and statistical history". Euphemia Vale Smith's *Newburyport* (1854) divided the town's history into periods which were given titles: settlement (1635-1764); incorporation (1764-1783); commercial prosperity (1783-1806); successive disasters (1807-1815); peace, but not prosperity (1815-1835); resuscitation, annexation, and city charter (1835-1854).

47. William Barry's *Framingham* (1874) contains sections entitled civil, ecclesiastical, and topographical. John S. Barry's *Hanover* (1853) has chapters on such subjects as "natural history," "Indians," "ecclesiastical history," "education," "military history," "incidents of the Revolution," "manufactures and trade," and "ship-building," before trailing off into two miscellaneous segments. Charles Brook's *Medford* (1855) has chapters on political, military, and ecclesiastical history, and on education, public buildings, and trade, before petering out in miscellany. It is evident that the topical format spurred at least some of the antiquarians to assemble their material into categories covering as many dimensions of local life as they could garner information for.

48. Jacob B. Moore, *Annals of the Town of Concord* (Concord, N. H.: Jacob B. Moore, 1824), pp. 53-54.

49. Deane, p. 165.

50. Nahum Mitchell, *History of the Early Settlement of Bridgewater* (Boston: Kidder and Wright, 1840), p. 4-5.

51. Ward, p. 3

52. Brooks, p. vi.

53. Coffin, p. 2; Felt, p. 1.

54. Felt, p. 1.

55. *Ibid.*, pp. 6-7.

56. *Ibid.*, p. 14; Lewis, pp. 25-33.

57. Felt, pp. 214-246.

58. *Ibid.*, pp. 55-58.

59. *Ibid.*, pp. 114-115.

60. Lewis, pp. 86-87, 160; Felt, pp. 140-152.

61. *Ibid.*, p. 95.

62. *Ibid.*, pp. 95-101.

63. *Ibid.*, pp. 89, 91-92.

64. *Ibid.*, pp. 199-211.

65. *Ibid.*, pp. 153-158, 194-195, 198-199.

66. *Ibid,* pp. 195-197.

67. Marjorie Stafford, *Subscription Book Publishing in the United States, 1865-1930* (Urbana, Ill.: M.A. Thesis, University of Illinois, 1943). Also: Downing P. O'Harra, *Book Publishing in the United States, 1860 to 1901, Including Statistical Tables and Charts to 1927* (Urbana, Ill.: M.A. Thesis, University of Illinois, 1928).

68. Felt, pp. 301-304.

69."Agreement with Bowen," May 17, 1824, Calcb Snow Papers, Massachusetts Historical Society.

70. James Savage to Lewis, May 22, 1829; Eastburn to Lewis, August 27, December 29, 1829, Lewis Papers, Essex Institute.

71. Coffin to Lewis, May, 1829, *ibid.*

72. Same to same, October 6, 1829, *ibid.*

73. "Agreement with Bowen," May 17, 1824, Caleb Snow Papers, Massachusetts Historical Society.

74. Solsom to Felt, June 25, 1834, Felt Papers, Essex Institute.

75. "Agreement with Bowen," May 17, 1824, Caleb Snow Papers, Massachusetts Historical Society.

76.    Snow, p. iii.
77.    Coffin to Lewis, May, 1829, Lewis Papers, Essex Institute.
78.    James Draper, *History of the Town of Plymouth*, 2d ed. (Boston: Marsh, Capen, and Lyon, 1835) p. iii.
79.    James Draper, *History of Spencer*, 2d ed. (Worcester, Mass.: Henry J. Howland, 1860 ), p.v.
80.    White to Lewis, August 11, 1829, Lewis Papers, Essex Institute.
81.    Farmer to Lewis, August 21, 1830, *ibid.*
82.    [?] to Lewis, September 24, 1829, *ibid.*
83.    Higginson to Felt, March 18, 1835, Felt Papers, Essex Institute.
84.    Folsom to Felt, February 1, 1831, *ibid.*
85.    Lewis to Felt, May 1, 1830, *ibid.*
86.    Birney to Coffin, June 8, 1850, Coffin Papers, Essex Institute.
87.    Morse to Coffin, October 9, 1845, *ibid.*
88.    James L. Loring to Coffin, April 2, 1845, *ibid.*
89.    [?] to Lewis, September 24, 1829, Lewis Papers, Essex Institute.
90.    Farmer to Lewis, October 16, 1829; also, August 21, 1830, *ibid.*
91.    Eastburn to Lewis, August 27, 1829, *ibid.*
92.    *North American Review* 42, (January-June, 1836, pp. 448-467 (Shattuck); 57, July-October, 1843, pp. 242-243 (Stone); 82, January-April, 1856, pp. 279-280 (Brooks); 83, July-October, 1856, pp. 52-66 (Bond), pp. 551-553 (Drake); 91, July-October, 1860, pp. 565-567 (Babson).
93.    *North American Review*, 42, January-June, 1836, p. 449.
94.    *Ibid.*, p. 453.
95.    *Ibid.*, p. 456.
96.    Two influential studies on the high incidence of geographic mobility are: Peter R. Knights, *The Plain People of Boston, 1830-1860* (New York: Oxford University Press, 1971) and Steven Thernstrom, *The Other Bostonians: Poverty and Progress in the American Metropolis* (Cambridge, Mass.: Harvard University Press, 1973).

**CHAPTER FOUR**

1.    From "Notices of the Press," in Benjamin Dorr, *A Memoir of John Fanning Watson* (Philadelphia: Collins, Printer, 1861), pp. 83, 84, 87.
2.    Watson to Willis, February 22, 1850, Willis Papers, vol. G, #44, Maine Historical Society.
3.    Deborah D. Waters, "Philadelphia's Boswell:  John Fanning Watson," *The Pennsylvania Magazine of History and Biography* 98, January, 1974, p. 5; Watson, "Diary of John F. Watson's Journey to New Orleans," Watson Papers (DMI 58X29.123-4), Historical Society of Pennsylvania.
4.    Waters, p. 11.
5.    Watson to Peters, April 8, 1823, Peters Papers, vol. 12, p. 24, Historical Society of Pennsylvania.
6.    Waters, pp. 17-18.
7.    Watson Papers (Am. 301, 381-382-383), Historical Society of Pennsylvania.

8. Watson to Du Ponceau, March 23, 1824, Gratz Collection, Historical Society of Pennsylvania.

9. Vaux to Watson, July 22, August 23, 1824, *ibid*. (AM 30163, 38-39-40).

10. Same to same, September 28, 1824, *ibid*. (AM 30163, 46).

11. Watson to Vaux, September 30, 1824, Vaux Papers, Historical Society of Pennsylvania.

12. Waters, p. 15; See Watson's note at the end of Rawle to Watson, September 28, 1825, Watson Papers (AM 30163), Historical Society of Pennsylvania.

13. Dorr, p. 29.

14. Everett to Watson, November 15, 1825, Watson Papers (AM 30163, III), Historical Society of Pennsylvania.

15. For evidence: Watson to Alonzo Lewis, July [?], 1831, Lewis Papers, Essex Institute.

16. Waters, p. 16; *Bucks County Patriot*, November 30, 1826, Watson Papers (AM 3013, 191), Historical Society of Pennsylvania.

17. Preface, "Historical Collections," *ibid*.

18. Watson to Smith, May 21, 1827, Library Company of Philadelphia Collection (Yi2-7299), Historical Society of Pennsylvania.

19. Watson to J. Jay Smith, September [?], 1829, Library Company of Philadelphia Collection (Yi2-7299), Historical Society of Pennsylvania.

20. Waters, p. 22.

21. Watson to Vaux, December 9, 1829, Society Collection, Historical Society of Pennsylvania.

22. John F. Watson, *Annals of Philadelphia* (Philadelphia: E.L. Grey, and New York: G. & C. & H. Carvill, 1830), pp. 633-634.

23. *Ibid*., pp. 1-35.

24. *Ibid*., p. 32.

25. *Ibid*., p. 34.

26. *Ibid*., pp. 36-48.

27. *Ibid*., pp. 51-58.

28. *Ibid*., pp. 59-94.

29. *Ibid*., pp. 95-109.

30. *Ibid*., pp. 111-115.

31. *Ibid*., p. 161.

32. *Ibid*., p. 163.

33. *Ibid*., pp. 164-165.

34. *Ibid*., pp. 171-182.

35. *Ibid*., pp. 183-190.

36. *Ibid*., p. 183.

37. *Ibid*., pp. 191-226.

38. *Ibid*., p. 220.

39. *Ibid*., p. 221.

40. *Ibid*., p. 227.

41. *Ibid*., pp. 227-236.

42. *Ibid*., pp. 237-244.

43. *Ibid*., p. 245.

44. *Ibid*., p. 257.

45.  *Ibid.*, p. 259.
46.  *Ibid.*, p. 261.
47.  *Ibid.*, p. 264.
48.  *Ibid.*, pp. 279-282.
49.  *Ibid.*, pp. 435-436.
50.  *Ibid.*, p. 437.
51.  *Ibid.*, p. 454.
52.  *Ibid.*, p. 470.
53.  *Ibid.*, p. 472.
54.  *Ibid.*, p. 477.
55.  *Ibid.*, p. 479.
56.  *Ibid.*, p. 485.
57.  *Ibid.*, pp. 438-493.
58.  *Ibid.*, p. 566.
59.  *Ibid.*, pp. 569-594.
60.  *Ibid.*, pp. 602-603.
61.  *Ibid.*, pp. 604-615.
62.  *Ibid.*, p. 617
63.  *Ibid.*, p. 622.
64.  *Ibid.*, p. 710.
65.  *Ibid.*, p. 712.
66.  *Ibid.*, pp. 676-693.
67.  Watson to Barker, July [?], 1830, Library Company of Philadelphia Collection. (Yi2-7370), Historical Society of Pennsylvania.
68.  Dreer  Collection,  vol.  186,  p.  3,  Historical  Society  of Pennsylvania.
69.  *Ibid.*
70.  *North American Review* 36, January-April, 1833, p. 395.
71.  *Ibid.*, p. 360.
72.  John  F.  Watson,  *Annals  of  Philadelphia*  2d  ed.,  2  vols. (Philadelphia:  the author, 1844), pp. iv-vii.
73.  *Ibid.*, pp. iii-iv.
74.  Dreer  Collection,  vol.  186,  p.  349,  Historical  Society  of Pennsylvania.
75.  *Ibid.*
76.  Watson to Horatio Jones, Jr., March 6, 1845, Society Collection, Historical Society of Pennsylvania.
77.  Neville B. Craig, *The History of Pittsburgh* (Pittsburgh:  J. H. Mellon, 1851).
78.  George H. Morgan, *Annals, Comprising Memoirs, Incidents, and Statistics of Harrisburg* (Harrisburg: G. A. Brooks, 1858).
79.  John  F.  Watson,  *Annals  of  Philadelphia*  3rd  ed.,  2  vols. (Philadelphia:  Whiting and Thomas, 1856-57), p. iii.
80.  Watson  to  Jenkins,  September  18,  1860,  Society  Collection, Historical Society of Pennsylvania.
81.  Originally  published  as  a  part  of  *Annals  of  Philadelphia*  (1830 edition), and then separately published in 1832.
82.  Dorr, p. 29.

83.   James Fennimore Cooper, *The Chronicles of Cooperstown* (Albany, N.Y.: H. & F. Phinney, 1838).

84.   James Fennimore Cooper and Samuel T. Livermore, *A Condensed History of Cooperstown* (Albany, N.Y.: J. Munsell, 1862), p. 9.

85.   Russel B. Nye, *Society and Culture in America, 1830-1860*, pp. 97-101: Nina Baym, *Novels, Readers, and Reviewers: Responses to Fiction in Antebellum America* (Ithaca, N.Y.:  Cornell University Press, 1984), pp. 23-24, 44.

86.   Cooper and Livermore, *A Condensed History of Cooperstown*, pp. v-vi.

87.   John B. Wilkinson, *The Annals of Binghamton* (Binghamton, N.Y.: Cooke and Davis, Printers, 1840), p. vii.

88.   Edward M. Ruttenber, *History of the Town of Newburgh* (Newburgh, N.Y.: autor, 1859), p. v.

89.   James Lemon, *The Best Poor Man's Country:   A Geographical Study of Early Southeastern Pennsylvania* (Baltimore:   Johns Hopkins University Press, 1972), pp. 98-149.

90.   John W. Reps, *Town Planning in Frontier America* (Princeton: Princeton University Press, 1969), pp. 181-223.

91.   Carl Bridenbaugh, *Myths and Realities:   Societies of the Colonial South* (Baton Rouge, La.:   Louisiana State University Press, 1952), pp. 147-152.

92.   Rhys Isaac, *The Transformation of Virginia, 1740-1790* (Chapel Hill:  University of North Carolina Press, 1982).

## CHAPTER FIVE

1.   For a survey of the impact of the war on civilian life in the Union:  George W. Smith and Charles Judah, eds., *Life in the North During the Civil War:  A Source History* (Albuquerque, N.M.:  University of New Mexico Press, 1966).

2.   Van Tassel, p. 150; also, pp. 149-154.

3.   James Schouler, *History of the United States of America under the Constitution*, 7 vols. (New York: Dodd, Mead and Company, 1880-1913).

4.   Van Tassel, p. 157.

5.   *Ibid.*, p. 159.

6.   *Congressional Record*, vol. 4, pt. 2, p. 1402, Senate Session, March 2, 1876; also, *ibid., vol. 4, pt. 1, p. 260, Senate Session, January 5, 1876*.

7.   John S. Hittel, *A History of the City of San Francisco* (San Francisco: A. L. Bancroft and Co., 1878).

8.   *Ibid.*, p. 5. For an example of the kind of address Congress called for:  Rev. Payson W. Lyman, *Historical Address Delivered at the Centennial Celebration in Easthampton, Mass., July 4, 1876* (Springfield, Mass.:   Clark W. Bryan and Co., 1877).

9.   George R. Rowell, *Forty Years an Advertising Agent, 1865-1905* (New York:  Printer's Ink Publishing Co., 1906), pp. 225-236; David J. Russo,

*The Origins of Local News in the U.S. Country Press, 1840's-1870's* (Lexington, Ky.: Journalism Monographs, #65, February 1980), p. 11.

10.   For an account of one such local society's "field meetings": David J. Russo, "The Deerfield Massacre of 1704 and Local Historical Writing in the United States," in Paul Fritz and David Williams, eds., *The Triumph of Culture: 18th Century Perspectives* (Toronto: A. M. Hakkert, 1972). pp. 325-326.

11.   Lyman Draper was the organization's Secretary from 1852 to 1891. For an assessment of Draper: William B. Hesseltine, "Lyman Copeland Draper, 1815-1891," *Wisconsin Magazine of History* 35 (Spring, 1952), pp. 163-176; for a book-length version: William B. Hesseltine; *Pioneer's Mission: The Story of Lyman Copeland Draper* (Madison, Wis.: State Historical Society of Wisconsin, 1954).

12.   D. S. Divine, *The Importance of Local History* (Madison, Wis., 1874), pp. 3-4.

13.   California Historical Society *Papers*, 1, pt. 1, pp. 1-2, 11-12.

14.   "Fifty Years of Historical Work in New Jersey," New Jersey Historical *Proceedings*, series 2, 13 (1895), pp. 311-312.

15.   Mississippi Historical Society *Publications*, 1 (1898), pp. 96-97.

16.   *Indiana History Bulletin*, 1, no. 5, pp. 35-38.

17.   Harlow Lindley, "A Systematic Study of Local History," *Michigan Historical Magazine* (1933), pp. 109-113.

18.   For a fuller account, see Russo, *The Origins of Local News.*

19.   Carl C. Weicht, "The Local Historian and the Newspaper," *Minnesota History*, 13 (1932), pp. 45-46.

20.   *Ibid.*, pp. 47-48.

21.   *Ibid.*, p. 50.

22.   *Ibid.*, p. 53.

23.   Winfield S. Nevins, "The Study of Local History," *New England Magazine* 8, new series, March-August, 1893, pp. 28-30.

24.   Claude S. Larzelerle, "The Study of Local History," *Journal of Education*, 66 (June-December, 1907), pp. 544-545.

25.   Charles A. Ellwood, "How History Can Be Taught from a Sociological Point of View," *Education*, 30, 1909-1910, pp. 300-303.

26.   *Ibid.*, p. 306.

27.   "Local History and the Civic Renaissance in New York," *The American Monthly Review of Reviews*, 16, July-December, 1897, pp. 446-449.

28.   *Ibid.*, p. 447.

29.   *Ibid.*, p. 448.

30.   *Ibid.*, p. 449.

31.   Herbert T. Wade, "What the Pageant Does for Local History," *Review of Reviews* 48, July-December, 1913, pp. 328-333.

32.   *Ibid.*, pp. 328-329.

33.   *Ibid.*, p. 329.

34.   *Ibid.*, p. 333.

35.   *Scribner's Magazine* 48, July December, 1910, p. 250.

36.   For Trumbull's activities as a paid genealogist: J. B. Trumbull Collection, Forbes Library, Northampton, Massachusetts.

37.  R. B. Pugh, "The Structure and Aims of the Vitoria History of the Counties of England," *Bulletin of the Institute of Historical Research* 40, 1967, p. 67.

38.  Lowell [Mass.] Historical Society *Contributions*, 2 (nos. 1 and 2 and 3) (October 1921), pp. 24-35.

39.  *Ibid.*, p. 24.

40.  "Town Histories," New Hampshire Historical Society *Proceedings*, 5 (1905-1912), pp. 262-270.

41.  *Ibid.*, pp. 262-263.

42.  *Ibid.*, pp. 263, 269.

43.  *Ibid.*, p. 269.

44.  *Ibid.*, p. 263.

45.  *Ibid.*, p. 264.

46.  *Ibid.*, p. 263.

## CHAPTER SIX

1.  *Dictionary of American Biography*, vol. 17, pp. 342-343.

2.  *Ibid.*, vol. 1, pp. 556-557.

3.  *Ibid.*, vol. 13, pp. 389-390.  "Old" Dunstable included territory on both sides of the Massachusetts, New Hampshire line and was later divided into new townships on either side of the border.

4.  Lucius Paige, *History of Hardwick* (Boston:  Houghton, Mifflin, and Co., 1883).

5.  *Ibid.*, p. v.

6.  *Ibid.*, p. vi.

7.  *Ibid.*, p. viii.

8.  James F. Hunnewell, *A Century of Town Life:  A History of Charlestown* (Boston: Little, Brown, and Co., 1888).

9.  *Ibid.*, pp. 1-2.

10.  Alfred S. Hudson, *The History of Sudbury* (Boston:  R. H. Blodgett, 1889), p. vii. Hudson's italics.

11.  *Ibid.*, p. 659.

12.  Henry S. Nourse, *History of the Town of Harvard, 1732-1893* (Harvard, Mass.:  Warren Hapgood, 1894), pp. i-iii.

13.  Josiah H. Temple, *A History of the Town of Northfield, Massachusetts* (Albany, N. Y.: Joel Munsell, 1875), pp. iv-v.

14.  George Sheldon, *A History of Deerfield, Massachusetts*, 2 vols. (Greenfield, Mass.: E. A. Hall and Co., 1895-1896), vol. 1, p. iv.

15.  *Ibid.*

16.  Margaret Whiting "Recollections of George Sheldon," p. 3, Sheldon Papers, Pocumtuck Valley Association Library, Deerfield, Massachusetts. This segment on Sheldon is excerpted from David J. Russo, "The Deerfield Massacre of 1704 and Local Historical Writing in the United States."

17.  Sheldon, vol. 1, pp. 324-325.

18.  Pocumtuck Valley Memorial Association *Proceedings*, vol. 4 (1901), pp. 241-242.

19.  *Ibid.*, vol. 7 (1921), p. 60.

20. Sheldon, vol. 1, p. 316.

21. *Ibid.*, pp. 100, 104-105.

22. John Williams, *The Redeemed Captive Returning to Zion* (1707; Springfield, Mass.: The H. R. Huntting Co., 1908).

23. Pocumtuck Valley Memorial Association *Proceedings*, vol. 4 (1903), pp. 385-386.

24. *Ibid.*, vol. 6 (1917), p. 369.

25. *Ibid.*, vol. 4 (1901), pp. 270-271.

26. *Ibid.*, vol. 5 (1906), p. 149.

27. For a general treatment of the continuing utopian impulse within local community-building: Page Smith, *As a City Upon a Hill: The Town in American History* (New York: Alfred A. Knopf, 1966), pp. 17-36, 41-54.

28. The efforts of several of these pioneering state historians are described in their surviving papers: James Lanman of Michigan, in the Woodbridge Papers, Detroit Public Library; Edward D. Neill of Minnesota, in the Neill Papers, Minnesota Historical Society; James G. M. Ramsey of Tennessee, in the Ramsey Papers, University of Tennessee; Charles C. Jones of Georgia, in the Jones Papers, Duke University, and the Jones Collection, University of Georgia; George R. Fairbanks of Florida, in the Fairbanks Papers, Florida State University; and Hubert H. Bancroft, in the Bancroft Collection, University of California-Berkeley.

29. Andrew Young, *History of Warsaw* (Buffalo: Sage Sons and Co., 1869).

30. George H. Tinkham, *History of Stockton* (San Francisco: W. H. Hinton, Printers, 1880).

31. J. Marmus Jensen, *History of Provo* (Provo, Utah: 1924).

32. Frederick Davis, *History of Jacksonville* (Jacksonville, Fla.: Florida Historical Society, 1925).

33. Isabella Brayton, *The Story of Hartford* [New York] (Glens Falls, N.Y.: Bullard Press, 1929).

34. In the Midatlantic area, **Pennsylvania:** Byberry and Moreland, 1867; Pithole, 1867; Phoenixville, 1872; Bethlehem, 1872; Chester, 1877; Altoona, 1880; Hanover, 1885; Waynesboro, 1900; Bethlehem, 1903; Connelsville, 1906; Athens, 1908; Catasaugua, 1914; Lancaster, 1917; Germantown, 1933 and Pine Grove, 1935. **New Jersey:** Princeton, 1879; Montclair, 1894 and Jersey City, 1902. **New York:** Portland, 1873; Moravia, 1874; Concord, 1883; Conesus, 1887; Dryden, 1898; New Paltz, 1903 and Poughkeepsie, 1905.

In the South, **Maryland:** Cumberland, 1878; Poconoke City, 1883 and Annapolis, 1887. **Kentucky:** Lexington, 1872; Maysville, 1936 and Lexington, 1939. **Missouri:** Independence, 1927. **Virginia:** Fredericksburg, 1908. **South Carolina:** Camden, 1905. **Georgia:** Columbus, 1929. **Florida:** Jacksonville, 1911 and Key West, 1912. **Alabama:** Greensboro, 1908 and Huntsville, 1916. **Mississippi:** Columbus, 1909.

In the Mid-West: **Michigan:** Howell, 1868; Vermontville, 1897; Howell, 1911; Leslie, 1914; St. Joseph, 1928 and Van Buren, 1930. **Ohio:** Barnesville, 1899; Marietta, 1903; Oberlin, 1933 and Bowling Green, 1933. **Indiana:** Evansville, 1897; Vicennes (2 Vols.), 1902 and Michigan City, 1908.

**Illinois:**    Peoria, 1870; Round Prairie and Plymouth, 1876; Bloomington and Normal, 1879 and Rockford, 1900. **Wisconsin:**    Madison, 1874 and Neenah, 1878. **Minnesota:** Red Wing, 1933. **Iowa:** Nevin, 1901 and Malvern, 1917.

In the Plains, Mountains, and Pacific coast:    **Kansas:**    Fort Riley, 1926 and Emporia, 1929. **Arizona:** Tucson, 1930. **Utah:** Lehi, 1913. **Colorado:** Pueblo, 1917. **California:** Monrovia, 1927.

35.    Elizabethtown (1889-1890), Paducah (1927), and Russelville, Kentucky; Old Point Comfort (1881), Virginia; Shephardstown (1931), West Virginia; Athens (1879), Georgia; St. Andrews (1922), Florida. In the Midatlantic region:    Easton (1906), Pennsylvania; Dover (1922), New Jersey; Pine Plains (1897), New York.

36.    Hamilton (1896-1901), and Lancaster (1898), Ohio; Remington (1894), Indiana; Sheshequin (1902), Pennsylvania.

37.    Philias Garand, *Historical Sketch of the Village of Clayton*, (Clayton, N. Y.: G. H. Bates, 1902).

38.    Uzal V. Condit, *The History of Easton* (Easton, Penn.:    G. W. West, 1889).

39.    James Hadden, *A History of Uniontown* (Akron, Ohio:    New Werner Co., 1913).

40.    John J. McLaurin, *The Story of Johnstown* (Harrisburg, Penn.:    J. M. Place, 1890).

41.    James Helmen, *History of Emmitsburg* (Frederick, Md.:    Citizens Press, 1906).

42.    Natalie Cooper, *History of Fort Wayne* (Fairmont, W. V., 1940).

43.    Maude Hearn-O'Pry, *Chronicles of Shreveport* (Shreveport, La.: Journal Printing co., 1928).

44.    Wallace A. Bruce, *History of Fort Wayne* (Fort Wayne, Ind.:    D. W. Jones, 1868).

45.    Richard Cordley, *A History of Lawrence, Kansas* (Lawrence, Kan.: E. F. Caldwell, 1895).

46.    I have selected Martin as a subject for scrutiny because he did not stand out and because his papers survive, revealing a good deal about the various aspects of a local antiquarian's work.

47.    [?] to Martin, March 18, 1869; James Wrigley (Librarian, Historical Society of Pennsylvania) to Martin, June 19, 1869; John Jordan (Historical Society of Pennsylvania) to Martin, January 10, 1872, Martin Papers, Historical Society of Pennsylvania.

48.    Draft statement in miscellaneous documents, *ibid*.

49.    On Milchsack's activities as an agent:    Milchsack to Martin, February 21, 27, March 5, 9, 1872, *ibid*.

50.    William H. Hutchings to Martin, April 16, 1874, *ibid*.

51.    [?] to Martin, May 5, 1874, *ibid*.

52.    Westcott to Martin, November 21, 1872, *ibid*.

53.    Pennypacker to Martin, April 26, 1874, *ibid*.

54.    The publisher turned out to be, not Lippincott, but another Philadelphia firm: O. Rogers.

55.    John Hill Martin, *Historical Sketch of Bethlehem* (Philadelphia: O. Rogers, 1872), p. 1.

56. Futhley to Martin, November 28, 1874, Martin Papers, Historical Society of Pennsylvania.

57. Same to same, April 12, 1872, *ibid*.

58. Same to same, May 6, 1872, *ibid*.

59. Martin to Davis, November 3, 1873, *ibid*.

60. J. W. Davis to Martin, July 9, 1874, *ibid*.

61. Edward A. Price to Martin, April 20, 1872, *ibid*.

62. R. M. Johnson to Martin, March 6, 1873, *ibid*.

63. John H. Brinton to Martin, March 18, 1874; H. G. Ashmead to Martin, March 23, April 14, 1874, *ibid*.

64. F. A. Dick to Martin, June 25, 1874, *ibid*.

65. H. G. Ashmead to Martin, September 24, 1874, *ibid*.

66. F. A. Dick to Martin, June 13, 1874, *ibid*.

67. Edward J. Willcox to Martin, November 25, 1872, *ibid*.

68. George Smith to Martin, November 23, 1874; E. Sayres to Martin, February 29, 1874, *ibid*.

69. For example: William Hubbell to Martin, August 20, 1874; [?] to Martin, July 20, 1874, *ibid*.

70. Harvey to Martin, September 2, 1874, *ibid*.

71. Futhley to Martin, October 18, 1873, *ibid*.

72. Martin to John J. Groff, October 18, 1872, *ibid*.

73. Groff to Martin, October 25, 1872, *ibid*.

74. For example: Lemuel Moss to Martin, March 7, 1873, *Ibid*. The individual proposed by Moss agreed to serve as a contributor: Horatio G. Jones to Martin, March 10, 1873, *ibid*.

75. Dick to Martin, December 25, 1872, *ibid*.

76. Miller to Martin, April 27, [?], *ibid*.

77. Westcott to Martin, [no date], *ibid*.

78. Justis to Martin, December 3, 1873, *ibid*.

79. Ashmead to Martin, April 7, 1873, *ibid*.

80. For example: Samuel Field to Martin, February 5, 1874; John Hill Brinton to Martin, May 19, 1874; [?] to Martin, May 9, 1874; [?] to Martin, May 22, 1874; [?] to Martin, September 7, 1874, *ibid*.

81. E. Darlington to Martin, June 11, 1873, *ibid*.

82. J. Smith Futhley to Martin, April 12, 1872, *ibid*.

83. William Platt to Martin, March 10, 1873; E. H. Engle to Martin, April 11, 1873; [?] to Martin, April 4, 27, October 23, 1873, *ibid*.

84. J. Smith Futhley to Martin, January 6, 1875, *ibid*.

85. [?] to Martin, March 8, 1871, *ibid*.

86. Strickland Knears to Martin, November 22, 1872, *ibid*.

87. Y. S. Walter to Martin, April 14, 1873, *ibid*.

88. A. E. Shanafelt to Martin, March 17, 1873; Joseph Taylor to Martin, April 30, 1872; [?] to Martin, November 17, 1873, *ibid*.

89. Ward Baker to Martin, November 12, 1872; W. B. Brownell to Martin, January 28, 1873, *ibid*.

90. [?] to Martin, April 1, 1873, *ibid*.

91. [?] to Martin, April 27, 1874, *ibid*.

92. [?] to Martin, December 6, 1873, *ibid*.

93. [?] to Martin, October 15, 1874, *ibid*.

94.  Cope to Martin, April 10, 1874, *ibid.*

95.  Same to same, November 15, 1874, *ibid.*

96.  Same to same, November 29, 1874, *ibid.*

97.  For example: Samuel Field to Martin, February 6, 1874, *ibid.*

98.  [?] Stacey to Martin, February 9, 1873, *ibid.* Also: William A. Todd to Martin, November 28, 1874; Thomas D. Thurlow to Martin, December 10, 1874; J. C. Taylor to Martin, December 26, 1874, *ibid.*

99.  Charles S. Daire to Martin, June 14, 1874, *ibid.*

100.  John H. Brinton to Martin, March 14, 1874, *ibid.*

101.  Y. S. Walter to Martin, November [?], 1873, *ibid.*

102.  Westcott to Martin, April 27, 1871, *ibid.*

103.  Martin to Westcott, April 24, 1873, *ibid.*

104.  Westcott to Martin, December 7, 187[?], *ibid.*

105.  John Hill Martin, *Chester and Its Vicinity* (Philadelphia: W. H. Pile, 1877), pp. 183-184.

106.  *Ibid.*, pp. 244-245.

107.  *Ibid.*, p. 303.

108.  *Ibid.*, p. 262.

109.  *Ibid.*, p. 344.

110.  *Ibid.*, p. 450.

111.  *Ibid.*, pp. 447-448.

112.  *Ibid.*, p. 472.

113.  Jones was the eldest son of the prominent Jones family whose letters from the 1860s have been edited by Robert Myers in *The Children of Pride* (New Haven: Yale University Press, 1972).

114.  Jones to D. Mason and Co., January 14, 1888, Jones Papers, Duke University.

115.  Same to same, February 22, 1888. Also: same to same, December 13, 14, 19, 20, 1888, March 2, 1889, *ibid.*

116.  Same to same, April 2, 1888, *ibid.*

117.  Same to same, April 9, 1888, *ibid.*

118.  Same to same, May 19, 1888, March 2, December 14, 1889, *ibid.*

119.  Same to same, December 30, 1889, *ibid.*

120.  Same to same, February 7, 1890, *ibid.*

121.  Same to same, March 4, 1890, *ibid.*

122.  Same to same, March 29, April 4, 1889, *ibid.*

123.  Same to same, April 23, 1889, *ibid.*

124.  Same to same, November 23, 1889, *ibid.*

125.  Same to same, February 26, 1890, *ibid.*

126.  An atlas that distinguishes the types of local and county political "territories" is: *Commercial Atlas and Marketing Guide* (Chicago: Rand, McNally Co., updated annually).

127.  The Midatlantic, and later the Midwest, by contrast, developed a mixed township-county system, in between that of the Southern county and the New England township. For a treatment of this subject: Richard Lingeman, *Small Town America: A Narrative History, 1620-Present* (New York: G.P. Putnam's Sons, 1980), p. 123.

**CHAPTER SEVEN**

1.   **Good examples, South:**    Brantz's *Baltimore*, 1871; Stevens' *St. Louis*, 1901.   **Mid-West:**   Farmer's *Detroit*, 1884; Conrad's (ed.) *Milwaukee*, 1893; Greve's *Cincinnati*, 1904; Orth's *Cleveland*, 1910; Goss' *Cincinnati*, 1912.   **Pacific Coast:** Hittell's *San Francisco*, 1878.

**Typical, South:**    Du Bose's *Birmingham*, Alabama, 1887; Wooldridge's (ed.) *Nashville*, Tennessee, 1890; Johnston's *Louisville*, Kentucky, 1896; Shepherd's (ed.) *Baltimore*, 1898; Martin's *Atlanta*, 1902; Amis' *Raleigh*, North Carolina, 1902; Rutt's *St. Joseph*, Missouri, 1904; Young's (ed.) *Memphis*, Tennessee, 1912.   **Mid-West:**    Whittelsey's *Cleveland*, 1867; Holloway's *Indianapolis*, 1870; Williams' *St. Paul*, Minnesota, 1876; Buck's *Milwaukee*, 1876-1881; Andreas' *Chicago*, 1884-1886; Robison's *Cleveland*, 1887; Crew's *Dayton*, Ohio, 1889; Kirkland's *Chicago*, 1892-1894; Moses' *Chicago*, 1895; Vrann's *Cleveland*, 1896; Kennedy's *Cleveland*, 1896; Goss' *Grand Rapids*, Michigan, 1906; Rockel's *Springfield*, Ohio, 1908; Woodbridge's (ed.) *Duluth*, Minnesota, 1910; Doyle's *Toledo*, Ohio, 1910; Butler's *Youngstown*, Ohio, 1921; Bruce's *Milwaukee*, 1936. **Mountains and Plains:** Vickers' Denver, 1880; Giles' Topeka, Kansas, 1886; Bentley's Witchita, Kansas, 1910.   **Pacific Coast:**    Hall's *San Jose*, California, 1871; Grant's *Seattle*, 1891; Guinn's *Los Angeles*, 1915; Sherer's *Glendale*, California, 1922; McGrew's *San Diego*, 1922.   **Mid-Atlantic:**    Stiles' *Brooklyn*, 1867; Raum's *Trenton*, New Jersey, 1871; Weise's *Troy*, New York, 1876; Wilson's *New York City*, 1892-1893; Young's (ed.) *Philadelphia*, 1895-1898; Lee's *Trenton*, New Jersey, 1895; Lawyer's *Binghamton*, New York, 1900; Killikelly's *Pittsburgh*, 1906; Harvey's *Wilkes-Barre*, Pennsylvania, 1909; Fleming's *Pittsburgh*, 1922; Garand's *Ogdensburg*, New York, 1927; Foreman's *Rochester*, New York, 1931-1934.

2.   Elbridge H. Goss, *The History of Melrose* (Melrose, Mass.: The City of Melrose, 1902).

3.   Samuel A. Eliot, *A History of Cambridge* (Cambridge, Mass.: *The Cambridge Tribune*, 1913).

4.   Nathaniel Shurtleff, *A Topographical and Historical Description of Boston* (Boston: Boston City Council, 1871); Horace Scudder, *Boston Town* (Boston: Houghton-Mifflin, 1881); Mark A. D. Howe, *Boston: The Place and the People* (New York: MacMillan and Co., 1903).

5.   *Dictionary of American Biography*, vol. 17, pp. 141-142.

6.   *Ibid.*, vol. 7, p. 556.

7.   J. Fletcher Williams, *A History of the City of Saint Paul* (St. Paul, Minn.: Minnesota Historical Society, *Collections*, 1876), vol. 4, pp. 3-5.

8.   *Ibid.*, p. 27.

9.   *Ibid.*, pp. 27-28.

10.   *Ibid.*, p. 16.

11.   *Ibid.*, p. 3.

12.   *Ibid.*, pp. 3-4.

13.   For a general description of this process: David R. Goldfield and Blaine A. Brownell, *Urban America: From Downtown to No Town* (Boston: Houghton-Mifflin Co., 1979), pp. 198-200.

14.   J. M. Guinn, *Historical and Biographical Record of Los Angeles and Vicinity* (Chicago: Chapman Publishing Co., 1901), p. 2.

15.   Charles T. Greve, *Centennial History of Cincinnati* (Chicago: Biographical Publishing Co., 1904), pp. 1-2. For an account of how Greve and his publisher prepared his history for publication: Biographical Publishing Co. to Greve, May 19, 20, June 8, 11, 14, 1904, Greve Papers, Cincinnati Historical Society.

16.   Zoeth Eldredge, *The Beginnings of San Francisco* (San Francisco, 1912).

17.   William Griffith, *History of Kansas City* (Kansas City: Hudson-Kimberly Publishing Co., 1900).

18.   Benjamin Lossing, *History of New York City* (New York: G. E. Perine, 1884).

19.   Charles Dahlinger, *Pittsburgh: A Sketch of Its Early Social Life* (New York: G. P. Putnam's Sons, 1916).

20.   Frank Moss, *The American Metropolis* (New York: P. F. Collier, 1897), pp. x-xi.

21.   W. H. Miller, *The History of Kansas City* (Kansas City: Birdsall and Miller, 1881), preface.

22.   *Ibid.*, p. 6.

23.   *Ibid.*

24.   *Ibid.*, p. 246.

25.   Griffith, pp. 57-62.

26.   Frederic Grant, *History of Seattle, Washington* (New York: American Publishing and Engraving Co., Publishers, 1891), p. 7.

27.   William E. Smythe, *History of San Diego* (San Diego: History Co., 1907), pp. 21-22.

28.   Joseph Kirkland, *The Story of Chicago*, 2 vols. (Chicago: Dibble Publishing Co., 1892-1894.

29.   *Ibid.*, pp. 144-145.

30.   *Ibid.*, p. 376.

31.   *Ibid.*

32.   *Ibid.*

33.   *Ibid.*, pp. 377-381.

34.   *Ibid.*, pp. 383-384.

35.   *Ibid.*, p. 227.

36.   *Ibid.*, p. 229.

37.   *Ibid.*, p. 445.

38.   *Ibid.*, p. 446.

39.   *Ibid.*, p. 448.

40.   *Ibid.*, p. 451.

41.   Charles P. Willard, *The Herald's History of Los Angeles City* (Los Angeles: Kingsley-Barnes and Neimer Co., 1901), p. 2.

42.   *Ibid.*, pp. 257-258.

43.   *Ibid.*, p. 354.

44.   Silas Farmer, *The History of Detroit and Michigan* (1884; reprint ed., Detroit: Gale Research Co.. 1969). The Farmer family developed an early map-making and publishing firm in Michigan. Silas Farmer worked on his history of Detroit for ten years, from 1874 to 1884, with the initial

intention of presenting a "Centennial" history in 1876. According to James Babcock of the Detroit Public Library (in 1967): "Rather than produce a superficial work, [Farmer] resolved, in the face of impatient subscriber reaction, to continue his researches [to produce after many delays] a veritable encyclopedia of Detroit" [unpaged Preface of 1969 reprint ed.]

45. *Ibid.*, p. v.
46. *Ibid.*, p. vi.
47. *Ibid.*, p. xii.
48. *Ibid.*, p. vi.
49. *Ibid.*, p. 48.
50. *Ibid.*
51. *Ibid.*, p. 49.
52. *Ibid.*, p. 62.
53. *Ibid.*, p. 63.
54. *Ibid.*, pp. 66-67.
55. *Ibid.*, pp. 74-76.
56. *Ibid.*, p. 204.
57. *Ibid.*, pp. 171, 221.
58. *Ibid.*, p. 348.
59. *Ibid.*, pp. 377-456.
60. *Ibid.*, p. 469.
61. *Ibid.*, p. 489.
62. *Ibid.*, p. 503.
63. *Ibid.*, pp. 507-510.
64. *Ibid.*, p. 508.
65. *Ibid.*, pp. 513-523.
66. *Ibid.*, p. 527.
67. *Ibid.*, p. 629, Farmer calls synagogues "societies" and rabbis "Reverends".
68. *Ibid.*, p. 644.
69. *Ibid.*, pp. 644-645.
70. *Ibid.*, pp. 648-649.
71. *Ibid.*, p. 666.
72. *Ibid.*, p. 670.
73. *Ibid.*, p. 765.
74. *Ibid.*, p. 793.
75. *Ibid.*, p. 802.
76. Thomas F. De Vas [?] to Westcott, December 3, 1867, J. T. Scharf Papers, Maryland Historical Society.
77. William S. Torr [?] to Westcott, June 26, 1868, *ibid.*
78. Egle to Westcott, May 2, 1874, *ibid.*
79. Westcott to J. T. Scharf, [November 1874?], *ibid.*
80. J. Larson to Westcott, February 6, 1869, *ibid.*
81. For example: W. W. H. Davis to Westcott, March 28, 1867; P. W. Sheafer to Westcott, June 16, 1868; [?] to Westcott, April 15, 1873; Richard Eddy to Westcott, February 5, 1874; Jonathan McAllister to Westcott, June 6, 1874; William H. Egle to Westcott, June 13, 1874; [?] to Westcott, February 24, 1876; Fred Graff to Westcott, April 8, 1876; John Jordan to Westcott, September 30, 1876; Josiah Thompson to Westcott, August 20,

1877; Edward Shippen to Westcott, November 16, 1877; Martha J. Smith to Westcott, March 6, 1878; Fred Graff to Westcott, December 5, 1879, *ibid*.

82.   Martin Griffen to Westcott, October 6, 1883, *ibid*.

83.   G. R. Flanigan [?] to Westcott, May 14, 1867; William S. Lorr [?] to Westcott, June 26, 1868; J. Larson to Westcott, November 24, 1868; M. F. Lobo to Westcott, [?] 1870; [?] to Westcott, March 7, 1870, *ibid*.

84.   For example: James H. Carr to Westcott, February 5, 1883, *ibid*.

85.   R. Shelton to Westcott, November 23, 1872, *ibid*.

86.   [?] to Westcott, May 16, 1869; G. W. Richards to Westcott, November 7, 1870; C. H. Plummer to Westcott, May 28, 1878, *ibid*.

87.   W. H. Yerkes to Westcott, March 28, 1876; [?] to Westcott, April 1, 1876, *ibid*.

88.   John W. Jordan to Westcott, January 17, 1870, *ibid*.

89.   James L. Mifflin to Westcott, February 18, 1867; Samuel Parrish to Westcott, March 25, 1868; W. W. H. Davis to Westcott, October 14, 1870; William J. Potts to Westcott, March 25, 1870; William H. Egle to Westcott, November 1, 1875; Theodore D. Emory to Westcott, January 28, 1878, *ibid*.

90.   Thomas A. McAllister to Westcott, January 20, 1868; same to same, May 31, 1868, [?] to Westcott, December 20, 1870, [?] to Westcott, November 12, 1871; Jonathan Neill to Westcott, July 20, 1874; John Bleight [?] to Westcott, March 18, 1880; McKenna [?] to Westcott, March 31, 1880; Charles H. Carr to Westcott, May 31, 1883; Edward Waln [?] to Westcott, July 7, 1883, *ibid*.

91.   H. S. Boardman to Westcott, March 27, 1884, *ibid*.

92.   J. Carson to Westcott, April 12, 1875, *ibid*.

93.   R. C. S. Davis to Westcott, November 17, 1867, *ibid*.

94.   Crawford Arnold to Westcott, December 29, 1866, *ibid*

95.   E. Armstrong to Westcott, February 26, 1867, *ibid*.

96.   Titus S. Emery to Westcott, February 19, 1867, *ibid*.

97.   A. McAllister to Westcott, January 6, 1867; William S. Gregory to Westcott, April 27, 1874, *ibid*.

98.   J. C. Martindale to Westcott, March 17, 1867; Charles Wister to Westcott, November 22, 1867; same to same, November 28, 1867; B. H. Coates to Westcott, April 10, 1869; D. M. Fox (Mayor of Philadelphia) to H. M. Phillips, February 27, 1870; James H. Castle to Westcott, May 9, 1871; Joseph Plankinton [?] to Westcott, July 17, 1871; Frank M. Etting to Westcott, January 2, 1873; Mayer Sulsberger to Westcott, May 26, 1874; J. E. Carpenter to Westcott, March 19, 1878; James T. Mitchell to Westcott, January 14, 1883, *ibid*.

99.   A later "serializer" was Joseph Jackson, whose regular contributions on the history of Philadelphia appeared sporadically in the Philadelphia *Public Ledger* during World War I. Contributors and readers responded in ways remarkably similar to the ways they responded to Westcott's writings four decades earlier. See: Joseph Jackson Papers (Box 24, Misc.), Historical Society of Pennsylvania.

## CHAPTER EIGHT

1.    William B. Lapham, *History of Woodstock, Maine* (Portland, Maine: Stephen Berry, Printer, 1882).

2.    *Ibid.*, pp. 3-4.

3.    William B. Lapham, *History of Paris, Maine* (Paris, Maine: authors, 1884).

4.    *Ibid.*, p. 3.

5.    William B. Lapham, *Centennial History of Norway* (Portland, Maine: Brown, Thurston, and Co., 1886), pp. v-vi.

6.    *Ibid.,* pp. vii-viii.

7.    William B. Lapham, *History of Rumford* [Maine] (Augusta, Maine: *Maine Farmer*, 1890), p. v.

8.    *Ibid.*, p. vi.

9.    William B. Lapham, *History of the Town of Whately, Mass.* (Whately, Massachusetts: the town, 1872), pp. 3-5.

10.    *Ibid.*, p. 4; *History of the Town of Northfield* (Albany, N.Y.: Joel Munsell, 1875), p. v.

11.    *Ibid.*; David J. Russo, "The Deerfield Massacre of 1704 and Local Historical Writing in the United States," p. 328, FN31.

12.    Josiah H. Temple, *History of Framingham, Massachusetts* (Framingham, Mass.: The Town of Framingham, 1887), Introductory Note.

13.    Josiah H. Temple, *History of North Brookfield, Massachusetts* (North Brookfield, Mass.: The Town of Palmer, 1887), pp. 3-4.

14.    Josiah H. Temple, *History of Palmer* (Palmer, Mass.: The Town of Palmer, 1889), pp. 3-4.

15.    Temple, *History of North Brookfield*, p. 6.

16.    Samuel Orcutt, *History of the Town of Wolcott* (Waterbury, Conn.: American Printing Co., 1874).

17.    Samuel Orcutt, *History of Torrington* (Albany, N.Y.: Joel Munsell, 1878); Samuel Orcutt, *The History of the Old Town of Derby, Connecticut* (Springfield, Mass.: Springfield Printing Co., 1880).

18.    Samuel Orcutt, *History of the Towns of New Milford and Bridgewater, Connecticut* (Hartford, Conn.: Case, Lockwood, and Brainard, 1882), p. iv.

19.    Samuel Orcutt, *A History of the Old Town of Stratford and the City of Bridgeport* (New Haven, Conn.: Tuttle, Morehouse, and Taylor, 1886).

20.    Orcutt, *History of the Town of Wolcott*, p. v.

21.    Orcutt, *History of Torrington*, p. vi.

22.    Orcutt, *The History of the Old Town of Derby*, p. ix.

23.    Orcutt, *A History of the Old Town of Stratford and the City of Bridgeport*, pp. iii-iv.

24.    Orcutt, *History of the Town of Wolcott*, p. iv.

25.    Orcutt, *The History of the Old Town of Derby*, p. vi.

26.    *Ibid.*, p. vii.

27.    *Ibid.*, p. vi.

28.   Abby  Maria  Hemenway,  *Vermont  Historical  Gazetteer*,  5  vols. (Burlington,  Vt.:    A.M.  Hemenway  and  others,  1867-1891),  vol.  1  (1867), Preface.

29.   Francis  H.  Babb,  *Abby  Maria  Hemenway  (1828-1890)*  (M.A.  Thesis, University of Maine, 1939), p. 28.

30.   *Ibid.*, p. 29.

31.   Ann  Douglas,  *The  Feminization  of  American  Culture*  (New  York: Alfred  A.  Knopf,  1977).  Douglas,  in  a  rather  muddled  account  of  women  and historical  writing  during  the  nineteenth  century,  argues  in  a  chapter entitled  "The  Escape  from  History"  that  antiquarian  local  history,  which  she mistakenly  assumes  to  have  been  written  "mainly  by  clergymen  and  women," "triumphed  over"  national  political  history  after  1850  (p.  181),  at  the  same time  that  she  argues  that  clergymen  and  women  turned  to  the  writing  of biography  to  escape  from  largely  male-defined  historical  inquiry  (pp. 188-189).

32.   The  *Quarterlies*  were  periodically  combined,  producing  five separate volumes altogether.

33.   Babb, p. 35.

34.   Hemenway  to  [?]  Gilman,  June  28,  1877,  Hemenway  Papers, Vermont Historical Society.

35.   As quoted in Babb, pp. 53-54.

36.   *Ibid.*, p. 54.

37.   *Ibid.*, p. 56.

38.   As quoted in Babb, p. 34.

39.   *Ibid.*, pp. 56-57.

40.   *Ibid.*, p. 60.

41.   *Ibid.*, pp. 52, 57, 60.

42.   *Ibid.*, p. 66.

43.   As quoted in Babb, p. 70.

44.   *Ibid.*, p. 36.

45.   Oren  Morton,  *A  History  of  Highland  County,  Virginia*  (Monterey, Va., 1911), p. 2.

46.   Oren  Morton,  *A  History  of  Rockbridge  County,  Virginia* (Staunton, Va.: The McClure Co., 1920), p. 2.

47.   Oren  Morton,  *A  History  of  Preston  County,  West  Virginia* (Kingwood, W. V.: Journal Publishing Co., 1914), pp. 4-5.

48.   Oren  Morton,  *Annals  of  Bath  County,  Virginia*  (Staunton,  Va.: McClure Co., 1917), p. vi.

49.   Morton, *Rockbridge County*, p. 1.

50.   *Ibid.*, pp. 1-2.

51.   Oren  Morton,  *A  History  of  Monroe  County,  West  Virginia* (Staunton, Va.: McClure Co., 1916), p. 5.

52.   Morton, *Highland County*, p. 1.

53.   On  this  point:    Carl  Bridenbaugh,  *Myths  and  Realities:  Societies of  the  Colonial  South*  (Baton  Rouge,  La.:  Louisiana  State  University  Press, 1952), pp. 5, 18, 135.

54.   Morton, *Monroe County*, p. 4.

55.   Oren  Morton,  *A  Centennial  History  of  Alleghany  County,  Virginia* (Dayton, Va.: J. K. Ruebush Co., 1923), Foreword.

56. Morton, *Monroe County*, p. 4.
57. *Ibid.*, p. 6.
58. Morton, *Highland County*, p. 2.
59. *Ibid.*, pp. 1-2.
60. Morton, *Rockbridge County*, Foreword.
61. Morton, *Alleghany County*, Foreword.
62. Morton, *Rockbridge County*, p. 3.
63. Morton to Joseph Ruebush, December 22, 1922, Oren Morton Papers, University of Virginia.
64. Same to same, January 12, 1923, *ibid.*
65. Same to same, March 3, 1923, *ibid.*
66. Same to same, May 7, 1923, *ibid.*
67. Same to same, May 23, 1923, *ibid.*
68. Same to same, June 19, 1923, *ibid.*
69. Same to same, November 13, 1923, *ibid.*
70. Same to same, November 1, 1923, *ibid.*
71. Same to same, November 13, 1923, *ibid.*
72. Same to same, February 11, 1924, *ibid.*
73. [Undated], *ibid.*
74. Same to same, June 24, 1925, *ibid.*
75. For example: Morton, *Alleghany County*, pp. 9-11, 19-25 (with his comments on the land grant system and on pioneer life).
76. White to Ruebush, [?], 1924, Oren Morton Papers, University of Virginia.
77. Thomas F. Walker to Morton, October 26, 1925, *ibid.*
78. For a biographical sketch: Morris L. Radoff's Foreword in J. Thomas Scharf, *History of Maryland*, 3 vols. (1879; reprint ed., Hatboro, Penn.: Tradition Press, 1967). Scharf, though trained as a lawyer, abandoned a legal career for journalism and became city editor of the *Baltimore Evening News* in 1874 and then the managing editor of the *Baltimore Morning Herald*. He later became commissioner of the Land Office, from 1884 to 1892.
79. John J. L. Findlay to Governor William T. Hamilton, December 5, 1879; W. N. Carter to Governor William T. Hamilton, February 10, 1880 (copy); George W. Brown to Hamilton (copy), January 21, 1880; James Haggerty to Hamilton (copy), January 20, 1880, J. T. Scharf Papers, Mayland Historical Society.
80. Crunvime to Scharf, February 4, 1882, *ibid.*
81. Bruch to Scharf, April 3, 1882, *ibid.*
82. Childs to Scharf, October 30, 1880, *ibid.*
83. Cockneel to Scharf, January 26, 1881, *ibid.*
84. Westcott to Shea, [undated; November 1873 [?]], *ibid.*
85. Same to same, [undated, [?] [1875] [?]], *ibid.*
86. Childs to Scharf, January 21, 1881, *ibid.*
87. For glimpses of their work together: Westcott to Scharf, February 11, March 7, 1884, *ibid.*
88. Shea to Scharf, January 31, 1882, *ibid.*
89. For example: James H. Man, (Office of the First Assistant Postmaster General) to John S. Schenck (an assistant of Scharf), July 12,

1881; Robert K. Martin (Civil Engineer's Office of the Baltimore City Water Works) to Scharf, June 13, 1881, *ibid.*

90. There is evidence of this scattered through Scharf's papers. See Introduction by Edward G. Howard, in J. Thomas Scharf, *History of Baltimore City and County* (1881; reprint ed., Baltimore: Regional Publishing Co., 1971), pp. iii-v, on the same point.

91. Billou to Scharf, December 28, 1882, *ibid.*

92. R. M. Johnston to Scharf, August 4, 1883, *ibid.*

93. James T. Owens to Scharf, October 1, 1887, *ibid.*

94. Form Letter for Contributors, January 25, 1881, *ibid.* For responses: Rebecca Conkey to Scharf, February 13, 1881; I. J. Ingle to Scharf, March 31, 1881; William Isaac to Scharf, April 3, 1881; David Wolfe to Scharf, April [?], 1881, *ibid.*

95. For example: Isaac A. Sheppard to Scharf, April 19, 1881; B. F. Newcomer to Scharf, July 7, 1881; James McSherry to Scharf, November 21, 1881, *ibid.*

96. For example: William Downey to Scharf, December 28, 1881, *ibid.*

97. J. B. Roberts to Scharf, April 21, 1881; C. A. Dana to Scharf, April 21, 1881, *ibid.*

98. A. Spenser to Scharf, November 18, 1880; James Hodges to Scharf, February 2, 1881, *ibid.*

99. Bradley Johnson to Scharf, May 8, 1875; Joseph Kinkley to Scharf, August 24, 1878, *ibid.*

100. Perine to Scharf, December 28, 1883, *ibid.*

101. Forney to Scharf, December 6, 1883, *ibid.*

102. Johnston to Scharf, December 8, 1883, *ibid.*

103. Lindulry to Scharf, May [?], 1886, *ibid.*

104. Van Tassel, pp. 161-165.

105. Dawson to Scharf, June 10, 1884, Scharf Papers, Maryland Historical Society.

106. *Ibid.* For comments on other matters involving the project on Westchester County: same to same, June 26, August 13, [undated], 1884, *Iiid.*

107. Same to same, May 5, 1888, *ibid.*

108. Westcott to Scharf, [undated] [1875?], *ibid.*

109. Williams to Scharf, November 13, 1889, *ibid.*

110. Scharf to Parkman (copy), December 16, 1882, *ibid.* (original in Massachusetts Historical Society).

111. Parkman to Scharf, December 21, 1882, *ibid.*

112. W. E. Foster to Scharf, May 5, 1884, *ibid.* Winsor's history as a model for others is a subject dealt with in Chapter 10.

113. Winsor to Scharf, April 23, 1881, *ibid.*

114. Drake to Scharf, March 2, 1876, *ibid.*

115. J. Thomas Scharf, *The Chronicles of Baltimore* (Baltimore: Turnbull Brothers, 1874), p. v.

116. *Ibid.*, p. vii.

117. J. Thomas Scharf, *History of Baltimore City and County*, (Philadelphia: Louis H. Everts, 1881), p. vii.

118. Similarly, *The History of Western Maryland*, 2 vols. (Philadelphia: Louis H. Everts, 1882) consisted of groups of chapters on various topics for each of the counties in the western part of the state, with Scharf even using some of the same language in his Preface.

119. J. Thomas Scharf, *History of Saint Louis City and County*, 2 vols. (Philadelphia: Louis H. Everts, 1883), vol. 1, p. iii.

120. *Ibid.*, p. v.

121. *Ibid.*, p. vi.

122. *Ibid.*, pp. ix-x.

123. *Ibid.*, p. x.

124. *Ibid.*, p. ix.

125. J. Thomas Scharf, *History of Philadelphia*, 3 vols. (Philadelphia: Louis H. Everts, 1884), vol. 1, p. iv.

126. *Ibid.*

127. J. Thomas Scharf, *History of Maryland*, 3 vols. (Baltimore: J. B. Piet, 1879)

128. *J. Thomas Scharf, History of Delaware*, 2 vols. (Philadelphia: L. J. Richards and Co., 1888)

129. J. Thomas Scharf, *History of Westchester County, New York, 2 vols.* (Philadelphia: L. E. Preston, 1886), p. v.

130. Scharf, *History of Baltimore*, pp. 281-282.

131. *Ibid.,* pp. 281-286.

132. *Ibid.,* pp. 778-794.


## CHAPTER NINE

1. Augustus Gould and Frederic Kidder, *The History of New Ipswich* (New Hampshire) (Boston: Gould and Lincoln, 1852), p. viii.

2. William Boyd, *History of the Town of Conesus* (New York) (Conesus, N. Y.: Boyd's Job Printing Establishment, 1887), p. 7.

3. George S. Cottman, "History to Order," *Indiana Magazine of History* 7, 1911, pp. 16-19. Unfortunately, Cottman is unidentified.

4. *Ibid.*, pp. 17-19.

5. Lewis F. Byington, ed., *History of San Francisco*, 2 vols. (Chicago: S. J. Clarke, 1931). Lewis is not the cultural anthropologist who later wrote about the "culture of poverty."

6. "Mug Books," *The Colophon*, part 17 (1934) [unpaged].

7. *Ibid.*

8. Stafford, *Subscription Book Publishing*.

9. *Ibid.*, pp. 81-82.

10. L. B. Hill, *Benjamin Franklin Lewis, 1842-1928: The Man and His Business* (Chicago: privately printed, 1938), as quoted in Stafford, *Subscription Book Publishing*, p. 82.

11. John Tebbel, *A History of Book Publishing in the United States*, 4 vols.(New York: Bowker, 1972-1981), vol. 2, p. 533.

12. John Tebbel, *History of Lewis, Clarke, Knox, and Scotland Counties, Missouri* (Chicago: Goodspeed Publishing Co., 1887), p. iii.

13. William Young, *Young's History of Lafayette County, Missouri* (Indianapolis, Ind.: B. F. Bowen, 1910), Preface.

14. *Portrait and Biographical Record of Buchanan and Clinton Counties, Missouri* (Chicago: Chapman Brothers, 1893).

15. *Ibid.*, Preface.

16. Stafford, *Subscription Book Publishing*, pp. 83-85.

17. *Ibid.*, p. 81.

18. O'Harra, *Book Publishing*, pp. 62-63.

19. *New York Daily Tribune*, Illustrated Supplement, July 15, 1901, p. 4, cols. 2-4, as referred to in *Ibid.*, pp. 62-63.

20. Lewis Publishing Co. to Wilson, January 20, 1896, Wilson Papers, University of Iowa.

21. Same to same, February 25, 1896, *ibid.*

22. Same to same, March 6, 1895, *ibid.*

23. Same to same, June 5, 1894, *ibid.*

24. Same to same, January 15, 1895, *ibid.*

25. Same to same, February 19, 1895, *ibid.*

26. Same to same, July 31, 1894, *ibid.*

27. W. G. Dunbar to Wilson, July 23, 1895, *ibid.*

28. Lewis Publishing Co. to Wilson, January 13, 1896; D. F. Smith to Wilson, January 18, 1896, *ibid.*

29. Lewis Publishing Co. to Wilson, February 18, 1896, *ibid.*

30. Same to same, May 8, 1895, *ibid.*

31. T. B. Du Bois to Wilson, May 2, 1896, *ibid.*

32. D. F. Smith to Wilson, May 7, 1899, *ibid.*

33. Lewis Publishing Co. to Wilson, January 19, 1895, *ibid.*

34. Same to same, May 1, 14, 1894, January 25, 1895, *ibid.*

35. T.B. Du Bois to Wilson, September 5, 1895, *ibid.*

36. Form Letter by Dayton and Hersey, November 9, 1895, *ibid.*

37. Order Form, June 1, 1894, *ibid.*

38. Lewis Publishing Co. to Wilson, May 14, 1894, *ibid.*

39. Same to same, July 22, 1894, *ibid.*

40. Same to same, June 25, 1895, *ibid.*

41. Same to same, May 1, 1899, *ibid.*

42. Same to same, September 3, 1894, *ibid.*

43. Same to same, September 15, 1894, *ibid.*

44. Same to same, March 18, 1895, *ibid.*

45. Same to same, November 3, 1894, *ibid.* Also: same to same, July 5, 1895, *Ibid.*

46. Same to same, September 13, 1895, *ibid.*

47. Same to same, December 4, 1894, *ibid.*

48. Same to same, July 1, 1895, *ibid.*

49. Form, December 21, 1895, *ibid.*

50. Lewis Publishing Co. to Wilson, September 28, 1894, *ibid.*

51. T. B. Du Bois to Wilson, July 25, 1895, *ibid.*

52. Lewis Publishing Co. to Wilson, May 17, 1895, *ibid.*

53. Same to same, January 19, 1895, *ibid.*

54. Order Form, June 1, 1894, *ibid.*

55. Lewis Publishing Co. to Wilson, January 19, 1895, *ibid.*

56. Same to same, December 12, 1894, *ibid.*
57. For example: Lewis Publishing Co. to Wilson, June 15, 1899, *ibid.*
58. Same to same, February 18, 1896, *ibid.*
59. Same to same, May 22, 1894, *ibid.*
60. Same to same, June 1, 1894, *ibid.*
61. Same to same, June 19, 1894, *ibid.*
62. Same to same, December 26, 1894, *ibid.*
63. Smith to Wilson, April 12, 1895, *ibid.*
64. Du Bois to Wilson, July 22, 1895, *ibid.*
65. Lewis Publishing Co. to Wilson, February 25, 1896, *ibid.*
66. Same to same, August 27, 1894, *ibid.*
67. Same to same, September 3, 1894, *ibid.* Also: same to same, October 25, 1894, July 23, August 24, 1895, April 15, June 3, 28, 1899, *ibid.*
68. For example: same to same, September 26, October 11, 15, 24, 1894, *ibid.*
69. Same to same, October 17, 1894, *ibid.*
70. Same to same, December 19, 1894, *ibid.* Also, same to same, January 2, 1895, *Ibid* .
71. Same to same, January 9, 1895, *ibid.*
72. Same to same, July 28, 1896, *ibid.*
73. Same to same, August 1, 4, 1896; F. W. Teeple to Wilson, August 1, 1896, *ibid.*
74. Du Bois to Wilson, August 5, 1896, *ibid.*
75. Lewis Publishing Co. to Wilson, August 18, 1896, *ibid.*
76. Du Bois to Wilson, August 26, 1896, *ibid.*
77. Same to same, September 7, 1896, *ibid.*
78. Same to same, September 22, 1896, *ibid.*
79. Lewis Publishing Co. to Wilson, May 22, 1894, *ibid.*
80. Same to same, June 10, 1895, *ibid.*
81. D. F. Smith to Wilson, December 27, 1895; Du Bois to Wilson, June 2, 1896, *ibid.*
82. Lewis Publishing Co. to Wilson, April 27, 1896, *ibid.*
83. D. F. Smith to Wilson, September 4, 1896, *ibid.*
84. Lewis Publishing Co. to Wilson, May 2, 1894, *ibid.*
85. Same to same, May 14, 1874, *ibid.*
86. C. A. Woodmansie to Lewis Publishing Co., November 3, 1894, *ibid.*
87. Smith to Wilson, June 29, 1895, *ibid.*
88. Lewis Publishing Co. to Wilson, April 25, 1895, *ibid.*
89. Du Bois to Wilson, June 10, 1895, *ibid.*
90. Smith to Wilson, November 7, 1895, *ibid.*
91. Lewis Publishing Co. to Wilson, June 5, 1894, *ibid.*
92. Same to same, February 19, 1895, *ibid.*
93. Du Bois to Wilson, May 26, 1895, *ibid.*
94. Same to same, September 5, 1895, *ibid.*
95. Smith to Wilson, May 2, 1896, *ibid.*
96. Same to same, January 13, 1895, *ibid.*
97. Du Bois to Wilson, August 14, 1895, *ibid.*
98. Smith to Wilson, January 29, 1895, *ibid.*

99.  Same to same, September 10, 1895, *ibid.*
100.  Du Bois to Wilson, November 27, 1895, *ibid.*
101.  Smith to Wilson, February 18, 1895, *ibid.*
102.  Du Bois to Wilson, January 8, 1896, *ibid.*
103.  Same to same, March 31, 1896, *ibid.*
104.  Same to same, June 2, 1896, *ibid.*
105.  Same to same, July 19, 1896, *ibid.*
106.  Same to same, November 17, 1895, *ibid.*
107.  Same to same, November 27, 1895, *ibid.*
108.  Smith to Wilson, January 16, 1896, *ibid.*
109.  Du Bois to Wilson, October 13, 1896, *ibid.*
110.  Smith to Wilson, February 13, 1896, *ibid.*
111.  Same to same, February 16, 1895, *ibid.*
112.  C. B. Ward to Wilson, May 21, 1895, *ibid.*
113.  Smith to Wilson, August 2, 1895, *ibid.*
114.  Du Bois to Wilson, February 13, 1896, *ibid.*
115.  Same to same, March 14, 1896, *ibid.*
116.  Same to same, May 2, 1896, *ibid.*
117.  Same to same, September 22, 1896, *ibid.*
118.  Smith to Wilson, March 25, 1895, *ibid.*
119.  Same to same, April 21, 1895, *ibid.*
120.  Du Bois to Wilson, August 6, 1895, *ibid.*
121.  Same to same, February 13, 1896, *ibid.*
122.  Same to same, October 13, 1896, *ibid.*
123.  Smith to Wilson, November 17, 1895, *ibid.*
124.  Same to same, December 27, 1895, *ibid.*
125.  Same to same, January 18, 1896, *ibid.*
126.  Du Bois to Wilson, February 29, 1896, *ibid.*
127.  The most influential of the many overall statements on the increasing standardization of Americans life is Robert Wiebe, *The Search for Order, 1877-1920* (New York: Hill and Wang, 1967).
128.  John W. Reps, *Views and Viewmakers of Urban America* (Columbia, Mo.: University of Missouri Press, 1984); Walter W. Ristow, *American Maps and Mapmakers: Commercial Cartography in the Nineteenth Century* (Detroit: Wayne State University Press, 1985). There was even an exposé of atlases to match those of Cottman's and Lewis' on local history: Bates Harrington, *How Tis Done: A Thorough Ventilation of Numerous Schemes Conducted by Wandering Canvassers Together with the Various Advertising Dodges for Swindling the Public* (1879; reprint ed., Syracuse: W. I. Pattison, 1890).

**CHAPTER TEN**

1.  Lewis, "*Mug Books*".
2.  Circular, December 31, 1879, Winsor Papers, Massachusetts Historical Society.
3.  *Ibid.*
4.  Circular on Sale of Winsor's *History of Boston, ibid.*

5.    Bynner to Winsor, August 30, 1880, #156, Winsor Letterbooks, *ibid.*

6.    Same to same, September 1, 1880, #162, *ibid.*
7.    Same to same, November 16, 1880, #242, *ibid.*
8.    Same to same, January 13, 1881, #88, *ibid.*
9.    Edes to Winsor, January 6, 1880, #31, *ibid.*
10.   Same to same, June 14, 1880, #45, *ibid.*
11.   Same to same, December 13, 1880, #28, *ibid.*
12.   Same to same, June 15, 1881, #39, *ibid.*
13.   Ellis to Winsor, July 22, 1881, #76, *ibid.*
14.   Winsor to Edes, August 3, 1881, #92, *ibid.*
15.   B. S. Ticknor to Winsor, August 3, 5, 1881, #91, 95, *ibid.*
16.   Same to same, August 4, 1881, #98, 99, 100, *ibid.*
17.   Same to same, August 13, 1881, #108, *ibid.*
18.   E. E. Hale to Winsor, January 13, 1880, #35, *ibid.*
19.   Poole to Winsor, January [?], 1880, #69, *ibid.*
20.   Same to same, September 25, 1880, #194, *ibid.*
21.   George E. Ellis to Winsor, October 29, 1880, #223, *ibid.*
22.   Charles Deane to Winsor, November 19, 1880, #247, *ibid.*
23.   Poole to Winsor, November 25, 1880, #255, *ibid.*
24.   Same to same, December 3, 1880, #15, *ibid.*
25.   Same to same, July 15, 1881, #68, *ibid.*
26.   Hale to Winsor, December 31, 1879, #1, *ibid.*
27.   Same to same, January 18, 1880, #63, *ibid.*
28.   Same to same, April [?], 1880, #184, *ibid.*
29.   Charles Deane to Winsor, June 11, 1880, #41, *ibid.*
30.   Edward Hale to Winsor, October 11, 1880, #205, *ibid.* For evidence that Winsor relied on his collaborators for suggestions:  Winsor to Charles Deane, January 15, 23, 27, October 8, November 17, December 1, 1880, Deane Papers, Massachusetts Historical Society; Winsor to George Ellis, January 17 (2), 19, 24, February 6, June 7, 1880, Ellis Papers, Massachusetts Historical Society.
31.   Winsor Letterbooks, vol. 5, part 1, Massachusetts Historical Society.
32.   Jewett to Winsor, January 15, 1880, #44-45, *ibid.*
33.   Same to same, January 17, 1880, #55, *ibid.*
34.   Same to same, January 22, 1880, #82, *ibid.*
35.   Same to same, January 23, 1880, #86, *ibid.*
36.   Same to same, January 15, 1880, #44-45, *ibid.*
37.   Same to same, January 22, 1880, #82, *ibid.*
38.   Same to same, January 24, 1880, #89, *ibid.*
39.   Osgood to Winsor, January 16, 1880, #52, *ibid.*
40.   Jewett to Winsor, May 5, 1880, #233, *ibid.*
41.   Osgood to contributors, May 10, 1880, #245, *ibid.*
42.   *Ibid.*
43.   Osgood to Winsor, July 31, 1880, #111, *ibid.*
44.   B. H. Ticknor to Winsor, August 11, 1881, #106, *ibid.*
45.   Stevens to Winsor, August 6, 1881, #101, *ibid.*
46.   Hale to Winsor, November 29, 1880, #5, *ibid.*

47.   Justin Winsor, *The Memorial History of Boston*, 4 vols. (Boston: James R. Osgood and Co., 1881-1882), Preface.

48.   Hale to Winsor, November 29, 1880, #5, Winsor Letterbooks, Massachusetts Historical Society.

49.   Winsor Letterbooks, vol. 5, p. 2, *ibid*.

50.   Jewett to Winsor, January 14, 1881, #89, *ibid*.

51.   Poole to Winsor, November 2, 1880, #228, *ibid*.

52.   Same to same, November 29, 1880, #3, *ibid*.

53.   Same to same, December 3, 1880, #15, *ibid*.

54.   Same to same, December 6, 1880, #20, *ibid*.

55.   Same to same, December 10, 1880, #25, *ibid*.

56.   Undated review, Winsor Letterbooks, vol. 3, #13, *ibid*.

57.   Howard L. Conrad, ed., 2 vols., *History of Milwaukee* (Chicago and New York: American Biographical Publishing Co., 1892), p. v-vi.

58.   Oscar Lewis was an editor of the *History of San Francisco*, 2 vols. (Chicago: S. J. Clarke, 1931).

59.   Bagley to Meeker and Hines, November 30, 1918, Bagley Papers (Outgoing), University of Washington.

60.   Bagley to William H. White, May 10, 1913, (Outgoing), *ibid*.

61.   Bagley to Colonel Aden J. Blethan, August 27, 1913, (Outgoing), *ibid*.

62.   Bagley to T. C. Elliott, June 15, 1914, (Outgoing), *ibid*.

63.   Bagley to S. J. Clarke, June 22, 1914, (Outgoing), *ibid*.

64.   Hines to Bagley, July 28, 1914, (Incoming), *ibid*.

65.   Bagley to Hines, August 1, 1914, (Outgoing), *ibid*.

66.   Bagley to T. C. Elliott, October 22, 1914, (Outgoing), *ibid*.

67.   Same to same, February 23, 1915, (Outgoing), *ibid*.

68.   Bagley to Thomas Huggins, May 4, 1916, (Outgoing), *ibid*.

69.   Bagley to [?] Farrar, October 10, 1916, (Outgoing), *ibid*.

70.   Bagley to Burke, November 20, 1915, (Outgoing), *ibid*. Bagley to Greene, February 19, 1916, (Outgoing), *ibid*.

71.   Same to same, March 2, 1916, (Outgoing), *ibid*.

72.   Clarence Bagley, *History of Seattle*, 3 vols. (Chicago:   S. J. Clarke, 1916), Preface.

73.   *Ibid*., p. 117.

74.   *Ibid*., pp. 597-598.

75.   *Ibid*., p. 599.

76.   *Ibid*., p. 455.

77.   *Ibid*., p. 477.

78.   *Ibid*., pp. 419-428.

79.   *Ibid*., pp. 452-453; 556-557.

80.   (Copy) Gregory to Becker, January 29, 1930, Gregory Papers, Box 4, Wisconsin State Historical Society.

81.   Becker to Gregory, January 17, 1930, *ibid*.

82.   Miller to Gregory, July 11, 1930, *ibid*.

83.   Rice to Preston, before December 9, 1930, *ibid*.

84.   S. J. Clarke to Preston, February 16, 20, 21, 26, 27, 28, 1931, *ibid*.

85.   Same to same, February 26, 1931, *ibid*.

86.   (Copy) Bolens to Clarke, February 25, 1931, *ibid.*
87.   Clarke to Preston, February 26, 1931, *ibid.*
88.   Bolens to Gregory, February 27, 1931, *ibid.*
89.   West to Clarke, June 16, 1932, *ibid.*
90.   Craig Rice to Preston, December 9, 1930, *ibid.*
91.   Brown to Gregory, January 19, 1931, *ibid.*
92.   Burton to Gregory, May 19, 1932, *ibid.*
93.   Earll to Gregory, January 18, 1932, *ibid.*
94.   Murphey to Gregory, April 7, 1932, *ibid.*
95.   Derthick to Gregory, January 18, 1932, *ibid.*
96.   Same to same, [?, 193?], *ibid.*
97.   Same to same, [?, 193?], *ibid.*
98.   Same to same, [?, 193?], *ibid.*
99.   John T. Lee to Gregory, March 22, 1932, *ibid.*

## CHAPTER ELEVEN

1.   W. Scott Robison, ed., *History of the City of Cleveland* (Cleveland: Robison and Cockett, 1887), pp. ix-x.
2.   T.J. Chapman, *Old Pittsburgh Days* (Pittsburgh: J. R. Weldin, 1900).
3.   *Ibid.*, Preface.
4.   Willard, *The Herald's History of Los Angeles City.*
5.   *Ibid.*, Preface. Willard's history at first appeared serially in the Sunday magazine of the *Los Angeles Herald* from July through December, 1901.
6.   Ralph Birdsall, *The Story of Cooperstown* (Cooperstown, N. Y.: Arthur H. Crist, 1917).
7.   *Ibid.*, Foreword.
8.   James Truslow Adams, *History of the Town of Southampton* (Bridgehampton, N. Y.: Hampton Press, 1918), p. xix.
9.   Henry K. Rowe, *Tercentenary History of Newton* (Newton, Mass.: The City of Newton, 1930), pp. iii-iv.
10.   Maria Letila Stockett, *Baltimore: A Not Too Serious History* (Baltimore: Norman Remington Co., 1928).
11.   *Ibid.*, Foreword.
12.   Roberta Frye Watt, *The Story of Seattle* (Seattle: Lowman and Hanford Co., 1931).
13.   *Ibid.*, p. xi.
14.   Henry R. Hamilton, *The Epic of Chicago* (Chicago: Willett, Clarke and Co., 1932).
15.   *Ibid.*, p. viii.
16.   William G. Bruce, *A Short History of Milwaukee* (Milwaukee: Bruce Publishing Co., 1936).
17.   *Ibid.*, pp. vii-viii.
18.   William W. Dewhurst, *History of St. Augustine, Florida* (New York: G. P. Putnam's Sons, 1881), p. iii.

## CHAPTER TWELVE

1. J. Franklin Jameson, "Early Days of the American Historical Association, 1884-1895," *American Historical Review*, 40, October 1934, p. 2.

2. Among other historical writings, Clarence Bowen, (Ph.D), was the author of the *History of Woodstock* [Connecticut], 6 vols. (Norwood, Mass.: Plimpton Press, 1926). On Adams: John Higham, "Herbert Baxter Adams and the Study of Local History," *American Historical Review* 89, no. 5, December 1984, pp. 1225-1239; John Higham, *History: Professional Scholarship in America* (New York: Prentice-Hall, 1965), pp. 11-14. Van Tassel, unaccountably, has national history "triumphing" merely with the founding of the AHA in 1884, a far too simplistic interpretation (Van Tassel, *Recording America's Past*, p. 179).

3. J. Franklin Jameson, "The American Historical Association, 1884-1909," *American Historical Review* 15, October 1909, p. 13.

4. Franklin, "Early Days of the American Historical Association, 1884-1895," p. 6. Indeed, Bancroft chose to be a life member (!) of the Association and sent Treasurer Bowen a check for $5.00. Bancroft to Bowen, August 20, 1885, Bowen Family Papers, American Antiquarian Society.

5. Jameson, "The Early Days of the American Historical Association, 1884-1895," p. 5.

6. *Ibid.*, pp. 27-29. Also: Chairman's (Clarence Burton's) Remarks, Sixth Conference of State and Local Historical Societies [1910], Clarence Burton Papers, Detroit Public Library. Amateurs such as Thomas Owen and Dunbar Rowland, directors of Alabama's and Mississippi's Department of Archives and History, respectively, were on the committee for particular meetings.

7. Jameson, "The Early Days of the American Historical Association, 1884-1895," pp. 29, 34.

8. *Ibid.*, pp. 31-32, 35.

9. For an assessment of the founding of the MVHA: James L. Sellers, "Before We Were Members The MVHA," *Mississippi Valley Historical Review*, 40, 1953-54, pp. 3-24.

10. Thwaites to Alvord, May 29, 1908, Thwaites Papers, Wisconsin State Historical Society.

11. A. H. Clarke, the publisher in Cleveland who published Thwaite's edited versions of *Early Western Travels*, as revealed in Thwaites to Houghton-Mifflin, March 20, 1909, *ibid.*

12. Thwaites to Alvord, May 29, 1908, *ibid.*

13. Thwaites to Clarke, June 1, 1908, *ibid.*

14. Sellers, "Before We Were Members" p. 21.

15. *Ibid.*, p. 7.

16. *Ibid.*, p. 8.

17. *Ibid.*, pp. 3-24, for an account until 1953.

18. Jameson, "The American Historical Association, 1884-1909," pp. 10-11; Jameson, "The Early Days of the American Historical Association, 1884-1895," pp. 8-9. Other amateurs elected to the presidency were: Justin

Winsor (1887), William F. Poole (1888), Henry Adams (1894), Charles Francis Adams (1901), Alfred T. Mahan (1902), and Theodore Roosevelt (1912).

19.     W. Stull Holt, "The Writing of Local History in America," *Middle States Association of History Teachers*, 33, 1935, p. 80.

20.     Hart to Wisconsin State Historical Society, January 2, 1902, Thwaites Papers, Wisconsin State Historical Society.

21.     Agenda, February 1, 1902, pp. 1, 3, *ibid.*

22.     Turner was in the history department at the nearby University of Wisconsin and was described by Thwaites as "one of my oldest and dearest friends." Thwaites to W. B. Parker, April 2, 1904, *ibid.*

23.     Thwaites to Hart, February 4, 1902, *ibid.*

24.     Hart to Thwaites, February 8, 1902, *ibid.*

25.     Same to same, March 6, 1904, *ibid.*

26.     Thwaites to Hart, March 11, 1904, *ibid.*

27.     Turner to Mrs. Thwaites, November 25, 1913, *ibid.*

28.     Holt, "The Writing of Local History in America," p. 81.

29.     Richard Hofstadter, *The Progressive Historians: Turner, Beard, Parrington* (New York: Alfred A. Knopf, 1968), p. 37.

30.     Rowland to Channing, January 6, 1923, (Outgoing), Rowland Papers, Mississippi Department of History and Archives.

31.     For accounts of the growing separation between amateurs and academics within the AHA: David D. Van Tassel, "From Learned Society to Professional Organization: The American Historical Association, 1884-1900," *American Historical Review* 89, no. 4, October 1984, pp. 929-956; Higham, "Herbert Baxter Adams and the Study of Local History"; Higham, *History: Professional Scholarship in America*, pp. 14-25. For an account of similar developments in Britain, where academic scholars nonetheless retained a stronger link to the world of the amateurs than was the case in the United States: Rosemary Jann, "From Amateur to Professional: The Case of the Oxbridge Historians," *Journal of British Studies* 22, no. 2 (Spring, 1983) pp. 122-147.

32.     *The Nation*, 98, #2534, January 22, 1914, (copy in Rowland Papers, Mississippi Department of Archives and History); Ray Allen Billington, "Tempest in Clio's Teapot: The American Historical Association Rebellion of 1915," *American Historical Review*, 78, April, 1973, pp. 348-369; Higham, *History: Professional Scholarship in America*, p. 20.

33.     Julian P. Boyd, "State and Local Historical Societies in the United States," *American Historical Review*, 40, October 1934, p. 29.

34.     *Ibid.*, pp. 36-37.

35.     William T. Alderson, "The American Association for State and Local History," *The Western Historical Quarterly*, 1, April 1970, p. 176.

36.     *Ibid.*, p. 181.

37.     Boyd, "State and Local Historical Societies in the United States," p. 27.

38.     Dixon Ryan Fox, "State History I," *Political Science Quarterly*, 36, 1921, pp. 572, 578.

39.     Dixon Ryan Fox, "Local Historical Societies in the United States," *Canadian Historical Review*, 13, 1932, p. 266.

40. Boyd, "State and Local Historical Societies in the United States," p. 33.

41. Holt, "The Writing of Local History in America," p. 80.

42. *Ibid.*, p. 79.

43. *Ibid.*

44. Fox, "State History I," p. 576.

45. Holt, pp. 77-78.

46. Higham, "Herbert Baxter Adams and Local History," pp. 1234-1236.

47. Examples of state historians who were involved in efforts of this kind are Professors Walter Fleming (John Du Bose Papers, Alabama Department of History and Archives), Edmond Meany (Edmond Meany Papers, University of Washington), William Folwell (Clement Lounsberry Papers, North Dakota State Archives).

48. Wayland to Ruebush, October 29, 1910, Morton Papers, University of Virginia.

49. John W. Wayland, *A History of Rockingham County, Virginia* (Dayton, Va.: Ruebush-Elkins Co., 1912), pp. vi-vii.

50. John W. Wayland, *History of Shenandoah County, Virginia* (Strasburg, Va.: Shenandoah Publishing House, 1927).

51. Tate to Wayland, December 24, 1927, Wayland papers, #4299, University of Virginia.

52. *Ibid.*, undate list in.

53. Keister to Wayland, December 11, 1929, *ibid.*

54. Wayland to Keister, January 31, 1933, *ibid.*

55. Blake McKelvey, *Rochester: The Water Power City, 1812-1854* (Cambridge, Mass.: Harvard University Press, 1945), p. xi.

56. Blake McKelvey, *Rochester: The Quest for Quality, 1890-1925* (Cambridge, Mass.: Harvard University Press, 1956), p. x.

57. McKelvey, *Rochester: The Water Power City, 1812-1854*, p. ix.

58. *Ibid.*, pp. v-vi.

59. Blake McKelvey, *Rochester: The Flower City, 1855-1890* (Cambridge, Mass.: Harvard University Press), p. vii.

60. McKelvey, *Rochester: The Quest for Quality, 1890-1925*, p. vii.

61. Blake McKelvey, *Rochester: An Emerging Metropolis, 1925-1961* (Rochester, N. Y.: Christopher Press, 1961), p. v.

62. *Ibid.*

63. McKelvey, *Rochester: The Quest for Quality, 1890-1925*, p. vii.

64. Lewis Atherton, *Main Street on the Middle Border* (Bloomington, Ind.: Indiana University Press, 1954).

65. Lewis Atherton, *Main Street on the Middle Border*, paperback ed., (Chicago: Quadrangle Books, 1966), p. xvi.

66. *Ibid.*, pp. xiv-xv, 33-64.

67. *Ibid.*, p. 3.

68. Higham, *History: Professional Scholarship in America*, pp. 33-34.

**CONCLUSION**

1.    For evidence of the mobility of business and professional groups since the 1930s:   Steven Thernstrom, *The Other Bostonians:    Poverty and Progress in the American Metropolis*, pp. 228-234. For a review of recent non-academic local histories:    David J. Russo, [review essay], *The New England Historical and Genealogical Register*, 130, October 1976, pp. 293-296.

2.    For a general treatment of this theme:    David J. Russo, *Families and Communities:    A New View of American History* (Nashville, Tenn.: American Association of State and Local History, 1974).

3.    W. Lloyd Warner, *Democracy in Jonesville:    A Study of Quality and Inequality* (New York:   Harper and Brothers, 1949), p. xiv.

# Bibliography

*Manuscripts*

Bagley, Clarence, Papers, University of Washington.

Bancroft, Hubert H., Collection, University of California (Berkeley).

Bowen Family Papers, American Antiquarian Society.

Burton, Clarence, Papers, Detroit Public Library.

Coffin, Joshua, Papers, Essex Institute.

Dean, Charles, Papers, Massachusetts Historical Society.

Dreer Collection, Historical Society of Pennsylvania.

Du, John, Bose Papers, Alabama Department of History and Archives.

Dunham, Josiah, (Zadock Thompson Papers), Vermont Historical Society.

Ellis, George, Papers, Massachusetts Historical Society.

Fairbanks, George R., Papers, Florida State University.

Felt, Joseph, Papers, Essex Institute.

Gratz Collection, Historical Society of Pennsylvania.

Gregory, John G., Papers, Wisconsin State Historical Society.

Greve, Charles T., Papers, Cincinnati Historical Society.

Jackson, Joseph, Papers, Historical Society of Pennsylvania.

Hemenway, Abby Maria, Papers, Vermont Historical Society.

Jones, Charles C., Papers, Duke University and University of Georgia.

Lewis, Alonzo, Papers, Essex Institute.

Library Company of Philadelphia Collection, Historical Society of Pennsylvania.

Lounsberry, Clement, Papers, North Dakota State Archives.

Martin, John Hill, Papers, Historical Society of Pennsylvania.

Meany, Edmond, Papers, University of Washington.

Moore, Jacob B., Papers, Harvard University.

Morton, Oren, Papers, University of Virginia.

Neill, Edward D., Papers, Minnesota Historical Society.

Peters Papers, Historical Society of Pennsylvania.

Ramsey, James G. M., Papers, University of Tennessee.

Rowland, Dunbar, Papers, Mississippi Department of Archives and History.

Scharf, J. Thomas, Papers, Maryland Historical Society.

Shattuck, Lemuel, Papers, Essex Institute.

Snow, Caleb, Papers, Massachusetts Historical Society.

Society Collection, Historical Society of Pennsylvania.

Sparks Papers, Houghton Library, Harvard University

Thompson, Zadock, (Josiah Dunham Papers), Vermont Historical Society.

Thwaites, Reuben, Papers, Wisconsin State Historical Society.

Trumbull, J. B., Collection, Forbes Library (Northampton, Massachusetts).

Vaux Papers, Historical Society of Pennsylvania.

Watson, John F., Papers, Historical Society of Pennsylvania.

Wayland, John, Papers, University of Virginia.

Williamson, William, Papers, Maine Historical Society.

Willis, William, Diary, Portland Public Library.

Willis, William, Papers, Maine Historical Society.

Wilson, Nathan, Papers, University of Iowa.

Winsor, Justin, Papers, Massachusetts Historical Society.

Woodbridge, William, Papers, Detroit Public Library.


*Published Writings (non-academic)*

Abbot, Abiel. *History of Andover* [Massachusetts] (Andover, Mass.:   Flagg and Gould, 1829).

Adams, James Truslow. *History of the Town of Southampton* [New York] (Bridgehampton, N. Y.: Hampton Press, 1918).

Adams, Nathaniel. *Annals of Portsmouth* [New Hampshire] (Exeter, New Hampshire: C. Norris, 1825).

Babson, John J.   *History of the Town of Gloucester* [Massachusetts] (Gloucester, Massachusetts: Proctor Brothers, 1860).

Bagley, Clarence. *History of Seattle*, 3 vols. (Chicago: S. J. Clarke, 1916).

Bancroft, George.   *The History of the United States of America from the Discovery of the Continent*, 10 vols. (Boston:   Little, Brown and Co., 1834-1875) (Chicago:   University of Chicago Press, 1966; ab. & ed. by Russell B. Nye).

Bancroft, Hubert H.   *The Works of Hubert H. Bancroft*, 39 vols. (San Francisco: A. L. Bancroft, 1882-1890).

Barry, John S.   *A Historical Sketch of the Town of Hanover* (Boston:   S. G. Drake, 1853).

Barry, William. *A History of Framingham* [Massachusetts] (Boston:     J. Munroe, 1847).

Biglow, William.   *History of   Sherburn* (Milford, Mass.: Ballou & Stacy, 1830).

Birdsall, Ralph. *The Story of Cooperstown* [New York] (Cooperstown, N. Y.: Arthur H. Crist, 1917).

Bliss, Leonard. *The History of Rehoboth* [Massachusetts] (Boston: Otis, Broaders, and Co., 1836).

Bond, Henry. *Family Memorials* (Boston: Little Brown, 1855).

Bouton, John Bell. *Autobiography of Nathaniel Bouton* (New York: Anson D. F. Randolph Co., 1879).

*Character and Life Work of Rev. Nathaniel Bouton* (Concord, N. H.: Mrs. Arthur E. Clark, 1902).

Bouton, Nathaniel. *The History of Concord* [New Hampshire] (Concord, N. H.: Benning W. Sanborn, 1856).

Bowen, Clarence. *History of Woodstock* [Connecticut], 6 vols. (Norwood, Mass.: Plimpton Press, 1926).

Boyd, William. *History of the Town of Conesus* [New York] (Conesus, N. Y.: Boyd's Job Printing, 1887).

Brayton, Isabella. *The Story of Hartford* [New York] (Glens Falls, N. Y.: Bullard Press, 1929).

Brooks, Charles. *History of the Town of Medford* (Boston: J. M. Usher, 1855.)

Bruce, Wallace A. *History of Fort Wayne* [Indiana] (Fort Wayne, Ind.: D. W. Jones, 1868).

Bruce, William G. *A Short History of Milwaukee* (Milwaukee: The Bruce Publishing Co., 1936).

Butler, Caleb. *History of the Town of Groton* [Massachusetts] (Boston: T. R. Marvin, 1848).

Byington, Lewis F., ed. *History of San Francisco* 2 vols. (Chicago: S. J. Clarke, 1931).

Campbell, William S. *History of Fayetteville* [Arkansas] (Fayetteville, Ark., 1925).

Caulkins, Frances. *History of Norwich* [Connecticut] (Norwich, Conn.: Thomas Robinson, 1845).

Chapman, T. J. *Old Pittsburgh Days* (Pittsburgh: J. R. Weldin, 1900).

Clark, George F.  *A History of the Town of Norton* [Massachusetts] (Boston: Crosby, Nichols and Co., 1859).

Coffin, Joshua.  *A Sketch of the History of Newbury, Newburyport, and West Newbury* [Massachusetts] (Boston: Samuel Drake, 1845).

Condit, Uzal W., *The History of Easton* (Easton, Penn.: G.W. West, 1889).

Conrad, Howard L., ed.  *History of Milwaukee*, 2 vols. (Chicago and New York: American Biographical Publishing Co., 1892).

[Cooper, James Fenimore].  *The Chronicles of Cooperstown* [New York] (Cooperstown, N. Y.: H. & E. Phinney, 1838).

Cooper James Fenimore and Samuel T. Livermore.  *A Condensed History of Cooperstown* (Albany, N. Y.: J. Munsell, 1862).

Cooper, Natalie.  *History of Prospect Valley* [West Virginia] (Fairmont, W. V., 1940).

Cordley, Richard.  *A History of Lawrence, Kansas* (Lawrence, Kan.: E. F. Caldwell, 1895).

Cottman, George S.  "History to Order," *Indiana Magazine of History* 7, 1911, pp. 16-19.

Craig, Neville B.  *The History of Pittsburgh* (Pittsburgh: J. H. Mellon, 1851).

Daggett, John.  *Sketch of the History of Attleborough* [Massachusetts] (Dedham, Mass.: H. Mann, 1834).

Dahlinger, Charles.  *Pittsburgh: A Sketch of Its Early Social Life* (New York: G. P. Putnam's Sons, 1916).

Davis, Frederic.  *History of Jacksonville* [Florida] (Jacksonville, Fla.: Florida Historical Society, 1925).

Deane, Samuel.  *History of Scituate* [Massachusetts] (Boston: J. Loring, 1831).

Dewhurst, William W.  *History of St. Augustine, Florida* (New York: G. P. Putnam's Sons, 1881).

Divine, D. S.  *The Importance of Local History* (Madison, Wis., 1874).

Dorr, Benjamin.  *A Memoir of John Fanning Watson* (Philadelphia: Collins, Printer, 1861).

Drake, Samuel. *The History and Antiquities of the City of Boston* (Boston: Luther Stevens, 1854).

Draper, James. *History of Spencer* [Massachusetts] (Worcester, Mass.: Henry J. Howland, 1841).

*History of Spencer* [Massachusetts] 2d ed. (Worcester, Mass.: Henry J. Howland, 1860).

Dunlop, Leslie W. *American Historical Societies, 1790-1860* (Madison, Wis., 1944).

Eldredge, Zoeth. *The Beginnings of San Francisco* (San Francisco, 1912).

Eliot, Samuel A. *A History of Cambridge* [Massachusetts] (Cambridge, Mass.: *Cambridge Tribune*, 1913).

Ellis, Charles. *The History of Roxbury Town* [Massachusetts] (Boston: Samuel Drake, 1847).

Ellwood, Charles A. "How History Can Be Taught from a Sociological Point of View," *Education*, 30 (1909-1910), pp. 300-306.

Farmer, John, and Jacob B. Moore. *Gazetteer of the State of New Hampshire* (Concord, N. H.: Jacob B. Moore, 1823).

Farmer, Silas. *The History of Detroit and Michigan* (1884; reprint ed., Detroit: Gale Research Co., 1969).

Felt, Joseph. *History of Ipswich, Essex, and Hamilton* [Massachusetts] (Cambridge, Mass.: C. Folsom, 1834).

Felt, Joseph B. *Annals of Salem* (Salem: W. & S. B. Ives, 1827).

Fessenden, Guy. *The History of Warren* [Rhode Island] (Providence, R. I.: H. H. Brown, 1845).

Folsom, George. *History of Saco and Biddeford* [Maine] (Saco, Maine: Alex G. Putnam, 1830).

Folwell, William. *A History of Minnesota*, 4 vols. (St. Paul, Minn.: Minnesota Historical Society, 1921-1929).

*Minnesota* (Boston and New York: Houghton, 1908).

Fox, Charles J. *History of the Old Township of Dunstable* [Massachusetts and New Hampshire] (Nashua, N. H.: Charles and Gill, 1846).

Garand, Philias. *Historical Sketch of the Village of Clayton* [New York] (Clayton, N. Y.: G. H. Bates, 1902).

Goodhue, Josiah. *History of the Town of Shoreham* (Middlebury, Vt: A. H. Copeland, 1861).

Goss, Elbridge H. *The History of Melrose* [Massachusetts] (Melrose, Mass.: The City of Melrose, 1902).

Gould, Augustus, and Kidder, Frederic. *The History of New Ipswich* [New Hampshire] (Boston: Gould and Lincoln, 1852).

Grant, Frederick. *History of Seattle, Washington* (New York: American Publishing and Engraving Co., 1891).

Greenleaf, Thomas. *Geographical Gazetteer of the Towns in the Commonwealth of Massachusetts* (Boston: Greenleaf and Freeman, 1784-1785 [issued in parts]).

Gregory, John G., ed. *Southwestern Wisconsin: A History of Old Crawford County, 4 vols.* (Chicago: S. J. Clarke, 1932).

*Southeastern Wisconsin: A History of Old Milwaukee County,* 4 vols. (Chicago: S. J. Clarke, 1932)

*West Central Wisconsin: A History,* 4 vols. (Chicago: S. J. Clarke, 1933).

Greve, Charles T. *Centennial History of Cincinnati* (Chicago: Biographical Publishing Co., 1904).

Griffith, William. *History of Kansas City* [Missouri] (Kansas City, Mo.: Hudson-Kimberly Publishing Co., 1900).

Guinn, J. M. *Historical and Biographical Record of Los Angeles and Vicinity* (Chicago: Chapman Publishing Co., 1901).

Hadden, James. *A History of Uniontown* [Pennsylvania] (Akron, Ohio: New Werner Co., 1913).

Hamilton, Henry R. *The Epic of Chicago* (Chicago: Willett, Clarke and Co., 1932).

Hanson, J. W. *History of Gardiner, Pittston, and West Gardiner* [Maine] (Gardiner, Maine: William Palmer, 1852).

*History of the Town of Danvers* [Massachusetts] (Danvers, Mass., 1848).

Harrington, Bates. *How Tis Done: A Thorough Ventilation of Numerous Schemes Conducted by Wandering Canvassers Together with the Various*

*Advertising Dodges for Swindling the Public* (1879; reprint ed., Syracuse: W. I. Pattison, 1890).

Hearn-O'Pry, Maude. *Chronicles of Shreveport* [Louisiana] (Shreveport, La.: Journal Printing Co., 1928).

Helman, James. *History of Emmitsburg* [Maryland] (Frederick, Md.: Citizens Press, 1906).

Hemenway, Abby Maria, ed. *Vermont Historical Gazetteer: A Magazine Embracing a History of Each Town, Civil, Ecclesiastical, Biographical, and Military*, 5 vols. (Burlington, Vermont: A. M. Hemenway and others, 1867-1891).

Hill, L. B. *Benjamin Franklin Lewis, 1842-1928: The Man and His Business* (Chicago, 1938).

Hittell, John S. *A History of the City of San Francisco* (San Francisco: A. L. Bancroft and Co., 1878).

Howe, Mark A. D. *Boston: The Place and The People* (New York: Macmillan and Co., 1903).

Hudson, Alfred S. *The History of Sudbury* [Massachusetts] (Boston: R. H. Blodgett, 1889).

Hudson, Charles. *History of the Town of Westminster* [Massachusetts] (Mendon, Mass.: G. W. Stacey, 1832).

Hunnewell, James F. *A Century of Town Life: A History of Charlestown* [Massachusetts] (Boston: Little, Brown and Co., 1888).

Jackson, Francis. *History of the Early Settlement of Newton* [Massachusetts] (Boston: Stacey and Richardson, 1854).

Jensen, J. Marmus. *History of Provo* [Utah] (Provo, Utah, 1924).

Kellogg, Martin. "The Local Units of History," California Historical Society *Papers*, vol. 1, pt. 1, pp. 1-13.

Kirkland, Joseph. *The Story of Chicago*, 2 vols. (Chicago: Dibble Publishing Co., 1892-1894)

Lapham, William B. *Centennial History of Norway* [Maine] (Portland, Maine: Brown, Thurston and Co., 1886).

*History of Rumford* [Maine] (Augusta, Maine: *Maine Farmer*, 1890).

*History of Woodstock, Maine* (Portland, Maine:   Stephen Berry, Printer, 1882).

Lapham, William B., and Silas P. Maxim. *History of Paris, Maine* (Paris, Maine, 1884).

Larzelerle, Claude S.   "The Study of Local History," *Journal of Education* 66, June-December, 1907, pp. 544-545.

Lewis, Alonzo.   *The History of Lynn* [Massachusetts] (Boston:    J. H. Eastburn, 1829).

Lewis, Oscar. "Mug Books," *The Colophon*, part 17 (1934), [unpaged].

Lincoln, Solomon.   *History of the Town of Hingham* [Massachusetts] (Hingham, Mass.: Caleb Gill, Jr. and Farmer and Brown, 1827).

Lincoln, William.   *History of Worcester* [Massachusetts] (Worcester, Mass.: Moses D. Phillips and Co., 1837).

Lindley, Harlow.   "A Systematic Study of Local History," *Michigan Historical Magazine* (1933), pp. 108-113.

Livermore, S. T.   *A Condensed History of Cooperstown* [New York] (Albany, N. Y.: J. Munsell, 1862).

"Local History and the Civic Renaissance in New York,"   *The American Monthly Review of Books*, 16, July-December, 1897, pp. 446-449.

Lossing, Benjamin.   *History of New York City* (New York:   G. E. Perine, 1884).

Lounsberry, Clement.   *Early History of North Dakota* (Washington, D.C.: Liberty Press, 1919).

Ludewig, Hermann.   *The Literature of American Local History:    A Bibliographical Essay* (New York, 1846).

Lyford, James O.   "Town Histories," New Hampshire Historical Society *Proceedings*, vol. 5 (1905-1912), pp. 262-270.

Lyman, Payson W.   *Historical Address Delivered at the Centennial Celebration in Easthampton, Mass., July 4, 1876* (Springfield, Mass.:   Clark W. Bryan and Co., 1877).

Mann, Herman.  *Historical Annals of Dedham* [Massachusetts] (Dedham, Mass.: author, 1847).

Martin, John Hill.  *Chester and Its Vicinity* (Philadelphia:  W. H. Pile, 1877).

*Historical Sketch of Bethlehem* [Pennsylvania] (Philadelphia:    O. Rogers, 1872).

Massachusetts Historical Society. *Collections* and *Proceedings*.

Matthews, Lyman.  *History of the Town of Cornwall, Vermont* (Middlebury, Vt.: Mead and Fuller, 1862).

McLaurin, John J.   *The Story of Johnstown* [Pennsylvania] (Harrisburg, Penn.: J. M. Place, 1890).

Meany, Edmond.  *History of the State of Washington* (New York:  Macmillan and Co., 1909).

Miller, W. H.   *The History of Kansas City* [Missouri] (Kansas City, Mo.: Birdsall and Miller, 1881).

Mitchell, Nahum.    *History of the Early Settlement of Bridgewater* [Massachusetts] (Boston:  Kidder and Wright, 1840).

Moore, Jacob B.  *Annals of the Town of Concord* (Concord, N. H.:  Jacob B. Moore, 1824).

*A Topographical and Historical Sketch of the Town of Andover* [New Hampshire] (Concord, N. H.:  Hill and Moore, 1822).

Morgan, George H.  *Annals, Comprising Memoirs, Incidents, and Statistics of Harrisburg* [Pennsylvania] (Harrisburg, Penna.: G. A. Brooks, 1858).

Morton, Oren.  *Annals of Bath County, Virginia* (Staunton, Va.:  McClure Co., 1917).

*A Centennial History of Alleghany County, Virginia* (Dayton, Va.:   J. K. Ruebush Co., 1923).

*A History of Highland County, Virginia* (Monterey, Va., 1911).

*A History of Monroe County, West Virginia* (Staunton, Va.:  McClure Co., 1916).

*A History of Preston County, West Virginia* (Kingwood, W. V.:  Journal Publishing Co., 1914).

*A History of Rockbridge County, Virginia* (Staunton, Va.:   McClure Co., 1920).

Moss, Frank. *The American Metropolis* (New York: P. F. Collier, 1897).

Nevins, Winfield S.  "The Study of Local History," *New England Magazine 8*, new series, March-August, 1893, pp. 28-30.

Nourse, Henry S.    *History of the Town of Harvard, 1732-1893* [Massachusetts] (Harvard, Mass.:  Warren Hapgood, 1894).

"On Local History," *Scribner's Magazine* 48, July-December, 1910, p. 250.

Orcutt, Samuel.   *The History of the Old Town of Derby, Connecticut* (Springfield, Mass.: Springfield Printing Co., 1880).

*A History of the Old Town of Stratford and the City of Bridgeport* [Connecticut] (New Haven, Conn.: Tuttle, Morehouse, and Taylor, 1886).

*History of Torrington* (Albany, N. Y.: Joel Munsell, 1878).

*History of the Town of New Milford and Bridgewater, Connecticut* (Hartford, Conn.:  Case, Lockwood, and Brainard, 1882).

*History of the Town of Wolcott* [Connecticut] (Waterbury, Conn.:  American Printing Co., 1874).

"Outline for a Survey of Local History," *Indiana History Bulletin* 1, no. 5 (March 1924), pp. 35-38.

Paige, Lucius.  *History of Hardwick* [Massachusetts] (Boston:   Houghton, Mifflin and Co., 1883).

*Portrait and Biographical Record of Buchanan and Clinton Counties, Missouri* (Chicago: Chapman Brothers, 1893).

Ramsey, James G. M.  *Annals of Tennessee* (Charleston, S. C.:   Walker and Jones, 1853).

Ricketson, Daniel. *The History of New Bedford* [Massachusetts] (New Bedford, Mass.: Daniel Ricketson, 1858).

Ripley, Franklin J. "Suggestions to Local Historians," Mississippi Historical Society, *Publications* 1 (1898), pp. 96-100.

Robison, W. Scott, ed.   *History of the City of Cleveland* (Cleveland: Robison and Cockett, 1887).

Rowe, Henry K.  *Tercentenary History of Newton* [Massachusetts] (Newton, Mass.: The City of Newton, 1930).

Rowell, George R.  *Forty Years an Advertising Agent, 1865-1905* (New York: Printer's Ink Publishing Co., 1906).

Rowland, Dunbar.  *History of Mississippi* (Chicago:   S. J. Clarke, 1925, 4 vols.).

Ruttenber, Edward M.  *History of the Town of Newburgh* (Newburgh, N.Y.: author, 1859).

Scharf, J. Thomas.   *The Chronicles of Baltimore* (Baltimore:    Turnbull Brothers, 1874).

*The History of Baltimore City and County* (1881; reprint ed., Baltimore: Regional Publishing Co., 1971).

*History of Delaware*, 2 vols. (Philadelphia: L. J. Richards and Co., 1888).

*History of Maryland*, 3 vols.   (1879; reprint ed., Hatboro, Penn.: Tradition Press, 1967).

*History of Philadelphia*, 3 vols. (Philadelphia: Louis H. Everts, 1884).

*History of Saint Louis City and County*, 2 vols. (Philadelphia:   Louis H. Everts, 1883).

*History of Westchester County, New York*, 2 vols. (Philadelphia:   L. E. Preston, 1886).

*The History of Western Maryland*, 2 vols.   (Philadelphia:   Louis H. Everts, 1882).

Schouler, James.   *History of the United States of America under the Constitution*, 7 vols. (New York:  Dodd, Mead and Co., 1880-1913).

Scudder, Horace.  *Boston Town* (Boston:  Houghton-Mifflin, 1881).

Shattuck, Lemuel.  *History of the Town of Concord* [Massachusetts] (Boston: Russel, Odiorne and Concord:  John Stacey, 1835).

Sheldon, George.  *A History of Deerfield, Massachusetts*, 2 vols. (Greenfield, Mass.: E. A. Hall and Co., 1895-1896).

Shurtleff, Nathaniel.  *A Topographical and Historical Description of Boston* (Boston:  Boston City Council, 1871).

Smith, Euphemia Vale. *History of Newburyport* (Newburyport: Danviell & Moore, 1854).

Smythe, William E. *History of San Diego* [California] (San Diego, Calif.: History Co., 1907).

Snow, Caleb. *A History of Boston* (Boston: Abel Bowen, 1825).

Staples, William R. *Annals of the Town of Providence* [Rhode Island] (Providence, R. I.: Knoles and Vose, 1843).

Stockett, Maria Letila. *Baltimore: A Not Too Serious History* (Baltimore: Norman Remington Co., 1928).

Stone, Edwin M. *History of Beverly* [Massachusetts] (Boston: J. Munroe, 1843).

Swift, Samuel. *History of the Town of Middlebury* [Vermont] (Middlebury, Vt.: A. H. Copeland, 1859).

Temple, Josiah H. *History of Framingham, Massachusetts* (Framingham, Mass.: The Town of Framingham, 1887).

*History of North Brookfield, Massachusetts* (North Brookfield, Mass.: The Town of North Brookfield, 1887).

*History of Palmer* [Massachusetts] (Palmer, Mass.: The Town of Palmer, 1889).

*History of the Town of Northfield* [Massachusetts] (Albany, N. Y.: Joel Munsell, 1875).

*History of the Town of Whately, Mass.* (Whately, Mass.: The Town of Whatley, 1872).

Thacher, James. *History of the Town of Plymouth* [Massachusetts] (Boston: Marsh, Capen, and Lyon, 1832).

*History of the Town of Plymouth*, 2d ed. (Boston: Marsh, Capen, and Lyon, 1835).

Thompson, Daniel P. *History of the Town of Montpelier* [Vermont] (Montpelier, Vt.: E. P. Walton, 1860).

Thompson, Zadock. *A Gazetteer of the State of Vermont* (Montpelier, Vt.: E. P. Walton, 1824).

*History of Vermont* (Burlington, Vt.: Chauncey Goodrich, 1842).

Throop, Benjamin.  *A Half-Century in Scranton* [Pennsylvania] (Scranton, Penn.: *Scranton Republican*, 1895).

Tinkham, George H.  *History of Stockton* [California] (San Francisco:  W. H. Hinton, Printers, 1880).

Torrey, Rufus C.  *History of the Town of Fitchburg* [Massachusetts] (Fitchburg, Mass.: J. Garfield, Printer, 1836).

Wade, Herbert.  "What the Pageant Does for Local History," *Review of Reviews* 48, July-December, 1913, pp. 328-333.

Ward, Andrew H.  *History of the Town of Shrewsbury* [Massachusetts] (Boston: Samuel Drake, 1847).

Washburn, Emory.  *Topographical and Historical Sketches of the Town of Leicester* [Massachusetts] (Worcester, Mass.: Rogers and Griffin, 1826).

Waters, Wilson.  "The Writing of Local History," Lowell [Massachusetts] Historical Society *Contributions* 2, no. 1, October 1921, pp. 24-35.

Watson, John F. *Annals of Philadelphia* (Philadelphia:  E. L. Carey and A. Hart, and New York: G. & C. & H. Carvill, 1830).

    2d ed., 2 vols. (Philadelphia, 1844).

    3rd ed., 2 vols. (Philadelphia: Whiting and Thomas, 1856-1857).

Watt, Roberta Frye.  *The Story of Seattle* (Seattle:  Lowman and Hanford Co., 1931).

Wayland, John W.  *A History of Rockingham County, Virginia* (Dayton, Va.: Ruebush-Elkins Co., 1912).

*History of Shenandoah County, Virginia* (Strasburg, Va.:  Shenandoah Publishing House, 1927).

Weeks, John.  *History of Salisbury, Vermont* (Middlebury, Vt.:  A. H. Copeland, 1860).

Weicht, Carl C.  "The Local Historian and the Newspaper," *Minnesota History* 13, 1932, pp. 45-54.

Wilder, David. *The History of Leominster* [Massachusetts] (Fitchburg, Mass.: Reveille Office, 1853).

Wilkinson, John B.  *The Annals of Binghamton* [New York] (Binghamton, N. Y.: Cooke and Davis, Printers, 1840).

Willard, Charles P.  *The Herald's History of Los Angeles City* (Los Angeles: Kingsley-Barnes and Neimer Co., 1901).

Willard, David.  *History of Greenfield* [Massachusetts] (Greenfield, Mass.: Kneeland and Eastman, 1838).

Williams, J. Fletcher.  *A History of the City of Saint Paul* [Minnesota], *Collections*, vol. 4 (St. Paul, Minn.: Minnesota Historical Society, 1876).

Williams, John.  *The Redeemed Capture Returning to Zion* (1707, Springfield, Mass.: The H. R. Huntting Co., 1908).

Williamson, William.  *The History of the State of Maine*, 2 vols. (Hallowell, Maine: Glazier, Masters and Co., 1832).

Willis, William.  *History of Portland* [Maine], 2 vols. (Portland, Maine:  Day, Fraser and Co., 1831-1833).

*History of Portland*, 2 vols., 2d ed. (Portland, Maine:  Bailey and Noyes, 1865).

Winsor, Justin.  *The Memorial History of Boston*, 4 vols. (Boston:  James R. Osgood and Co., 1881-1882).

Worthington, Erastus.  *The History of Dedham* [Massachusetts] (Boston: Dutton and Wentworth, Printers, 1827).

Young, Andrew.  *History of Warsaw* [New York] (Buffalo:  Sage Sons and Co., 1869).

Young, William.  *Young's History of Lafayette County, Missouri* (Indianapolis, Ind.: B. F. Bowen, 1910).

## PUBLISHED WRITINGS (ACADEMIC)

Alderson, William T.   "The American Association for State and Local History," *The Western Historical Quarterly* 1 April, 1970, pp. 175-182.

Atherton, Lewis.   *Main Street on the Middle Border* (Bloomington, Ind.: Indiana University Press, 1954).

Main Street on the Middle Border, paperback ed. (Chicago:   Quadrangle Books, 1966).

Babb, Francis H.   *Abby Maria Hemenway (1828-1890)*, (M.A. Thesis, University of Maine, 1939).

Baym, Nina.   *Novels, Readers, and Reviewers:   Responses to Fiction in Antebellum America* (Ithaca, N.Y.:   Cornell University Press, 1984).

Billington, Ray Allen.   "Tempest in Clio's Teapot:   The American Historical Association Rebellion of 1915," *American Historical Review* 78, April, 1973, pp. 348-369.

Boorstin, Daniel J.   *The Americans*, 3 vols. (New York:   Random House, 1958-1973).

Boyd, Julian P.   "State and Local Historical Societies in the United States," *American Historical Review* 40, October 1934, pp. 10-37.

Bridenbaugh, Carl.   *Myths and Realities:   Societies of the Colonial South,* (Baton Rouge, La.:   Louisiana State University Press, 1952).

Callcott, George H.   *History in the United States, 1800-1860:   Its Practice and Its Purpose* (Baltimore:   Johns Hopkins Press, 1970).

Cohen, Patricia C.   *A Calculating People:   The Spread of Numeracy in Early America* (Chicago:   University of Chicago Press, 1982).

Cohen, Patricia C.   "Statistics and the State:   Changing Social Thought and the Emergence of a Quantitative Mentality in America, 1790 to 1820," *William and Mary Quarterly 38*, 3rd series   January 1981, pp. 35-55.

*Commercial Atlas and Marketing Guide* (Chicago:   Rand, McNally, updated annually).

Daniels, Bruce.   *The Connecticut Town:   Growth and Development* (Middletown, Conn.:   Wesleyan University Press, 1979).

*Dissent and Conformity on Narragansett Bay:   The Colonial Rhode Island Town* (Middletown, Conn.:   Wesleyan University Press, 1983).

*Dictionary of American Biography,* 21 vols., Allan Johnson & Dumas Malone, eds. (New York: Charles Scribner's Sons, 1928-1937).

Douglas, Ann. *The Feminization of American Culture,* (New York: Alfred A. Knopf, 1977).

Dunlap, Leslie W. *American Historical Societies, 1790-1860* (Madison, Wis., 1944).

Fitzgerald, Frances. *America Revised:    History Schoolbooks in the Twentieth Century* (Boston: Little, Brown, and Company, 1979).

Fox, Dixon Ryan.    "Local Historical Societies in the United States," *Canadian Historical Review* 13, 1932, pp. 263-267.

"State History I," *Political Science Quarterly* 36, 1921, pp. 572-585.

Fritz, Paul, and David Williams, eds., *The Triumph of Culture:   18th Century Perspectives* (Toronto:  A. M. Hakkert, 1972).

Gay, Peter. *A Loss of Mastery:   Puritan Historians in Colonial America* (Berkeley, Calif.: University of California Press, 1966).

Goldfield, David R., and Blaine A. Brownell. *Urban America:    From Downtown to No Town* (Boston: Houghton Mifflin Co., 1979).

Hesseltine, William B.    "Lyman Copeland Draper, 1815-91," *Wisconsin Magazine of History,* 35 (Spring 1952), pp. 163-176.

*Pioneer's Mission:   The Story of Lyman Copeland Draper* (Madison, Wis.: State Historical Society of Wisconsin, 1954).

Higham, John.    "Herbert Baxter Adams and The Study of Local History," *American Historical Review* 89, no. 5, December 1984, pp. 1225-1239.

Higham, John. *History:    Professional Scholarship in America* (New York: Prentice-Hall, 1965).

Hofstadter, Richard. *The Progressive Historians:    Turner, Beard, and Parrington* (New York: Alfred A. Knopf, 1968).

Holt, W. Stull.    "The Writing of Local History in America," *Middle States Association of History Teachers* 33, 1935, pp. 76-83.

Isaac, Rhys. *The Transformation of Virginia, 1740-1790* (Chapel Hill, N.C.: University of North Carolina Press, 1982).

Jameson, J. Franklin.    "The American Historical Association, 1884-1909," *American Historical Review,* 15, October 1909, pp. 1-20.

"Early Days of the American Historical Association, 1884-1895," *American Historical Review* 40, October 1934, pp. 1-9.

Jann, Rosemary. "From Amateur to Professional: The Case of the Oxbridge Historians," *Journal of British Studies* 22, no. 2 (Spring, 1983) pp. 122-147.

Knights, Peter R. *The Plain People of Boston, 1830-1860,* (New York: Oxford University Press, 1971).

Kraus, Michael. *The Writing of American History* (Norman, Okla.: University of Oklahoma Press, 1953).

*The Wrtiting of American History,* rev. ed., David D. Joyce, ed. (Norman, Okla.: University of Oklahoma Press, 1985).

Laslett, Peter. *The World We Have Lost* (London: Methuen, 1965).

Lemon, James. *The Best Poor Man's Country: A Geographical Study of Early Southeastern Pennsylvania* (Baltimore: Johns Hopkins University Press, 1972).

Lingeman, Richard. *Small Town America: A Narrative History 1620-Present* (New York: G. P. Putnam's Sons, 1980).

Lockridge, Kenneth. *A New England Town: The First Hundred Years* (New York: W. W. Norton, 1970).

McKelvey, Blake. *Rochester: An Emerging Metropolis, 1925-1961* (Rochester, N. Y.: Christopher Press, 1961).

*Rochester: The Water Power City, 1812-1854* (Cambridge, Mass.: Harvard University Press, 1945).

*Rochester: The Flower City, 1855-1890* (Cambridge, Mass.: Harvard University Press, 1949).

*Rochester: The Quest for Quality, 1890-1925* (Cambridge, Mass.: Harvard University Press, 1956).

Mendyck, Stanley G. *'Painting the Landscape': Regional Study in Britain during the Seventeenth Century* (Ph.D. Dissertation, McMaster University, Hamilton, Ontario, 1983).

Meyers, Robert M., ed. *The Children of Pride* (New Haven, Conn.: Yale University Press, 1972).

Nye, Russell B. *George Bancroft* (New York: Alfred A. Knopf, 1945).

*Society and Culture in America, 1830-1860* (New York:   Harper and Row, 1974).

O'Harra, Downing P.   *Book Publishing in the United States, 1860 to 1901, Including Statistical Tables and Charts to 1927.* (M. A. Thesis, University of Illinois, 1928).

Plumb, J. H.   *The Death of the Past* (Boston:  Houghton-Mifflin Co., 1970).

Pugh, R. B.    "The Structure and Aims of the Victoria History of the Counties of England," *Bulletin of the Institute of Historical Research* 40, 1967, pp. 65-73.

Reps, John W.    *Town Planning in Frontier America* (Princeton, N.J.: Princeton University Press, 1969).

*Views and Viewmakers of Urban America* (Columbia, Mo.:   University of Missouri Press, 1984).

Ristow, Walter W.    *American Maps and Mapmakers:   Commercial Cartography in the Nineteenth Century* (Detroit:   Wayne State University Press, 1985).

Russo, David J.    "The Deerfield Massacre of 1704 and Local Historical Writing in the United States," in Paul Fritz and David Williams, eds., *The Triumph of Culture: 18th Century Perspectives* (Toronto: A. M. Hakkert, 1972), pp. 315-333.

*Families and Communities:   A New View of American History* (Nashville, Tenn.:  American Association of State and Local History, 1974).

*The Origins of Local News in the U.S. Country Press, 1840s-1870s* (Lexington, Ky.:  Journalism Monographs, 65, February, 1980).

Sellers, James L.   "Before We Were Members—The MVHA," *Mississippi Valley Historical Review 40,* 1953-54, pp. 3-24.

Smith, George W., and   Charles Judah, eds.   *Life in the North During the Civil War:   A Source History*   (Albuquerque, New Mexico:   University of New Mexico Press, 1966).

Smith, Page.   *As a City Upon a Hill:   The Town in American History* (New York: Alfred A. Knopf, 1966).

Stafford, Marjorie.    *Subscription Book Publishing in the United States, 1865-1930* (Urbana, Ill.:  M.A. Thesis, University of Illinois, 1943).

Tebbel, John.   *A History of Book Publishing in the United States, 4 vols.* (New York: Bowker, 1972-1981).

Thernstrom, Steven.  *The Other Bostonians:  Poverty and Progress in the American Metropolis* (Cambridge, Mass.: Harvard University Press, 1973).

Van Tassel, David D.  "From Learned Society to Professional Organization: The American Historical Association, 1884-1900," *American Historical Review* 89, October, 1984, pp. 929-956.

*Recording America's Past:  An Interpretation of the Development of Historical Studies in America, 1607-1884* (Chicago:  University of Chicago Press, 1960).

Vaughan, Alden, and Edward W. Clark, eds.  *Puritans among the Indians: Accounts of Captivity and Redemption*  (Cambridge, Mass.:  Harvard University Press, 1981).

Warner, W. Lloyd.  *Democracy in Jonesville:  A Study of Quality and Inequality* (New York:  Harper and Brothers, 1949).

Waters, Deborah D.  "Philadelphia's Boswell:  John Fanning Watson," *The Pennsylvania Magazine of History and Biography* 98, January 1974, pp. 4-52.

Weisberger, Bernard.  *The American Newspaperman* (Chicago:  University of Chicago Press, 1961).

Wiebe, Robert.  *The Search for Order, 1877-1920* (New York:  Hill and Wang, 1967).

Wish, Harvey.  *The American Historian:  A Social-Intellectual History of the Writing of the American Past* (New York:  Oxford University Press, 1960).

Zuckerman, Michael.  *Peaceable Kingdoms:  New England Towns in the Eighteenth Century* (New York:  Alfred A. Knopf, 1970).

# Index

**About the Author**

DAVID J. RUSSO is a Professor of History at McMaster University in Hamilton, Ontario. He is the author of *Families and Communities: A New View of American History*, and *The Origins of Local News in the U.S. Country Press, 1840-1870s*, and journal articles on historical topics.

| DATE DUE | | | |
|---|---|---|---|
| | | | |
| | | | |
| | | | |
| | | | |
| | | | |
| | | | |
| | | | |
| | | | |
| | | | |
| | | | |
| | | | |
| | | | |
| | | | |

Russo    214697